THE URBAN SEA
Cities of the Mediterranean

Dennis Hardy
Photographs by Jane Woolfenden

Enquiries concerning these terms should
be addressed to Blue Gecko Books.
bluegeckobooks@ymail.com

British Library Cataloguing In Publication
Data. A catalogue record for this book is
available from the British Library.

ISBN: 978-0-9575685-0-1

Design and formatting by
Barbara Velasco (Papel Papel)

Printed and bound by
Lightning Source UK

to Jane

Have you ever reflected what an important sea the Mediterranean is?

James Joyce, 1905, in a letter from Trieste.

CONTENTS

PREFACE

As an 18-year old, waiting to go to university, I had a yen to travel round the Mediterranean. Long before the days of the internet I sent off for a timetable produced by the Turkish Hellenic shipping line and duly planned my route. It was possible then to catch a train at London Victoria, cross the Channel on a packet boat and head southwards across France to Marseille, one of the numerous ports visited by a Turkish Hellenic steamer. I had visions of basking in the sun by day and sleeping under the stars on deck at night.

Alas, shortly before I left, Israel and its neighbours engaged in one of the region's periodic wars and anxious parents persuaded me to delay my trip until the following summer. Fifty years later I made it. By now, though, I was no longer so keen on the prospect of sleeping on deck.

One other difference was that, with other commitments, I could not be away for much more than a week at a time. With the wonderful Turkish Hellenic service long since disbanded, and with some of the most colourful ports no longer even served by international ferries, I resorted to the option of fifteen separate trips—each of a week or so.

Half a century had passed since my original plans. Although I knew that I would find a different place, the Mediterranean still held its fascination for me. The dire poverty in southern Europe in the middle of the last century would have eased, and there had been time for the raw wounds of post-colonial adjustments in the countries of North Africa and the eastern Mediterranean to have healed. Of course, terrorism has since reared its head and extremists (political and religious) are not that eager to welcome westerners, especially with cameras.

To add to it all, just as the Mediterranean has done throughout its long and volatile history, it came up with not just one but two new surprises. One was the so-called Arab Spring, with all its uncertainties as well as hopes, and the other the collapse of the Greek economy and ripple effects through neighbouring countries along the southern rim of the Eurozone.

The only constant factor in this ancient region, I soon discovered, is change itself. All those years have passed in its human history—millennia not just mere centuries—yet upsets are still a part of life. This restlessness, of course, is just one of the things about the Mediterranean that makes it such an intriguing place to visit.

One could spend a lifetime drifting between its bordering countries, always with the sea in view. But even these staccato visits were enough to reveal some truly amazing stories, invariably centred on the ancient cities that line the shores.

I was drawn to these locations because this is where most of the important events in the region have happened. Through a series of vignettes, insights are offered of exceptional places. The story of the Mediterranean, one quickly concludes, is the story of its cities—it is truly an urban sea.

ACKNOWLEDGEMENTS

This book has been in my mind for a long time and I owe a debt to many friends and colleagues who have offered ideas and encouragement. Perhaps I could single out just two. While sharing the odd bottle of fine wine, Gregory Andrusz and I have discussed many of the issues that I have now written about and, like the good tutor that he is, he has invariably followed up our evenings with suggestions for further reading. In turn, over several decades, Edmund Penning-Rowsell, has been a constant source of inspiration, always encouraging me to go that extra mile. I am grateful to them both for their longstanding friendship and support.

In the course of collecting material in the UK and in a variety of Mediterranean cities, I have been helped by numerous librarians, museum curators and guides, as well as government and other officials. A special mention must be made of the John Rylands University Library in Manchester, where I was able to find many of my secondary sources. Later in the project I was fortunate to have access to the impressive resources of the South Australia State Library.

There are particular cities where I have been helped by people who know them so much better than I do, and I have noted their various contributions in the relevant sections. I would also like to record my appreciation of the British Academy for the award of a grant to support my visits to four cities in the southern Mediterranean.

I am indebted to Steve Chilton, a former colleague at Middlesex University (and subsequently Chairman of the Society of Cartographers), for so willingly agreeing to draw the essential map of the Mediterranean.

In the production stage, my thanks are due to Nicola Markus for introducing me to the wonders of modern publishing, and to Barbara Velasco for her patient and skilful conversion of my manuscript into its present format.

Last but certainly not least, my wife, Jane, has supported me throughout the project, talking through ideas and encouraging me in those moments when the thought of visiting yet another city seemed all too much! In one particular respect, the book would certainly not be the same without her major contribution, as she has taken all of the photographs and laboriously prepared them for publication. This study of the Mediterranean has been a joint project and all the more enjoyable for her involvement. As a modest recognition of this and more, it is only fitting that I dedicate the book to Jane.

INTRODUCTION

The Mediterranean is an urban sea. Across its waters have come ideas as well as people, trade as well as war. And it is cities where these have emanated and cities where these have arrived.

At the crossroads of continents, nothing in the Mediterranean is what it first seems. It is an intriguing part of the world: Africa to the south, Asia to the east, Europe to the north. Human development in this region has occurred over millennia, producing a mix of cultures that is unique and often volatile. The apparent serenity of azure waters belies an underlying restlessness and hidden currents of change: cultural and political, historical and religious, geological and geographical. There is no easy way to make sense of it all. Many writers have approached the subject from their own separate perspectives and the bookshelves are heavy with worthy volumes; the best of these are warmly acknowledged in the pages that follow.

Writers and artists, inspired by the setting, have reflected on the meaning of the Mediterranean. Trieste.

My own approach takes a different tack. I have been drawn specifically to the cities of the region, each of which has its own revealing story to tell. The book takes the form of a series of *vignettes* which in themselves offer specific insights but which together form a bigger picture.

The cities around the shores of the Mediterranean are like sentinels, looking out to sea but also guarding their respective hinterlands. They are invariably old places, with histories often extending over millennia rather than mere centuries. Moreover, from classical times they have been on the frontline of most of what has happened in the region. Little has passed them by. Some of the stories they have to tell are quite extraordinary and all are eventful. Particular cities have at times changed the course of history, whether through the conquest of rival states or encouragement of scientific discovery and artistic endeavour.

In other cases, and at other times, cities have themselves been at the receiving end of change, coming under foreign occupation and forcibly turned towards new paths of development. Either way, their respective histories are inextricably linked to the changing fortunes of the Mediterranean as a whole. That is why the first chapter provides an overview of the region, showing the integral place of cities and how they have been shaped by their location at the crossroads of three of the world's continents. The Mediterranean, it will be seen, is at once a blessed home for its cities as well as one of recurring crisis; the best of all worlds but also the worst.

With this duality in mind, it is time to set forth on the long journey around the largely landlocked waters. In deciding which cities to visit, some of the most obvious examples—Athens and Rome, Istanbul and Jerusalem, Barcelona and Venice—have been deliberately passed by. This, of course, is not because they are insignificant but, on the contrary, because their stories are already familiar. Instead, 'second-tier' cities have been chosen. It will be seen that their own stories are no less illustrative of broader themes than those of better-known neighbours. The reader will find that I use the term 'city' loosely to describe any settlement (usually large but not always so) that has exercised a decisive influence on the course of events in the region.

Thus, our journey starts in Gibraltar, at the very entrance to the inner sea, with the Mediterranean on one side and the Atlantic on the other. The main settlement on 'the Rock' is least of all like a city but, if only because of its strategic location, it offers a natural beginning for a voyage of this sort. From Gibraltar, heading east along the coast of Spain, we then alight on Alicante. Together with its neighbouring settlements, it tells vividly of the impact of incoming tourists and 'retirees' from northern Europe, a modern episode layered over a long and varied history that has not always been benign. Next, into France and to Marseille, modern and vibrant, a fascinating place that is European in character combined with the influence of longstanding links to North Africa. In many ways, it has successfully blended past and present, Europe and Africa, to become one of the most dynamic cities in the modern Mediterranean.

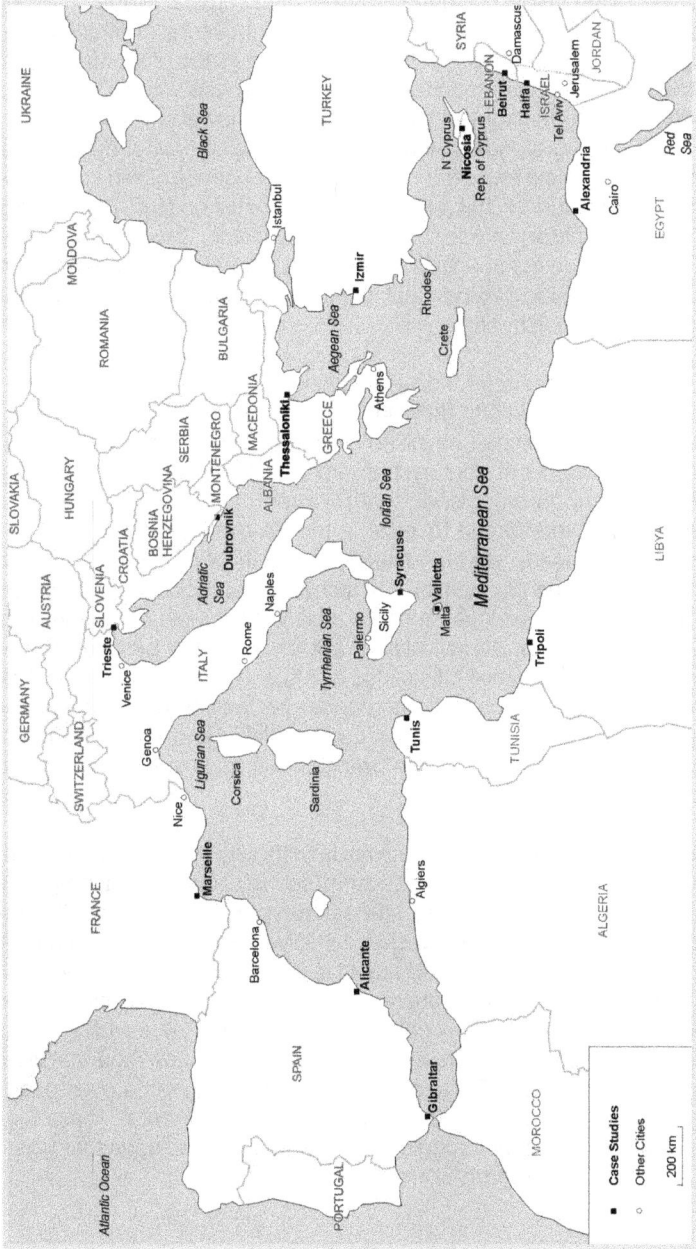

Cities of the Mediterranean.

After Marseille, one crosses the plains of northern Italy to Trieste, still bearing the hallmarks of historic ties with Central Europe in its imperial heyday and with more than a whisper of Slavic cultures to the east. If only because of its unique pedigree, it is a cuckoo in the Mediterranean nest, too good to miss. Following the coastline southwards to Croatia, we next stop at Dubrovnik, once with its own commercial empire a rival even to mighty Venice. Like the latter, however, Dubrovnik is now set in aspic, its imperial pretensions long past and resigned instead to the gaze of a steady stream of tourists attracted by an iconic townscape. Then south-eastwards to northern Greece, and to Thessaloniki, inextricably linked to its Balkan neighbours and for long under Ottoman rule. For most of its history it was known as Salonica and was home to large communities of Jews, Muslims and Christians. For centuries they lived peaceably side by side, until two tragic episodes in the twentieth century brought that all to a violent end.

From Europe to the eastern Mediterranean, known more exotically as the Levant, we stop first in Izmir. Formerly Smyrna, it prospered as an important port for the Ottoman Empire. In its heyday, its mixed population was treated with tolerance and it was only in the twentieth century that ethnic differences became an issue that threatened its future. In an episode that mirrored the fate of Salonica, the Greek citizens of Smyrna were forced to leave in terrible circumstances. Leaving behind this tale of human tragedy, we then make our way to Beirut—only to find that there is no relief here, for the city is itself a watchword for modern conflicts. Once the 'Paris of the Mediterranean', Beirut offers a classic example of the twin processes of war and reconstruction, and today is still finely poised between the two. For geopolitical reasons, an Israeli city is also a 'must' and Haifa, an ancient port with a modern role, reveals much of contemporary as well as past interest. Not least of all, Haifa shows how world politics can suddenly and dramatically change a city's realm of influence—in this case, truncating a once extensive hinterland that extended deep into Iraq.

Beyond Israel, the trail takes us westwards to the Arab states along the fringes of the Sahara, following the path of the seventh-century soldiers bearing the message of Islam. This stretch of the journey starts in Egypt with Alexandria, its very name enough to lure any traveller who wishes to delve into a seemingly timeless past, although now offering little to remind one of its days of glory. Further west, between the sea and the sands of the Sahara, is Tripoli. Like many of its Mediterranean counterparts, the city has been conquered repeatedly by invading forces, until the coming of Libyan independence and the start of a new and volatile chapter in its history. Then there is Tunis, a city of the Maghreb, once overshadowed by neighbouring Carthage and, much later, colonized by the French. These three cities have each featured in recent struggles in the region—the episode that was dubbed (at least at the outset) the Arab Spring.

Finally, no odyssey of the Mediterranean can be complete without venturing seawards to its islands. From the many venues that could be chosen, ferries are taken to three—to Sicily, Malta and Cyprus. Sicily is the largest island in the Mediterranean and Syracuse was once not only its capital but one of the great cities of the region. Now it languishes in a backwater, largely overtaken by events which favoured its Sicilian rivals, surrounded by relics from the past. Just a short journey to the east takes us to Malta and to its capital Valletta. In Mediterranean terms this is a young city—founded as recently as the sixteenth century. Yet, in spite of its relatively short history, it can tell of tempestuous events as well as offering a modern lesson that small can indeed be beautiful. Valletta is, indeed, one of the treats in store. For our last visit we travel further east, to the conflict-ridden island of Cyprus, with its segregated communities of Turks and Greeks. In the interior is the divided city of Nicosia, demonstrating all too vividly timeworn differences between Islam and Christianity, East and West.

Having largely encircled the Mediterranean, it will be time to reflect on the experience. This is not just a question of looking back, and the theme of the final piece, 'Arab Spring, European Winter', is intended to signify that the region is one of continuing drama. The full impact of contemporary political and economic events is not yet known.

Mediterranean cities have never been far from the eye of the storm, nor are they now. Yet always in the past a parting of the clouds has eventually given way to new vistas. There is no crystal ball to foretell what might yet emerge, but in seeking to chart a way forward the collective evidence of these fifteen cities can at least offer a sense of perspective.

CHAPTER 1

CROSSROADS OF CONTINENTS

There was a time when the Mediterranean was rightly thought of as *Middle Earth*.[1] It is a small sea but around its shores many of the world's earliest achievements could be found. Events later shifted the centre of human activity to more distant lands but the name, of course, has stuck. In spite of its diminished importance, the region retains a powerful presence on the world map, not least of all because of its renowned cities. These places are where much has happened in the past and where history continues to be made.

Compared with maritime settings in other parts of the world, Mediterranean cities are huddled together in a remarkably compact area. No city is far from another; their various fortunes have always been closely intertwined. They share the same sea but there is more than that: three continents face each other across the water.

The Mediterranean is at one of the world's major crossroads and the cities themselves have been shaped in no small measure by being in this unique location. Their natural setting, exceptionally long histories and constant interactions have combined to produce remarkable places. They have at times been reduced to ashes and risen again; they have known years of legendary wealth and then abject poverty; they have welcomed the arrival of new groups and later expelled them without remorse.

With so much that is shared, one is tempted to ask whether Mediterranean cities can be regarded as a separate group in the world's urban panoply. One must be careful not to see patterns where none exist for, for as one wise observer has noted in a veiled warning: 'It is difficult to explain the repeated impulse to piece the Mediterranean mosaic together...'[2] At the same time, it is hard to escape the fact that certain factors, which occur only in this region, have had a profound effect on its cities. It can reasonably be argued that some of these factors are evident in other regions too, but not necessarily in the same ways. As a result of their particular form and concentration, a group of cities has evolved which in many respects is unlike anywhere else. There is, indeed, a compelling case for a Mediterranean *genre*.

Like their urban counterparts elsewhere, cities in this region perform routine functions as markets and commercial centres, as locations for industry and housing, and few have escaped the ubiquitous mark of modernity. At the same time, compared with other parts of the world, these cities of Middle Earth have all been fired in the same kiln; they share a similar geography, a connected history and a unique location at the meeting point of three continents. For these reasons one looks for what it is that makes them more like each other than cities elsewhere. What is it that makes them 'Mediterranean cities'? In this first chapter, we begin to see some of the reasons for their commonalities.

Stereotypical images of the Mediterranean continue to lure people to its shores. Amalfi Coast & Dubrovnik.

NATURE'S BOUNTY

As a result of cataclysmic upheavals of the Earth's surface in the distant past, the Mediterranean found its present form as a sea within a largely enclosed basin, fringed by mountains and desert. To add to this powerful sense of physical enclosure, it shares from one end to the other a distinctive and traditionally benign climate, and this, in turn, has endowed the region with its own, recognizable vegetation; one only has to think of the Mediterranean to scent its fragrant herbs, to visualize lush fruits against whitewashed walls.

The Inner Sea

The sea is everything it is said to be: it provides unity, transport, the means of exchange and intercourse...[3]

The Mediterranean is a product of its own images, an azure sea bathed in eternal sunshine. Even allowing for flights of fantasy, it really is a sea that sparkles in a light that is unusually bright and clear: 'the shadows are rigidly projected and only the distant prospect shimmers frail and vague in the heat haze.'[4] Little wonder that generations of artists have been drawn to its shores and that such a prospect retains an allure for visitors. Nor is it just its appearance that lends such an aura; by definition it is a largely landlocked sea, in the middle of the once known world. The human universe has grown since the name was first coined but nothing can change the essential geography of the Mediterranean, surrounded by no less than three continents. It remains, even now, at the heart of an important cross-section of the world's cultures.

The sea itself is the defining feature of the region, once a barrier but more often a bridge between the nations that surround it. Yet even the most cursory glance at a map of the Mediterranean reveals that it is a sea like no other. For one thing it is smaller than the world's great oceans; indeed, 'the Mediterranean is an absurdly small sea; the length and greatness of its history make us dream it larger than it is.'[5] Its absolute size, however, can be deceptive.

Some 3500 kilometres from east to west and with complex indentations on the European side, it is an ocean in microcosm. 'Its character is complex, awkward and unique...the Mediterranean is not even a *single* sea, it is a complex of seas.'[6] Within its boundaries there are, in fact, two distinct basins separated, east from west, by a largely submerged sill that runs between Sicily and Tunisia, once a geological land bridge between Europe and Africa.

There are also separately named seas, worlds of their own to the sailors and fishermen who know their every current: the Alboran between Spain and Morocco; the Ligurian, Tyrrhenian and Adriatic surrounding Italy; the Ionian and Aegean abutting either side of Greece; and the Levantine in the eastern Mediterranean.

And, although in many parts quite shallow, it plunges in places to very considerable depths: midway between Sicily and Crete the waters descend more than 6000 metres.

In spite of its hidden complexities, in most respects it looks and behaves like a vast lake; ancient Arab cartographers thought of it as 'the inner sea'. Indeed, at one stage in its geological history that really was the case; the pre-historic Tethyan Ocean, precursor to the Mediterranean, was literally an inner sea, albeit far larger than its modern counterpart. Just like a lake, too, the Mediterranean is a sea almost without tides. This has for long been a factor in the silting of its various estuaries and, more recently, its sluggish waters have left it vulnerable to serious problems of pollution. Yet for all the similarities, the Mediterranean is not, of course, a fully-fledged lake and even though the gap that connects it to the open waters of the Atlantic is very narrow, without it the smaller sea would not be as it is. A combination of silting by its rivers and its modern use for dumping man-made waste would have left it in an even sorrier state than one finds now. Moreover, the volume of water supplied by its inflowing rivers is more than lost by a high rate of evaporation in the sea itself. Salvation, which has ensured its continuing survival, comes in the form of a two-way flow in the narrow channel between Gibraltar (tenuously connected to the European mainland by a sandy isthmus) and the North African coastline, with one current taking salty waters from the Mediterranean and the other bringing in fresh supplies from the Atlantic. The importance of this link is recognized in the grandness of the classical description of the headlands that face each other from different continents, the Pillars of Hercules. Historically, these were seen as markers, like the columns of a gateway between the Mediterranean and the terrors of the rough seas and unknown lands that lay beyond. Only the most intrepid sailors, led by the Phoenicians, at first dared to sail into the darkness beyond their known world.

In reality, there was always darkness and danger within its boundaries as well as beyond. Many a mariner has been deceived by its familiarity, wrongly believing that it would be an easy sea to traverse, only to be faced by sudden storms whipped up in one of the many strong winds that have their origins in the surrounding mountains and deserts. The history of the Mediterranean is chequered with tales, both real and fictional, of sailors battling heroically, and sometimes tragically, in the face of fierce seas: the mythical Jason led the Argonauts in his ship, the Argos, through a series of adventures, against all earthly odds; Scylla and Charybidis were the two monsters on either side of the Strait of Messina, between Italy and Sicily, daring sailors to steer too close to one or the other; and even St. Paul was unable to prevent the ship that was carrying him from running aground in one of Malta's deceptive bays. In Shakespeare's play, *The Tempest*, set in the Mediterranean, Scene 1 tells of a storm raging and the noble passengers from Naples fearing for their lives. 'Now would I give a thousand furlongs of sea for a furlong of barren ground,' wished the faithful adviser, Gonzalo.[7] Such a sentiment was no more than an echo of the prayers of earlier generations, for the Mediterranean was more often than not an awesome place. The Egyptians, who excelled in most things but were not outstanding mariners, regarded it as 'the Great Green Sea', and sensibly confined their trips to relatively short distances along the Levantine coast. For Homer's Greeks it was 'the wine-dark sea': 'a source of danger to be feared and propitiated as much as to be used and navigated'.[8]

Like all seas it is the stuff of legends, of heroism and cowardice, of war and peace. It is like an ever-changing stage set, framed by the natural contours of the coastal lands around its edge. Reflecting its formation at a time of geological upheaval, these surroundings are predominantly mountainous, the main exception being the long stretch of the Sahara that reaches to the coast in the south-east. Nothing, though, is forever, and, at the junction of European and African tectonic plates, this is by no means a stable landmass. Active volcanoes and periodic earthquakes remain part and parcel of life in the Mediterranean, their impact sometimes barely noticeable but at other times cataclysmic. The iridescent outpourings of Vesuvius that engulfed Pompeii are enshrined in Mediterranean history, while other cities, too, have been reduced to rubble by catastrophic earthquakes. For these places, the setting is less benign than it first seems.

Halcyon Days

You are aware not so much of a landscape coming to meet you invisibly over those blue miles of water, as of a climate.[9]

The sea is the defining feature of the region but the very name of the Mediterranean also describes (in other parts of the world too, along a similar latitude on both sides of the Equator) its characteristic climate. It is a global climate type, of which this region is the most extensive exemplar: 'the largest area of dry summer subtropical climate is on the border lands of the Mediterranean.'[10] In people's minds at least, and in certain ways in practice, the climate has a unifying and generally beneficial effect: 'the very word Mediterranean signified sunny skies and balmy weather...'[11] Sunshine and warmth continue to draw people to the area, even though the annual cycle is surprisingly varied.

It is best known for its hot, dry summers and mild (though often cool), wet winters. The changing experience of summer and winter provides a natural backcloth to cyclical activities; thus, 'from one end of the sea to the other people have found summer the time for travel and war and winter the season for agriculture and repair at home.'[12]

Typically, a Mediterranean climate avoids most of the extremes one finds across the neighbouring land masses. Inevitably, though, over such an extensive region there are geographical variations, with critical differences in rainfall and temperatures from one part to another. More extreme conditions can be expected in the east than in the west, although the general characteristics of a Mediterranean climate prevail across the whole sea and its surrounding lands. This distinctive climate is, in its way, no less a defining feature of the region than the sea itself; the climatologist, Allen Perry, for instance, claims unambiguously that its regular seasons 'impose a unity on the Mediterranean environment.'[13] Because of the dominant climate, travellers journeying from one part of the Mediterranean to another would have found much that was familiar: 'their journey simply meant finding in a new place the same trees and plants, the same food on the table that they had known in their homeland.'[14]

It is easy, sometimes deceptively so, to draw connections between climate and cultural behaviour: such as the architecture that has been adapted to its surroundings, offering cool interiors for the hot summers, with pastel-painted buildings and a propensity to outdoor life that many see as typifying the Mediterranean. A single chair, well-worn from years of use, carefully placed outside a house so that the owner can watch the world go by, is as much a feature of this part of the world as a white shrine on a hill or a fishing boat moored in a tiny harbour. Invariably, amongst visitors from northern Europe at least, the Mediterranean is invoked in terms of its sunny disposition, ignoring the harsh conditions created by drought for those who have to farm the land and ignoring, too, the fact that for several months of the year it will be cool and wet. Even such an astute observer as Goethe was seduced by the sunshine and the lively street life with its market stalls; and he dreamed of taking back to his temperate Germanic homeland a little of the magic air he breathed.[15]

Like so much else that defines the region the climate bears the marks of its surrounding continents. This mainly works in its favour, with more days of sunshine than the rest of mainland Europe and less arid conditions than the interior of the Middle East and the Sahara. Sometimes, though, it is the extremes that break through, with bitter winds bringing winter snow from the north and north-east and, in contrast, the searing heat of the desert extending well north of its provenance. Best known of the winds which temporarily import foreign climates is the *mistral*, which draws cold air from the Alps down the Rhone valley to the Camargue and Marseille, before blowing out to sea, to the islands of Corsica and Sardinia, sometimes even reaching the North African coastline.

The *mistral* is a cultural as much as climatic phenomenon, its constancy over several days having a discernibly unsettling effect on those who live in its path; when it eventually ceases the quiet itself feels intrusive. Other winds, from the north that bring lower temperatures into the region include the *tramontana*, which mainly affects the west coast of Italy but sometimes Corsica and even Spain as well, and the *bora*, which in winter sweeps down the coast of Croatia. More benign are the summer winds from the north in the Aegean Sea, known locally as the *etesians* by the Greeks and *meltemi* by the Turks. The *etesians* were known in classical times and the Greeks believed that they would endure for forty days each summer.

From the opposite direction, the *sirocco* carries the heat of the desert from the Sahara, reminding southern Europe of the proximity of Africa. As it sweeps across the sea it gathers moisture to produce almost unbearably hot and humid conditions that drain the energy from those caught in its path. Typically, it will bring with it red sand, which it then deposits in a fine layer across whole landscapes. The *sirocco* is the best known of the winds from the south but there are related ones, like the *leveche*, that originates in Morocco and brings dry, scorching conditions to southern Spain. Further east, the winds from the desert are known as the *khamsin*, carrying (mainly from Egypt) sand and dust and very high temperatures.

Other winds have more local impacts, often associated with particular islands. The *leveccio* is largely restricted to the north coast of Corsica, where it can be evident throughout the year. Not surprisingly, given its location between the Atlantic and Mediterranean, Gibraltar also attracts its own micro-climate. The *levante* blows mild, humid air from the east, across the Rock of Gibraltar, where it is responsible for heavy cloud formations downwind of the island; while the *vendavales* are typically the harbingers of thunderstorms.

There is something evocative about these various winds that cut across the sea, demonstrating more than other climatic elements an often unwanted connectivity between the surrounding continents. The Mediterranean is contained but not isolated and, somehow, these winds from the interior are like invisible threads that bind the sea and its coastline to the more distant lands beyond.

Olives and Oregano

The familiar prospects of vines, olives, cypresses… the odour of thyme bruised by the hoofs on the sun-drunk hills.[16]

Along with the sea and climate, the vegetation that flourishes around the Mediterranean completes Nature's trinity. It is, in itself, no less a defining feature of the region. Although no single plant species can be found over the whole of the Mediterranean, and although most occur in neighbouring regions too, there are at least four that together help to define its limits.

Best-known as an enduring feature is the olive tree, evident no less at the time of the classical civilizations than in the present landscape, and a constant staple of the local diet. The olive is perhaps the nearest one finds to a perfect match with the Mediterranean climate, even though it originated in the more extreme conditions of Anatolia to the east. Unlike most vegetation, it thrives in the summer drought, when the oil accumulates in the precious fruit and the tree roots delve deep to find just enough water to sustain growth. No other plant in the region is so well integrated with its natural surroundings and is so much a part of the way of life that 'some would say it *is* the Mediterranean'.[17]

It is its persistence and its refusal to thrive elsewhere that has fascinated one dedicated olive grower, who is also an author, Carol Drinkwater.[18] In her book, *The Olive Route*, sub-titled *A Personal Journey to the Heart of the Mediterranean*, she describes her search for the origins of olive cultivation and its subsequent effects on the life of the region. She journeyed first to Lebanon to see for herself trees reputed to have been planted 6000 years ago and still bearing fruit, and she contemplates how the young saplings might themselves have been carried from central Anatolia. How then, she speculates, might the precious oil — used for lighting as well as nourishment — have been exported to other parts of the Mediterranean, encouraging a trade in shipping and the rise of foreign ports?

Typical coastal scene. Dalmatian Coast.

From Lebanon she ventures to other olive-growing countries — to Syria and Turkey, to Malta and Tunisia, to Libya and Greece, to Crete and Israel — questioning all the time the spiritual meaning of a tree that has outlived civilizations and has witnessed the destructiveness of humans.

As well as the olive, there are three other indigenous plants — the holm oak, the Aleppo pine and the scrub woodland known as the *maquis*. The incidence of forests is now quite localized, although this vary paucity adds to their distinctiveness: the famous pines of Rome (immortalized in 1924 in the stirring musical composition by Respighi), the cedars of Lebanon, the cork forests of Sardinia, the citrus groves of Sicily and plantations of exotic date palms in parts of the eastern and southern Mediterranean. Beyond these areas, instead of mature woodland, the *maquis* has become more typical, along with its even more degenerate offshoot, the *garrigue*.

Such landscapes consist of a scattering of small trees and tough, evergreen shrubs with outcrops of bare rock and loose stone. In spite of its inferior nature, both the *maquis* and *garrigue* have a romantic appeal as another defining feature of the region. Partly, this is because of its very wildness, accentuated by the sound of the wind brushing through the dry vegetation and of the busy call of the cicada and of owls at night. Even more evocative are the haunting scents of the indigenous shrubs and herbs: mint and rosemary, thyme and oregano, sage and fennel—not to mention the clumps of wild lavender that add colour as well as fragrance to the landscape.

No less typical than the natural vegetation are the crops of the farmers, whether the vine (which also grows well beyond the region)[19] or hard grains that are found especially along the coastal plains of North Africa. Figs and peaches, tomatoes and aubergine, onions and garlic, lemons and oranges can be seen from one country to another, carefully tended in gardens and small plots as well as in commercial plantations. It is a colourful harvest as well as one that provides the basis of a typical Mediterranean diet. Many a visitor to the region has extolled the virtues of such simplicity, where the fruits of the earth find their way, directly and without complication, onto the plate.[20] To supplement this diet, catches from the sea were once more plentiful but with diminished stock the harvest is more specialized.

Perhaps it is food as much as any other feature that is indicative of the region's character and which seeps most obviously into the life of its cities. The sea, climate and vegetation provide the natural setting for a culinary *mélange* that is truly Mediterranean. More than anything else it transcends the various cultural and geographical differences to produce ingredients and dishes that would be recognizable anywhere within the region. Bread, olives, tomatoes and wine will be found in any of the Mediterranean countries, cooked and presented in various ways but all to a common formula. *Hummus*, made from chickpeas, olive oil and sesame seeds, is an Arab staple that has become no less popular in southern Europe; lamb is cooked slowly with fruits and succulent vegetables in Greece as in Morocco; the aubergine is mashed to a paste as well as roasted in slices in Lebanon as well as southern France; lemon, sea salt, rosemary and garlic are seasonings used everywhere in large quantities.

It is a diet that reflects not only what Nature provides but also what the various cultures have brought with them in long-forgotten times of invasion and colonization; invariably, there are elements from each of the adjoining continents on the table at any one time. Well-stocked markets, a profusion of colour; restaurants spreading out *al fresco* onto cobbled quaysides and in market squares; and family tables in private houses, set in the shade of a protective vine—these are all common sights from Spain to Israel, from Turkey to Algeria. Eating in the Mediterranean is as much a cultural as a purely culinary experience.

CULTURAL RICHES

If one is to ask what it is that makes Mediterranean cities different from cities elsewhere, it is their longevity; most of them have extraordinarily long histories. Important cities in other parts of the world might be dated in centuries or even in decades, but in this region it is not uncommon to trace their first occupation over millennia. Nor is it uncommon to link their emergence to a sequence of striking cultural achievements. In a remarkably concentrated area, here one finds the legacy of some of the earliest civilizations, not to mention the historic and continuing influence of the three major monotheisms—Judaism, Christianity and Islam. The sheer intensity of it all is unique and its cities still reveal signs of this remarkable history, whether in its ubiquitous ruins or in the drama of religious architecture.

Civilized Traces

The Mediterranean is a miracle... a body of water that might have been deliberately designed, like no other on the surface of the globe, as a cradle of cultures.[21]

The Nile is one of the great rivers to flow into the Mediterranean and, if only for its impact on history, by far the most important. Yet, in spite of its obvious significance, its influence as an early source of civilization must be shared with the more distant, inland river valleys of the Tigris and Euphrates in Mesopotamia. Cultural innovation from the latter spread westwards across deserts and mountains to the Levant, later fusing with developments in the Nile itself. At the confluence of these twin streams, the Mediterranean was for long seen as the centre of the known world, if not the very seat of civilization; 'all the world', claimed the American geographer Ellen Churchill Semple, 'is heir to the Mediterranean.'[22] Semple's claim would today be seen as exaggerated but it does at least illustrate a popular and enduring view of the region.

Some of the earliest building blocks of modern civilization have their origins in pre-history, emerging very slowly and often quite independently in different places Agriculture was the key to it all, for the natural cycle of crop growth in fields and the domestication of animals forced people to settle. Once that happened, other things followed: the storage of surpluses and the keeping of records; the development of writing and a profession of scribes; the making of pottery and invention of weaving; the emergence of villages and then larger settlements, each with its own ruling class and, subsequently, laws; the formalization of religion and a priestly caste; and trade and exchange, first over short distances between neighbours followed by longer land routes and across the sea. All of this took place over very many years, measured in millennia, becoming increasingly evident, at least in a rudimentary form, around much of the Mediterranean between the fifth and third millennia BC.[23]

To take things to a higher level of development, conditions had to be right and progress more concentrated. Major river valleys were ideal, their overwhelming advantage being the propensity to flood each year, bringing fresh supplies of fertile silt and exceptional productivity. It was this which (along with Queen Cleopatra) caught the eye of Mark Antony on his expedition to Egypt, who then felt impelled to explain it all to Caesar in Rome:

> *The higher Nilus swells*
> *The more it promises: as it ebbs, the seedsman*
> *Upon the slime and ooze scatters his grain,*
> *And shortly comes the harvest.*[24]

Irrigation in this way was a natural process but it was soon discovered that its benefits could be enhanced with man-made modifications; the development of these new methods themselves required greater social discipline and gave birth to the science of engineering. In turn, with the accumulation of larger surpluses, urban centres expanded and the organization of society became more complex, while trade was progressively extended beyond its own boundaries. Certainly, by the third millennium BC this process of development and diffusion was well underway in Egypt (a little later than in Mesopotamia).

Ancient Egyptian civilization endured over the best part of three millennia, with periods of rise and fall as different dynasties prospered and waned. During its heyday it introduced to the world cultural innovations that were to have a lasting influence: in writing and art, architecture and metal working, pottery and music. The focus for much of this activity was its cities, strung out like a necklace along the Nile from the mountains and deserts of the upper valley to the Mediterranean delta. In spite of its geographical extent, the whole of the riverine domain was under single rule, in sharp contrast with earlier forms of society where there was, typically, little contact even between one village and another. To unite it in this way was itself a mighty achievement but that was only the start of an irresistible process of diffusion, through which the spoils of this newfound civilization were to be shared across the Mediterranean.

In fact, the Egyptians themselves were not the main carriers, being content to restrict their own shipping largely to the safe waters of the Nile. Their forays onto the open sea were generally confined to short-haul sailing assignments, following the line of the coast and probably venturing no further north than modern-day Syria; there they collected supplies of wood, oil and wine. They were quite content, instead, to allow for most of their trade to be conducted by the ships of neighbouring powers, notably the Phoenicians, Canaanites, Cretans and, later, the Greeks. Gradually, shipping routes were extended further westwards, to more distant parts of the Mediterranean; while, by land, slow-moving caravans crossed the deserts, spreading news of all that was happening along the Nile.

After ancient Egypt, the beacon of civilization was next lit on certain islands and pockets of the mainland across the sea to the north, in the area that is now modern

Greece but which then embraced the Anatolian coastline as well. The Greek contribution to civilization proved to be of inestimable worth, not only across the Mediterranean but elsewhere in Europe and beyond. 'The result was not merely a torrential outpouring of ideas and images in drama, poetry, sculpture, painting, logic, mathematics and philosophy; but a collective life more highly energized, more heightened in its capacity for aesthetic expression and rational evaluation than had ever been achieved before.'[25]

An observer at the time would have noticed that some of the first stirrings were taking place on the large island of Crete, where its people proved exceptional not simply in copying what had been done already but also adding their own discoveries. Without river valleys to provide a natural economic base, the Cretans were forced to respond to the challenging environment of mountains and dusty plains that are more typical of most of the Mediterranean. Crete had for long been settled but mainly as a farming community, and things only began to change with the assertion of Minoan supremacy and developments that lasted for probably little more than half a millennium, until about 1450 BC. At first the Minoans looked east for inspiration, and the writing that it used for records in about 1900 BC is similar to a system already in use in Syria. It is almost certain, too, that refugees from the Levant brought with them craft skills and versions of the arts derived from both the Nile and Mesopotamia. The people of Crete proved to be adept at working with bronze and copper, and their knives were made with shiny black obsidian, imported from nearby Anatolia. Trade was an important part of their culture and for several centuries Crete served as the commercial crossroads of the eastern Mediterranean.[26] It was not essentially an aggressive culture but an effective navy was used to clear the surrounding seas of pirates and to gain control of neighbouring islands. The Minoans built magnificent palaces, most famously at Knossos, and 'enjoyed a degree of luxury unprecedented in history and not to be equalled until the dissipated days of the Roman Empire.'[27] Through the invention of the potters' wheel they shaped unique pottery which they decorated with exquisite designs, while their jewellery was no less spectacular. Compared with most of their Mediterranean successors, the Minoans have enjoyed a good press and their influence was generally benign:

> *This extraordinary civilization—talented, cultivated and extremely rich—ruled an empire covering most of the islands of the Aegean and until about 1400 BC exercised a powerful influence over the whole eastern Mediterranean, leaving traces as far afield as Transylvania and on the Danube, as well as in Sardinia and the Aeolian Islands just off the northeast coast of Sicily.*[28]

The historian of the Mediterranean, David Abulafia, credits the Minoan civilization with being the first 'wealthy, literate, city-based culture' of the Mediterranean world, in preference to the Egyptians who largely lived within the boundaries of the Nile.[29] However, in spite of their dominance and civilized ways, it all came to a sudden end. A severe volcanic eruption on nearby Santorini undoubtedly had an impact on Crete and, perhaps in a weakened state, it proved vulnerable to invasion by a force then in the ascendancy, the Mycenaeans. This latter group had made its way through mainland Greece from the north, as much as a millennium before, eventually settling in the mountain stronghold of Mycenae, in the Peloponnese, and in other settlements in that region.

As well as ousting the Minoan rulers, the Mycenaeans built their own, ornate palaces, they gained a worthy reputation for craftsmanship, and then spread their culture through Greece and more widely across the Mediterranean from the Levant to Italy. Mycenaean hegemony, however, was to last for little more than two centuries, after which there was something of an interregnum before civilization flowered once again. This time it was the famous Greek city states, such as Athens and Sparta, Corinth and Thebes, that took up the challenge.

From the eighth century BC, these aspiring city states made their presence felt: with the sword they forced their way into new lands, through their scribes they spread the art of alphabetical writing, and with coinage they facilitated trade. It was a powerful combination and Hellenic influence soon extended well beyond the Greek heartland. Colonies were established along the coast in Asia Minor, as western outposts in southern Italy and Sicily, and even as far west as Marseille and Catalonia. Greek colonies were a bit like a modern franchise, much the same from one to another with their city walls and recognizable layouts within. Most of the investment of time and skills went into the civic areas, the religious precinct of the *acropolis* and the political and commercial district of the *agora*. Typically, less attention was paid to the surrounding streets and housing, and even legendary Athens could evoke surprise amongst contemporaries for its mundane appearance:

> *The road to Athens is a pleasant one, running between cultivated fields the whole way. The city is dry and ill-supplied with water. The streets are nothing but miserable old lanes, the houses mean, with a few better ones among them. On his first arrival a stranger would hardly believe that this is the Athens of which he has heard so much.*[30]

No doubt, though, even a sceptical observer such as this would have drawn breath as he raised his sights to the magnificent, white marble structures of the Acropolis on the skyline. This was the Greek answer to the pyramids, an architectural expression of what mattered most. No less would visitors have marvelled at the city's intellectual and artistic achievements, and the refinement of democracy, reaching its apotheosis in the fifth century. Modern critics point to the social divisions that restricted participation in the pleasures of that 'golden age', but none can deny the advances that were made—in politics and the arts, in philosophy and mathematics. Nor can it be denied that these represented step changes for the development of humanity and that later generations well beyond

Greece were to share the spoils. The Greeks, a truly Mediterranean people, were to leave an indelible mark throughout the region and in the West more widely.

From Egypt and the Aegean the scene then shifts westwards, to the new city of Rome; this was the Mediterranean's third growth point for civilization and probably the most far-reaching and enduring in its impact.

To a much greater extent than its predecessors, Rome spread its culture by force of conquest, dominating not only the whole of the sea (rightly becoming known as *mare nostrum*) but also lands far to the north and east. Even today, the city at the heart of this spectacular display of power can still demonstrate through its 'broken towers and mouldered stones' a tangible link with its past, although the more impressive legacy lies in the soaring of the imagination when one merely thinks of Rome.[31]

Under the Romans, for the first (and, as time has shown, the only) time, the Mediterranean fell progressively under single rule. Through the success of their disciplined armies and efficiency of their administrators, one territory after another was drawn into their orbit. They changed the political map of the Mediterranean and established Rome as the centre of the known world. For a contemporary view of how this was perceived we can turn to Strabo, a Roman citizen of Greek descent, with a grasp of geography ahead of his time. His understanding of the world was matched only by his innate curiosity. Why, he asked, had the Earth's surface been so arbitrarily divided into different continents?

> *The writers who have divided the habitable world according to continents divide it unequally. Africa wants so much of being a third part of the habitable world that, even if it were united to Europe, it would not be equal to Asia; perhaps it is even less than Europe.*[32]

When Strabo refers to the 'habitable world' he is implicitly locating civilization as the preserve of Europe and Asia, and within those continents seeing it concentrated very much around the Mediterranean itself (implicitly, with Rome as the hub).

He suggests that Africa would like to be a part of this although, elsewhere in his books, collectively entitled *Geographica*, he also acknowledges that Africa (particularly, the fertile western half of the Mediterranean seaboard) was coveted by Europeans. Strabo, who was well aware of the epic struggles for supremacy between the Romans and Carthaginians, alluded to tensions between the two continents that have continued as a recurring feature of Mediterranean life.

Roman power (if not for all of that time, supremacy) endured for the best part of a millennium, more or less the first 500 years being the time of the Roman Republic and the second (until towards the end of the fifth century AD) the Roman Empire. For much of this era, control of the Mediterranean lands was complete and the sea

Ruins around the Mediterranean provide a tangible link with the classical past, spanning the gap of millennia.
Leptis Magna & Sabratha.

itself was used extensively for commerce, military and governmental traffic; little wonder it was commonly referred to as 'our sea', or even the 'empire ocean'[33]. Rome itself was not for all of this time the sole capital and the emperor Constantine was responsible for creating an eastern branch of the empire, centred on Byzantium (renamed Constantinople in 330). Towards the end of the days of Empire, dominion was in fact divided between West and East, centred on Rome and Constantinople respectively. The Eastern or Byzantine Empire survived for another millennium—as long as the period of former Roman supremacy—espousing the Greek language and traditions, combined with Orthodox Christianity, until it was in turn taken over and its lands incorporated in the Ottoman Empire.

The Mediterranean, from one side to the other, set the innermost boundaries for Rome's expansionist plans and, even if they had not chosen to go further afield, controlling the boundaries of the sea alone would have been an unrivalled achievement. Territorial acquisition, however, was only part of the story for alongside military might there was a comparable expansion of trade, with sea traffic heavier than it had ever been before. This would not have been possible without ever-improving methods of exchange, from coinage to harbour administration, from a good system of law to an efficient taxation system. Nor would it have been possible without well-constructed ships, effective docking facilities and an outstanding infrastructure of roads and bridges to connect the ports with their hinterlands. The more that trade as well as military control increased, the more the Mediterranean 'displayed a certain unity in style and life.'[34]

In spite of the Roman tendency to sweep all before them, there was at first a willingness to incorporate certain elements of earlier Greek life; in time, though, they had more than enough of their own culture to transmit. Starting with their language, Latin proved to be of enormous sophistication, demonstrated in acclaimed writings by the likes of Virgil and Horace and later used to lend a common structure to the evolving languages of conquered European nations. The Romans also produced paintings and sculpture of lasting note, and advanced the arts of cooking and gardening. Of all their contributions, though, it must surely be in their architectural and engineering innovations that the Romans made their most visible contribution to future generations. In the hands of the Romans, buildings changed their shape, the most novel difference being in the use of the arch and, employing the same principles, the vault. Mighty new structures, like the Colosseum became possible, as did the aqueducts and bridges that were a Roman trade mark. In their cities a certain uniformity crept in, just as it had with the Greeks before them. One could reasonably expect, from one city to another, paved roads from the countryside to enter through well-fortified gates, each following a straight axis into a standardized central square, the forum. That would be very much a public space and usually the scene of a market, with colonnades along each side to offer shelter from the elements. Close to the forum was the temple of the three gods of the Capitol (Jupiter, Juno and Minerva); the senate as the local seat of government and the basilica to administer justice; and (depending on the size of the settlement) an amphitheatre, circuses, latrines and baths. Cities had never been like this before and even with the demise of Roman power in the fifth century they were to bequeath, around the Mediterranean and well beyond, a formidable legacy.

For centuries after the fall of Rome the West largely turned its back on the past, in many ways regressing rather than building on early achievements. It was not until the late-thirteenth century that a new respect for learning was born, flourishing first in Italy—centred initially on the artistic powerhouse of Florence—and over the next few centuries spreading through the rest of Europe. Such was the Renaissance, the 're-birth', a far-reaching cultural movement that derived its inspiration from classical sources and the power of rational enquiry. For so long neglected, it was time to look again to the ruined temples and broken columns along the shores of the Mediterranean to rediscover the very origins of European culture. Much had been lost in the intervening years before this new generation of scholars and artists found inspiration in rediscovered ancient texts, mostly in Greek and Latin, which told of long-forgotten achievements.

The Renaissance is personified by the likes of Leonardo da Vinci and Michelangelo, who drew on images of the past and portrayed them in their own idealized making. They and fellow artists pored through revived versions of the Bible, they shared a new interest in Greek history and mythology, and in the well-documented exploits of the Romans. Arab influences (largely through Greek translations) were revisited too but the main interest of artists and writers, architects and musicians, was to be found in the Judaeo-Christian legacy. Cities on the Italian mainland thrived in this period of awakening, prospering from the lucrative trade that the Mediterranean could offer. Venice and Genoa, rival city states, led the way in capturing rich markets and securing their presence across the whole of the region.

They were well placed to capitalize on the lively trade between the Levant and continental Europe, although—on account of the sharp rivalry between the two cities, the constant nuisance and threat of piracy, and the opposition of the Turks who competed for control of the same waters—their resultant wealth was well earned. In their heyday, both Venice and Genoa were favoured by merchants, the harbours were full, the city fathers invested in grand buildings of religious and municipal importance, and the arts were generously supported. Later, when shipping routes bypassed the Mediterranean, both cities declined and Venice, especially, assumed the sad disposition of 'marine melancholy' that somehow defines its character.[35] Its very location on a series of islands, embraced by the still and often grey waters of the facing lagoon, exudes a sense of decay—indeed, of a city slowly sinking into the sea.

In spite of later decline, it was the Renaissance that established the Mediterranean forever in Western thought as the cradle of civilization, giving a sense of perspective (albeit partisan) to the disjointed histories of the past. And it was the Renaissance, even after it had passed its zenith, that encouraged later generations (starting in the late-sixteenth but mainly in the eighteenth and early-nineteenth centuries) to go a step further and make their own cultural pilgrimage to Mediterranean lands. Samuel Johnson struck a popular chord in the eighteenth century, in the midst of a classical revival in Europe, when he famously declared that 'the grand object of travelling is to see the shores of the Mediterranean'.[36]

Most vividly, such pilgrimages were embodied in the idea of the Grand Tour, a fairly standard itinerary favoured by young aristocrats, usually men in the first place but, later, ladies with a chaperone. Such an experience was considered in European elitist circles an essential part of a young person's education, offering direct exposure to some of the artefacts—from ancient times as well as more recent works of the Renaissance—that defined the roots and essence of Western civilization. The Grand Tour was especially favoured amongst the English upper classes, where young men would all have received in their schooling a grounding in the classics, but it became popular too amongst wealthy counterparts in other countries. Typically, an itinerary would include visits to Venice and Florence, Rome and Naples, as well as the archaeological sites of Herculaneum and Pompeii; and for the more adventurous there would be extended tours to take them to the ruins in Sicily and even, in the nineteenth century (with the ending of Turkish rule), to the very heartland of Greece.

From being simply building rubble, ruins took on a new and more profound meaning. Perhaps no-one has better interpreted this than the English novelist, Rose Macaulay, in *Pleasure of Ruins*. Writing after the end of the Second World War her interpretation of ruins has a sense of desolation and poignancy, as well as pleasure and discovery; seeking to shrug off the impact of the recent past, she describes her work as 'less ruin-worship than the worship of a tremendous past.'[37] In her search for ruins she casts the net wider than the Mediterranean, although it is the sites of classical civilizations along its shores that draw her most. She is, after all, a child of her times and can speak of her Western heritage with pride and certainty, in a way that contemporary authors would find more difficult:

> *In the ruin-loving dreams of western man it is Greece and Italy which have always mainly enshrined those wistful, backward-gazing dreams. Perhaps because it was there that our civilization was cradled and grew; we yearn back to these vestiges of our past. Perhaps because we have been bred in a classical culture, given from our youth up to understand that there was the glory of the world; hypnotized, our eyes dazzle with it. Here were Socrates, Plato, Pericles, Praxiteles; here was Troy, here Athens, the Islands, there Magna Graecia, and the tremendousness of Rome. Nothing can compete...*[38]

Macaulay's travels include visits to the Turkish ruins of Troy and Ephesus, to Tyre in Lebanon and Leptis Magna in Libya, to New Paphos in Cyprus and the sites of Delos and Bassae in Greece, and to Paestum in Italy. It is the ruins themselves that

Orientalism has been a constant source of fascination for European visitors. Tunis.

she holds in awe, in preference to the buildings that they once were. She marvels, for instance, at the solitary beauty of the remains of Apollo's temple at Bassae, in the Arcadian mountains, and she would undoubtedly have preferred what she saw then to the artificiality of more recent restoration. Decay has its own appeal. No matter that columns have collapsed and surfaces are weathered, it is here that the very essence of the past is to be found; as symbols of a lost civilization such ruins present 'the stunning impact of world history on its amazed heirs'.[39] And everywhere the Mediterranean landscape provides a fitting backcloth, whether it is the shimmering sea or windswept mountains, an isolated promontory or clusters of fig trees and olive groves.

The Place of Faith

There is only one religion, though there are a hundred versions of it.[40]

As well as the political and cultural forerunners of modern life, the Mediterranean also saw the flourishing of three of the world's great monotheisms: Judaism, Christianity and Islam. Not all three originated on the shores of the Mediterranean, nor were they later confined to its boundaries, but all were to play an important part in the early and continuing history of the region as a whole and its cities in particular.

First came Judaism, its precise origins by no means sharply defined but indicated in the Old Testament and at least partly borne out by archaeological remains; it was left to the Greeks to write the first histories, as such. The story would have it that God designated Abraham to be father of his 'chosen people' and to spread the word of this new beginning. The Almighty then communicated with Moses, pronouncing a set of rules, including the Ten Commandments. Jewish kings, such as Saul, David and Solomon added a political and military dimension, enabling religious influence to be extended further afield. Much of its early history was located in the eastern Mediterranean, centred on the two kingdoms of Judah and Israel (the latter largely confined to the north of the modern state).

From there the Jews later dispersed over a much wider area of the Mediterranean, drawn by trading opportunities and driven from one place to another by successive persecutions. The start of this diaspora, a constant feature of Jewish history, can be dated to around 300 BC;[41] first northwards into Syria and western Turkey, and south and westwards to Egypt and Libya on the North African coast. Some six hundred years later, on the eve of the Roman adoption of Christianity, the diaspora had reached most of the Mediterranean lands.[42]

Even where the Jews were initially welcomed, mainly for their trading and financial skills, they invariably suffered later persecution. Much of this opposition stemmed from proponents of other dominant religions, especially Christianity along the European shores and, to a lesser extent, Islam elsewhere. Jews were banished, first from France and later from Spain and Portugal, the result being a return flow of migrations back across the Mediterranean; this particular body of Jews was known as the Sephardim and the name became used more widely to describe all Jews in the region. In between their various expulsions, they were to play an important part in the commercial life of the various cities of the Mediterranean.

Meanwhile, the diaspora had already taken other Jews—the Ashkenazim—in large numbers northwards into central and eastern Europe. Persecutions have been an inseparable feature of Jewish history, culminating in the Holocaust of the Second World War, and, partly in response, the creation

Religion accounts for so much of what has happened around the Mediterranean, and continues to do so. Beirut & Dubrovnik.

of the State of Israel as a homeland immediately after. In Israel, religion and national identity have been conflated, with significant consequences (as we will see in many of the cities to be visited) for the geopolitics of the Mediterranean and the Middle East.

Following Judaism, the second of the great monotheisms to set roots in the region was Christianity. In this case, there were no ambiguities about its origins, being linked directly to the life and death of Jesus Christ and located in the joint territories of modern Israel and the West Bank.

From the outset it was immersed in conflict, the ruling Romans taking exception to the very idea of worshipping just one God, a sufficient provocation to engage in legendary methods of persecution. In time, of course, the Romans themselves trod the road to Damascus and in the fourth century adopted Christianity as the official religion of its vast but, by then, ailing Empire.

Long after Rome itself had fallen into decline, Byzantium, renamed Constantinople, kept the beacon of Christianity burning in that part of the Mediterranean for a further millennium. Until it finally fell to the Ottoman Turks in 1453, Constantinople was the centre of a vast Empire, just as Rome had been in an earlier era, reaching back along the Danube valley into the heart of Europe, eastwards into Asia Minor and across the sea to North Africa. It was constantly at war with the soldiers of Islam, and when it finally fell it was to Muslim invaders.

Christianity was also riven with internal divisions, the most enduring being between the Greek-speaking Orthodox faction in the eastern territories and the Latin brand of Catholicism to the west. Although this caused grief to the devout, it was not without benefits to the rest of the civilized world and, especially, to the Mediterranean lands: 'it was thus able to transmit across a rather chaotic period, from the fourth century onwards, a whole complex of Graeco-Roman values which were not entirely buried by Christian orthodoxy.'[43] The spread of Christianity also brought with it some outstanding religious architecture, its very magnificence intended to impress believers and non-believers alike. Across the Mediterranean, Christianity announced its presence through its buildings.

In Constantinople, the vast structure of the Hagia Sophia—which was to remain the largest cathedral in the world for nearly a thousand years—dates from the sixth century and served not only as the church for the Patriarch of Constantinople but, no less, as a symbol of Christianity itself in the Byzantine Empire. Elsewhere, in Jerusalem and Rome, in Sicily and Seville, monumental cathedrals were to mark the dominance of the religion of Christ. On a more domestic scale, churches made their mark in innumerable towns and villages, while monasteries were established in remote mountain strongholds. So, too, one can still see small shrines, dotted through the countryside and by the sea, bringing succour to farmers and sailors alike as they go about their work. Following both Judaism and Christianity, the most recent of the three Mediterranean monotheisms is the religion of Islam. Its own origins were located well to the east, in what is now Saudi Arabia, when the Prophet Mohammed in the seventh century told of a different path to righteousness. Mohammed's teachings spread quickly, remarkably so, and within a century of its birth, Islam had been adopted far and wide across the Mediterranean: along the eastern seaboard in Palestine, Syria and Turkey; into North Africa through what is now Egypt, Libya, Tunisia, Algeria and Morocco; then across the sea to Spain and Portugal.

Later, following the fall of the Byzantine Empire, it reached into parts of the Balkans.[44] Islam was linked closely (although not exclusively) with Arab culture, bringing westwards in its train a variety of new forms of architecture and art, cooking and costume. During Europe's so-called 'dark ages' it was left to the followers of Islam to promulgate scientific invention and cultural refinement. Some of the mosques built in the region were not only every bit as impressive as rival cathedrals and synagogues, but their very presence demonstrated new building techniques that enabled the inclusion of giant domes and towering minarets, soon to become familiar features of the Mediterranean skyline. No less distinctive was some of the grander domestic architecture, typified by houses around an inner courtyard, each with its own shaded garden and fountain.

In their different ways, each of the three monotheisms brought lasting changes to the region, many for the good; together, they introduced a host of ideas and artefacts, customs and cultural traditions that make the Mediterranean unique. The problem is that doctrinal difference has also proved to be a source of enduring conflict, leaving a legacy of outstanding issues still to be resolved.

THEATRE OF WAR

In some respects, the very word Mediterranean is a synonym for human achievement. Yet there is also a darker side, for where else has there been such incessant and bloody conflict, from the time of earliest occupation to the present day? Nation against nation, cities plundering cities, the banners of ethnicity and religion on the battlefield, foreign powers fighting their own wars in the region, not to mention pirates and terrorists. Here one see the very best and worst of the human spirit.

Ancient Rivalries

North against south meant Rome against Carthage; east against west meant Orient against the Occident, Islam against Christendom.[45]

There are seemingly endless permutations that shape the complex history of conflict between one set of interests and another. Every empire itself created a myriad of oppositions, resulting in the confrontation of whole armies, in the cumulative impact of raiding parties, in fierce and bloody battles at sea, in the razing of conquered towns and wholesale massacre of populations. It was through the various Mediterranean empires that civilization was spread but the reverse side of that is an unending story of humanity at its militaristic worst.

The Minoans and Mycanaeans, Greeks and Romans, Carthaginians and Moors, Venetians and Turks, all took to the sea — to defend their boundaries or to acquire new territories. From the earliest times it has been a place of warfare. Cities have at different times been on the side of conquerors as well as captives, they have gained as well as lost. Sometimes they succumbed to enemy attacks, their fortunes plundered, whole populations massacred and buildings set on fire; at other times, their own navies sailed from the various harbours to protect trade routes, to ward off potential attacks and to return with bounty. In the cities that prospered from war, the shipyards were busy with orders for new fleets and then with repairs after battle.

No matter how far back one looks the story is much the same. The Bible itself, records warring factions and outright atrocities. In the Old Testament, the Lord urged little restraint in clearing the way for the Israelites to settle in Palestine, in the south-eastern corner of the Mediterranean (known then as the Great Sea). Cross the valley of the Jordan, he commands Joshua, and 'from the wilderness and this Lebanon as far as the great river, the river Euphrates, all the land of the Hittites to the Great Sea toward the going down of the sun shall be your territory'. Joshua and his armies duly obeyed and 'utterly destroyed' everyone who stood in their way.[46] Later, it was King David who continued the struggle, annihilating the resentful Philistines and establishing Jerusalem as the capital of his nation. In due course, the Israelites were themselves defeated by the Assyrians and King Nebuchadnezzar destroyed the capital, though the Israelites were able to return to their spiritual homeland in the sixth century BC. Disputes over the legitimacy of the occupancy of Jerusalem and its surrounding lands have, of course, continued ever since.

Meanwhile, the Egyptian civilization, by then well into its third millennium, had already passed its peak. For most of its long history it had been remarkably self-contained but in its decline it fell prey to outsiders: first the Persians, who arrived from the east, and then Alexander the Great, who hailed from Macedonia and in the fourth century BC usurped the earlier conquerors before continuing his own extraordinary campaigns, that took him eastwards as far as the Himalayas. In his thirteen years as king, Alexander not only suppressed dissent amongst the Greek city states but he pushed back the Persians and brought the whole of the eastern Mediterranean under Hellenic influence if not total control; Anatolia, Syria, Phoenicia, Judea, Gaza and Egypt were all to fall to his advancing armies.

Alexander was an exceptional commander but, even without his exploits, the history of ancient Greece is replete with tales of historic battles on land and at sea. Although the fifth century BC is recalled (by Athenians at least) as a golden age, it was also a time of recurring warfare—against external forces and also, internally, between city states. Externally, the legendary enemy was the Persian Empire, and it was left to a handful of Greek city states, led by Athens but also at times with the support of Sparta and Corinth, to engage the opposing forces. At Marathon, the Athenian army, greatly outnumbered by the Persians, achieved a famous victory, but it was not enough to stop the return of the invaders a few years later. On this second occasion, the Athenians were assisted by the Spartans and were better prepared, having used the pause in hostilities to build their own, impressive navy. The Persian forces were, again, overwhelming in number and it was finally at sea that the Athenians battered their way to ultimate victory. Later in that same century, the battles were internal but no less fierce, this time between competing city states in the Peloponnesian War. The contemporary Greek soldier and historian, Thucydides, has provided a seminal record of this quarter-century long conflict, telling of the terrible destruction of farmland and cities as well as human life, an episode that led eventually to the decline of Athens itself. There had been nothing like it before, claimed Thucydides, for this war:

> ... *not only lasted for a long time, but throughout its course brought with it unprecedented suffering for Hellas. Never before have so many cities been captured and then devastated, whether by foreign armies or by the Hellenic powers themselves (some of these cities, after capture, were resettled with new inhabitants); never had there been so many exiles; never such loss of life—both in the actual warfare and in internal revolutions.*[47]

The problem for the Greeks was that they never presented a united front, fragmented in the face of an external enemy and at other times at war with each other. In contrast, although the Romans also had more than their fair share of internal disputes, they were able to close ranks when it counted; their military effectiveness and cohesion was at the very heart of their expansion across the Mediterranean. First they had to see off the Etruscans, in 510 BC, who had ruled that part of Italy during the previous century. With this done, Rome was still, in its early history, a relatively weak state, and must have seemed easy game at the time for an invading Greek army led by King Pyrrhus of Epirus. In the ensuing battle, in 270 BC, the losses were so great on both sides that a victory for the invaders amounted only to a 'Pyrrhic' victory; in any case, within five years the Greeks had been forced to retreat totally from the Roman hinterland.

The most telling opposition, instead, came from North Africa, in the form of the Carthaginians, forcing Rome to engage in the costly but ultimately victorious Punic Wars. There was an enormous loss of life on both sides, culminating, in 146 BC, in the total destruction by the Roman army of the city of Carthage (with a reputed population of some 750,000). Rome had, by then, taken valuable territories from the Carthaginians, including Spain, and, with its newly won control of the sea as well as land, 'it was Rome, not Carthage, which would be mistress of the Mediterranean in the centuries that followed'.[48]

In spite of its dominance and seemingly relentless territorial expansion, Rome was never, for any length of time, wholly at peace with itself or with others. Its history in the last days of the Republic and in the era of the Empire that followed is one of intermittent civil strife and an unremitting story of battles abroad. As the Empire gained control not just of the whole of the Mediterranean but of lands well beyond, it left in its wake revealing evidence of massacres, pillage and cities razed to the ground. Its own armies incurred massive losses but these were always more than matched by the destruction inflicted on their enemies. Onwards they marched and across the sea they sailed, until there was no part of the Mediterranean that was beyond the reach of Rome. When jurisdiction of the Empire was later divided between west and east, Rome and Constantinople, control of the inland sea was complete.

Crescent and Cross

The encounter between western Christendom and Islam after 1099 [the fall of Jerusalem to the Christians] created a malign heritage for both communities. Each battle, siege, despoliation or defilement fuelled opposing narratives.[49]

With the rapid growth and spread of Islam from its Middle Eastern birthplace in the seventh century, coupled with the eastern march of Christianity, the two great religions became locked into a collision course. Both belief systems rested on an assumption that theirs could be the only one and that followers of the other were infidels. The geography of their respective areas of dominance ensured that the eventual battlegrounds would be primarily in southern Europe and in the eastern Mediterranean, although North Africa would become of increasing importance too. To illustrate this seemingly inevitable clash of cultures we can look at what happened in the series of military campaigns known in the West as the Crusades.[50]

In the event, it was the westward march of the Islamic Seljuk Turks, who hailed from the steppes of Central Asia, which brought the two religions face to face. Renowned for their skills on the battlefield, the progress of the Turks into Asia Minor was gradual but relentless. Eventually, as they came increasingly under threat, the Byzantine Christians responded and an army was sent from Constantinople in 1071 with the aim of turning back the invaders. A battle was fought at Manzikert, in eastern Turkey, in which the Christians were defeated; because of its far-reaching consequences this is seen as 'one of the most decisive encounters of history'.[51]

An immediate consequence was an appeal by the Byzantines to fellow Christians for military aid, but even before an effective response could be mounted the invaders had continued on their way, occupying most of the eastern Mediterranean coast, including Antioch, one of the five patriarchates of the Eastern Orthodox Church. Alexandria and Jerusalem had already been ceded and, only Rome and Constantinople still remained free of Islamic rule.

The divided city of Nicosia is a modern reminder of an ancient conflict between Christianity and Islam.

Once again, an appeal was made for assistance from the West, this time by the Byzantine Emperor, Alexius I. Witnessing the fragility of this eastern bulwark, and only too aware of existing incursions by warriors of Islam into southern Europe from North Africa, the Pope in Rome, Urban II, responded by calling for defenders of the Cross to rally to the holy cause. In so doing, he ushered in the first of what proved to be no less than seven Crusades, fought at various times between 1096 and 1365.

The whole episode has traditionally been portrayed in the West as an heroic struggle against the barbarism of the infidels, a battle between Good and Evil fought on the dry plains of the eastern Mediterranean. Significantly, in Muslim history the same campaigns were seen as little more than skirmishes, just temporary obstacles in the way of the onward advance of Islam.

If the truth is to be measured in terms of outcomes, it is the latter interpretation that is probably more accurate, for the whole of the contested area fell progressively to the Crescent and not to the Cross.

Undoubtedly, there remains more than a whisper of romance in the adventures of knights and their followers making the long and arduous journey from their homes in the West to fight in hostile conditions, ostensibly for a noble cause. There, in alien lands, they built great forts and flew the flag of the Cross from the battlements. Courage would not have been in short supply and there were, indeed, some famous, albeit short-lived, victories that encouraged the writing of fine stories and epic poems. Of all the historic events, it is hard to imagine one that would have more readily excited the popular imagination than the First Crusade, which saw the recapture, in 1099, of Jerusalem from the Saracens (the soldiers of Islam).[52]

Nothing could have been more symbolic—Jerusalem was in its way a metaphor for paradise in Christian mythology—and yet there was little about the record of conquest that is either romantic or mystical. It was, in fact, a tale of hideous atrocities, where every non-believer found in the city was massacred; Jews as well as Muslims were put to the sword in a frenzy of killing.

This, the marauders believed, was justified as a Holy War; after all, was it not written in the Book of Revelation that the angels of the Lord wielded sickles across the land and threw their harvest into the 'great wine press of the wrath of God'? And was it not also written that 'blood flowed from the wine press, as high as a horse's bridle'?[53] If the streets of Jerusalem were to run with blood that was, surely, no more than God's command and the resultant Kingdom established in the city was no less exalted because of its violent birth.

Just as the first of the Crusades started on an exceptionally violent note, the last brought it all to a symmetrical close: it was 'the most shameful of them all [and] it set back the course of progress in the Mediterranean by the best part of a century.'[54]

This time, in 1365, it was the turn of the ancient city of Alexandria to bear the brunt of the assault; even resident Byzantine Christians were treated as the enemy by the campaigners from the West, in the same way as the infidels. There was nothing remotely divine about the tactics used: 'The slaughter was indiscriminate. The important Christian and Jewish communities suffered as much as the Muslim majority; churches and synagogues as well as mosques were put to the torch. Five thousand prisoners were captured and sold into slavery.'[55]

In between the first and last of the Crusades there were other dramatic events, none more than within the Christian camp itself, divided between the soldiers of Rome and Constantinople. Years of brooding enmity between the two culminated in 1205 in the capture by the western contingent of the Byzantine capital itself. Nothing played more into the hands of the watching Saracens than the sight of Frankish-led forces taking the city by storm.

It was not just the event itself but the manner of it that shocked watching Christians and Muslims alike: a barbaric 'orgy of vandalism and brutality'[56] that left Constantinople desecrated and Byzantine rule in a weakened state, even more vulnerable to eventual occupation by the Saracens.

By the time that Alexandria was plundered in the final Crusade, the region was in many ways no more stable than when the first soldiers had appeared more than two and a half centuries earlier. The Byzantine Empire—the only enduring Christian force that might have been able to check the continuing advance of the Saracens—was by then well into decline. Any lingering notion in the West that the Muslims could somehow be forced to retreat from the shores of the Mediterranean was already a distant dream.

As if to mark the end of an era, in the following century, in 1453, the walls of Constantinople itself were breached, this time by the Saracens, and it became a Muslim city, the new capital of the expanding Ottoman Empire. The future of the eastern Mediterranean was, in this way, set for many centuries to come.

Brigands at Sea

Torrid summer then reigns uncontested in the centre of the Mediterranean, the best time for shipping, piracy and war.[57]

For most of its occupied history, the sea itself has been a relatively lawless domain. Across the Mediterranean, beyond the reach of conventional custodians of law and order, pirates have brazenly ruled their own borderless realm. Valuable commodities like metals and silks, spices and grain, carried by merchant ships from port to port, for centuries offered rich pickings for opportunistic marauders. No less lucrative was the practice of kidnapping travellers and holding them in exchange for a ransom. With the pirates adept at manoeuvring their ships and skilled in hand-to-hand fighting, no merchant trader was safe from attack; nor were the well-stocked warehouses in the ports.

As the confidence of pirates grew, towns and cities were the scene of successful attacks from the sea, at times even threatening whole city states and nations. In desperation, it was not uncommon for governments to buy security through what would now be regarded as protection money. Pirates were, indeed, a fact of life in this region from the time of the first settled nations; as early as the second millennium BC there are signs that the Egyptians were troubled by such raiders. Certainly, by the time that Thucydides wrote of the Peloponnesian War in the fifth century BC, pirates were undoubtedly a force to be reckoned with:

> *For in these early times, as communication by sea became easier, so piracy became a common profession both among the Hellenes and among the barbarians who lived on the coast and in the islands. The leading pirates were powerful men, acting both out of self-interest and in order to support the weak among their own people. They would descend among cities which were unprotected by walls and indeed consisted only of scattered settlements; and by plundering such places they would gain most of their livelihood.*[58]

In his characteristically laconic style, Thucydides goes on to say that, far from being a shameful occupation, piracy was then regarded as 'quite honourable'. It was not uncommon for newcomers arriving by boat to be asked whether they were pirates, and not to take offence if they were. In later episodes, it is evident that, as the practice spread across the Mediterranean, this surprisingly tolerant approach was not to endure. In 68 BC the Romans were affronted when pirates ransacked their port of Ostia, an event which led to far-reaching changes in the very governance of the Republic. Rome's most distinguished soldier, Pompeius Magnus, seized the opportunity to claim supreme powers and, although constitutionalists objected, he silenced the opposition by clearing the sea of pirates within three months.

The pirates returned, of course, when the attention of Rome was diverted by new campaigns, and they continued until the nineteenth century to terrorize one part of the sea or another. From time to time their influence was especially marked, as it was after the capture of Crete by Muslim invaders in the ninth century, when the large island became 'a nest of pirates and the centre of the Mediterranean slave trade'.[59] Meanwhile, further to the west, Muslim pirates constantly harassed regular shipping and mounted raids on Christian settlements along the coast, in southern France and Italy. Rome itself was overrun by pirates in 846 and in the following century so, too, was the important maritime city state of Genoa—leaving only Venice strong enough to withstand the threat.

Later still, Muslim pirates gained a notorious reputation along the Barbary Coast of North Africa; acting, as they did, on behalf of client states, they were more generally known as corsairs. The rise of the Barbary pirates can be found in the wake of the expulsion of the Moors from Spain, over a long period but especially from the end of the fifteenth century. These conditions created a natural breeding ground for a new generation of buccaneers, 'ruined, disaffected and longing for revenge'.[60] Those of their Christian victims who took the brunt of the raids learnt to respond in kind, and Sardinians, Maltese, Genoese and Greeks were all responsible for their own brigands of the sea.

Fernand Braudel, the pioneer historian of the Mediterranean, saw an inverse relationship between the occurrence of warfare and outbreaks of piracy. Thus, the suspension of major hostilities after 1574 was followed by a new outbreak of lawlessness: 'on the water, the end of conflict between the great states brought to the forefront of the sea's history that secondary form of war, piracy.'[61] Sometimes, he contends, pirates were, in effect, working for a particular power and were then properly known as privateers; sometimes, too, he sees in their actions an attempt to save their communities from starvation rather than simply engaging in illegal acts as a means of personal gain. In other instances, notably in the case of the perennial conflict between Islam and Christianity, it almost takes on the form of a proxy war: 'in the sense that the entire Mediterranean was an arena of constant conflict between two adjacent and warring civilizations, war was a permanent reality, excusing and justifying piracy.'[62]

The seventeenth century was another time of active piracy in the region. This episode included the involvement of a growing number of disaffected European seamen as well as a new generation of Muslim corsairs from Barbary.[63] The best of the pirates were good seamen and skilled with sail, which proved altogether faster and more effective than the traditional, oar-driven galleys hitherto favoured along the Barbary Coast. So long as they enjoyed continuing success, the Mediterranean could never enjoy a settled existence. Over a thirty-year period, for instance, Sicily suffered attacks from pirates on more than eighty occasions, and with such uncertainties no ship could set sail from a Mediterranean port without fear of its cargo being forcibly removed.

In spite of periodic attempts to clear the sea of these marauders, various incidents continued until early in the nineteenth century. The Barbary Coast was still the source of greatest nuisance, so much so that things finally came to a head when the American navy intervened. America's own trade along that coast was at risk and (unlike other nations) its government was not prepared to pay the high rate of tribute demanded by pirates to guarantee safe passage. Two wars ensued, the second with the support of the Dutch and British navies, spelling the beginning of the end for the long history of piracy in the Mediterranean. The French colonization of North Africa that followed brought a new regime to the lands along that coastline and led to the final expulsion of the remaining pirates.

Sea of Encounters

For the inmost sea of all the earth is shaken with his ships... [64]

Piracy presented a persistent nuisance but the scale of disruption was as nothing compared with the large-scale battles that have taken place in and around the Mediterranean under the flags of warring nations. For many of the maritime cities, hardly a century can have passed without the sound of galley oars approaching the shore or the sight of billowing sails on the horizon. In more recent times, there would be powerful destroyers with heavy artillery, with fighter planes overhead. Time and again, this busy sea has been host to legendary encounters, becoming one of the world's most heavily visited theatres of warfare.

'I see wars, horrible wars, and the Tiber foaming with much blood.' [65] Virgil's evocative lines tell of an earlier period but are also a reminder of the constancy of the Mediterranean as a place of war. Time and again the sea has witnessed fierce and bloody battles, some of which are long forgotten but others proved turning points in world history. In the sixteenth century, for instance, the Battle of Lepanto was, in certain respects, a continuation of the saga of the Crusades; it was also a portrayal of warfare conducted with methods that were already outmoded. [66] On the one side were the Ottoman Turks, flying the flag of Islam and dominant in the eastern Mediterranean, their influence to be increased in 1571 with a famous victory in wresting Cyprus from the Venetians. Not only did Ottoman control of the Levantine ports yield a monopoly of trade but the West was forever in fear of an advance into southern Europe. Rome itself, the Christian capital, was constantly in the sights of successive Ottoman leaders; while Spain—although it had seemingly shaken off the hold of the Moors after a long period of occupation— was always wary of further threats from North Africa. In response, the Christians believed that the best way to defend was to strike back, a belief that led to a new alliance of naval forces.

Led by the charismatic Spaniard, Don Juan, the Christian League (as the alliance was named) lost no time in assembling its fleet and seeking out the Ottoman navy. Fighting ships were gradually adopting new designs but the technology was still essentially traditional, comprising galleys (which relied on a single deck of oars in battle, with metal bows for ramming), galleons (wholly reliant on sail, cumbersome but bristling with artillery) and galleasses (with a more balanced combination of oars and guns). The two fleets were to join battle off the coast of Greece, at Lepanto, in October 1571: 'gun upon gun, ha! ha! gun upon gun, hurrah!' [67] Through clever tactics the ships of the League manoeuvred themselves into dominant positions and by the end of the day, victory was theirs.

The loss of lives could be measured in thousands and the destruction of ships in hundreds. Most of the losses were on the Turkish side, amounting to 113 galleys sunk and 117 captured, with 30,000 sailors killed and another 8,000 taken prisoner.[68] Blood had spilled into the waters of the Mediterranean before but this was, by any measure, a fearful day:

> *The greater fury of the battle lasted for four hours and was so bloody and horrendous that the sea and the fire seemed as one, many Turkish galleys burning down to the water and the surface of the sea, red with blood, was covered with Moorish coats, turbans, quivers, arrows, bows, shields, oars, boxes, cases and other spoils of war, and above all many human bodies.*[69]

More than two centuries later, lines were again drawn, but this time between European powers at war with each other—the navy of the French Republic, led by Napoleon, matched against all and sundry.[70] Napoleon himself hailed from a Mediterranean island, Corsica, and in an era of conquest he saw the sea as a natural stage on which to advance his expansionist cause. One of his various maritime exploits rested on a plan to rein Egypt into the French empire and, ultimately, to make a move on to India to challenge the British for overall control. His campaign started well enough, with the French commander typically taking the initiative faster than his enemy.

On his way across the sea, his navy quickly swept aside token resistance from the Order of the Knights of St. John, enabling his ships to re-provision on the island of Malta. From there they made their way to the Egyptian coast, landing near Alexandria and rapidly capturing he city. Cairo was then in his sights and in the exotically named Battle of the Pyramids, the French army was victorious. Meanwhile, the British fleet, under Admiral Nelson, was in close pursuit. After a false start that led him first towards Syria, Nelson found the enemy ships at anchor in the Nile delta and took advantage of favourable weather and currents to make an immediate attack. In a fierce, overnight battle—the Battle of the Nile—most of the French fleet was destroyed, including Napoleon's flagship, *L'Orient*. The French were not, at that stage, ousted from Egypt but their navy was defeated and Napoleon's line of communication broken. His plans for further conquest in that region and to the east were effectively over. For a child of the Mediterranean it was an emotionally wounding as well as a strategically damaging blow.

Twice in the twentieth century, in each of two world wars, the region again became a major theatre of operations. Like a duelling ground on a grand scale, on sea and on land, it was where the opposing alliances chose to fight. For the surrounding nations and their cities, there was a heavy price to pay for being at the crossroads of continents. Thus, during the First World War, with Turkey a member of the German-dominated alliance that included Austria-Hungary, the sounds of gunfire would soon be heard along the shores of the eastern Mediterranean.

It was widely believed by the western allies that the Ottoman Empire was in its dying days, a simplistic view which cost their forces dear; the Turks, inspired by the revolutionary modernizer, Mustapha Kemal, were still more than capable of producing a highly effective fighting force. Nothing showed this more than the fatal events that surrounded the allied landings on the Turkish peninsula of Gallipoli.[71]

At a strategic level, the idea of a thrust from the south was sound enough. If, as the western allies believed, Turkey was vulnerable, it should have been possible to force a way through from the sea, as intended, first to capture Constantinople and then to link with Russian forces to the north. Tactically, though, the mission was a disaster. Gallipoli, the finger of land between the eastern Aegean and the Dardanelles (the entrance to the Black Sea), was chosen for two landings, one by a British-led force and the other by Australian and New Zealand troops (the Anzacs).

Both landings failed to meet their objective, the British immediately coming under fire and suffering numerous casualties as they fought to remain on the beach, while the Anzacs landed in the wrong place and found themselves trapped beneath high cliffs. For ten months, the allied forces dug in on the peninsula, until finally, in January 1916, the campaign was called off and the surviving troops retreated to a fleet of rescue ships.

By then, more than 100,000 soldiers from the armies of both sides had died in battle and another quarter of a million were injured; as well as these, an additional 90,000 fell victim to dysentery and frostbite. It represented a major defeat for the invading forces, who were shown to have been prepared neither for the searing heat of summer nor the biting cold of winter. Not only was the mission to fail in its territorial aims but, sensing that the tide had turned in favour of the German alliance, Bulgaria joined the war on that side.

A quarter of a century after the tragic events of Gallipoli, in the Second World War the Mediterranean was again the arena for fighting by foreign forces.[72] Its strategic importance this time was twofold: the western allies were determined to retain control of the Suez Canal, while the Mediterranean was once more perceived as the launch pad from which to pierce the vulnerable southern front of Europe. Few parts of the region escaped the reach of one side or the other—the Allied or Axis forces—not least of all the islands (such as Malta, Sicily and Sardinia) which served as important supply points and havens to repair and regroup. As a major battleground, though, there is little to compare with the fierce fighting that took place in the North African desert terrain, especially of Tunisia, Libya and Egypt.

It all started with the hold that Italy (as part of the Axis) enjoyed as a colonial power in Libya, and from where it mounted an attack on Egypt; pressing eastwards it was at one point almost within view of Alexandria. Against superior numbers, Allied forces pushed back the Italian advance and gained control of a number of Libyan towns, including the port of Tobruk. The apparent weakness of Italian forces led to the direct intervention of the Germans, under General (later Field-Marshal) Erwin Rommel. He quickly reversed the situation, putting Tobruk (held largely by

Australian forces) under siege and gaining control of much of Libya, with Egypt then clearly in his sights.

It was only with the appointment of the British General Montgomery and the later arrival of American forces that the tables were once again turned, leading to the departure of Rommel himself from this desert theatre of war. By May 1943, the previously dominant German-led army was forced to surrender and over 250,000 German and Italian troops laid down their arms.

The desert war was over but not without an enormous tally of casualties on both sides; once again, in this latest episode of history, the shores of the Mediterranean were witness to fierce conflicts and consequent loss of life. Along this same coastline, battles had been fought many times before, by the Carthaginians and Romans, by Arabs and Berbers, by generations of pirates, and by colonial powers forcibly taking possession of the whole of the North African coastline and its vast hinterland. There are few, if any, of its cities that cannot tell of successive chapters of conquest and destruction in their own long histories.

EBBS AND FLOWS

Because of its location at the meeting place of three continents, the whole history of the Mediterranean has been bound up with cultural interaction and continues to be so.

Migrant groups like the Mycenaeans made their way southwards through Greece to the Aegean from distant lands in the north and east; the founding of the state of Israel ushered in the arrival of Jews from central and eastern Europe, joining those already in the region; dominant nations have persistently looked for opportunities to extend their boundaries in pursuit of richer farmland and other resources; wars and colonization have led to large-scale territorial acquisitions across continents. Nothing has ever stood still and in the modern era the situation is no less fluid. Trade has been a constant element in the mix, not only as a source of great wealth but also a reason for the traffic of peoples.

Now there are two additional forces at work: one is an ostensibly benign flow of northern Europeans to the sunny shores of the Mediterranean, some of it for tourism but, increasingly, also as a place to live; the other results from the sheer pressure of population growth, poverty and political instability on the African continent and in the eastern Mediterranean, leading to a relentless drift of migrants into southern Europe and beyond. It is a region of ebbs and flows—of goods and finance, people and ideas. As we will see in the chapters to follow, cities themselves have been central to this process—serving as communicators between cultures and shapers of destiny, not merely passive receptors but also instruments of change.

Commercial Considerations

The Mediterranean... became probably the most vigorous place of interaction on the face of this planet...[73]

Initially, trade routes were confined to the shores of the Mediterranean itself, with carriers invariably using the sea rather than difficult journeys across land. Unsure of themselves, the early navigators stayed close to the coastline, sailing from port to port. Longer distance routes across the sea came later, before more intrepid sailors ventured beyond the Pillars of Hercules and into the Atlantic. In this widening of networks, the Phoenicians played the lead role; these were the world's original mariners, famed for their boat-building as well as navigational skills. From their home ports of Tyre and Sidon, Byblos and Arwad, along the coast of what is now Lebanon, they sailed throughout the Mediterranean and bravely into the unknown seas beyond. To assist their trade they established outposts along the North African coast (including the famed city of Carthage) and on islands including Cyprus, Sardinia, Corsica and Sicily, while the port of Cadiz extended Phoenician influence into the seemingly limitless waters of the Atlantic. As the Mediterranean's first merchants, the Phoenicians were an important economic force from the middle of the second millennium BC until the end of the eighth century BC; and 'thanks above all to the luxury goods they provided, they were also a force for civilization. From their Levantine home, as well as from Cyprus, Egypt, Anatolia and Mesopotamia, they would bring ivory and rare woods, superb drinking vessels of gold and silver, flasks of glass and alabaster, seals and scarabs of precious and semi-precious stone.'[74] Nor were the Phoenicians only sailors, for they earned an even more lasting reputation as the likely inventors of a workable alphabet, one that was more useable than the largely indecipherable Egyptian hieroglyphics. It was this alphabet that was soon to be adapted by the Greeks and thence brought more widely into European use.

Even within the confines of the Mediterranean, trade was from the earliest times varied and lucrative. Each of the three adjoining continents supplied an extraordinary variety of merchandise—timber and minerals, grain and oils, fabrics and jewellery, dried fruit and precious stones. The sea was at the hub of this trade, the scene of an intricate network of shipping routes and thriving harbours. Beyond its shores, there were even more lucrative opportunities, drawing merchandise from the surrounding hinterlands and exchanging it for prized goods from the Mediterranean itself. Until the advent of fast and reliable shipping, much of this trade was carried overland from the main ports. Responding to these opportunities, every city worth its name was equipped to play its part, looking both to the sea and to land routes for its income. Typically, the city fathers would invest in an impressive harbour, large enough to accommodate a variety of shipping at any one time. Around the quays were warehouses and merchants' offices, chandlers and repair yards, while the larger ports also hosted finance and insurance houses. Successive empires were built on the profits from commerce, and control of the routes was essential.

Of the ancient imperial powers, Egypt's interest in the Mediterranean was the most localized, being largely limited to the Levant and using other fleets to do their bidding. The Greek city states, however, established new routes to the western lands, although nearby Anatolia and the Levant remained of greater importance. It was left to the Romans to gain control of the whole sea, which they did very effectively in the second century BC, a momentous achievement which David Abulafia describes as a milestone in the region's history:

> *Single rule over mare nostrum ensured freedom of movement and resulted in cultural mixing in the Mediterranean on a scale never seen before or since.*[75]

Certainly, subsequent powers could not match the reach of the Romans. In spite of the dominance of Constantinople, the Byzantines did not exploit the potential of the sea to extend their power. Later, in spite of the formidable Ottoman navy, the Turks were seldom able to control the waters beyond the Mediterranean's eastern basin. Meanwhile, Arab influence in North Africa and the Levant was very much land-based and marine power was not a feature of their presence in the region. In later centuries, some of the city states (notably, Barcelona, Venice and Genoa) used their powerful navies to secure the trade on which they depended, but there was never any question of their controlling the entire sea as the Romans had done. Napoleon had pretensions to do so but he was seen off by the British at the battles of the Nile and Trafalgar, while the British themselves were more interested in safeguarding their own trade routes, within the Mediterranean and *en route*, through the Suez Canal, to the Orient. Mussolini later invoked his nation's Roman heritage to support his claim that North Africa represented Italy's 'fourth shore', but he lacked the military power to enforce it.

In any case, after centuries of being relatively unchallenged, a real 'sea change' had set in, long before the likes of France, Britain and Italy viewed the Mediterranean as theirs for the taking. Its centrality in the world order was questioned as early as the fourteenth century, when bubonic plague swept through the region and decimated half the population. In spite of the dramatic impact at the time, recovery was remarkably swift and it continued to prosper until the advent of more deep-seated changes. Unlike the plague, which was sudden and decisive, these later changes first appeared in the sixteenth century and gathered pace over a long period so that, by the twentieth century, the Mediterranean had become something of a backwater in the global economy. As David Abulafia has concluded (albeit tentatively): 'there is some strength in the argument that after 1500, and certainly after 1850, the Mediterranean became decreasingly important in wider world affairs and 'commerce'.[76]

First came the impact of geographical discovery, when the world map of shipping routes was redrawn in the wake of exploration by Portuguese explorers and others. As a result, the Mediterranean could no longer enjoy its former mercantile monopoly.

Much later, the opening of the Suez Canal in 1869 further reduced the importance of the Mediterranean, which became little more than a thoroughfare for long-distance shipping. Moreover, associated with each of these changes but for other reasons too, by the twentieth century the balance of world power had long shifted from the Mediterranean to north-west Europe, most notably, to Britain, France and Germany. Holland and Austria-Hungary had earlier shared in this geopolitical shift, but the former missed out on the Industrial Revolution while the latter was a victim of the First World War.

In addition to the above factors, the relative economic decline of Mediterranean was also, in no small measure, due to modern industrialization. From the end of the eighteenth century, certain European nations, and later America, engaged in a new form of industrial production, based on coal and iron together with a plentiful water supply. These natural resources had to be nearby, meaning that an area like the Mediterranean was unable to compete. As a result, the Industrial Revolution passed it by and its maritime cities were left to function primarily as trading hubs and local service centres.

Do not come to this region, advises the Greek urban geographer, Lila Leontidou, and expect to find replicas of the cities of northern Europe or North America.[77] Industry came late, in the past fifty years or so, and where it occurs is typified by extensive petro-chemical plants and the processing of imported materials. Container ports have been developed on new sites along the coast, replacing old harbour landings. In spite of new developments, the region remains on the economic margins, certainly compared with its heyday. For geopolitical as well as economic reasons, in the headier days of the European Union the idea was floated of integrating the whole of the region in a combined Euro-Mediterranean free trade bloc. During his French presidential candidacy, in 2007, Nicolas Sarkozy gave the idea impetus: '... the Mediterranean', he declared, 'is a key to our influence in the world...'[78]

A year later, installed in office, Sarkozy convened a conference of EU and Mediterranean leaders in Paris that ratified the formation of the Union for the Mediterranean (or 'Club Med' as it was popularly known). The French President had hoped to limit its membership to the countries surrounding the sea but the conference insisted it should include the whole of the EU. Extending from the Arctic to the Sahara was hardly going to be manageable, but that was nothing compared with events that unfolded in the following year, with the collapse of the Greek economy.

Overnight, the EU turned in on itself, struggling to retain its own unity let alone drawing in even more problematic neighbours. 'Club Med' remains formally in being but, to all intents and purposes, the countries of the Mediterranean have been left once again to chart their own different futures.

The Lotus-Eaters

And round about the keel with faces pale, Dark faces pale against that rosy flame, The mild-eyed melancholy lotus-eaters came.[79]

Life in the Mediterranean is not all trade and commerce. It was Homer who first introduced the notion of a group of lotus-eaters in a hidden corner of Greece, happily imbibing the juice of a narcotic plant, largely immune to the rest of the world. The theme much later appealed to Tennyson, who took his readers to 'a land in which it always seemed afternoon', and who (in the above verse) described 'faces pale' and a 'mild-eyed melancholy' demeanour.[80]

In this depiction there is surely a metaphor for those pale-faced invaders from northern Europe who presently come to the Mediterranean *en masse*, in search of a place that is always afternoon. Both Homer and Tennyson spoke of a particular group enjoying in their own terms an idyllic existence, but the main difference now, as in everything, is one of scale. The lotus-eaters of the current century share the quest for a place where the sun always shines and the troubles of the world are forgotten, but now they arrive on charter flights and in people carriers with trailers, carrying the baggage of everyday life that they so often purport to be leaving behind.

For more than half a century, the Mediterranean has been a mecca for mass tourism, typically accommodated in new hotels designed for package holidays but also in villas and campsites, not to mention the floating hotels of cruise ships. Sun-starved Swedes burn on the beaches, German families lay out their towels in the best spots by hotel pools, British youths maraud in numerous bars that sell cheap alcohol; the inner sea has become the favourite playground for visitors from the north, just a couple of hours away through budget airlines. It is, in fact, the most frequented tourist region on earth.[81] Not surprisingly, the resultant impact on the fragile environment of the Mediterranean and its cultural traditions has become critical.

Sheer numbers alone pose the greatest threat. At the start of the present millennium, the Mediterranean shores were receiving some 200 million visitors per year, and this figure excludes the very significant number of tourists from within the reception countries who like to enjoy their own coastline.

Although many Europeans now choose to travel further afield, to long-haul destinations, the number of visitors to the Mediterranean is expected to rise to 350 million by 2020, partly a result of second and third holidays in a year as more people enjoy a greater disposable income.[82]

The sheer number of tourists, in all seasons, has transformed towns and villages around the Mediterranean. Dubrovnik & Calvi.

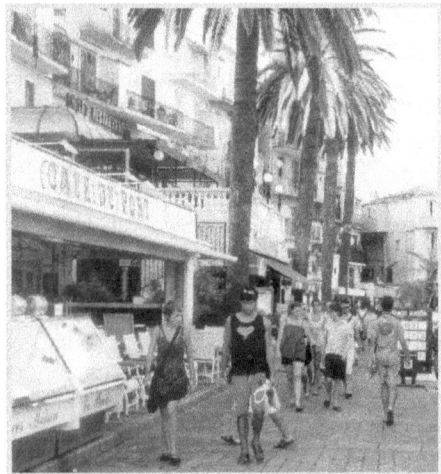

At present, the largest number of visitors is from Germany, followed by the United Kingdom, with many too from Scandinavia, the Netherlands and Belgium; in the future, a growing number will arrive from eastern and central Europe. Spain and Italy are, traditionally, the main venues for mass tourism, with Greece, Turkey and Cyprus competing fiercely, and countries like Croatia and the Red Sea resorts of Egypt growing rapidly. The only exceptions to the general pattern are those places where western visitors are not encouraged, such as Syria and Algeria, as well as countries undergoing political change; elsewhere, there are few stretches of the Mediterranean coast that are not treated as fair game for tourist development.[83]

Little opportunity has been lost to cram development around the shores of the Mediterranean. Haifa & Benidorm.

Apart from the obvious physical impact of mass tourism, there is a high price to pay in terms of loss of cultural traditions and even identity. A Greek island, for instance, that has for centuries based its life on the fruits of land and sea, now finds itself with a runway across a precious strip of flat land and the arrival of visitors who greatly outnumber the indigenous population. Or, no less typical, a once quiet bay along the Spanish coast becomes the site of intense urbanization, lined with high-rise hotels and apartments, its young people with little option but to take jobs as waiters and chamber-maids.

This is true, tourism advocates will say, but with these changes has come greater prosperity for previously remote and poor areas:

> *The tourist industry generates over 50% of GDP in the Balearics and Corsica, and... in Cyprus, which is the third largest Mediterranean island, tourism represents some 50% of the service sector, employs 12% of the working population and produces 40% of export earnings. In Malta, tourism is also the island's principal industry, generating 30% of GDP and 25% of exports.*[84]

Such figures always look compelling until one adds the hidden costs, like the damage that is done to the social fabric of communities and the impossible demands made on natural resources. Islands, especially, record a serious water deficit and often have to import fresh supplies to cater for tourists. Some look for salvation in the form of desalination but this is itself a vast consumer of energy and probably not sustainable in the long term. To some extent in the wake of short-term visits, the Mediterranean has also become a favoured destination for outsiders who decide to settle there permanently.

Holidays will often lead to familiarity with an area and provide an opportunity to look for affordable properties. The benign climate is a powerful draw, but so too (in the early stages at least of this new migration, less so now) was the prospect of cheap properties and lower costs of living. With the expansion of the European Union, the flow of people across national boundaries has been eased and many have taken advantage of this to move south, to a new home by the sea. Apart from localized exceptions, like Marseille and Barcelona with their own buoyant economies, the attraction to incomers from the north is not primarily one of jobs. There is a view that the Mediterranean could become like southern California, the home of high-tech industries in the sun, but the evidence so far points more to a likeness with Florida, popular with retirees.[85]

For a majority, it seems, the motive in moving to this region is to find a place for retirement, and a characteristic destination is a villa with its own swimming pool and a barbecue permanently sited alongside. 'Ex-pats', so the stereotype suggests, move from house to house, sharing cold beers with their neighbours and outdoing each other with stories of how bad things are back home.

For those who choose to stay in their own enclave, contact with the indigenous population might be limited to the briefest of exchanges at the supermarket checkout or with a local plumber. In a book with the telling title, 'Sunset Lives', the authors spoke at length to residents in four locations around the Mediterranean who have chosen to retire there.[86]

By and large, most people believed they had made the right move, although for some it was clearly wrong and for others it might have worked better had they chosen a different location. A common complaint was that, as further incomers arrived, their neighbourhood, inevitably, had become more urbanized and some of the early attraction of being in a pristine setting was lost. This was especially evident in one of the survey locations, the Costa del Sol, in southern Spain, which has witnessed a rapid growth of tourism as well as new housing. Class, as in everything, is a factor, and, in contrast with Spain, there was a higher level of satisfaction amongst residents in an up-market location like Tuscany—popularly known as Chianti-shire, because of the large proportion of settlers from the fashionable English Home Counties and often, too, from former colonies.

There is a continuing drift from impoverished rural areas to the cities. Izmir.

Significantly, these 'sunset lives' were surveyed in the 1990s, still on the lower slope of a rising curve of permanent migration from northern Europe. The past ten years will have brought many changes, particularly to the lower end of the market, in the form of higher densities of development and the use of properties for holiday rentals. More recently, the weakening of the pound against the euro will have created problems for residents from outside the euro-zone (mainly from the UK), who rely on pensions and other income from their home country.

The sunny climate will continue to compensate in kind, although even that has its downside; for health reasons people are becoming more wary about exposing themselves too much to the sun, while climate change is only likely to worsen the effects of a perennial water shortage in the region. Euro-migrants are still making their way in large numbers to the Mediterranean and, even if the honeymoon is over, the marriage of north and south will almost certainly survive. Dutch émigrés will live alongside Germans, British next to Swedes, in what can be thought of as a new Euro-rainbow coalition of cultures, perhaps in itself something of a latter-day utopia for a continent that has seen so much of its history at war.

Drifting North

Stagnating economic development and high natural population increase will remain the main incentive to move abroad, to Al Kharisch, as Europe is called.[87]

Traditionally, the natural poverty of the land around the sea has limited the population that can be supported. An obvious response has been for people to leave the region, in search of work and a new life. In the late-nineteenth and early twentieth centuries, countries in southern Europe (notably Spain, Italy and Greece) experienced this kind of exodus on a mass scale. Many of their people crossed the Atlantic to find new homes in North and South America. Of all the migrant populations, more came from Italy than anywhere else, reaching up to 700,000 each year in the decade before the First World War.[88] Later in the twentieth century, particularly from the 1950s when the north European economies recovered from the war and started to grow, many migrants from these southern countries were attracted there instead. In addition, young Turkish workers were drawn to the thriving German industrial market, while North Africans from former French colonies crossed the sea to France. The postwar period also saw a fresh wave of long-haul migrations—especially from Italy, Greece and the former Yugoslavia—to Australasia and Canada.

In human terms, migration can be a painful experience, not only for those who venture abroad but no less for those left behind. Typically, it is the younger and bolder members of a community who leave, with a disproportionate number of older people remaining. With their lifeblood flowing away, farms on the very margins of viability might finally be abandoned and whole communities left with little to sustain them. The 'picturesque' sight of old folk chattering in a village square or gazing out to sea is just the top layer of a deeper set of meanings, with the disappearance in our own lifetime of ways of life that had previously endured for centuries.

More recently, the demographics of the Mediterranean are changing. Most of those countries of southern Europe which not so long ago were net exporters of young people have experienced a remarkable change, with new and unprecedented reductions in birth rates. Spain and Italy, for instance, in spite of the traditional influence of the Catholic Church and its strictures on the use of birth control, have bucked the trend of large families.

This is true, too, of other countries like Greece and (to a lesser extent) France, which are typically abandoning the custom of women marrying young and maximizing their opportunities for childbirth. Women now seek other roles in society, and families are choosing to restrict numbers in order to enjoy the fruits of consumerism. In spite of people living longer in these countries, the trend is towards a levelling and then a modest decline in overall population totals. All of this, inevitably, tends to reduce the former tendency for out-migration.[89]

Rapid population growth in countries in the southern and eastern Mediterranean is not matched with sufficient jobs. Alexandria.

In contrast, population levels are still rising rapidly in the southern and eastern Mediterranean, extending from Morocco to Turkey. Although the current rate of growth in these countries has slowed, the actual increases projected are still very significant. Between 1990 and 2025, the total in these countries is expected to double, from 194 million to 374 million.[90] Turkey will see an increase from 58.5 to 102.7 million, Egypt from 54.5 to 105.4 million and Algeria from 39.1 to 49.3 million. Not surprisingly, the numbers of young people will increase disproportionately; in Syria, the percentage of those under the age of 15 will rise in this same period to 49%, in Algeria to 46% and in Libya to 44%.

On the eve of the Arab Spring, Tarek Osman, himself an Egyptian, lamented the decline of his country over the past half century and pointed, especially, to its rapidly-growing population. With over 70% of the total population under the age of thirty, he feared a steady exodus of some of its most talented individuals.[91]

The prospect of continuing growth in these countries has given rise to growing concerns amongst their northern neighbours, who fear the effects of large-scale migrations. Moreover, it is not just from the Mediterranean rim that inward migration comes but also from a much deeper hinterland. Young men and women from West Africa regularly make their way, illegally, to the Spanish territory of the Canary Islands, in the hope that they can move from there to the European mainland. Others come north across the Sahara to join a growing number of migrants from the Maghreb, using the regular ferries as well as their own makeshift boats to enter, illegally, the countries of the European Union. Similarly, there are well-worn tracks from Central Asia and the Middle East, using Greek islands like Chios and Lesvos as stepping stones en route to the rest of Europe.[92]

Fears in the north are compounded by the fact that most of the migrants are Muslim. Without exception, the fastest growing countries in the region are Islamic and it seems inevitable that an increasing number of their people—invariably young men—will seek jobs in Europe. Little wonder that the Mediterranean specialist, Russell King, observes that 'demography lies at the heart of Mediterranean destiny' and that:

> *The Mediterranean is now a demographic frontier between two entirely different population systems. This demographic fault-line is also a divide between two very different economic and politico-religious regimes.*[93]

Crossing this fault-line can be a life-changing experience for those on both sides. In *Andalus*, Jason Webster provides a fascinating insight into the marginal world of illegal migrant workers from Morocco in southern Spain.[94] He starts with a nail-biting account of being chased from a market garden, a labyrinth of plastic tunnels, where he discovered the employment of unauthorized migrants in intolerable conditions. Mafia-style organizations were responsible, he believed, for a racket on a large scale, in which migrants had to pay to get work and then were lucky if they were themselves paid at a fair rate or at all. They worked for long hours in the exceptionally high temperatures of enclosed growing areas and were, effectively, prisoners at the mercy of the gang-masters. Violence and intimidation was an everyday part of their lives.

It is not surprising that such an emotive subject attracts conflicting views. At one extreme, a populist response (exploited and articulated by far-right political parties) is invariably to see such migrants as a threat to the established societies of southern Europe. Racism is evident in various ways in the southern cities, from physical attacks on migrants to political graffiti. At the other end of the spectrum, there is an intellectual, post-colonialist stance that mocks bourgeois values and accounts for modern migrations in terms of continuing inequities between North and South. Iain Chambers is one such theorist, who has written a book on some of the cross-currents of contemporary Mediterranean life.[95] In seeking to understand modern population movements, Chambers is undoubtedly right to set these in an historical context, a continuation of past processes. Its various peoples have, from the earliest times, been on the move, constantly leaving one homeland in search of another.

The Mediterranean, he contends, is 'a sea of migrating cultures, powers and histories [that] continues to propose a more fluid and unstable archive, a composite formation in the making, neither conclusive nor complete'.[96] Chambers is also right to see the wider picture, 'where the Occident and the Orient, the North and the South, are evidently entangled in a cultural and historical net cast over centuries, even millennia'.[97]

In other respects, though, Chambers makes no obvious attempt to explain why it is that Europeans view the spectre of uncontrolled migration from poorer countries, ideologically opposed to western society, with fear. Is it enough merely to dismiss such views as 'moral panic'?[98] The fact remains that growth in North Africa and the Levant, even at a reducing rate, is still substantial, and both sides need to discuss how it can best be accommodated. It remains to be seen whether and how the new democratic regimes in North Africa will address the problem.

CHAPTER 2

SUNBELT CITIES

The idea of a sunbelt first emerged in the United States, where there has for many years been a steady drift southwards of people and jobs from the northern 'rust-belt'. Cities like Detroit, once a byword for economic buoyancy, found themselves locked into a spiral of irreversible decline. There was, too, for those who were footloose, the appeal of moving from the northern states to a more amenable climate, with the added advantage that land was cheaper.

Europe is not North America, yet, in spite of differences in detail, a comparable trend can be discerned. In limited cases (as we will see in Marseille) there has been a movement of jobs from the north but, in the main, the exodus has been of people seeking longer vacations and retirement in the sun. Freedom of movement in the European Union has made this easier than in the past. Seen from Scandinavia in winter, and from other north European countries, the prospect of living in a warm climate is appealing. Only in recent years, with the global financial crisis and severe problems in the Eurozone, has the ideal been tarnished. A collapse in the property market combined with diminished returns from investments for retirement has left many in a quandary.

It is not enough, though, to dwell only on the recent past, for in the Mediterranean events can best be understood against a much wider backcloth. Thus, the three cities in this chapter have each evolved in distinctive ways over long periods. They are all Mediterranean cities but they are also individual places; they have much in common yet they have also taken different paths.

The first of these, Gibraltar, is something of an anachronism in the modern world, preferring an archaic form of colonial status and protection by the United Kingdom, to assimilation with neighbouring Spain. It is a place that is very much in search of its own identity. In contrast, Alicante is passionately Spanish, preferring to gloss over a long period of Moorish occupation yet now opening its doors to an influx of new residents from northern Europe. In spite of its national loyalties, even here there are signs of a regional movement, linked to the neighbouring city of Valencia.

Finally, there is Marseille, which has always vied with Paris and likes to assert itself as the city of the future. It has a chequered history but is now remaking itself, with an ambitious development programme and an enviable record in attracting inward investment. Marseille seems to have taken on Barcelona for the title of capital of the modern Mediterranean.

GIBRALTAR

Gibraltar is as good a place as any to start this odyssey and, geographically, better than most. Its location is everything, literally at the crossroads of oceans as well as continents: between Europe and Africa, between the Atlantic and the Mediterranean. From a vantage point high on this rocky outcrop one gets a very real sense of the closeness of these different worlds. The erstwhile British Prime Minister, Benjamin Disraeli, visited Gibraltar as a young man in 1830 and found the population 'infinitely diversified', witnessing 'Moors with costumes radiant as a rainbow or an Eastern melodrama, Jews with gaberdines and skull-caps, Genoese, Highlanders and Spaniards...'[1] No longer so exotic it still speaks of this historic mixing of cultures.

Mohammed and the Mountain

You do not need to be religious to understand why many have found spirituality in its extraordinary topography, nor an expert in defence to appreciate its strategic value. Since the dawn of humanity the eternal rock has exerted a steady magnetism.[2]

It is hard to miss the irony in a visit to Europa Point, the southern tip of Gibraltar (and, indeed, almost the southernmost point of Europe). One might be forgiven for thinking that the name of this promontory has a modern ring about it, coined perhaps by an image-maker seeking to promote one of the island's attractions for tourists; in fact, this landmark has been known as such for centuries. The most striking feature of the headland now is an impressive mosque, its minaret rising high above the ground, its white walls dazzling in the translucent atmosphere. This is clearly no ordinary mosque and, indeed, it was presented to the Muslim community of Gibraltar by King Fahad of Saudi Arabia. Known as the Ibrahim-al-Ibrahim Mosque (or the Mosque of the Custodian of the Two Holy Mosques), no expense was spared in its making and it was opened to worshippers in 1997. The buildings in the complex are impressive enough in themselves but it is the powerful message conveyed that leaves the most lasting impression.

Could there, one might ask, be a more symbolic location for such a mosque than Europa Point? Once Gibraltar was peopled wholly by Muslims, until the Spaniards claimed it for their own and expelled the worshippers of Islam. When they did so they appropriated an early mosque on this very headland and converted it to a Catholic shrine; a large chapel was added and it became the Shrine of our Lady of Europe.[3] It is reputed that sailors passing through the narrow strait, from one sea to the other, would cross themselves and offer prayers for a safe passage. Now, some five hundred years later, a mosque has returned, not instead of the shrine but on different ground, its minaret visible from the opposite shore of Africa. Perhaps tellingly, the Christian place of worship has become engulfed within a nearby housing estate. In one sense, Islam and Christianity are still poised alongside each other but the balance is uneven. When the call to prayers is made from the towering minaret, one cannot help but muse on whether it can be heard across the continent to the north as well as on the African mainland just a short distance to the south. Should one see it more as a restored tie to the past or as a portent for the future? Is Gibraltar a southern outpost of European hegemony or a bridgehead into its heartland?

The symbolism of a prestigious mosque at the southernmost tip of Europe cannot easily be missed.

Such musings are, in their very nature, speculative but the realities of the past are incontrovertible. Less than a hundred years after the Prophet Mohammed's teachings signalled the birth of Islam, the soldiers of righteousness sailed from the African mainland and were soon to claim the largely barren and thinly inhabited outcrop, then known as Mons Calpe. They landed first on the nearby Spanish mainland but were quick to see the strategic advantages of this natural spur as a base for their subsequent exploits. Unlike most of the Mediterranean, Gibraltar had not featured in the colourful history of the preceding, classical empires and there was little to impede the invaders. For centuries, Mons Calpe had been used, if at all, to launch small fishing boats and to graze goats on the steep and thinly-pastured slopes. Its real history only begins with the arrival of the Moors in the year 711.[4]

The Moorish occupation was a dramatic event, heralded by the landing of 8000 troops (composed largely of Berbers from North Africa, led by a freed slave, Tariq-ibn-Zeid) and was to last for more than seven centuries. One of the first actions of the invaders was to rename the occupied land, Jebel Tariq, the mountain of Tariq, after the conqueror. The name was later corrupted by the British to Gibraltar. More tellingly, the Moors were the first to see in their new territory its potential as a natural fortification. Its striking features were heaven-sent. First, the stronghold is defensible from any assault mounted on the mainland. Although not an island it is connected by a low strand, a mile in length, over which the Gibraltarian defenders from their high ground would always have an advantage. The mountain itself is impregnable from the landward approach, with a slope rising sheer over more than 300 metres (and, further, to a summit of 426 metres). It has proved no more accessible on the eastward side, facing the Mediterranean, where steep cliffs have deterred successive invasion attempts; just once an invading army reached the peak from this side but, unsupported from the ground, it failed to secure its advantage. Only to the south, on Europa Point, are there gentler slopes, and on the westward side too where there was sufficient land to build a settlement — the town of Gibraltar — alongside the natural harbour. It is a dramatic landform, its impact enhanced by the sight of a comparable mountain, Mons Abyla (later known as Jebel Musa), facing it from the African coast. Together these are the celebrated Pillars of Hercules, for generations of sailors the gateway to the Mediterranean.

To the Muslim invaders, Gibraltar's attraction was as a secure base and bridgehead for their subsequent conquest of the mainland rather than as an end in itself. Progressively, they worked their way across the southern half of Spain, endowing the country with a powerful legacy of Islamic culture. At the height of their powers, known as Al-Andalus, the Moors controlled a vast area, extending westwards into Portugal and in the other direction across the Pyrenees to France, seemingly with the rest of Europe in their sights. Gibraltar was a mere stepping stone, albeit important for that. A fort was built soon after it was settled and, later, a more substantial castle on the same site, although it was to be several centuries before it was engaged in battle.

Gradually, the Moors started to lose their hold over the mainland and were forced to retreat southwards to what remained of the ancient province of Granada. With Spanish armies now in the ascendancy, Gibraltar itself was soon to come under attack. In fact, in spite of the weakened state of the Moors, its capture proved to be far from easy. Having to confront the steep slopes was the most obvious obstacle but not the only one. As well as its formidable height, the limestone bedrock of Gibraltar had produced a myriad of caves and tunnels that were cleverly used by the defending forces to store supplies and reinforce the external fortifications. Rather than making direct attacks and most likely inflicting heavy losses, the invaders chose to mount a siege that would lead to surrender. The Spanish army was duly triumphant but, little more than twenty years later, in 1333, the Moors recaptured the territory through their own, highly effective, siege. A precarious existence followed until the Moors were once again ousted and Gibraltar fell permanently to the Christians in 1462.

In spite of the long period of Muslim occupation, there is not in modern Gibraltar the tangible legacy of Islamic culture that one finds in many of the cities on the Spanish mainland. The town of Gibraltar itself, first named Madinat Al-Fath, dates from the twelfth century and one searches, largely in vain, for clues to reveal evidence of this early period. There are, for instance, the remains of what is still known as the Moorish Castle, with its square tower (the largely brick-built Tower of Homage) visible from the town below. Beneath Gibraltar's cathedral, excavations have revealed the site of a mosque and, nearby, an Arab bath-house has been restored.

These are, however, slender reminders of a culture that elsewhere on the Iberian Peninsula bequeathed outstanding examples of architecture and art. At a time when the rest of Europe was floundering in the so-called 'dark ages', it was left to the Muslims to nurture the growth points of civilization and to lay the foundations for a later revival across the continent. In contrast, while this was happening in other locations, Gibraltar was seen as no more than a useful base for the Moorish advance, a mere garrison town.

Rock of Empire

Thou art the rock of empire, Set mid-seas between East and West, That God has built.[5]

The Spanish 're-conquered' Gibraltar in the name of Catholicism and, thirty years later, in 1492, regained the important city of Granada; the resident Muslims, if not slaughtered in the process, were subsequently forced to return across the sea. Those who converted to Christianity, the Moriscos, were allowed to remain until the early seventeenth century, until they, too, were banished. It was seen (after the event if not at the time) as a holy war, the *Reconquista*, the expulsion of the infidel; just as the Muslims had many centuries before seen their own conquest as the start of a conversion that they believed would one day embrace the whole of Europe.

In spite of its almost spiritual associations, the re-conquest of Gibraltar proved hardly to be the start of a glorious era. Apart from opposing factions amongst the Christian conquerors, which led to civil wars and further sieges, as first one group and then another sought control, there was a difficulty in attracting new settlers to replace the banished Muslims. One outcome was the establishment of a penal settlement, with prisoners used to rebuild and extend the broken defences, and subsequently to settle in the town. In addition to the prisoners, being either Christian or Jewish was the only strict qualification for residency, and, in time (with the expulsion of the Jews from Spain) only the former remained. Rather like the Muslims had done before them, the Spanish viewed Gibraltar primarily as a fortification, and even that was not pursued with vigour. Some work was done to strengthen the defences, but not enough to stop a raiding party of Turkish pirates from pillaging the town in 1540. Spain was to have grander aspirations in that period, as it embarked on lucrative explorations to the New World; in the broader scheme of things, there was little regard for this miniscule territory, an island in all but name. There remained in the Hispanic psyche an almost mystical fear of further invasions from North Africa, but little was done to ensure the viability of Gibraltar and to develop trade links with its former enemies:

> *It had been unhappily lost for a long time, but now by the grace of God was restored. As any idea of a serious invasion receded Gibraltar tended to become a place of pilgrimage rather than a fortress. The new rulers of Spain were unable to re-orient their ideas to see that Gibraltar had a new function and a different future as soon as the Moorish threat was ended.*[6]

Further work to enhance the fortifications was undertaken towards the end of the sixteenth century but, in the mistaken belief that this would be enough to protect Gibraltar for the foreseeable future, things were then allowed to decay. Instead of developing Gibraltar into a vibrant port, at the entrance to the Mediterranean, it took on the appearance of a neglected backwater. The world was passing it by. Little wonder that England, with its own territorial ambitions and growing reliance on sea power, showed more than a passing interest in this largely forgotten corner of Spain.

'The rock of empire'.

It was in the middle of the seventeenth century that the English republican leader, Oliver Cromwell, considered taking Gibraltar from the Spanish as a way of improving the efficiency of his country's naval operations in the region. Nothing came of it at the time and England embarked instead on an ill-judged occupation of Tangier, on the African coast, only to rue the absence of a good harbour and the vulnerability of the city to repeated attacks from the surrounding mountains. Gibraltar was quietly forgotten until, some years later, as part of the Grand Alliance of continental nations ranged against the French and Spanish, a naval blockade forced its surrender. The ignominious event was dismissed by the French with the disdainful observation that 'it is impossible to imagine how careless the Spaniards are'.[7] Careless or not, the Spanish garrison was duly disbanded and in August 1704 Gibraltar was formally occupied in the name of Queen Anne, and the terms of occupation were later ratified, in 1713, in the Treaty of Utrecht. In spite of constant opposition by Spain to the appropriation of what is, to all intents and purposes, a natural adjunct to the mainland, the Rock (as it is patriotically known, conveying a provocative sense of solidity and permanence) has remained in British hands ever since.

After years of neglect during the period of Spanish control, the local population might have hoped for early signs of recovery; if so, they were to be greatly disappointed. The new occupation could not have got off to a worse start. In spite of a proclamation that rights and religions would be respected, the garrison of some 1800 men wasted little time in plundering the newly acquired territory. A product of sheer indiscipline after weeks at sea, combined with a mob fervour of anti-Catholicism, the new occupiers set about their conquest with a barbarous appetite:

> *They profaned all the churches except the principal one, which was zealously defended by the curate Padre Juan Romero. But the greatest disorders were committed at the hermitage of Our Lady of Europa; they treated the Holy Image with derision and cut off the head of the Infant she held in her arms... Many females experienced insults and outrages, whence arose numerous sanguinary acts of vengeance on the part of the inhabitants, who murdered the perpetrators and threw their bodies into wells and sewers. In this deplorable state of things the unfortunate citizens... determined on quitting for ever the place of their birth rather than submit to foreign domination.*[8]

Although order of a sort was gradually restored, Gibraltar retained the character of a distant garrison town with little interest in civilian welfare and with no apparent plans for its future. By the middle of the eighteenth century the local population numbered fewer than 2000—about the same size as the garrison—comprised mainly of Jews (largely from Morocco), Genoese, British, Spanish and Portuguese. Gibraltar was by then known as something of a sanctuary for political refugees fleeing their own countries. During the nineteenth century, the town itself (although still small) steadily grew in size although its population was greatly outnumbered by the garrison, which housed as many as 30,000 troops and their families. This growth, however, was not matched by a proper system of sanitation and, coupled with the high densities and arid conditions for much of the year, Gibraltar experienced periodic epidemics. Some 10,000 people died from yellow fever in the course of the century, and a smaller but still considerable number from cholera. It was a particularly virulent outbreak of the latter, in 1865, that led belatedly to the replacement of a rudimentary network of sewers and the establishment of an effective sanitary commission.[9]

Distant and poorly served it may have been—and certainly not the healthiest place on earth—yet it gradually won a place in the hearts of the British public. Strangely, at the time of its occupation, it was seen by friend and foe alike as not much of a conquest and hardly worth the trouble and expense of administering it. Politicians in London condemned it as a costly venture and feared a repeat of the Tangier debacle. Ironically, it was the possibility of Spain recapturing the Rock that hardened opinion in favour of its retention. Most notably, for four years from 1779 to 1783, the garrison successfully resisted a legendary siege by the Spanish, prosecuted from land and sea. Greatly outnumbered by opposing forces and not helped by the delay of naval reinforcements, the public at home revelled in tales of remarkable ingenuity and heroism by the defending garrison. When the British Prime Minister, Charles Fox, a few months after the siege ended, reported on the event in Parliament there was only one speech he could make: Gibraltar symbolized the greatness of Britain and would never be sacrificed:

> *Give up to Spain the fortress of Gibraltar, and the Mediterranean becomes to them a pool in which they can navigate at pleasure, and act without control or check. Deprive yourselves of this station, and the states of Europe that border on the Mediterranean will no longer look to you for the maintenance of the free navigation of that sea; and having it no longer in your power to be useful, you cannot expect alliances.*[10]

Gibraltar has since assumed a status that is symbolic as well as real: a British possession, with rights of sovereignty that no politician would lightly concede. From time to time an incident flared up, with Spain reasserting its own claim of control, but for the most part the arrangement forced through at the time of the Treaty of Utrecht has held firm. Confirming Britain's hold, at least until the Second World War, the Rock retained the strategic role that had originally been anticipated. Little more than twenty years after Prime Minister Fox urged the retention of Gibraltar on a willing Parliament, it was to play its part in supporting the efforts of the British navy in the Napoleonic Wars. The decisive Battle of Trafalgar was fought at sea to the west of the Rock, and the body of Admiral Lord Nelson was later brought to Gibraltar until repairs could be carried out to his battered flagship, HMS Victory, prior to the onward journey of the nation's hero to his last resting place in England. Throughout the rest of the century, Gibraltar settled into its routine as a garrison town and as a base for naval supplies and repairs, functions that were enhanced when new dockyards were built early in the twentieth century. These were later to be heavily used in the Second World War, when Gibraltar was instrumental in maintaining control of the western Mediterranean and supporting the war effort in

North Africa. As a relatively safe haven, a generation of fighting men and women were to enjoy temporary respite from ongoing battles in the region on land and at sea, and for them Gibraltar became a fond memory.

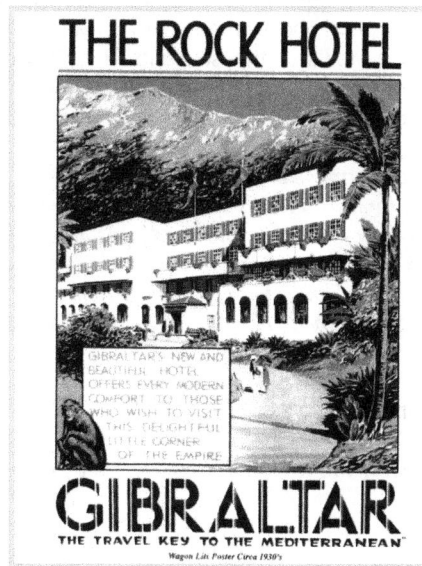

THE ROCK HOTEL

GIBRALTAR'S NEW AND
BEAUTIFUL HOTEL
OFFERS EVERY MODERN
COMFORT TO THOSE
WHO WISH TO VISIT
THIS DELIGHTFUL
LITTLE CORNER
OF THE EMPIRE

GIBRALTAR
THE TRAVEL KEY TO THE MEDITERRANEAN
Wagon Lits Poster Circa 1930's

As well as its essential military role, over the years Gibraltar also attracted a growing number of civilian visitors, usually on their way to more distant colonial destinations. After its turbulent start the town lost its reputation as a place of unruliness and ill-repute, so much so that by the end of the nineteenth century it could be described as 'thoroughly respectable and extremely dull'.[11] It took on the appearance of a typical British colony, the Union Jack flying from the castle on the skyline, a constant naval presence at anchor in the harbour, and the social routines of garrison life.

Undeterred by poor relations with Spain, the families of the garrison chose each summer to cross the parched countryside on the mainland to reach the cooler mountain town of Ronda; the main hotel there still bears the name of Reina Victoria. It could well have been India, where the same pattern of retreating to amenable hill stations was earlier established as a salient feature of colonial life. The opening of the Suez Canal in 1869, although a triumph of French engineering, was to serve British interests and add to the importance of Gibraltar itself, with merchant shipping using the harbour as an essential link on the route to the Orient. While the ships took on fresh supplies, passengers disembarked, in many cases witnessing for the first time a cosmopolitan population and enjoying the novel experience of a warm climate.

The colonial connection continued into the first half of the twentieth century, with Gibraltar remaining a favoured destination for genteel visitors who felt secure in a place where the Union Jack fluttered overhead. There were regular sailings from London, Liverpool and Southampton, for which first class passengers paid a return fare of £18. To meet this obvious demand, a new hotel was opened in 1932, an imposing white building combining elements of Art Deco and Orientalism, set in sub-tropical gardens with views of the sea and Africa beyond. The Rock Hotel proudly proclaimed in its publicity brochure that its luxury facilities were not the only reason why people should stay there:

> *And by no means last in importance to British visitors there is the satisfaction of feeling that in Gibraltar one is under the Union Jack; that here is to be found complete security and safety, outward signs of which are Khaki-clad British troops; the many old guns in the Alameda Gardens and elsewhere; the passing of a military band; stolid British policemen; distant bugle calls; the firing of Salutes from the King's Bastion—all constant reminders of the fact that the Rock is a British possession.*[12]

A Hundred Different Costumes

It is a curious sight at evening this thronged street, with the people in a hundred different costumes…[13]

Visitors to Gibraltar—especially in the past when the observation of different races was more of a novelty—invariably commented on the cultural diversity that they witnessed. William Makepeace Thackeray made a visit in 1846 and that was his immediate reaction:

> *Suppose all the nations of the earth to send fitting ambassadors to represent them and your imagination may figure the Main Street of Gibraltar… swarthy Moors, in white or crimson robes; dark Spanish smugglers in tufted hats, with gay silk handkerchiefs round their heads; fuddled seamen from men-of-war, or merchantmen; porters, Galician or Genoese; and at every few minutes' interval, little squads of soldiers tramping to relieve guard at one of the innumerable posts in the town.*[14]

Gibraltar is even today, albeit to a lesser extent, the Mediterranean in microcosm, a mixing of cultures that at times is so unobtrusive as to be hardly noticed. It would be misleading to suggest unbroken harmony, for in the Mediterranean conflict is never far away, but Disraeli was right to comment favourably on the diversity he experienced on his own visit to the Rock, in 1830. As a Jew himself he knew firsthand the meaning of discrimination and, finding a community of such mixed races and religions apparently living at peace with each other, it was little surprise that he described Gibraltar as 'a wonderful place'.[15]

The Jews, as elsewhere in the Mediterranean, have had a chequered history on the Rock. So long as the Moors controlled most of Spain the Jews continued to prosper on the mainland, with an estimated population of more than 200,000 in the fifteenth century. It was the largest concentration of Jews in the region but was not to last. The Reconquista was hailed by the Spanish as a victory for Christianity and, as well as expelling the hitherto powerful Muslim invaders, they also decided to cleanse their land of the alien Jews. In 1492, in the newly captured Al-Hambra of Granada, it was decreed that all Jews would be given a choice of baptism or immediately leaving the country. About half of the community fled westwards, into Portugal, although within five years in the face of forced baptism most chose to leave there too. Some found their way to North African cities, where they enjoyed greater tolerance, and were later to develop trade links with Gibraltar as a conduit to European markets.

More than two centuries after the Spanish decree the issue of Jewish residency was still an issue, and Spain insisted in the Treaty of Utrecht that Britain's occupation of Gibraltar should exclude both Jews and Moors. Britain assented at the time but was soon to allow the settlement of both groups, if not for liberal reasons then certainly for self-interest as both could contribute in their own ways to the effective operation of the territory. The Jews, in particular, would exploit their trading links along the North African coast and elsewhere in the western Mediterranean. Provoked by this non-compliance of the terms of Utrecht, Spain in 1826 mounted a fiercely fought but ultimately unsuccessful siege to loosen Britain's hold. With its failure, the matter of exclusion was now effectively closed, and the number of Jewish settlers increased to some 1500 (nearly half of the civilian population) by the middle of the nineteenth century. During the Second World War the Jews, along with the rest of the civilian population, were evacuated (in the case of the Jews, mainly to Britain) and only a minority returned after the war. There is now a community of some 600, in Gibraltar's total population of 30,000.

The legacy and contemporary influence of this Jewish community is greater than its modest numbers would suggest. There are still four synagogues in the town, with small but devout congregations, and a scattering of Kosher stores. Some of the people speak their own language, Ladino, a mixture of Spanish and Hebrew (the Mediterranean equivalent of Yiddish).[16] On the Jewish Sabbath, families congregate in the public squares, on their way to and from the synagogues: the men in dark suits and wide-brimmed hats, the women in long skirts and with their heads covered. Typically, the community is loyal to its religious heritage but also to the place that has provided sanctuary; on the surface at least, they appear to mix easily with other racial and religious groups. Evidence of their commitment to Gibraltar has been helped by the high profile of some of its leading families and, most notably, the reputation of Sir Joshua Hassan, who was at one time Chief Minister. In that office he gained the support of the whole population for taking a tough stand against Spanish diplomatic attempts to regain the territory. Hassan's family had been in Gibraltar since the eighteenth century, coming originally, like many fellow Jews, from one of the towns along the Moroccan coast. His wife's family hailed from Minorca, another common source of immigration for Jews who had, earlier, most probably lived in Spain. Now, claimed Hassan, 'we consider ourselves Gibraltarians irrespective of where we come from. We get along very well together.'[17]

Other races, too, have made their mark on Gibraltar's development. The Moors and the Spaniards, of course, had good reason to do so as previous landlords of the Rock, and their presence is still very much in evidence. So too, of course, is the enduring influence of the British, its resident population consisting both of descendants of the former garrison and more recent 'ex-pats' who prefer to soak up the sun in a familiar culture rather than in neighbouring Spain.

On his modern-day Mediterranean odyssey, Paul Theroux found much to despise in Gibraltar but he warmed to the mingling of so many different cultures: 'There was a strong sense of community in Gibraltar, which made it much odder for me to reflect that I was in a place that was both a racial hotchpotch and also deeply paranoid about admitting aliens.'[18]

Unwanted Legacy

It has always been difficult for people to recognise the end of an era in which they are themselves living.[19]

In spite of its natural advantages, and its exotic history with the mingling of cultures, Gibraltar is not a beautiful place. Britain has made sure of that. There might well have been tea parties on the lawn of the Governor's residence, and cocktails on the decks of fighting ships as the sun went down, but there is also a less attractive side to the island's colonization. From the time of its inauspicious arrival, when drunken troops rampaged through the streets, to the piecemeal though relentless addition of naval fortifications and its supporting infrastructure, this Mediterranean haven was transformed into an inherently unattractive dockyard town.

Gibraltar has many virtues but it is hard to be positive about the appearance of its imperial legacy. For Evelyn Waugh, making his way round the Mediterranean in 1929, a visit to Gibraltar was a low point of his trip. 'I will not say that I did not know any town could be so ugly as the town of Gibraltar; to say that would be to deny my bitter visits in the past to Colwyn Bay, Manchester and Stratford-on-Avon'.[20] Theroux, in a more recent observation, was clearly no more enamoured: 'It is pretty clear that shrunken, bankrupt Britain finds Gibraltar too expensive to run, no more than an inconvenient relic of a former age. It even looks it.'[21]

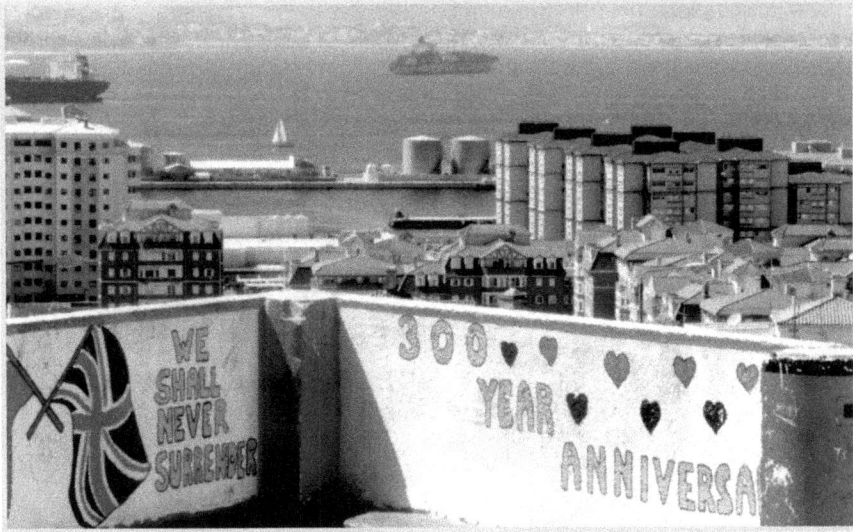

A mural on a housing estate defiantly proclaims continuing allegiance to Britain.

The signs of this are still apparent. Partly they are to be found in the debris of a discarded military infrastructure: blocked-up tunnels into the hillside that once served as ammunition stores; rusting fences with peeling notices, forbidding entry to overgrown sites that presumably once defended this corner of the Empire; empty storage yards and derelict buildings visited only by noisy sea-birds. Partly, too, it can be seen in the low-grade housing estates on some of the upper slopes, built in the 1950s for dockyard workers and looking more as if they had been planned for a windswept corner of the British Isles. Even with the diminished presence of the Ministry of Defence, with its utilitarian designs intended for use in any part of the world, the Mother Country has clearly not exported the best of town planning practice. Nor has modern Gibraltar achieved much on the traffic management front. In spite of its restricted scale and the opportunities for a sustainable transport system, cars and motor-cycles reign supreme, the result being that it is a noisy and congested place with valuable space given over to extensive and visually obtrusive car parks.

The cultural legacy is little better than the physical; in some ways, the whole place is in a time-warp and even the churlish service and over-pricing is a reminder of Britain before anyone had heard of competition and customer care. Charm is in short supply, starting in the Disney-sounding Main Street, no more than a long parade of shops selling tax-free products. It attracts large numbers of British visitors, many of them 'ex-pats' living in mainland Spain, and the numerous pubs and cafés, almost without exception, sell various permutations of fish and chips, steak and kidney pies and all-day breakfasts.

One has to pinch oneself to remember that this is the Mediterranean. In fact, it becomes so only if one climbs the various flights of steps, away from Main Street. There one finds a quiet backwater of vernacular housing, with brightly coloured bougainvillea draped over walls embedded with ornately patterned tiles, and shutters pulled tight against the afternoon sun.

In an alley a Moroccan cafe owner cooks skewers of lamb over a charcoal fire, an old lady in black sits in the street on a chair too small for her, and a bearded Jew wearing a kappel passes a hijab-covered Muslim woman in the narrow thoroughfare. In such cameos is a sense of what Gibraltar as a whole might have been without its long history of external control.

Aspects of Gibraltar's tourism.

It is likely that time will gradually erase some of the rawness of the most recent period of conquest. For now, though, the Rock is remaking itself in its own way. The old dockyards are still busy with repairs, for merchant rather than naval shipping, but the future of the economy lies more in the service sector. Tourism is one obvious source of growth, although Gibraltar has yet to decide whether to go more 'up market' or remain as a mecca for trippers — from the mainland and from the cruise ships that moor outside the harbour — who come to take photos of red pillar boxes with the sovereign's crest and to drink tax-free beer. More recently, Gibraltar has gained a reputation for financial services and, with its long background in trading and connections in this region, this could well play a bigger part in the future. [22]

Certainly, if one is to measure Gibraltar's renaissance by the volume of property development the signs are unmistakeable. New apartment blocks overlooking the harbour, and offices and retail schemes in the old districts, are all very much in evidence, sometimes excessively so as tiny building plots on the lower slopes are crammed and buildings become ever taller. Like all places with a finite supply of land, there is an obvious temptation to spread onto sites reclaimed from the sea, exemplified in this case by a new marina with a predictable assortment of restaurants and bars along the quays.

There are also attempts to improve the general environment, through the conservation and rejuvenation of some of the historic buildings and sites. The lanes and alleys behind the harbour lend themselves to this kind of reconstruction and new street signs tell their own story of a colourful past: Horse Barrack Lane and Tank Ramp, Flat Bastion Road and Victualling Office Lane. The Grand Parade Ground lives on (although now a car park), as does the Government House Garden; so, too, there's the Grand Battery and Grand Casemates Square (another car park).

In spite of such flirtations with heritage, it is not easy to fall in love with Gibraltar. Its muddled past mixes uneasily with a confused present. Each day, thousands of Spanish workers from the mainland pour across the isthmus, crossing the airport runway and threading their way in cars and motor-cycles through the narrow streets. These are followed by the day trippers, and a smaller number of more discerning visitors, in panama hats and linen suits, who come to stay in Gibraltar for a few days, sipping chilled sherry beneath canopies of wisteria and recalling the days when Gibraltar really was a staging post for a great Empire. Nothing is quite as it seems.

The Muslim mosque and the Catholic shrine, the Sephardic Jews in family groups on a Saturday, all seemingly at peace one with another. People from various nations have made this strange place their home, going about their business at what is truly a crossroads of continents. There is a strong sense of loyalty to their tiny land that is not always so evident elsewhere. Perhaps it is just too easy to be critical of its obvious blemishes, and to miss qualities of co-existence that are harder to find in other cities more closely akin to a Mediterranean stereotype.

Seen against the wider backcloth of the region, Gibraltar remains something of a geopolitical anomaly. It is, to all intents and purposes, geographically a part of Spain and yet any form of unification is fiercely resisted by the Gibraltarians.[23] Contrary to the post-colonial practice of seeking full independence, its people prefer to remain as one of the last bastions of a largely disbanded Empire;[24] and as the years go by its own sense of political and cultural identity increases. Nothing did more to harden its resolve and unify its people than Spain's closing of the frontier for sixteen years, from 1969 to 1985.

There is no sign of an early change in its status as a British Overseas Territory and, while it remains a thorn in the Spanish flesh (just as Britain would be less than pleased if Spain controlled the Isle of Wight), and the United Nations has decreed that a political agreement is overdue, there is no overwhelming reason why the situation cannot continue indefinitely. There are bigger geopolitical fish in the Mediterranean Sea, and Gibraltar is less likely to trigger a crisis than other places yet to be visited.

Reflecting on the end of an era?

ALICANTE

Alicante is a tale of three cities. It is, historically, a Moorish city, the legacy of more than seven centuries of Islamic culture still a part of the present; the name itself is derived from the Arabic, meaning 'city of light'.

It also bears the imprint of a more recent invasion, this time from the north, in the form of Europeans lured by the sunshine and opportunities to make their home by the Mediterranean. In spite of these various incursions, it remains, at heart, a Spanish city with traditional ways blending with the modern. Alicante is not alone in Spain in telling this three-part story and that in itself makes it all the more worth recounting.

'From Hot Africa'

That arid square, that fragment nipped off from hot Africa.[1]

Our excursion to Gibraltar revealed the proximity of the African continent and pointed to an obvious route for the invasions of the Spanish mainland in the eighth century. Following sporadic raids, the year 711 marked the first permanent landing of a Moorish army and shortly after, in 712, a decisive battle saw the defeat of the defending King Roderic. Toledo, the capital city at the time, quickly fell to the Moors, followed, in remarkably short order, by most of the Iberian Peninsula. The occupying Christian Visigoths, who had earlier invaded from the north, were routed and Moorish Spain, Al-Andalus, was born.

The North African leaders of the occupation brought with them a fervent belief in the new religion of Islam; and yet, in spite of a missionary zeal, they proved willing to tolerate Christianity and Judaism alongside. Only those who spoke out against the Koran faced martyrdom. Sometimes deals were made with local leaders, allowing whole fiefdoms to continue their Christian practices in exchange for submission. Alicante was one of the cities where such an arrangement was negotiated.

Many Christians across the Iberian Peninsula in due course were persuaded, if not effectively forced, to become Muslims and by the second half of the tenth century followers of the newer religion formed the majority of the population in Spain. It was an extraordinary process of conversion although time was to show that it would later be reversed, when the Moors were eventually forced to retreat from the mainland.

As a sign of the acclaimed superiority of Islam, grand mosques were built, like the magnificent structure at Cordoba. The architecture of such buildings brought from the East a style and methods of construction previously unknown to the Christians. Nor was architecture the only scientific import, for the Moors were no less responsible for diffusing earlier discoveries that had either not reached this far corner of the Mediterranean or had long been forgotten:

> *The scientific and philosophical learning of Greek and Persian antiquity was inherited by the Arabs in the Middle East. Translated, codified, elaborated by Arabic scholars, the corpus was diffused throughout the culturally unified world of classical Islam in the ninth and tenth centuries until it reached the limits of the known world in the west. And there, in Spain, it was discovered by the scholars of the Christian west, translated into Latin mainly between 1150 and 1250, and channelled off to irrigate the dry pastures of European intellectual life.*[2]

The Moors had much to celebrate and to share, and yet their rule was not without its difficulties. Over many centuries and covering a vast area it was, perhaps, inevitable that Moorish supremacy would be progressively challenged, so much so that the very boundaries of occupation receded steadily from their northern limits. Sometimes it was internal factions amongst the conquerors themselves that was the source of their problems; at other times there were determined, though initially localized, attempts to reclaim the land for the Christians. In retrospect, if there was a golden age for the Moors it was in the tenth century, when for nearly fifty years Al-Andalus enjoyed the stable rule of a single leader, Abd al-Rahman III. The city of Cordoba epitomized the progress that had been made, with a population that might then have exceeded 100,000 — on a par with the other great Mediterranean city of that age, Constantinople, and another rival, Cairo. It 'has no equal in the Maghrib, and hardly in Egypt, Syria or Mesopotamia', claimed a contemporary visitor.[3] Nor was it just its overall size that impressed, for 'the space occupied by its markets, the cleanliness of its streets, the architecture of its mosques, the number of its baths and caravanserais' were no less a source of wonder.[4] Cordoba also earned a reputation as a place of scholarly endeavour, in fields such as medicine and mathematics, literature and philosophy, geography and astronomy.

If descriptions of Cordoba in its heyday offer more than a hint of paradise — one can almost hear the sound of water trickling from the fountains in the shaded courtyards and, beneath the colonnades, the muffled conversations of learned scholars — then like all utopias it was to be shortlived. Within just a few years of its golden age, the ruling family was challenged by disgruntled Berber militia, frustrated by their meagre share of the spoils, and Cordoba itself fell victim to internal fighting — as did other cities in the south of the country. The golden age was over although Moorish dominance was not; indeed, for a time a stricter regime resulted with the arrival from Morocco of more orthodox sects: the Almoravids, Almohads and Marinids. But the writing was on the wall and one has only to look at the diminishing area under Moorish control to see an inexorable trend. In 1050 the Moors controlled as much as three quarters of the Iberian Peninsula, a century later only half and by 1250 just a narrow arc along the southern coast of Spain extending inland barely to the north of Granada. The Christian advance was now relentless and two centuries later, in 1492, under the leadership of Ferdinand of Aragaon and Isabella of Castile, the last Moorish king was forced to surrender this remaining territory. Seen as a holy crusade, the *Reconquista* was by then complete. Those Muslims who wanted to stay in Spain were forced to convert to Catholicism, but they still faced persecution and in 1610 were themselves made to leave the country.

The Moorish fortifications overlooking the city date from the ninth century.

Where was Alicante when all of this took place? In one sense it had barely thrown off the shackles of earlier periods of conquest, most notably by the Carthaginians and then the Romans. During the seven centuries when the Romans controlled the Iberian Peninsula, Alicante was known as Lucentum. It then passed into the hands of the Visigoths, before the arrival of the Moors.

As a southern coastal town with a good harbour, it was always going to be vulnerable to Moorish occupation, just as it had been to earlier invasions. The Moors could not be stopped although a local treaty allowed the Christian community to quietly continue its ways. One can only think of this as a time of sullen acquiescence by the people of Alicante, for the treaty was not designed to prevent the invaders from entering the town at will and turning it to their own advantage.

As a constant reminder of the new turn of events, the inhabitants would have had to look each day to the massive fortifications built above the city in the ninth century, on the rocky promontory of Mount Benacantil. Known since the *Reconquista* as the Castle of Santa Barbara (signifying the feast day on which it was captured from the Moors) most of the original features have been replaced by later modifications to the battlements and, more recently, by extensive landscaping. It would be facile to attribute this to a deliberate attempt to erase all traces of the foreign invaders as the damage was, in fact, done in the course of subsequent conflicts between different Spanish factions. After the Moors were ousted there were fierce internal conflicts—fought between the armies of Castile and Aragon—during which the fort was repeatedly destroyed and subsequently rebuilt. It is not hard to see why opposing forces have always sought control of this mountain stronghold, if only because of its strategic position and obvious location for cannons, high above the city, a vantage point with views for miles in all directions.

View of the historic core of the city.

Elsewhere within the city, for different reasons, there seems to have been little interest in retaining too many signs of the Moorish legacy. The largest mosque inherited from the past was demolished to provide the foundations for the Church of Santa Maria, an ornate Gothic symbol of Catholicism reasserting itself. Alicante, like other cities in Spain, has, in one way or another, done its best to erase half a millennium of its history. The Moors arrived in the eighth century and their departure was marked in 1244 by the signing of the Treaty of Almizra, when, as part of the *Reconquista*, Alicante was restored to Christianity within the Catholic province of

Castile. We know much of what happened since then but remarkably little of the period before, when the town was occupied by the Moorish invader. Buildings offer few clues and one has to look to other evidence to discover something of the influence of the earlier culture. Jason Webster is an Englishman abroad, living in Valencia and the author of a book, *Andalus*.[5] His thesis is that the trappings of so many centuries of occupation cannot simply have disappeared. It was inevitable, he contends, that some of the Moorish occupiers would have been assimilated; there were, after all, many farmers brought over from North Africa to irrigate the fields and introduce new crops like oranges and rice. Many of the soldiers, too, when their fighting days were over, settled on the land. Marriages took place between cultures and, when a decision was taken to expel the remaining *Moriscos*, it was difficult for the authorities to know who they actually were. Webster makes the point that many people in southern Spain retain obvious Moorish features and to travel south is to see more of the outstretched hand of Africa. Often it is a feeling as much as hard evidence and, in the words of an earlier visitor to this part of Spain, 'the Moorish air increases as we drive south towards Alicante. Palms fringe the beaches and white towns.'[6]

Walk through the streets of Alicante (or any other traditional city along that coast) today and one cannot miss the sense that there is still more than a hint of the continent to the south about it. Food is always a good indicator of different cultural influences and even in the national dish of *paella* there are Arabic derivations in the word itself and distinctly North African flavours in the cooking. Little cafes with Moroccan names offer skewered meat grilled over barbecues and one is never far from the scent of strong Arabic coffee. In the narrow streets of the old town, use is made in the houses of decorative ceramic tiling and here and there one can see the odd inner courtyard. Date palms line the coastal esplanade, offering shade to the townsfolk who tread the mosaic of literally millions of small tiles. The people of Alicante themselves, although predominantly Hispanic, sometimes bear the darker skin and Islamic headwear of North Africa. These are all fragments but, even without such scattered evidence of a long period of occupation, there are other signs in Alicante that the Moorish episode is certainly not forgotten. Scratch just a little below the surface, and strong feelings are quite soon revealed. Pageantry is an important feature of Spanish life and the nearest one gets to a record of this hidden era is through an annual depiction of 'Moors and Christians'. It is an amazing spectacle that can only be seen for its therapeutic rather than historical value, giving vent to the shame and hatred of being for so long a conquered people.[7]

The pageant consists of a series of enactments and battles between Moors and Christians, staged in the streets in different parts of the city on various days each year from March to December. It culminates on the sixth of the latter month, when the people of Alicante, dressed in either Christian or Moorish costume, parade together through the narrow streets of the historic district to commemorate the date when the city was recovered from the Moors in 1247. On this morning (and on other mornings during the year, when there are related events organized in different neighbourhoods) loud music is played to awaken and encourage Alicante's residents to make their way to the city square and await the entry of the opposing armies. The participants themselves, dressed in brightly coloured, flamboyant costumes, then engage in simulated battles. To the sounds of exploding gunpowder and patriotic music, battle is joined, but in the ensuing chaos the spectator is assured in the tourist literature that 'the Christians always seem to win'. Once this pre-destined victory is secured, fireworks are set off and there is much merriment into the early hours.

This annual celebration is not for the faint-hearted. At a time when most of Europe is treading carefully around multi-cultural sensitivities, it is not every city that would host such an event. It is more understandable, however, if one sees it in the context of Hispanic culture, where pageantry and the use of public spaces remain important aspects of civic life. Based on her experience of South America, Clara Irazabal has shown how public places can be used to express and even to seek the realization of political aspirations: such spaces acquire a symbolic meaning, 'a collective imagery of memories, histories and meanings'.[8]

While the characterization of Christians and Moors, depicted in almost cartoon form in their annual battles, is not an overtly political event it clearly has a deeper resonance. As well as addressing the still tender wounds of their shared past, this might also be seen as a way of confronting modern-day fears of the rise of Islam. In taking to the streets in this way, people express publicly what elsewhere is spoken only in whispers.

Residents of Alicante point warily to evidence of a renewed invasion from the south, this time through a steady flow of immigrants, mainly from Morocco and Algeria. Some arrive with the correct papers to take up work in the market gardens and on the many construction sites along the coast but others are there illegally, opening themselves to exploitation by unscrupulous employers.[9] A regular ferry service from Alicante to Algeria is tangible evidence of continuing links.[10] Although the number of new arrivals from North Africa (and also from south of the Sahara) is not overwhelming, their presence is certainly in evidence and it takes only a few groups on street corners to ignite local concerns.

Across the country as a whole, numbers add up and there are now some 750,000 Muslims in Spain, many from the Maghreb. Africa really is just a short distance away and, whether real or imagined, people feel vulnerable. In recent years, there have been racist incidents at international football matches in Spain, featuring black players in teams from other countries. It may seem irrational but, even after so many years since the Moors left, the wounds of a conquered people have not totally healed.

The New *Mediterraneans*

Anyone, regardless of birth or residence, can become a Mediterranean. 'Mediterraneity' is acquired, not inherited…[11]

Invading armies have in the past come from the north as well as from Africa: witness the conquest by the Germanic Visigoths of the whole area that is now Spain. At that time, from as early as the fifth century, these primitive warriors made their way slowly and with difficulty over the Pyrenees and across the arid plains; nor were they the only ones for there were other tribes from the north with designs on the Peninsula—the Vandals, the Sueves and the Alans all preceded them and had to be ousted by the Visigoths. Today the modern invader from northern Europe arrives daily on a succession of flights at Alicante's busy International Airport, *El Altet*. A look at the 'Arrivals' screen quickly reveals their provenance: Manchester and Malmö, Berlin and Belfast, Copenhagen and Cork, Ostend and Oslo, Hamburg and Helsinki. Many of the carriers are budget airlines that specialize in this lucrative traffic, responding to an all-year demand for a quick and cheap escape from the less amenable climate of northern Europe. Their passengers arrive pale and expectant, returning invariably burnt by the sun and flushed with an excess of alcohol.

The marauding northerners stay for varying periods. First the annual influx was largely seasonal and restricted to a summer vacation for a week or two; then a single excursion was supplemented by second and third holidays, usually for shorter periods out of season; and, as well, by weekend breaks to celebrate a family event or for a spell of sustained drinking and 'clubbing'. These different patterns of holiday-making are still very much in evidence but one can now add other groups of incomers who choose to stay longer. Some of these new arrivals have bought second homes, where they come to spend their holidays; and retired people who find that they can live more cheaply in Spain in hotels and rented accommodation over the winter months. Additionally, there are many from the north who have chosen to make their permanent home in sunny Spain, joining a rapidly growing 'ex-pat' community. Taken together, vacationers and home-makers alike, it has all called for new hotels and villas on a massive scale and this has resulted in a conglomeration of buildings and infrastructure along a once unspoiled coastline that, even until the 1950s, was marked by little other than fishing villages.The rate and extent of this transition has been remarkable. When Rose Macaulay in 1947 made a solo trip along the coast in a motor car she was able to observe a landscape that had changed little for centuries.[12] An Englishwoman abroad on her own, and behind the wheel of a car, was an unusual sight and wherever she stopped she invariably attracted a gathering of curious onlookers. She drove from the border with France in the north, along the whole coastline as far as Portugal, and saw only one other car with a GB number plate in her entire journey. Even ten years later, apart from a few fashionable resorts, the scene would have been much the same although by then the careful observer might have spotted the first signs of change.

Spain was still a poor country, with many of its people forced to leave their homes in search of work in neighbouring European countries. The dictator, General Franco, who had ruled the country since the end of the Civil War in 1939—inheriting not just an impoverished nation but also one devastated and split by years of internal conflict—had, until the late 1950s, done little to improve material conditions. He nursed an ideal of a landowning peasantry with a traditional notion of community, loyal to the Fatherland. Even Franco, however, in the face of growing disaffection and the possibility of political instability, was eventually forced to address the grim realities of widespread poverty.

Foreign investment was encouraged and in 1959 a small but decisive measure to scrap visas for visitors quickly eased the way for mass tourism. In the following decade, the number of visitors to Spain rocketed—from 3 million in 1959 to 34 million in 1973—most of them lured by the prospect of cheap holidays in the sun. Developers and tour operators were quick to see the benefits of a virtual absence of land-use controls coupled with a plentiful supply of cheap labour, and in these conditions the new phenomenon of package holidays emerged. Air strips were laid and hotels built, the latter often poorly constructed and not always finished in time for the first visitors. For these pioneering tourists—several decades before the availability of long-haul flights—a holiday in Spain was an adventure, a world apart from their everyday experience.

Tourism in the 1960s eased the Spanish economy out of a tight spot but in most respects it came at a heavy price. Much-needed new jobs were created but the traditional way of life was swept aside and many local inhabitants found it difficult to adapt.[13] On the environmental front it proved an unmitigated disaster. An absence of good master planning, dubious local political practices, poorly regulated construction and an inadequate infrastructure led to an unending line of coastal development, much of it of the worst kind. Commentators, like Paul Theroux, vie to write the most lurid prose to describe it:

> *The utterly blighted landscape of the Spanish coast—Europe's vacationland, a vile straggling sandbox... The landscape was obliterated, and from the edge of the Mediterranean to the arid gravelly inland slopes there were off-white stucco villas. There were no hills to speak of, only sequences of stucco rising in a hill shape, like a collapsing wedding cake. There were no people, there were few cars, and after dark only a handful of these houses were lit. In the poorer, nastier coves there were campsite communities and the footprint foundations in cement for caravans and tents.*[14]

It is not, of course, everywhere the same and to get a true impression one has to look closely at the different areas. The lengthy Spanish coastline as a whole along the Mediterranean is comprised of separate tourism regions, with names like Costa Brava and Costa del Sol. Alicante is in the centre of the Costa Blanca, a stretch of some 200 kilometres that includes a variety of neighbouring resorts. Many who arrive at Alicante's international airport make their way to places along the coast such as Albufereta and Playa de San Juan.

Another close neighbour along this stretch of coastline is Benidorm, one of the busiest resorts in Spain and in many ways a byword for all that has gone wrong in the race to cram as much as possible along the shoreline of the once pristine sea. When Rose Macaulay passed through it in 1947 she was charmed by what she saw, its 'sandy bay like a crescent moon' and she observed how the buildings were 'crowded very beautifully round its domed and tiled church on a rocky peninsula'.[15]

Things were soon to change beyond recognition and now its high-rise buildings around the bay say it all, exuding all the charm of a South London housing estate. Benidorm is, sadly, not exceptional in the sense that modern seaside resorts around the world too often reject any notion of good taste and environmental sensibility, as if popular enjoyment demands a total rejection of conventional standards. But if there were a league table of the very worst then Benidorm would surely take the prize. Or would it, for every cloud, it would seem, has a silver lining?

Although it is hard to find much to redeem it — and in environmental terms nothing at all — promotional literature sells Benidorm in summer as 'one big party', a mecca of bars and night clubs. For these same reasons, estate agents proclaim its attraction as a place to buy properties for holiday rentals. It might not be everyone's idea of a place in the sun but it has certainly cornered a lucrative market.[16]

Alicante itself, capital of the Costa Blanca, offers a more balanced diet, not least of all because it was already a city in its own right before the coming of mass tourism and has not, in that sense, been totally overwhelmed. It attracts a permanent stream of holiday-makers — including a growing number of visitors from cruise ships — but the city and its environs have also gained a reputation as one of the most favoured venues for permanent homes. Along the coast on either side of Alicante and inland, ever closer to the mountains, in neighbouring villages and resorts one sees all the signs of a massive building programme.

An estimated 30,000 British 'ex-pats' now live here permanently, and to these must be added at least as many from other European countries.[17] The reasons are not hard to see as it seems to tick all of the boxes that incomers are looking for, or at least those boxes identified by a group of geographers who have made a study of why northern Europeans move south.[18]

One obvious reason is the attractive climate — long hours of sunshine throughout the year (nearly 3000 hours annually in Alicante) and warm temperatures in winter. Rain tends to come in bursts without the endless drizzle and low cloud cover that is familiar in Belfast or Brussels and which this new generation of Euro-sunseekers are happy to leave behind. Another attraction that many cite is the availability of good golf courses that can be used in all seasons, something that Alicante boasts of with a number of renowned locations.[19] Sometimes new housing is integrated within one of these courses, effectively a gated community in landscaped grounds and with the clubhouse as a social gathering point. Another attraction is the proximity of a good airport, with frequent flights of two to three hours to most cities in northern Europe.

The cost of living in Spain has risen sharply in recent years but under most headings it is still regarded as cheaper than, say, the UK or Sweden. Finally, because of its earlier holiday associations, settling in Alicante is not a step into the unknown. Many will have been there before and, if they do decide to make a permanent move, they will soon find a readymade network of clubs and organizations to help them settle in. For the more timid, it might almost be possible to live in a ghetto with other sunseekers, untroubled by the nuances of a foreign language and unfamiliar ways.

Bonalba is one such mecca, several kilometres to the north-east of the city, and an integrated site for golf and housing. One enters the estate through an arch that spans the road, a point of transition from the outside world into this modern nirvana of easy living. Individual streets are gated, adding to the sense of arrival and enclosure.

One of a number of residential estates around a golf course in the Alicante region.

The rows of villas are colourful and gardens are planted with sub-tropical vegetation, while on the higher slopes are much denser clusters of apartments. Some of the properties have direct views over the different greens although, it seems, many of the occupants have little interest in golf as such.[20] It is a mixed community in various ways: for some it is their permanent home but others are there only occasionally, while in terms of nationality there can be few parts of Europe that are not represented. Dutch families live next to British, Germans alongside Swedes, Belgians with Danes.

There are teams of Polish construction workers and popular rumours of Russian money funding much of the new development along this coastline. Such a world would have been inconceivable at the end of the Second World War and even for many years after that, at least until the collapse of the Soviet Union. It ought to be an obvious source of celebration but it raises as many questions as it answers: about purpose and meaning, about exclusion and motives. Not everyone stays, and their reasons for returning home will be as telling as those that brought them to Spain in the first place.

Spanish Customs

Spain is essentially a Latin country. There's far too much emphasis today on Al-Andalus and the Moors.[21]

Spain is a proud country and successive waves of occupation by foreign powers have not diminished an enduring sense of national identity; indeed, this very history may, unintentionally, have nurtured it.

Before the arrival of the first invaders the Peninsula was peopled by Iberians and so it is again, albeit with many alien strains added along the way and with powerful regional variations. Alicante has experienced as much cultural change as any city and yet it remains an unmistakeably Spanish place. How can this be?

Part of the answer may lie in the fact that for Alicante the Reconquista started earlier than for many other cities in the south. It was reclaimed in the thirteenth century for the Castilian crown although in just half a century it was transferred into the smaller Aragonian Kingdom of Valencia. Two centuries later, in 1490, it was granted a City Charter by Ferdinand the Catholic, in part as recognition of its growing importance as a port for the region: an outlet for the rich produce of the inland valleys and plains, and a gateway for imports to Castile. No less was the port recognized for its strategic role when Spain was under attack, as it was in 1691 when the French navy bombarded Alicante constantly for seven days.

During the War of Spanish Succession at the start of the eighteenth century Alicante backed the unsuccessful contender and, along with the rest of Valencia, lost some of its rights as a result. More tangibly, the British navy (playing its own part in that war) left the city with a seriously damaged Castle of Santa Barbara. A century later Alicante was again at war, when Napoleon tried, largely without success, to control the city and was later ousted by an alliance of forces in the Peninsular War.

Tossed around in this turbulent sea of Spanish history, from the thirteenth century onwards, the different roles played by Alicante can still be seen throughout the city. Even as one approaches it, the dual road signs for 'Alacant' as well as 'Alicante' tell of divided loyalties, for the former is Valencian (generally regarded as a variant of Catalan) and the latter Castilian. In spite of this dual use of language and a call for closer cultural ties with their Catalan neighbours to the north, few would argue that it amounts to a serious attempt to separate the region from the rest of Spain. These subtleties are, in any case, largely lost to the outsider, who will see in Alicante all the hallmarks of a modern Spanish city.

The marine skyline is broken by a towering hotel, totally out of scale with its surroundings.

Whether one approaches it from the interior or along the coast the scene is not pretty. Spanish cities have no obvious limits and well before one enters the official boundaries the mountain landscape is scarred by quarries and electricity pylons, and by extensive sheets of white plastic that provide cover for countless rows of tomato plants. Factories and construction yards are sited indiscriminately along the highways and low-cost housing estates—straight off developers' conveyor belts, reminiscent of an earlier era—are dense, uniform and repetitive. Even the inner suburbs are dreary, often a mix of dark brickwork and a crude and poorly weathered brand of Modernism, offering little respite from the heavy traffic that heads towards the centre. Some of the neighbourhoods are the home of different ethnic groups who have come to Alicante, alongside indigenous workers and their families. Closer to the centre there are some good examples of careful conservation and impressive civic features but also some anomalies, like a towering hotel that breaks the coastal skyline for no obvious reason, diminishing from various views the impact even of the watchful Castle of Santa Barbara.

There is the ubiquitous marina, not unlike many others to be found elsewhere in Mediterranean cities, although the tawdry development along its quays is already looking sadly dated. The marina has replaced the historic harbour, the commercial facilities of the latter having been relocated southwards to a less prominent location. Like most major planning schemes the new harbour has attracted divided views, the main source of opposition being because the authorities decided that once they obtained permission (and European Union funding) they would do something quite different. Much to the consternation of nearby residents as well as conservationists the new plans called for massive storage silos, fuel tanks, a cement production plant and a chemical factory to produce bio-fuels. All of this was in addition to its intended function as a container and ferry port.

View of marina from the mountain fortress.

Inland, between the old harbour and modern city, on the lower slopes of Mount Benacantil, is the historic district of *El Barrion Santa Cruz*, once marking the limits of the mediaeval town. Stepping briskly through the tiny red light district, past prostitutes eating pizzas from cardboard boxes, tourists wander along narrow lanes and into bustling squares. It is a mixture of attractive, vernacular housing — the kind of backcloth that would appear on a flamenco poster in the local tourist office — and ornate churches that proclaim in no uncertain terms the traditional dominance of Catholicism in this part of the world.

Onwards, the ground rises and one finds a route upwards across a hillside covered with low trees and shrubs, to the Castle of Santa Barbara, the flag of Spain flying from the diminished battlements. Below, the city is laid out like a history lesson. Immediately beneath the castle, the old quarter marks the limits of past scenes of negotiation and conflict, first with the Moors and then as part of the *Reconquista*. And just beyond that the site of the old harbour evokes memories of successive foreign navies arriving to take control of one of the best natural havens along that stretch of the Mediterranean.

Aspects of everyday life in Alicante.

The mountain with its fort, the houses and shops huddled below, and the harbour vulnerable to invasion: the three focal points of Alicante's past. It is not difficult to see where the modern city begins, with its gridiron layout and higher buildings, as well as massive new dock facilities beyond. Further still, along both stretches of coast, to east and west, there is the high-rise development that is so much a feature of the Spanish littoral. Inland, it is sprawl and a damaged landscape that tell the contemporary story. Alicante has undergone massive change—its population is now more than 300,000—and there are few signs that municipal planning has really had very much to do with it.

It is only when one comes down from the mountain and looks at the everyday street scene that one really gets a sense of how the city works. The working day follows a routine that is distinctly Spanish, shaped by generations of cultural tradition and the related dictates of climate. It seems to get off to a slow start, with office workers making their way through the streets, like office workers everywhere clutching a plastic container of coffee and perhaps a croissant too.

Those who are not tied to the workplace might find their way to the Esplanada or one of the little squares, where the municipality provides chairs that can be moved into the morning sun: a time to read the newspapers, chat with neighbours or begin a game of chess.

Nearby, in the city's downtown, is the food market, a large enclosed building that attracts daily shoppers in search of fresh produce, the hum of activity giving life to the whole neighbourhood. Lunch is late and leisurely, an institution supported by a legal requirement that all cafes and restaurants provide an affordable *menu del dia*. After lunch, well into the afternoon, there is time for a few more hours of work and shopping, before the evening *paseo*, when families and friends parade along favoured thoroughfares. Only when the sun is well and truly down is it time for dinner, with restaurants and bars typically staying open until well into the night.

Alicante is all of this, a working city as well as a popular venue for visitors; it does some things well and others badly; at its heart is a core precinct of cherished history but on its periphery the city is boundless; the old harbour is now a marina and its new counterpart is dominated by ill-placed heavy industry; it values its own traditions but these are challenged by an increasingly cosmopolitan population.

Like most modern cities, Alicante is full of contradictions and, like any place that is growing fast, some of its future is as yet uncertain. Long gone are the days when it was a strategic stronghold, or when its main function was simply to ship oranges and almonds from the old port. Yet it is still very much in the path of people on the move: an influx of newcomers from northern and eastern Europe and the prospect that these may one day be matched by even more settlers from the south. Alicante remains poised, no less than in the past, between the relative fortunes and aspirations of neighbouring continents.

MARSEILLE

If one were to nominate a candidate for the title of 'capital of the modern Mediterranean' it is hard to think of a better contender than Marseille. This southern French city would not always have aspired to this status, but in recent years it has shrugged off a mediocre if not murky past to stake a serious claim for the crown. It has a vitality about it that is inescapable, a magnificent setting, and a cross-section of cultures; it has a long history but wears this lightly; and everywhere are signs that it is investing in a bold future.

Marseille: le vieux port.

Perhaps, of all the cities on this itinerary, this one illustrates most vividly the ongoing connections between North and South, Europe and Africa. These links can be seen tangibly in Marseille's mixed population, in its apparent unity but also underlying divisions, and most colourfully in the daily traffic of ferries to and from Tunisia and Algeria.

In spite of roots that stretch back over twenty-six centuries it is thoroughly modern; it belongs to the Mediterranean but is just three hours by TGV from Paris; it has all the hallmarks of a major European city although when the warm *sirocco* blows red dust from the Sahara the southern continent comes closer. Where better to continue to unravel the complexities of the Mediterranean?

'Port of the Empire'

Le port de Marseille est le rendez-vous du monde entier...[1]

The Rhône is one of the great rivers to flow into the Mediterranean. On its way to the sea, it cuts through a large slice of its country's interior, rising high in the French Alps and joining another impressive river, the Saône, in the city of Lyon. From there the combined waters flow southwards in a single valley that is the home of famous vineyards and fruits that grow well on the gentle slopes; of heavy industry and massive cooling towers; and following its easy contours the main roads and railways leading to and from Paris. The broad river itself is a navigable waterway until it approaches the Mediterranean, where things tend to clog up in the delta region of the Camargue and, even with the help of canals, only light shipping can now find its way through to the sea. There is no longer an obvious port of note at the mouth of the Rhône (Arles used to be so until the sea receded) and one has to look along the coast to the east, to Marseille, to find the first natural harbour, known as *le vieux port*, in a magnificent setting framed by sun-tinged mountains. It was, in fact, the exceptional qualities of this harbour that first attracted the interest of foreign invaders.

Although the Greeks were not especially noted for navigating far from their own waters, an exception was to be found in Phocaea, the Ionian city on the shores of Anatolia. Their mariners proved better equipped to make longer voyages and in 600 BC they sailed into the western Mediterranean to found the settlement which they named Massalia, forerunner of Marseille. Its potential as a trading port was immediately recognized, not only by the Phocaeans but also by the hostile Carthaginians. Thucydides notes in passing that, in the course of establishing themselves on the Gallic mainland, the former were powerful enough to defeat the Carthaginian navy.[2] Subsequently, Massalia sought the protection of the Romans until that empire, too, eventually waned and the hitherto prospering port suffered at the hands of successive invaders from the north (the Visigoths, Ostrogoths and then the Franks). In time, under the Franks, the city regained a degree of independence and the port once again flourished, this time as a valuable link between the countries of the Mediterranean and the French interior.

It remained largely autonomous until the thirteenth century, when it was conquered by the Count of Anjou, although it was still to retain various rights and privileges. Two centuries later, as part of Provence, the city was formally incorporated within the nation state of France. Perhaps because of its long history of relative independence, Marseille proved to be a rebellious city with successive attempts to loosen the hold of Paris. It was hardly surprising that in due course it would lend its support to the Revolution that swept the country in the late-eighteenth century, with the anthem sung by its soldiers on their long march to Paris immortalized as the *Marseillaise*.

As well as political distractions, progress was also hampered at times by serious outbreaks of bubonic plague. Because of its exposure as a port to outside influences, and a failure to enforce effective quarantine restrictions, Marseille was periodically affected by *la peste*. The last of the major epidemics, in 1720, was the most devastating of all. It struck first in one of the poorest and most densely packed neighbourhoods and spread quickly from house to house.

Celebrations of empire: Colonies d'Afrique and Colonies d'Asie

Attempts were made to place a cordon round the city but by then some of the surrounding villages were already affected. In any case, limits on movement also prevented the import of fresh meat and vegetables, and malnutrition was added to the city's suffering. While most of the victims fell to the disease within the first few months, it was four years before it finally ran its course. By then, the plague had claimed as many as 40,000 lives (from a total of some 100,000 within Marseille and its immediate hinterland). In spite of this number of mortalities, the city recovered quickly and went on to prosper during the rest of the eighteenth century. The pre-plague population level was soon restored and by the eve of the Revolution stood at 120,000.[3]

During the nineteenth century, Marseille went on to enjoy even greater prosperity, stimulated now by French expansion into North Africa, together with the part it played in a more extensive process of colonial acquisition in sub-Saharan Africa and beyond. It was this emergent empire, more than other factors, which most obviously shaped the modern history of Marseille. From the time of the first conquest, Algeria in 1830, to the later control of Tunisia and Morocco, the city performed a vital role in facilitating the movement of people as well as trade between the two continents. Colonization requires intricate systems of organization, and many of the specialist trading, banking, insurance and other businesses that oiled the wheels of the expanding empire were sited in Marseille. The city's role was further enhanced after 1869, following the opening of the French-built Suez Canal, leading to shorter shipping routes across the Mediterranean to the nation's colonies in Indo-China and other destinations in Asia. Marseille proudly assumed the title of 'port of the empire' and posters for shipping carried the motif, 'gateway to the Orient'. As well as its varied cargo, in 1900 its busy port was handling some 370,000 passengers (increasing to 850,000 by 1930).[4] To mark its self-proclaimed primacy, the city's leaders thought it fitting to host an exhibition on the French Empire, to take place in 1906; in the event, this proved to be the first of two, with the second held some years later, in 1922.[5]

The 1906 exhibition—*L'Exposition Coloniale Nationale de Marseille et Le Congrès Colonial*—was four years in the making and from the outset endowed with a dual purpose: one was educational, to spread knowledge to ordinary citizens about France's distant colonies, and the other was primarily economic, intended to encourage more trade and business for the city. French government, since the rule of Napoleon, has been heavily centralized and the decision of Marseille to take the lead in this way was at first coolly received in Paris; indeed, it was only when the exhibition was already well underway and assured of success that the French President and government ministers deigned to pay official visits. In fact, the distinguished visitors could not have been other than impressed by what they found, just as were the crowds who preceded them. The exhibition was laid out over some thirty-six hectares of parkland within easy reach of the city centre. Visitors who walked through the gates were immediately drawn along a wide avenue with pavilions on either side, leading to a monumental building at the end,

Le Palais de l'Exportation. The frontage of *Le Palais* extended over 140 metres and was approached between a splendid array of fountains; within it was a variety of exhibits, many of them designed to show how French industry was well equipped to provide the necessary infrastructure for colonial development. For the ordinary visitor, who would never have seen anything like this before, displays of photos and actual objects helped to bring it all to life.

Within the separate pavilions for the different colonies, the fare was altogether more exotic. Typically, there would be some natives in traditional costume and speaking unknown languages, and in some of the exhibition areas were wild animals that had never been seen before on French soil.[6] Elsewhere in the grounds were replica native settlements and performances of music and dance. To portray Marseille's nearest colonies, Algeria and Tunisia, there was even a village with typical white houses as well as an attempt to re-create the mysteries of a souk; visitors could also peer into the holy space of a mosque and listen to the call to prayer from a minaret alongside. Under the auspices of *Le Congrès Colonial*, specialist sessions were organized for scientists and industrialists, ranging over a variety of subjects such as commerce, shipping, transportation and mining. Taken together, the 1906 exhibition and congress were seen as a great success, attracting more than two million visitors and confirming Marseille's pre-eminent role in serving the cause of Empire. Not least of the achievements was its demonstration to politicians and bureaucrats in Paris that even a provincial city like Marseille was capable of organizing a national event to the highest of standards.

In the wake of the city's success, plans were soon laid for a sequel to take place in 1916, although because of the First World War this was subsequently delayed until 1922. The same site was used and the event followed a comparable dual format, with both educational and commercial activities. Differences were mainly of detail, with changes made as a result of experience gained in 1906, and to take account of new technological and political developments. Following a transfer of rights in the postwar peace settlement, Morocco was formally embraced within the Empire and portrayed for the public alongside neighbouring Algeria and Tunisia. Much to the enjoyment of visitors, more use was made of moving images, made possible by recent advances in cinematography. There was also more emphasis on the scientific and commercial congress, which itself attracted 10,000 delegates (compared with 2000 in 1906). Overall, the 1922 event was even more of a success than the first one, with more than three million visitors drawn from Marseille and the region but also this time from further afield as well. Even as far away as Paris, the message must have got through once again that Marseille was a city to be reckoned with, playing a vital role in the nation's mighty empire.

With these various imperial functions and at the meeting point of so many cultures, past and present, it is understandable that the population of Marseille has always been cosmopolitan. A contemporary account in the eighteenth century described the crowded harbour (with as many as 900 ships at anchor) and the colourful scene on the quayside.[7] It seemed at the time as if the whole world was there, with Turks and Armenians, Greeks and Arabs, and Africans from south of the Sahara, all in their national dress and speaking their own languages. Around the harbour it was like an oriental bazaar, with every kind of product sold from the merchants' stores and laid out on rugs in the open: carpets and silks, jewels and daggers, exotic fruits and flowers, and the squawking of brightly plumaged parrots and cockatoos. The vitality of the harbour was at the heart of the city's cosmopolitanism but there were other factors in its multi-cultural history too. Like much of the south-east coast of France, which was for long periods under Italian influence if not direct rule, Marseille has traditionally had sizeable communities from Genoa and Piedmont in particular, and many families today still claim Italian roots. Another significant minority comes from Corsica, an island fiercely independent in spirit, but historically linked to Marseille as the nearest mainland port. In the middle of the twentieth century, some of the main criminal syndicates in the city were reputedly Corsican. Over the years, the city also attracted immigrants from Spain (including many Jews at the time of their expulsion in the fifteenth century) and Greece, as well as from the Levant. Around the time of the First World War, tens of thousands arrived from Armenia, fleeing massacres at the hands of the Turks, and from Russia as a result of the Bolshevik Revolution. Most dramatically, too, there was a reverse flow of migrants with the disintegration of the empire towards the end of the 1950s, mainly from Algeria but also from Tunisia and Morocco. The colonial incomers included not only indigenous peoples from the Maghreb but also disaffected former French settlers, known as the *pieds noirs*. Returning colonialists also arrived in large numbers from former French islands in the Indian Ocean and from Indo-China.

The cosmopolitanism of Marseille remains today a feature of the city and can be seen in everyday observations in the different coloured skins and names, in an enticing variety of cuisines, in shops catering for various ethnic groups, and in contrasting fashions and decor.[8] Synagogues, churches and mosques all do good business. On the face of it, the city benefits from this kaleidoscope of cultures, and for most people it works well enough. Unemployment is higher amongst ethnic groups than the rest of the population, although not as high as in other major French cities. There is, however, a darker side to it, in the form of a strong presence of extreme right political factions, characterized around the turn of the last century by the rise of Jean-Marie Le Pen's *Front National*. Although not a single-issue party, the *Front National* prioritized the ending of further immigration and disparagement of those already in the city, in particular, Jews and Africans. For several decades Le Pen enjoyed a strong presence in Marseille and was himself a French Presidential candidate in five national elections, famously coming second in 2002, ahead of the Socialists. His campaign in that year attracted worldwide attention.

Poor and colorful Marseille, home to north African Muslims and Jews, ethnic Italians and Armenians, and generations-old French residents, offers one telling story of how Le Pen rose so stunningly in the polls. Nationally, Le Pen captured almost 17 percent of the first-round vote. But here, in France's

*southeastern Bouches-du-Rhone region, Le Pen led with 22.4 percent—
almost 6 percentage points ahead of Chirac. In Marseille, the second largest
city in France, almost one in four voters backed him.*[9]

Just a year after the attack on the twin towers of the World Trade Centre, Le
Pen was able to exploit powerful anti-Arab emotions, although many attributed his
success more to a promise of strong government. In Marseille, he even enlisted some
North African and Jewish followers, who found common ground in the prospect of
a more decisive government and themselves agreed that further immigration should
be halted. 'We have to limit immigration,' said Rojbi, a first-generation Tunisian who
arrived in France 20 years ago. 'Immigration only brings bad and negative things
to people living here. I'm honest. I pay my taxes. But these new people give a bad
name to North Africans.'[10]

Marseille has a brittle edge and it is, perhaps, not surprising that the likes of Le
Pen have found fertile ground amongst disaffected elements of its population, who
fear that their elected politicians are not listening to them. Slogans daubed on walls
in the city's poorer districts can be as much expressions of frustration on a range
of underlying issues (such as housing and jobs) as about racism as such. This is
a European phenomenon, by no means confined to Marseille, but with each new
ferry bringing more prospective immigrants from Africa there is a very real sense
of being on the front line. The city's ability to absorb further change and to resist
pressures to veer towards one extreme or another will, above all, define its future.
It may also set an example, or not, for the rest of the Mediterranean where cities
have tended to become less rather than more multi-cultural. Thessaloniki, Izmir,
Beirut, Alexandria, Nicosia were all once cities where races mixed easily, but where
minorities have since been forced to leave. Marseille, so far at least, seems, in
relative terms, to have bucked this recent trend.

La Belle France

*I am convinced that Marseille is the most beautiful city in France. It is so different from
all the others…*[11]

Marseille is so obviously Mediterranean, the sea itself shaping much of its
character, but it is also a typical French city with tree-lined boulevards, baroque
monuments and fashionable apartments. Inevitably, the two sets of influence,
Mediterranean and French, have at times pulled in different directions. Proud of its
independent character, Marseille was not always quite sure if it wanted to be part
of the nation state. One can see the case: a southern city with a northern capital,
the two regions geographically different and far apart. In the event, the mantle of
France was all-embracing and, although Marseille has managed to retain a strong
Mediterranean feel, the stamp of *la France* is unmistakeable. Typically, in its grand
buildings and public spaces it exhibits some powerful symbols, none more so than
the cathedral located high above the harbour, *Notre Dame de la Garde*.

For visitors arriving by air or on one of the sea ferries, few cities can rival this spectacular introduction; the Opera House in Sydney Harbour and Christ the Redeemer above Rio de Janeiro are obvious exceptions but in its iconic impact the Notre Dame is every bit their equal. Standing on a pine-covered hill to the south of the harbour, the cathedral can be seen across the whole city. Built to a mixed Roman-Byzantine design, its dominance is enhanced by a ten-metre high statue of the Virgin and Child, gilded in gold leaf, rising from its uppermost tower. The cathedral is best seen at night, when the whole structure is illuminated. No less impressive, perhaps, is that, like other iconic features in the city, it remains important to the everyday lives of the population with, in this case, a steady flow of devotees daily making their way up the hill to attend Mass and other services. In a part of the world where religion has for so long played a crucial role in its history, and where mosques now occupy a more pervasive presence on the Mediterranean skyline, this is a reminder of the continuing hold of Catholicism. There is, as well, a second cathedral near the waterfront, to the north of the old harbour, designed a few years before the Notre Dame by the same architect, Jacques Henri Espérandieu. This, the *Cathédrale de la Major*, built in the same exotic style as its successor, is also a massive structure and when the area around is redeveloped it will exercise its own special impact on the skyline.

The Notre Dame de la Garde dominates the Marseille skyline.

No single architect in Marseille was to play a more important role in bringing a sense of *la gloire* of the Second Empire than Espérandieu; in his way, he can be seen as a provincial counterpart of Baron Haussmann, who was working at the same time on his grand schemes in Paris. After his success with the *Cathédrale de la Major*, Espérandieu was then commissioned to design another monumental structure, the *Palais Longchamp*. The site for the palace marked the eastern terminal of the Canal de Provence, which had been linked to Marseille thirty years before, and which from that time assured the growing city of a regular supply of water. Ostensibly a decorative water tower, it became far more than that, flanked by two arcs of colonnades and classical sculptures, with ceremonial steps leading down to a formal lake. On either side of the central tower, the two wings were designed for the museums of Natural History and Fine Arts. The palace was opened in 1869 in appropriate fashion, to the sounds of a concert orchestra and fireworks, in the same year as the first ships sailed through the Suez Canal. After that, Espérandieu undertook one more important assignment, the *Palais des Arts*, completed in the year of his death in 1874. It was another decorative, neo-classical structure, to accommodate students of music and fine art, as well the city's main library, and represents that architect's final contribution to Marseille's rich heritage from the Second Empire.

Ceremonial stairway leading to the main railway station.

In addition to Espérandieu's legacy there were, in the middle and second half of the nineteenth century, other major works that helped to shape the modern development of the city. Individual buildings of note like the *Préfecture* and the *Bourse du Commerce* were also designed in the elaborate style associated with the Second Empire. Perched on a high site with extensive views towards the sea, Marseille's main station, St. Charles, was opened in 1848, although it was not until 1926 that an impressive stairway was added to link it more easily to the rest of the city. Other developments were more directly related to the extension of the harbour.

Especially as a result of the nation's colonial ventures, *le vieux port* was proving inadequate to the task and steps were taken in the middle of the century to create modern facilities to the north. In 1853 the first of a series of new docks was opened in the area known as La Joliette, with new warehouses and refineries alongside.[12] Taking a lead from Paris, it was also a time for cutting through some of the old districts to create new boulevards. The most significant of these projects was the Rue de la République (originally named Rue Impériale and designed by the uncompromising Baron Haussmann himself) to link the old and modern ports more effectively and to provide a new focus for business. It was Haussmanesque to the letter, driving a straight line through a crowded neighbourhood and forcing the removal of some 16,000 residents. Although the urban renewal process in Marseille was by no means as comprehensive as in Paris, the legacy of a number of broad avenues is still there to see. Preceding the Rue de la République, the Canebière— a kilometre in length—has always been the city's favourite, but it would take an outsider, Joseph Conrad, to taunt that if such a grand boulevard had been in Paris the latter would be thought of as 'un petit Marseille'.[13]

By the end of the century, Marseille was prospering: it had seen in barely fifty years the completion of a massive programme of infrastructure development that was by then bearing fruit. Nor was it solely a city of commerce; with greater prosperity came more investment in culture. Marseille's long-established opera house, for instance, enjoyed a national reputation for the quality of its productions. When the building was destroyed by fire in 1919 it was rebuilt in a characteristic classical mode, with six tall columns and ornamental stonework along the façade, in keeping with other grand buildings in the city. Progress continued in the early decades of the twentieth century, although development slowed down in the interwar period, as it did across the world; the city's reliance on the docks and associated industries had left it particularly vulnerable.

To add to its growing economic problems, it was then that various mobsters gained a hold over business and political life, giving Marseille a reputation that was likened to Chicago. Even after the Second World War it continued to suffer a negative image, and later images in the two 'French Connection' films starring Gene Hackman convinced those who had not seen the city for themselves that Marseille was wallowing in drugs and with armed gangsters on every corner. No modern city is without crime but Hackman's Marseille was even then as far from the truth as Jack the Ripper's London. Likewise, the city suffered from an image of racial enmities, with right-wing politicians portraying a false picture of an immigrant population as numerous as that of the indigenous *Provençals*. More problematic, because more realistic, was Marseille's lingering record of damaging industrial disputes, sufficient to deter potential investors for some years to come.

In the postwar years there was also the legacy of a period of German occupation to address. Although Marseille emerged from the war in better shape than many European cities, it was not without its own lasting wounds. Significantly, the occupying forces inflicted substantial damage, particularly on the northern flank of the old harbour, along the waterfront and in the densely-packed housing on the slopes behind (the district known as *Le Panier*). The military reason for wholesale destruction was to clear the area of resistance activities, but in the course of doing so the character of a colourful historic area, where many of the city's immigrants lived, was lost too.

No doubt an outcome of agreement between the Nazis and the Vichy Government, the *Hôtel de Ville*, located on the waterfront in this district, was spared. In France, such institutions are invariably at the heart of the city and their architecture will, typically, communicate a fitting sense of grandeur.

That was certainly true in this case, with the symbolic centre of local leadership overlooking the harbour, housed in a splendid baroque structure dating from the seventeenth century. It is now at the centre of a new programme of urban regeneration, designed to revitalize the whole of the previously run-down area around it.

The Hôtel de Ville survived wartime destruction of the harbour front and is now the focus of regeneration alongside.

The likes of the *Hôtel de Ville* are predictable landmarks but there is one renowned building in Marseille that stands apart from its more traditional counterparts, namely, Le Corbusier's *Unité d'Habitation*, widely seen as one of the great triumphs of Modernism. It is perhaps fitting that some twenty years before its completion, Le Corbusier and fellow modernists set sail from Marseille on the cruise ship, *Patris II*, bound for Athens and the 1933 CIAM Congress.[14]

Their shared vision of the future bore little relation to the kind of development that was commonplace at the time and it was not until 1954 that the people of Marseille could see for themselves what had then been so avidly discussed. For the first residents, the modernist rhetoric of creating cities in the sky was at least matched in Le Corbusier's new residential structure by uninterrupted views of the sea, in an area that was still relatively open. Today it is simply one building in a cluster of mixed development, a couple of kilometres south of the city centre. Perhaps because of its accurate portrayal of the future, the eighteen-storey slab block is at first sight quite unexceptional, its basic form now familiar in most modern cities.

At the time, though, it was hailed as a social as well as physical breakthrough in the provision of mass housing, with novel features including a roof garden, a crèche, and an internal 'street' of shops and a gym.

Le Corbusier's Unité d'Habitation, completed in 1954.

The whole building was set on pilotis so that the ground level could be used for circulation and landscaping. Of course, the reality is that the idealism that made it different at the time was subsequently ignored by cost-conscious public authorities around the world, stripping the concept of its finer qualities and condemning future generations to unsuitable high-rise living. Some of the modern French banlieues, including the poorer suburbs of Marseille, with their enormous slab blocks and little in the way of amenities, exemplify where it all went wrong. The *Unité d'Habitation*, once a sign of things to come, is today part of the past.

City in the Sun

Allez à Marseille. Marseille vous répondra.[15]

For a place that is generally not thought of as being in Europe's premier league, it will come as a surprise to many that Marseille, with a population of 1.6 million, is France's second city (third, behind Lyon, only if one includes that city's more extensive metropolitan area). But it is not statistics that will impress the visitor, so much as an immediate sense of being in a real place. Where else can one encounter the salty smell of the fish market even before you exit the Metro?

Aspects of everyday life in Marseille.

Make your way through the dimly lit tunnel from the underground platforms and suddenly emerge into the brightest of daylight, with the old harbour immediately in front of you and the fish stalls along the quayside. Sea bass and tuna, scallops and sea urchins, along with baskets of lemons and herbs: all are laid out on well-scrubbed tables, attended by vendors with weathered faces, shrewdly eyeing the day's catch and bantering with buyers in the sharp dialect of the region.

Close to the stalls are the ferries that sail regularly to the islands across the bay, along with rows of yachts bobbing alongside wooden jetties. The old harbour enjoys one of the most beautiful settings of any major city, with steep slopes on opposite sides and apricot-hued buildings banked up to conceal the narrow stairways and lanes between. Even as one leaves by boat there is the final attraction of historic fortifications on either side of the harbour mouth, Fort St. Nicholas to the south and Fort St. Jean to the north.

One can see why artists have for long favoured this alluring stretch of coastline, where the sun invariably shines and the sea literally sparkles. There was a time, around the turn of the nineteenth century, when nearby Estaque was in vogue as an artists' colony, with the likes of Cézanne and Renoir, Braque and Dufy immortalizing scenes across the bay from clifftops covered with wild flowers, and the village itself portrayed in various guises. Cézanne's mother had a house in Estaque and the painter was naturally drawn to the area, recording a visit made in 1870 when he observed that 'the sun here is so terrific that objects appear silhouetted not only in white or black, but in blue, red, brown, violet'.[16]

Amongst his best-known works is the view across the bay of Marseille, a dramatic collage of sea, sky, roofscape and mountains, all bathed in sunlight. In 1882 he received a visit from another experimental Impressionist, Auguste Renoir. The latter was totally captivated: 'it must surely be the most beautiful place in the world', he declared.[17] He was no less inspired by the progressive techniques of Cézanne, so much so that his depiction of the olive groves around the village, *Les Oliviers d'Estaque*, is believed to reflect something of Cézanne's own use of bold horizontal and vertical brushwork. Cézanne's influence was to extend to later painters too, notably Georges Braque, who made a number of visits between 1906 and 1910 and took the former artist's style into the more abstract versions of first Fauvism and then Cubism. Raoul Dufy followed a similar route, joining Braque in Estaque in 1908 and sharing his admiration of Cézanne but also with a determination to develop his own distinctive style; it is impossible to watch a scatter of little yachts on the blue waters of the bay without thinking of Dufy.

The sea is at the heart of everything, accounting for the growth of Marseille in the first place and serving ever since as its defining image. Within the city, it is fitting that from all directions one descends gently towards the water, passing through contrasting districts along the way. The route from the airport, for instance, takes one past some poor neighbourhoods where many of the immigrants and minority groups have clustered, living in crowded tenements and ugly slab blocks that represent an unenviable feature of French urban planning. In contrast, approaching from the south, one soon joins the *Corniche*, which snakes along the coast and into the very heart of the city, skirting the fashionable *arrondissement 8*, with its white villas and gardens with sub-tropical vegetation. Within the older neighbourhoods, buildings are splendidly French, six or seven storeys high, with ornate iron balustrades and large windows revealing heavy drapes and gloomy baroque interiors. Alternatively, one can slice through the centre of Marseille towards the old harbour, along the *Rue Canebière*, traditionally seen as a line between the predominantly North African population to the north and Europeans to the south.

Sea and land, past and present, peoples of north and south: it remains a place of opposing forces but, by and large, the modern city finds a way through. Unlike other Mediterranean cities its history is not overbearing; it has a long and interesting past but the record on the ground is not exceptional. For a thousand years, Marseille was under Greek and then Roman control, and yet there is little to see from this period; the city is not adorned with the ruins of temples and amphitheatres, public baths and aqueducts. Some observers, like the French writer, Prosper Mérimée, have rued the absence of sites of antiquity.[18]

Until recently, Marseille has not even been a favoured destination for tourists although this is now fast changing. Modern visitors can at least resort to some of the city's museums, in particular for the classical period the *Musée d'Histoire de Marseille* within a shopping complex close to the old port. Many of the remains on display were discovered in the course of excavations for the present development, and the *jardin des vestiges* includes a section of the classical ramparts, port buildings and a necropolis. Elsewhere, there are further signs of the city's history but these tend to be incorporated into the present fabric rather than set apart. In one sense, this loose attachment to the past has worked in its favour for it has not been constrained from looking to the future.

Even within the past decade, Marseille has emerged as Europe's exemplar of a thriving sunbelt city. In 2001 a new TGV service brought it within a three-hour train ride from Paris. Suddenly, the South was on the doorstep of the capital and this latest transport revolution hastened a growing realization that this might, in fact, be a good place for Parisians to live and work. Just as in the United States, where there has been an irreversible population drift to the warmer southern states, something of the same trend has been happening in France. Footloose high-tech firms, as well as finance and service sector activities, find in Marseille an attractive alternative to the congestion, high property prices and less conducive climate of the north.[19]

One has only to look at the bustling contemporary street cafes and bars to see how popular it has become with young professionals. Step back from the old port and one finds in the narrow streets that unique blend of gourmet food shops and high-class fashion boutiques that one associates with Paris: a waft of fresh coffee from a tiny store alongside a shop displaying contemporary household products, a colourful collage of Mediterranean fruit piled high blends happily with a neighbouring window of oriental fabrics. And everywhere restaurants that tell as much as anything about its location: fish bars around the harbour, menus with traditional Provençale cuisine drawn from the surrounding mountains, steaming *tagines* in North African kitchens, and cafes that cater for the many Corsicans and other ethnic groups who have made the city their home. Moreover, although far from being an urban utopia, it is a city that works. When they are not crippled by strikes, French public services are efficient and, unlike many modern cities, the streets are cleaned regularly. The traffic is heavy but there is an excellent public transport system and the city is well connected with the outside world through its modern docks, the international Marignane Airport and St. Charles railway station, as well as motorway links to the rest of Europe.

La Joliette is the locus for the Euroméditerranée project.

Currently, to gain a glimpse of the future, the most ambitious project is that which is expansively named *Euroméditerranée*. Initiated in 1994 the plan is to revitalize with the support of public capital a large swathe of the inner city, from the area around the docks at La Joliette to the main railway station of St. Charles and its environs.

Recently this core area (itself covering over 300 hectares) has been extended northwards by a further 170 hectares. More than 40,000 people will live in the combined area, along with 30,000 downtown jobs. Little wonder it is proclaimed as the largest area of urban redevelopment in southern Europe; certainly, there is nothing comparable anywhere else around the Mediterranean, exceeding in its scope even the earlier redevelopment of Barcelona.[20]

La Joliette, the heart of the nineteenth-century docklands, has already been largely transformed, with a massive programme of refurbishment and renewal. Its giant warehouses have been converted into fashionable apartments and offices, as well as chic restaurants and bars, and a former grain silo is now an events venue. A modern tramway system was introduced in 2007 and, through a variety of new roads and tunnels, the area will be efficiently linked to air and rail networks. In contrast with other cities, commonly abandoned by shipping, the docks themselves are thriving, with car ferries departing daily for Corsica and North Africa and a constant flow of container traffic. At the other end of the regeneration axis, St. Charles Station is at the centre of a complex series of works to enhance its setting and revitalize the whole district.

The station itself is a grand edifice, located on a hill with panoramic views of the city; the recent scheme has seen the restoration of its monumental steps and classical statues that were added to the original structure to celebrate the magnificence of the French Empire. Beyond St. Charles, the whole traffic circulation system in the district has been reconfigured to improve flows, and a boost has been given to the nearby university environment, previously cut off from the rest of the city by traffic and railway sidings. As well as all this, Marseille prepared with typical energy and aplomb for its role in 2013 as the European Capital of Culture, yet another sign that its seamy reputation has become a thing of the past.

Meanwhile, beyond the city's north-western boundaries, Marseille has benefited from plans laid in the 1960s for a petro-chemical complex at a coastal location near the small town of Fos. This, like the later *Euroméditerranée* within the city itself, was a public sector led initiative. Following the original investment, it has seen the addition of new dock facilities for large oil tankers and other cargo ships, and the development of adjoining land for processing and related industries. It is intended that *La Métropole*, as it was called, will progressively draw new development along the axis from Marseille to create an economically powerful sub-region.

Not only will Marseille strengthen its position as France's most important southern metropolis but, along with its other attributes, it will also be recognized more widely as one of the Mediterranean's leading port cities. There are some heavyweight rivals but it is clear from promotional material that Marseille sees Barcelona as its closest competitor. Both are rounded cities with a healthy balance of commerce and culture, both have known years of poverty and neglect, and both are currently enjoying the advantages of a deliberate process of planning and regeneration.

On most counts, Marseille is doing well. It is in every sense a city that is modern yet one in which tradition is not forgotten; a city that makes plausible attempts to come to terms with cultural diversity; and one where the presence of mountains and sea still offer a unique natural setting. As a thriving Mediterranean city, not perfect but very liveable, it is hard to find a more instructive example of what is possible in this region than Marseille.

CHAPTER 3

BALKAN RIM

As one heads east, the hinterland of the Mediterranean coastline changes. Spain, France and Italy—always with a key interest and involvement in European affairs—give way to the region known as the Balkans. The Latin cultural tradition to the west is replaced by Slavic, and this part of the continent is commonly perceived as being less like Europe than the heartland countries. It has a long history of ethnic and religious conflict and even as recently as the 1990s the Yugoslav wars brought old enmities to the surface. With its mountainous terrain and uncertain loyalties, this was for long regarded as a difficult if not dangerous place to visit, all of which gives its cities an added edge of intrigue.

The shoreline of the Balkans illustrates the fact that while the sea itself imposes its own generic character on the maritime cities across the whole of the Mediterranean, the contrasting character of the various interiors adds its own nuances. All of the Mediterranean cities have a commercial mission and all have hosted a mix of cultures over the years. This gives them a distinctive stamp that all of them share. Yet each serves its own particular hinterland, which varies significantly from one part of the region to another. The outcome is that in any one city its generic features are modified by localized factors.

The first of the three cities to be visited in this region is Trieste, an unusual city that is poised between Latin cultures to the west, Slavic to the east and Germanic to the north. It is located at the very gateway to the Balkans and during the Cold War it occupied a contested position between the two competing power blocs. The Austrian Habsburgs long ago saw the potential of Trieste as a warm-water port to serve their landlocked empire. Nearly a century after the collapse of Austria-Hungary, Trieste—now a part of Italy—still retains more than a hint of *mitteleuropa*.

Dubrovnik, to the south of Trieste, is more than it first appears. Contrary to its present demeanour, this is a city with a past as an important trading nation that enjoyed unrivalled access to the Balkan interior. Subsequently it rested on its laurels, renowned now as no more than a place of exceptional architectural qualities. After a turbulent period during the Yugoslav wars of the 1990s, the old city has been restored and tourists have returned. But its days of true grandeur have long passed.

Finally, on the eastern edge of the region, is Thessaloniki. Once a model of ethnic diversity—where Greeks, Turks and Jews lived peacefully alongside each other—

the dream became a nightmare in the twentieth century. First the Turks were forcibly evicted and then the Jews fell to Nazi occupiers. Only recently has Thessaloniki fully emerged as a modern Greek city, second only to Athens. But, as in the past, it still looks to its Balkan hinterland for much of its wealth and cultural diversity.

TRIESTE

In search of some of the more telling cross-currents of culture and history, a visit to Trieste is a 'must'—even though for much of the twentieth century it acquired a reputation as something of a Mediterranean backwater, one of Europe's forgotten cities. Tucked into the northern reaches of the Adriatic, close to the border between Italy and Slovenia, Trieste speaks more eloquently of its earlier role as the warm-water port of the Austro-Hungarian Empire than of its post-imperial experience. Until recently it looked somewhat out of place on a coastline dominated by the splendours of neighbouring Venice and by the sprightly tourist resorts in Croatia to the south. It seemed that age had finally caught up with Trieste, leaving it to reflect quietly—perhaps rather sadly—on a more elegant past. Yet nothing in the Mediterranean is forever, and there is now a new spring in the old lady's step and a reluctance to accept that better days cannot return.

Contradictions of Place

Curiously enough, Trieste is the least interesting city, from a visitor's point of view, that I know.[1]

Trieste, as the above view indicates, has not infrequently been seen by visitors as a rather dull place, a poor relation along the coast from Venice. Timing, of course, is everything and had this visitor made his observation just before rather than immediately after the First World War, he would undoubtedly have found a very different city. In any case, taking a wider perspective, nothing could be further from the truth for there are few places in the Mediterranean that are more intriguing. Far from being dull, it can be seen as poised on the cusp of contrasting worlds, a place where nothing is quite as it seems.

Even its very location is full of contradictions. For a start, is it favoured through being at the head of the Adriatic, with the whole of the Mediterranean beyond; or disadvantaged, on the road to nowhere, off the main shipping routes? Does it benefit from exceptional natural advantages, in the form of its deep-water harbour; or is it hampered by the abutting *karst* landscape, bleak and rugged, once a formidable barrier against the outside world?

Should we look beyond the *karst* and across the Alps, to a rich Central European hinterland, or eastwards to the historically troubled Balkans? Does it have the vitality of a cosmopolitan city, at the meeting point of three of Europe's major population groups—Slavs, Latins and Teutons—or is it somehow just beyond the boundaries of them all? Is Trieste the queen of the Adriatic; or is its lot always to be overshadowed by proud Venice, as it was in earlier times by the Roman port of Aquileia and, more recently, the nearby industrial rival of Koper?

In seeking to understand these various contradictions, the reality one finds is that both geography and history have dealt Trieste a mixed hand. At times, the city has undoubtedly gained from being where it is, strategically placed between the rest of the Mediterranean and the European mainland to the north. At other times, this very location has been to its disadvantage, pitting it against more powerful rivals and in a politically unstable zone between western Europe and the Balkans. Its fortunes have oscillated with the swings of geopolitics in the wider region. To take an instance, after the Second World War, Trieste found itself more or less on the line between the capitalist West and communist East, in a fold of the so-called Iron Curtain. Not unlike the situation in Berlin, Allied forces faced, in this case, the army of communist Yugoslavia's Marshall Tito, with neither side willing to cede authority to the other. In the event, an international agreement was reached in 1947, which established the city and surrounding land as an independent entity, the Free Territory of Trieste. For a few years the city proudly flew its own flag and traded in its unique currency but there was a touch of Ruritania about the situation. It was in any case a shortlived claim to self-rule, for with sustained Soviet opposition and the unremitting claims of Tito's Yugoslavia, a new agreement soon had to be negotiated. As a result, Trieste once again became a part of Italy (as it had been before the war), while its rural environs were ceded to its communist neighbour.

People on the streets battling against the force of the bora. (Istrianet.org)

Nothing is straightforward in Trieste, and even in terms of micro-geography it raises questions. It is blessed with a fine harbour, a feature recognized, and often coveted throughout its history, and yet the city for much of its history was remarkably inaccessible on the landward side. The reason for this is the inhospitable karst landscape, characteristic of this region but also a generic term for a limestone platform where mildly acidic water seeps into the bedrock to cause collapses and resultant hollows known as *dolinas*. With the river system confined to the subterranean depths, the surface is left typically dry and rugged, most of it a wilderness of little value to farmers and only in the hollows can anything of worth be grown. Cold winds blow across the plateau in winter and travellers have traditionally seen it as a hostile place, to be crossed as speedily as possible.

Even those who find beauty in it are never wholly convinced: it is at the same time 'a sad and beautiful place [that] has nothing to do with the Mediterranean and never has done'.[2] As one nears Trieste, the karst plateau drops steeply to the city below but it is not an easy route. Although the road winds down through hairpin bends, the railway is forced to make a much longer journey, just a few kilometres above the city at one stage before it turns away in favour of 30-kilometres of gentler gradients.

Nor, in spite of its Mediterranean location, is Trieste especially blessed by its climate. The summers are hot and unusually sultry, the sea perfectly still and brooding; in winter, 'it can suggest somewhere cruel, on the Black Sea or in the Baltic'.[3] Winter is the time when one is most likely to experience the *bora*, the fierce wind that sweeps through the city, bringing cold from the Alps and from the endless plains of eastern Europe; once there were ropes along the main thoroughfares so that people on the pavements would not be swept off their feet.[4] Pines were planted on the slopes above Trieste to offer protection but the wind was not to be deterred. Sometimes it persists for days, playing on the emotions and reputedly (like the mistral in southern France) leaving the people in its path strangely unsettled.

Apart from its micro-geography, the very location of Trieste has shaped its destiny; although it is at the crossroads of cultures there is a sense in which these various groups have neutralized rather than enriched each other. In its heyday, as a bustling port, things were different and the city attracted a mix of races, many of them working in one occupation or another along the waterfront:

> *Albanians, Turks, ear-ringed fisher-people from the Venetian lagoons, giant Montenegrins, Greeks with baggy trousers and Byronic headgear—talking and squabbling and singing in many languages, drinking in their particular taverns, living in their specific quarters of the town.*[5]

For centuries, too, much of the business of Trieste was managed by established families of Jews, who remained there until most were massacred by the Nazis during the Second World War.[6] Yet even before the Jewish persecution relations between different groups in the city had become less harmonious, partly a by-product of economic decline but also a result of deliberate actions by the dominant group. After the Italians took control of Trieste in 1920, its new fascist government was quick to take issue with the Slovenian minority (which then amounted to nearly one third of the city's population and up to 90% in the surrounding country districts).

It was in keeping with the nationalistic aims of the fascists to champion racial purity, but their actions were also rooted in centuries-old feelings that the peoples of the 'West' were somehow superior to the Slavs of the 'East'; a line reinforced by the Church of Rome on one side, and Orthodox Christianity and Islam on the other. Irrational though this perception of superiority might have been, Trieste has even today retained a sense of being a city 'on the edge', between one set of cultures and another. Only very recently, with Slovenia gaining membership of the European Union, are there signs that this longstanding prejudice will slowly be eroded.

History, too, is a tale of mixed fortunes, of times when it was shunned but also of days of glory. Certainly, there is little in its early episodes to indicate the better times that lay ahead. It was settled originally by an Indo-European tribe known as the Carni but, like most other Mediterranean cities, it was to be overrun by a succession of conquerors. First came the Histri and then the Palaeo-Veneti, before the inevitable arrival of the Romans, in 177 BC. In the scheme of things, for the Romans, Tergeste (as it was named) was not a major prize, although it was accorded the status of a colony. At the time of the conquest, the settlement was little more than a small port trading with nearby communities in staple commodities like olives, wine, fish and salt. Under the Romans it enjoyed protection but it was the nearby city of Aquilea that was favoured as a more important stronghold of that far-flung empire.

With the demise of Rome, Trieste then fell into the hands of the Byzantines, performing the function of a military outpost for the Orthodox Christians of the eastern Mediterranean. This episode lasted for three centuries, before the advance from the north of the Franks, and the appropriation of the city as part of their powerful European kingdom. Even after their departure, Trieste found itself subservient to Aquilea, and it was not until the end of the twelfth century that it experienced independence as a free commune. Freedom, though, came at a price and the city this time found itself open to attacks by the seemingly invincible Venetians, enjoying their inexorable rise to become one of the most powerful states in the Mediterranean. For two centuries, Trieste lived in constant fear of annexation (and was, in fact, actually occupied by the Venetians for a short period) until, confronting the realities of the situation, a decision was taken by the city to seek the protection of the Austrians. A petition was submitted to Leopold III von Habsburg, Duke of Austria, to cede to his kingdom and the move was formalized in 1382. This proved to be a seminal moment, for most of Trieste's subsequent history was to be intimately linked to that nation's rulers in Vienna. In geopolitical terms, the city re-orientated itself and, instead of remaining a provincial outpost, it was later to emerge as a vital cog in the machinery of a great empire. As a result of its diplomacy it became, effectively, a part of *mitteleuropa*, unlike any other city in the Mediterranean.

Imperial Destiny

There in the lee of a wilderness Habsburg Trieste was built, in the eighteenth and nineteenth centuries, with all urban refinements.[7]

The marriage of a humble Mediterranean city into one of Europe's most powerful courts was always going to be a strange one: not only socially uneven but also in mixing the warm blood of the south with the measured demeanour of the north. Trieste's whole being had previously been bound up with the sea, while Vienna's natural hinterland was the Danube. It was an unlikely match but also a marriage of convenience—for Trieste the promise of security, for the Habsburgs the prize of their own passage to the oceans of the world.

In the fourteenth century, when the relationship was cemented, it was clear that Trieste had chosen well for even then the Habsburgs were clearly aspiring to greater things. The origins of the family were to be found in an inauspicious castle of the same name in a Swiss canton, dating from the eleventh century. Three centuries on, by the time that the citizens of Trieste bid for protection, the Habsburgs had, through a mixture of judicious marriages and treaties, extended their domain into the heart of Europe. Amongst the many titles that came with the territory was that of Emperor of the Holy Roman Empire, grand-sounding but largely honorary as head of the union of Christian states formed by Charlemagne in 800 AD. The ambitious family was not, however, to be satisfied with a so-called empire over which it had very little direct control; progressively, when opportunities arose, it proved adept in adding more tangible acquisitions.

At one stage, before the dynasty split into two factions, Austrian and Spanish, Habsburg monarchs ruled lands as far apart as Portugal and Bohemia, and from Italy to the Low Countries. Few of the royal courts of Europe at that time were wholly beyond Habsburg influence. It was an astonishing story and the ever-extending web of territories could only be good news for Trieste. With the Austrian branch of the dynasty centred in Vienna, the port could soon claim something of a monopoly over trade across its vast hinterland of central and eastern Europe.

Trieste had been given an important role to play and it grew steadily over a long period until, early in the eighteenth century, it was marked out for something even bigger, with the status of a Free Port. This brought it greater independence and also led to more trade being directed through its warehouses. Later in that same century, Trieste benefited further from the ascendancy of a new ruler, Maria Theresa of Austria. On the face of it, Maria Theresa was an unlikely patron: reputedly the mother of sixteen children and holder of numerous titles—notably, Archduchess of Austria, Queen Regnant of Hungary, Croatia and Bohemia, and Holy Roman Empress by marriage. In fact, she proved to be a skilled strategist and modernizer, who amongst other achievements saw the potential of Trieste as a vital part of her still emerging empire. Most noticeably, it was Maria Theresa who put her name to a whole new district of the city, still known as the *borgo teresiana*, the Theresian Quarter.

Planned in Vienna, the intention was to break new ground in urban design, to create 'a merchant city that was also a garden city, full of greenery and fountains, while obeying careful imperial laws concerning sanitation, safety and proportions'.[8] It was a bold venture, comprising an area of fifty rectangular blocks, and including the new *Canal Grande*, which brought seagoing shipping into the very heart of the city. Merchants were attracted by the tall buildings, which could accommodate warehouses and offices on the lower floors and living accommodation above, while the neo-classical style with touches of Baroque lent a sense of grandeur which was no less appealing.

The Canal Grande is part of Maria Theresa's legacy to Trieste.

New piers were built along the harbour front and a lighthouse was added to assist the extra shipping. In addition to strengthening the physical infrastructure, Maria Theresa made further wise moves with an eye to the future. She was responsible for the establishment of a nautical school (to be run by Jesuits), and, putting religious prejudice to one side, she encouraged the settlement of Jews to run the businesses of the growing port. 'All of a sudden Trieste became a proper port, equipped for ocean traffic'.[9]

The Emperor Napoleon disrupted progress with no less than three invasions of the city during his rampage through Europe but in the years that followed the best was yet to come. For more than a hundred years, until 1914 when the First World War changed everything, Trieste flourished like never before or since, gaining a reputation as a city of culture as well as commerce. Everything seemed to go right for it, and with the formation of the Austro-Hungarian Empire in 1867 Trieste could now look for patronage to Budapest as well as Vienna. As the nineteenth century unfolded, new developments encouraged further growth. Seaborne trade would have increased in any case but it certainly did no harm to see the appearance in 1836 of Austrian Lloyd (Österreichischer Lloyd), the highly successful company which took a lead in the development of merchant shipping to and from the port. The opening of the railway in 1857, linking Trieste with Vienna, was another vital step. Trieste was also to become for a while the base for the Austro-Hungarian navy, as well as an important industrial centre for shipbuilding and repairs. Then came the Suez Canal, in 1869, and no more were there limits to the port's destinations; the inland Empire had become truly global in its reach.

One of the delights of researching the cities of the Mediterranean is not only to visit them but also to unearth some truly classic accounts of their history. Jan Morris's *Trieste and the Meaning of Nowhere* is one such treasure, and the sense she evokes of the city in its heyday surely cannot be bettered. Trieste, claims Morris, was one of the great achievements of Habsburg imperialism: 'its design was logical, its buildings were substantial, its streets were spacious, its manner was amply complacent, for it was a mercantile city, a port city, built for the job'.[10] It was not, though, simply its functionalism that distinguished it, so much as its whole ambience. Trieste was a city of great squares, with statues of dignitaries, and bands playing under the trees, with numerous cafes where people sipped strong coffee and watched the world go by. Symbolism played its part and key institutions like the Austrian shipping line; the major commercial insurance company, *Assicurazioni Generali*; the headquarters of the Imperial Maritime Government; the General Post Office; and the grand station where trains arrived from the imperial capital, were all housed in monumental buildings designed to impress. Most of all, life revolved around the ships that came and went, a time when 'anyone in the whole empire who wanted to travel overseas came down here to take ship'.[11] The Piazza Grande (today the Piazza dell'Unita d'Italia), which faces onto the harbour, would host passengers biding their time in the cafes and promenading in small groups, the women in fine silks, the men in resplendent uniforms of the sort that would be seen now only in a Gilbert and Sullivan production. Then it would be time to board, on a voyage that would take them down the Adriatic and on to an exotic Mediterranean destination like Alexandria, through the Suez Canal to the Orient, or westwards across the ocean to America.

Symbols of Trieste's grandeur before 1914.

Many ports are simply equipped to handle goods and people on arrival and embarkation, but in its heyday Trieste was a buzzing city of culture too. The wealth it generated and its important connections made it much more than a mere place of transit. There was a time when concerts and operas attracted full houses, and when intellectuals from across Europe gathered in the coffee houses and in the shade of trees around the squares to discuss art and politics, music and science. James Joyce was one such habitué, living in Trieste intermittently for eleven years between 1904 and 1920. In between scratching out a living for himself and his young family, he wrote some of his best-known works: *Dubliners, A Portrait of the Artist as a Young Man and Exile*, and it was there that he started *Ulysses* and found inspiration for *Finnegans Wake*. His job as a teacher of English was mundane enough but even in that he was fortunate to discover that one of his students was the Italian author, Italo Svevo, whose work Joyce much admired. When he was not teaching, he easily found the company of fellow intellectuals and, money permitting, enjoyed going to international concerts and theatrical productions.[12]

There were some superficial likenesses in the seaboard city with Joyce's native Dublin, but it was not that which excited him so much as the differences and, in particular, its cosmopolitanism.

James Joyce, immortalized crossing the Canal Grande.

Like other western intellectuals, his imagination was captured by the sight of strange costumes from the mysterious Balkans and North Africa, from Turkey and the Middle East; of boxes piled high on the quays, laden with exotic foodstuffs and pungent spices from India and beyond; of warm winds carrying the scents of herbs and blossom from nearby gardens; and the aroma of freshly-ground coffee arousing thoughts of Vienna and the intrigues of Central Europe.[13] Watching the boats lined up along the quays he was fascinated by their timelessness:

> *They are the same old galley-looking affairs which were in use during the Middle Age. The men row the row-boats from the standing posture. Inside the great bosom of the brow every sailing ship has an image of some saviour, Saint Nicholas or the Madonna or Jesus walking on the waters.*[14]

Such days have long passed. The start of a long period of decline for the city was marked by a sudden and dramatic event, not in Trieste itself but in another imperial possession to the south, Sarajevo. While undertaking a tour of duty to the Balkan territory of Bosnia-Herzegovina, the nephew and heir to the Emperor, Archduke Franz Ferdinand, and his wife Sophie, both fell victim to an assassin's bullets. Their bodies were brought back in a warship across the sea to Trieste, where they were carried in procession through the streets, before the onward rail journey to Vienna. For the silent crowds along the route, there was time for reflection although few would have anticipated the full chain of events to follow. In an already combustible situation, the assassination triggered immediate responses amongst opposing European alliances that led inexorably to the conflagration of the First World War. Amongst the many consequences of the war, the Austro-Hungarian Empire was dissembled and Trieste overnight lost its patronage. In the peace negotiations that followed the conflict, Italy seized the opportunity to annex the city and its surrounding farmlands, at a stroke breaking the link with the Central European hinterland that had for long served Trieste so well. No more would it be a prosperous port for an inland empire; instead, Trieste found itself in a marginal location in a country with an uncertain political future. Decline set in and it is only very recently that one can see the start of a renaissance, albeit in a very different form from the grandeur of its mercantile past.

A City Undone

Trieste makes one ask sad questions of oneself.[15]

Trieste was not alone in the twentieth century in losing its very *raison d'être*. In the aftermath of two world wars, other cities, too, were to see their economic and political lifeline cut away as the map of Europe was redrawn. A former hinterland could disappear overnight at a postwar conference table; by such means, indeed, it was Trieste's misfortune to become a classic example of what geographers call a 'shrinking city'.[16] So long as it remained within the Austro-Hungarian Empire its continuing prosperity would have been assured. There was still a role for it to play as a conduit to the rest of the world, meeting the needs of commerce if not, too, a more selective passenger traffic. Trieste's patrons in Vienna and Budapest would also have ensured that the city kept pace with modern port developments elsewhere, and that it continued to be well served by key institutions befitting its status. After 1918 the reality, of course, was very different. With the Empire dissolved and its patronage ended the good days were over.

Fresh investment dried up, a situation aggravated by Trieste's marginal location in its new universe; Italy, of which it became a part in 1919, had its own priorities. Under the banner of *Italia irredenta*, the aspiring young nation saw it as no less than a spiritual mission to bring Trieste back into the fold as a rightful possession. It was a mission championed by the ascendant fascists at that time, led by Benito Mussolini. The irony is that, although the 'return' of Trieste was of enormous symbolic significance, and although on occasion the city was portrayed as a spearhead for Italy's colonial ambitions in the Mediterranean and Africa, for the most part it was marginalized in favour of Rome and other historic centres that were more obviously at the heart of Italy. In any case, investors were hardly going to be attracted to a location with such an uncertain future, so strongly contested even then by its Slav neighbours.

Once again one can turn to Jan Morris for a sense of Trieste's dilemma during much of the twentieth century. For the six decades or so that Morris knew the place it was 'more or less stagnant'. If it had not been a port, she concludes, 'Trieste would have been nothing much, and the sense that it is nothing much, now that its great days seem to be gone, is what has made it feel so wistfully unfulfilled.' Becoming part of Italy was not to be its redemption because by then, cut off from its past, Trieste had no 'organic purpose'. It was simply not needed and there were other ports in a better position to handle the nation's trade.[17] Within the city itself the symbols of decline were everywhere to see:

> *The great steam locomotives do not hiss in the station now, the Südbahn station master no longer welcomes important personages in his tight-buttoned livery; there is no express to Vienna any more... The last passenger liner sailed long ago. The schooners, steamboats and barges have disappeared. No tram has crossed the piazza for years... The Governor's Palace is now only the Palace of the Prefect and the Lloyd Austriaco headquarters, having metamorphosed into Lloyd Triestino when the Austrians left, are now government offices... Those silken and epauletted passengers, with all they represented, have vanished from the face of Europe, and I am left all alone listening to the band.*[18]

After the Second World War, during the long years of the Cold War, Trieste was reduced to the furtive role of a black marketeer, turning a blind eye to the illicit trade across the nearby Yugoslav border for a population eager to buy luxury items from the West. Its buildings had become drab and peeling, its people largely ignored. Under Tito's communist regime, new industrial centres and shipbuilding yards were developed to the east and south along the Adriatic coast, with Trieste ill-equipped to compete. In the other direction, tourists could always be relied on to flock to Venice and coastal resorts nearby but few were attracted to Trieste. When Paul Theroux visited the city in the early 1990s he claimed that he could see no tourists but that seems not to have surprised him; why, indeed, he asked, would tourists come to Trieste?[19] Theroux's observation was undoubtedly exaggerated although it is a fact that in 2000 the only international flight to its small airport came from Munich, while the once prestigious and busy rail service from Vienna had long been scrapped. Even Jan Morris, for all her emotional attachment to Trieste, had to admit that:

> *It is not one of your iconic cities, instantly visible in the memory of the*

imagination. It offers no unforgettable landmark, no universally familiar melody, no unmistakable cuisine, hardly a single native name that everyone knows. It is a middle-sized, essentially middle-aged Italian seaport, ethnically ambivalent, historically confused, only intermittently prosperous, tucked away at the top right-hand corner of the Adriatic Sea.[20]

It is hard to believe that only a century ago the city was still flourishing at the heart of a great empire, and the stirring sounds of the Viennese waltz could be heard in its fashionable squares. In stark contrast, much of the period since then has been mundane if not downright miserable, in the face of repeated episodes of war, the persecution at times of its own minorities, and a relentless process of economic decline as its traditional functions disappeared. Even when the Iron Curtain was drawn back there was still more hardship to come, with Yugoslavia's civil wars in the 1990s spilling over the border, bringing refugees and further uncertainties to Trieste. It is only very recently that the city has at last been given a chance to breathe freely and to contemplate its own future.

A Most 'Un-Italian' City

I walked out and sensed that I was no longer in Italy. It hardly looked like the Mediterranean any more.[21]

Trieste has been part of Italy for most of the period since 1919 and yet it is still seen as something of a cuckoo in the nest: 'at the eastern limit of Latinity and the southern extremity of Germanness' if not, too, 'the western extremity of Slavdom'.[22] So much is the city on the margins of its homeland that in a poll in 1999 it was found that some 70% of Italians did not know it was in Italy at all.[23] It was as if their country ended in the environs of Venice and, even for the informed traveller, it is hard to envisage that much of note lies 120 kilometres or so further east. No-one visits Trieste by chance. Leaving the motorway, it is a long and winding descent across pine-covered slopes before one reaches a city that at first resembles a foreign land. This, surely, is no longer Italy, nor even part of the Mediterranean. The buildings are grand, the street scene formalized, and the smartly-dressed people who take the air on the sea front bear all the hallmarks of compatriots in *mitteleuropa*. Trieste, even now, has a touch of Vienna-by-Sea.

Yet, having been for so long in the doldrums, trapped in its own memories, a fresh wind is now blowing through the city. With the ending of the Cold War and then the termination of the Yugoslav civil wars of the 1990s, the very meaning of Trieste's location has changed. Instead of being in a remote corner of Italy that the past century's history had passed by, it now finds itself at the crossroads of a new map of Europe. To the west, as previously, are the wealthy markets of 'old' Europe, but now, to the east, a whole new world is opening up. With the eastwards extension of the European Union, trade and labour is free to search for the most lucrative markets, unrestricted as they used to be by rigid boundaries and tiresome customs controls. The motorway that cuts across the once largely impenetrable *karst* slopes above Trieste is busy with trucks travelling to and from Poland and Romania, Bulgaria and Turkey, while a northern spur links it to the old hinterland of Austria and Hungary. Additionally, modern port developments are attracting a new generation of international shipping. Few cities could be in a better position to take advantage of what is little short of a commercial revolution, and Trieste's institutions are, once again, well placed to provide financial and logistical services. Local officials take pride in the fact that the first of a new category of region designated by the European Union is based on the strategic location of Trieste at this important crossroads.[24]

The Opera House remains a hub of the cultural life of Trieste, as do the many coffee shops.

On the ground, evidence of a newfound prosperity is there to see. Its grand buildings of the past are, almost without exception, in an exemplary state of repair and work is ongoing to improve their surroundings. Some of the former harbour warehouses and offices are being converted to new uses, mainly for apartments, and there are attractive conference facilities.

Many of the shops and hotels are as finely appointed as any in Europe, and fashion-conscious Italians in the streets are heavily adorned with the very best of designer labels. Yet even within a short distance of the main piazzas, there is a buzz about the neighbourhoods where 'real life' goes on at its own pace. It is nearly a century since formal ties with Austria-Hungary ended but old ways die hard. Coffee shops remain central to the life of the city and traditional establishments sit easily alongside contemporary versions that appeal to a younger generation.[25] Trieste is a city that has plenty to occupy it and (unlike so many Mediterranean settlements) is certainly not overwhelmed by tourists. The fine features of the Piazza dell'Unita d'Italia and the Grand Canal remain as much for the pride and enjoyment of its resident population as for visitors. Likewise, the city has lost none of the cultural vitality prized of old; the Giuseppe Verdi opera house continues to stage international productions, as do the various theatres. There are numerous museums with a changing programme of exhibitions that includes recognition of distinguished foreigners who were once resident here (like James Joyce and the explorer, Sir Richard Burton) as well as subjects relevant to its own proud history.

At times, Trieste feels like the Italian city that it is, but, equally, the long hand of Vienna and Budapest has never entirely let go. No less, in some of the quarters, there are Slovenian shops and bars, a reminder of yet another element in the city's background and of its proximity to the country that in the past century claimed Trieste for itself. If aspects of identity are sometimes in doubt, one thing is certain: Trieste is not like any other Mediterranean city. Absent is the spontaneity that marks so many of its neighbours across the sea; absent too is the 'edge' that one senses in a place like Marseille or Beirut. In other respects, however, it has made its own distinctive mark on this little corner of Europe and, having endured a particularly troubled period in its long history, is now well positioned to open a new chapter.

DUBROVNIK

For much of its history the capital of the former Ragusan Republic, Dubrovnik tells a compelling story of the Balkans. Through its very location, on the Dalmatian coast and now within Croatia, Dubrovnik cannot be other than a Balkan city. Devastated at one point by a catastrophic earthquake, it has repeatedly suffered from the ambitions of neighbouring powers and bouts of ethnic infighting; the complex boundaries that surround it reveal their own history of fiercely contested issues of autonomy. For all these reasons, Dubrovnik brings to the shores of the Mediterranean an insight of the troubled soul of this wider region.

The very name of that swathe of south-eastern Europe has innocent enough origins, referring to a wooded range, the Balkan Mountains, extending from central Bulgaria to eastern Serbia. Travellers made their way over the low mountains on journeys from the cities of western Europe to Constantinople. Such innocence, though, has long been lost in the use of the term to describe a region renowned for its boundary wars, ethnic conflicts and resistance to external control; the fact that it is also a major earthquake zone has added a further dimension to its reputation for instability. For the rest of Europe the Balkans is a restless corner of the continent— the home of Orthodox Christianity and Catholicism as well as Islam, and not so long ago part of the Ottoman Empire—traditionally regarded as alien and backward.[1] When Rebecca West visited the area in the 1930s she confessed that 'violence was, indeed, all I knew of the Balkans'.[2] In keeping with its unwanted reputation, even the name has been corrupted to 'balkanization', referring generically to a process of fragmentation resulting from various groups seeking ever smaller areas of autonomy. Dubrovnik's place in the Mediterranean has been shaped, at different times, by all of these forces emanating from its hinterland.

A Very Balkan Place

Dubrovnik has thrived on divisions and conflicts...[3]

As befits a city of the Balkans, even the origins of Dubrovnik are remarkably complex and, in spite of the availability of a renowned set of archives, there are still issues of conjecture.[4] Most would agree, though, that its early history is linked to that of a nearby Roman settlement, Epidaurum, located some thirty kilometres along the coast to the south. Epidaurum, peopled mainly by settlers from the Italian mainland across the Adriatic, met a sorry end some time in the seventh century, probably as a result of being overrun first by barbarian tribes from the north and later by Slavic Croats and Serbs. By then without the protection of the Roman Empire, the population was forced to leave Epidaurum in favour of a new site to the north, which they named Ragusa. The fact that there was already a small fishing community alongside, known as Dubrovnik and occupied by Slavs, did not deter the migrants. It was a favoured location, with good harbours as well as being defended from the interior by mountains. The first use of the name, Dubrovnik, to encompass both settlements, was recorded in a charter of 1215 although in the outside world it continued to be known as Ragusa for many centuries to come (mainly in the context of the Ragusan Republic).

Christianity has always played an important part in the life of Dubrovnik.

With the demise of the Romans it proved wise to seek the patronage of another power, in this case the obvious choice being the Eastern Orthodox Church of Byzantium, centred on Constantinople. Both of the groups that settled in and around Dubrovnik had been converted some years earlier to Christianity and the so-called Byzantine Empire was already well entrenched along the Dalmatian coast; for these reasons, the eastern branch of the Church seemed the natural successor to Rome. Although united in this way by religion and its new reliance on Constantinople, the emergent joint settlement was from the outset divided along lines of ethnicity.

The migrants from Epidaurum were predominantly of Latin stock and brought with them a Roman model of organization. In contrast, the minority Slavs already living there, mainly fisherfolk, had not before been exposed to the more sophisticated ways of the incomers. There was also a third ethnic group, the Vlachs, who came from Italy. Most of the Vlachs had from an early date drifted inland to remote parts of the Balkans, away from the long arm of imperial Rome; there they lived and worked as semi-nomadic shepherds, although some remained in small settlements by the sea. The biographer of Dubrovnik, Robin Harris, recognizes the prevailing diversity in describing the coastal settlement in the ninth century as 'a modest but growing community, heavily shaped by Roman culture, Byzantine administrative habits and Christianity'.[5]

As elsewhere in the Mediterranean, the development of cities was periodically interrupted by the unwanted interest of neighbouring powers. Dubrovnik (to include Ragusa) did well to secure external support; from as early as the eighth century it found itself threatened by invaders from North Africa. Twice the invaders were repelled, once with the help of a Frankish force and the second time following the arrival of the Byzantine fleet. Protection, however, was not always so effective and in the tenth century the settlement was largely destroyed by fire, as were other places along the Dalmatian coast, as a result of raids by the Macedonian-Bulgarian Tsar, Samuilo. It was also for a time troubled by Norman invaders, based in southern Italy; and, increasingly, from the interior by the more powerful Serbs, who (as a sign of things to come) were eager to secure an outlet to the sea. The most persistent enemy, though, came from elsewhere in the Adriatic, from the great city of Venice, capital of an emergent Mediterranean empire. Venice took over at the start of the thirteenth century as the dominant power in the region, as Byzantium passed its own zenith, exercising direct control over Dubrovnik for the next 150 years and presenting a continuing threat for longer than that. Nor was that the end of Dubrovnik's susceptibility to the interests of external powers: first, Hungarian influence replaced Venetian, and then, when that waned, the city voluntarily sought protection from the Muslim rulers of the Ottoman Empire.

In spite of its vulnerability, the city leaders were skilled in the art of diplomacy and managed successfully to tread a middle way between the extremes of reliance on a powerful patron and effective independence. From the time of the departure of the Venetians in the fourteenth century, what had become known as the Ragusan

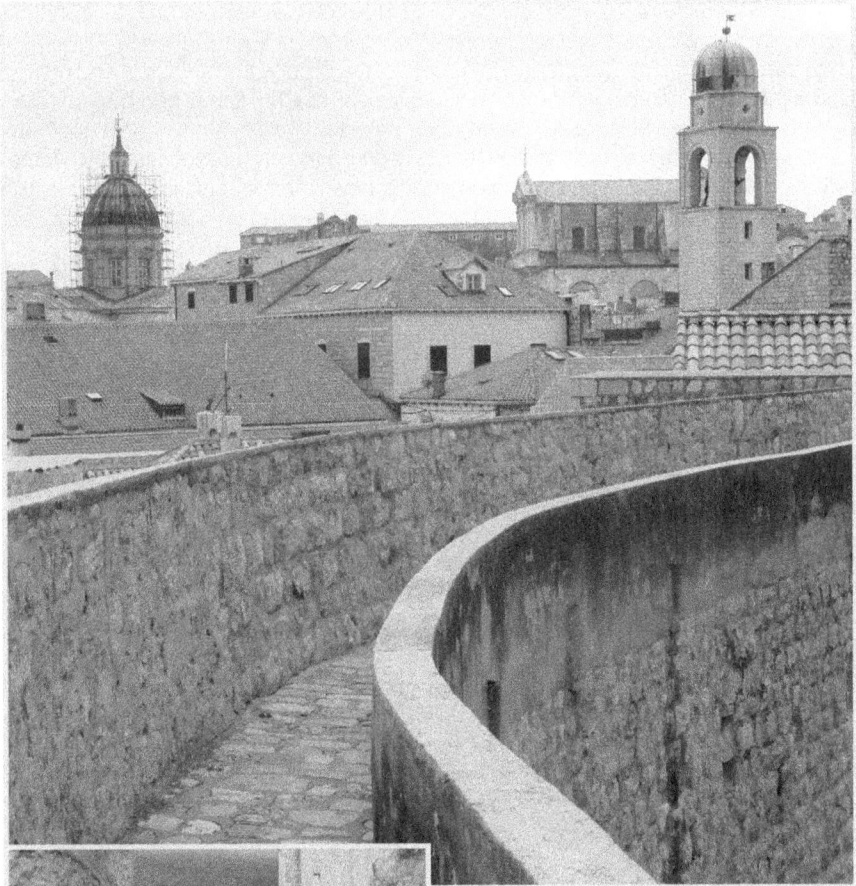

Dubrovnik's fortified walls are a reminder of the city's tempestuous past.

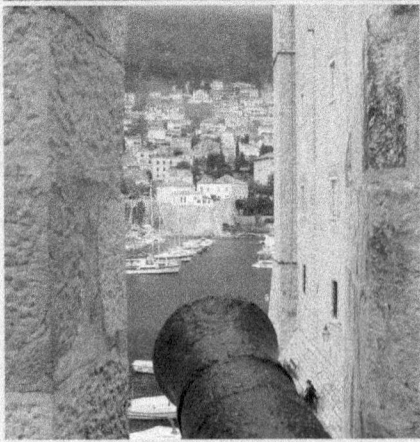

Republic enjoyed relative autonomy as a city state for nearly five hundred years. During this time it gained a worthy reputation as a significant trading nation, its success resting on a foundation of sound laws and liberal domestic policies. In commercial terms, it could draw in one direction on the extensive hinterland of the Balkans and in the other on the open seas. No other Adriatic port had such good contacts in the Balkan interior, importing to the landlocked communities essential supplies, such as salt, and exporting by sea valuable resources like silver and other minerals. The roads were poor but caravans could regularly be seen making their way slowly up the steep slopes of the bordering mountains, bound for remote settlements in Bosnia and Serbia, and beyond these further east to Bulgaria and Constantinople. An extensive network of trading colonies and bazaars was developed throughout the region, adding considerably to the wealth and influence of the Republic.

It was, however, as a maritime city that Dubrovnik was best known. In its heyday, it had its own merchant fleet and traded not only within the Mediterranean but across more distant oceans too; some 200 trading vessels flew the flag of the Republic, most of them built in the city's own shipyards. During the sixteenth century its fleet was the largest in the Mediterranean, ahead of Venice and Genoa. There were regular routes to England (which exported large quantities of wool) and eastwards to India, as well as long voyages to the western coast of South America.[6] Ragusan ships were to be seen in most of the world's main ports and the term *argosy* was used uniquely in the English language to describe their provenance.[7] Merchants visiting Dubrovnik were invariably impressed with its order and efficiency, with its long-established portfolio of trading institutions, with the reliability of its contracts and other marine documents, and with the skills of its shipbuilders. It gained a worthy reputation as a good place to do business. Nor was that all it was famed for, its prosperity, in turn, leading to a flowering of the arts and generous support for science and invention. The fact is that the diminutive Republic punched above its weight, achieving a status that was belied by its limited territory and small navy. Its importance, contends Harris, was a result of the city's 'strategic influence at the intersection between the Mediterranean basin and the Balkans, between Christendom and Islam, and between West and East'.[8] Location was certainly one thing but it was the clever use made of it that brought the port international renown.

From a high point in the sixteenth century the declining influence of the Republic was gradual but inexorable, resulting largely from the shift of power and prosperity away from the Mediterranean to the countries of northern Europe. Increasingly, its valuable trade routes were taken over by Dutch, British and French shipping. This structural decline was relentless but even this was overshadowed in 1667 by a sudden and cataclysmic event, a major earthquake that in a space of minutes led to wholesale destruction of the city. The earthquake came as a surprise although it should not have done, for the wider region had already experienced a number of serious tremors. Nothing in the Balkans is straightforward and, true to character, the reasons for its vulnerability to such earth movements are enormously complex. The Dalmatian coastline was slowly sinking—which accounts for its many islands parallel to the shoreline, the result of the sea flooding former valleys—but the rate was uneven and along different axes so that change was difficult if not impossible to predict with precision. From at least the fifteenth century, Dubrovnik itself had experienced periodic earthquakes, one of them, in 1520, being particularly destructive. Warnings these might have been but nothing was to compare with what happened on the morning of 6 April 1667, the date of the event that is still recalled as the Great Earthquake.

Destruction of the city was all but total, the main exception being the massive outer walls. Those buildings that survived the quake itself were then enveloped by fires that devoured the timbers. Dust and smoke covered everything and some 3000 lives were lost. Water seeped quickly from the wells and even the sea drained from the harbour, the outward current tearing ships from their moorings and smashing them against the jetties. In the wake of such widespread devastation, the authorities were unable to exercise control over the city and for a time it was doubtful if order would ever be restored. After an uncertain period they succeeded, but by then they had to contend with overtures from opportunistic rivals, in particular Venice, seeking to gain from its weakened state.

Once again, the republic proved adept at maintaining its independence and, remarkably, in spite of all that had happened, little time was lost in planning for Dubrovnik's reconstruction, a process that continued into the following century. By the time of its completion, the result was a restored city, with its old fortifications and most of the original street layout intact, but with a little thinning out of plots to create some new public spaces. The main difference came with the addition of some splendid new buildings, in a distinctive baroque style reflective of the period, including a rebuilt cathedral that symbolized for the people the whole process of recovery and renewal. It is these essential features of this post-earthquake restoration that have survived into the present century.

In spite of the achievement of rebuilding the city, the slow economic decline that was already underway before the earthquake, could not be stalled.[9] The eighteenth century is described by Harris as Dubrovnik's 'sunset years', although, compared with what was to follow, any changes then were hardly discernible. Some years later, during the Napoleonic Wars, the situation changed dramatically and the republic's much-admired diplomatic skills were finally out-manoeuvred by a wilier adversary. An immediate outcome was that the city was taken over by the French and in 1808 the republic was formally dissolved. In turn, of course, French expansionism was finally ended on the fields of Waterloo, and at the subsequent peace conference; Dubrovnik, by then a mere pawn on the international chessboard, was ceded to Austria. The ensuing century, under Austrian (and then joint Austro-Hungarian) rule, proved a sorry time for the city. Its merchant fleet had been largely lost at the hands of the French and, in an attempt to recover its position, a bid for free port status was later rejected by its rulers in Vienna in favour of the rival ports of Trieste and Rijeka. Some of its misfortune, however, was of is own making with the port authorities proving remarkably slow to see the coming dominance of steam power. In spite of its past reputation as a maritime power, Dubrovnik obstinately continued to invest in sail. Amidst great pomp and ceremony, the emperor Franz Joseph 1 in 1875 travelled from Vienna to launch the largest sailing ship ever constructed in the city's shipyards.[10] Yet far from announcing to the world its maritime revival, the event merely confirmed that its primacy at sea was over. Instead, its economic future would be built on different foundations, first as a favoured venue for visitors from the courts of Vienna and Budapest. Soon, however, even this modest start in modern tourism would be interrupted.

With the subsequent collapse of the Austro-Hungarian Empire after the First World War it was, once again, a time to redraw boundaries and change allegiances. Potentially, there were many permutations, reflecting a variety of religious, linguistic and ethnic identities, including the possibility of an independent state of Dalmatia. In the event, the mother of all compromises was reached when the whole region inhabited by the South Slavs was organized within a single kingdom of Serbs, Croats and Slovenes.

As a footnote to this grand scheme of things, the historic name of Ragusa was finally consigned to the records, in favour of the modern use of Dubrovnik. Further geopolitical changes were to follow during the Second World War, when Dubrovnik was forced to join the so-called Independent State of Croatia, distinguished from its Orthodox Christian and Muslim neighbours by the predominantly Catholic allegiance of its population. During the war, Croatia was occupied first by the Italians, then the Germans and from October 1944 by Tito's partisans, prior to the formation of the postwar communist state of Yugoslavia. Strong internal leadership of the new nation and the backing of the Soviet Union held it together for nearly half a century, until the fragility of the arrangement was finally exposed. As part of the wider collapse of European communism, the weakening of central controls led, first, to the fragmentation of Yugoslavia, followed by an intense series of civil wars. Once again, the integrity of Dubrovnik was dependent on the machinations of more powerful neighbours, although by now its own, long-admired diplomatic skills were to count for little.

Ghosts of the Past

Was this Europe's past or its future?[11]

To the outside world, the eruption of violence in the former Yugoslavia in the 1990s came as a surprise; somehow, a civil war in Europe in modern times, fought on so many fronts on the basis of extreme and seemingly arcane strains of nationalism, appeared to belong to an earlier age. Within the Balkans, however, there was little to surprise anyone. Old feuds are not forgotten, and ethnic ambitions may have been stalled for generations but they had certainly not gone away. With the plug of communist control removed the volcano exploded.

The story of Dubrovnik in the 1990s is part of a grand narrative, in which Serbia planned to retrieve most if not all of the former Yugoslavia, under the mantle of a Greater Serbia. At the same time, there were also numerous sub-plots, intricate and interwoven, and smaller entities were as much caught up in these as in the main storyline. Language, religion and history (real and imagined) were the tinder-boxes lit in this period and, depending on where the wind was coming from, there was nowhere to hide from the flames. Robert Fox is a journalist who travelled in the region on the eve of its civil wars and who could sense its combustibility:

> *The paradox of Yugoslav nationality is summed up in its languages and faiths. The principal language is Serbo-Croat, which Serbs depict in the Cyrillic alphabet and the Croats in the Latin. The other official languages are Slovenian and Macedonian. Minorities speak Albanian, Magyar, Italian, German and Turkish. One third of the population, principally in Croatia and Slovenia, is Catholic, two-fifths Orthodox and a sizeable minority is Muslim. Religion is still a powerful emblem of regional and ethnic separatism and protest.*[12]

Another commentator on the wars, Misha Glenny, confirmed how the past was never far from people's minds, expressed now through issues of nationalism: 'The nationalist sinews in this region have been exercised and strengthened by centuries of violence and uncertainty. '[13]

One has only to look at Dubrovnik's place on the political map to get a sense of its inescapable involvement in the destiny of the region. The most striking feature is its location in a long, thin wedge of Croatian territory that follows the coastline, hemmed in by rugged mountains that have always been difficult to cross. On the other side of these mountains its nearest neighbours are the states of Bosnia-Herzegovina and Montenegro, with Macedonia and Albania only a short distance further to the south. Belgrade, capital of the former Yugoslavia and now Serbia, had always seemed a world away. In the heyday of the Ragusan Republic, the city state itself held other territories along the Dalmatian coastline and, with difficult communications inland, it might well have emerged further as perhaps the capital of a linear, maritime state. Indeed, when Napoleon's forces occupied this part of the world he delved into history for the name of Illyria to describe a more extensive Adriatic province.

Geography, though, and political logic, were not enough and an Illyrian Movement in the nineteenth century championed the cause of Croatian independence. There were dreams of creating a new nation with boundaries well to the east but also with a strong hold on the coast, including the possession of Catholic Dubrovnik. Once again, the innate skills of Dubrovnik's diplomats were called for and, rather than resist, the prospect of moulding its future as part of an aspiring Croatia made good enough sense at the time. Independence, however, was a long time in coming and Croatian nationalists had to endure Habsburg followed by joint Austro-Hungarian domination, then a kingdom ruled by a Serbian monarch, before settling for republic status in the postwar Yugoslav Federation. Only in 1991 did the Croatians find the opportunity to finally break free and declare autonomy, an act that brought them into immediate and direct confrontation with neighbouring Serbia. By then, Serbia was led by the arch-nationalist, Slobodan Milosevic, who refused to countenance the transfer of the Serbian minority in Croatia to the rule of an ancient enemy. Even within living memory the Serbs recalled with bitterness the part played by Croatia, in league with the Nazis, during the Second World War. No love was lost on either side, and in an explosive mix of nationalism and recriminations a fierce and bloody war quickly followed.

Before long, most of the other states in the former Yugoslavia were caught up in the conflagration; it seemed that conventional rules of combat were set aside as all parties seized the chance to settle old scores. In the eyes of the Serbs, Dubrovnik, as part of Croatia, counted as the enemy. Because of its special architectural qualities, an attempt was made to keep the city out of the line of fire as a demilitarized zone. This sensible proposal was ignored in favour of military priorities and, and as part of the wider conflict the city itself soon came under direct and deliberate fire. The reasons were historical as well as contemporary. In the previous couple of decades, Dubrovnik had positioned itself as a popular holiday destination for Europeans from the north, with tourism emerging as the main source of its economic wellbeing. Compared with the Soviet Union and its immediate satellites, Tito's Yugoslavia was not an overly dogmatic communist state and visitors from the West were encouraged to take vacations in the country as a source of hard currency.

One of the attractions of Dubrovnik itself was its historic townscape, beautifully preserved and in summer invariably seen against the sparkling waters of the Adriatic. Such were its qualities that the 'Pearl of the Adriatic', as it proclaimed itself,[14] in 1979 (still part of Yugoslavia) won international recognition as a UNESCO world heritage site. In spite of its well-preserved fortifications, the city was no longer of military importance (and, indeed, had not in its long history assumed an aggressive role) so it was expected that it would be spared from enemy attack. As events showed, such expectations were seriously misplaced and, from October 1991 until it was recaptured by the Croatian army in April 1992 the city was a sitting target for enemy fire; artillery was quickly lined up along the ridge of Mount Srd, the historic backdrop to the city which had traditionally afforded protection. Two out of three buildings in the historic core were either damaged or totally destroyed, the iconic sites and other mainstays of the tourist industry were especially targeted, and shells were also directed onto the city's surrounding infrastructure. From being a prized UNESCO heritage site, Dubrovnik quickly became a war zone, re-designated as a site at risk

The renowned roofscape, badly damaged by Serb and Montenegrin artillery in the 1990s, is now largely restored.

It was a modern war but attended by ghosts of the past. The fact that more than 80% of the city's population saw themselves as Croats, and only 7% Serbs, was not enough to deter Serbia from claiming territorial rights. In the years before the conflict, Serbian nationalists in Belgrade had been building an intellectual case that Dubrovnik's rightful place would be within an emergent Greater Serbia. The case convinced few except Serbian extremists but, on the eve of armed conflict, rumours spread amongst the Serbian minority in the city, claiming that they were at great risk from a massacre by the Croatian majority. There was no evidence to support this and, indeed, both groups remained largely united within the city, in the face of a common enemy. Incoming shells were indiscriminate and civilians died in the conflict as well as defending forces. When hostilities opened, a cruel twist was to be found in the fact that Serbian forces were augmented by Montenegrins, who supported the cause of a Greater Serbia and who had once before been responsible for attacking the city. In retaliation for Dubrovnik's alleged connivance with the French at the time of Napoleon, Russia with its Balkan ally, Montenegro, had then laid siege to the city. With the citizens unable to escape, they fired cannons from the surrounding slopes and set fire to buildings within and beyond the walls. This historic precedent would not have escaped the memories of Dubrovnik citizens when once again it was the Montenegrins who put the city under siege and led artillery bombardments on their homes.

The attacks on Dubrovnik served no obvious military purpose and are generally regarded as outright acts of cultural vandalism. In war, though, symbolism is important and the aggressors were well aware that the very name of Dubrovnik was associated with unique qualities of architectural history, admired by the rest of the world. Through destroying this heritage they were making the unequivocal point that nothing would be allowed to stand in the way of Serbian claims. The damage done was unquestionable but, from his firsthand experience as a war reporter, Misha Glenny suggests that responsibility lay not only with the aggressors. In siting gun emplacements on the city walls, he contends that the Croat defenders invited return fire and were quick to exploit pictures of the resultant damage for propagandist purposes.[15] Either way, Dubrovnik was a sitting target and suffered human casualties (measured in hundreds) as well as extensive physical destruction. Even after the siege was lifted and the Croats forced back the attackers, this strip of coastline remained for several years more a dangerous and uncertain place. Remarkably, though, at the earliest opportunity plans were laid for rebuilding Dubrovnik, just as had been done at various times before in its long history, and by the end of the troubled decade a sizeable proportion of repairs and restoration had been completed. In an extraordinary change of scene, from a war zone to a holiday idyll, tourists were once again returning to the city in large numbers. For fresh cohorts of holidaymakers, from Germany and England, Sweden and France, it was almost as if this brief but terrible episode had never happened.

Trading in Heritage

The old town is a great city reduced in scale to human proportions.[16]

The modern trade of Dubrovnik is tourism. It helps to have an iconic historic core but visitors are attracted no less by the nearby coastal hotels and beaches, and opportunities to sail between the many islands. After its period of enforced closure, Dubrovnik is once again thriving as one of the Mediterranean's major tourist destinations. The city has always enjoyed a good press so it comes as a surprise to find one astute observer in its modern history who responded negatively, not so much to what she saw as what the city stands for. Rebecca West, one of the liveliest literary figures of the twentieth century, made three visits to Yugoslavia shortly before the Second World War and wrote a perceptive account of the region at that time. 'I can't bear Dubrovnik', she declared. 'I find it a unique experiment on the part of the Slav, unique in its nature and unique in its success, and I do not like it. It reminds me of the worst of England.'[17] It transpired that West could not abide its past—the price Dubrovnik paid for protection from a succession of great powers, and its steadfast resistance to allow a place in the city for Orthodox Christianity (in spite of its earlier affinity with Byzantium)—but she happily conceded that in architectural terms it really was a very special place: 'as precious as Venice, and [it] deserves comparison with the Venice of Carpaccio and Bellini, though not of Titian and Tintoretto'.[18]

The modern Grand Hotel Imperial has its origins in Austro-Hungarian tourism at the end of the nineteenth century.

Most visitors to Dubrovnik have shared the latter view, that Dubrovnik is, indeed, one of the jewels of the Mediterranean. Napoleon's captor of the city, General Marmont, arrived with the arrogance and disdain of a conqueror only to be seduced by Dubrovnik's charms.[19] It was a pattern repeated later in the century, when the Austrians, too, succumbed to the lure of its warm waters and spectacular scenery. Sensing a commercial opportunity, the President of Austrian Lloyd, the shipping company based in Trieste, in 1893 announced plans to build a prestigious hotel capable of meeting the needs of wealthy visitors. Four years later, distinguished guests from Vienna and Budapest arrived on the SS *Graf Wurmbrand* for the official opening of the Grand Hotel Imperial, located just outside the old city walls. Townsfolk gathered in the streets to marvel at the sight of a building illuminated wholly by electric lighting, while within the guests took advantage of various health treatments as well as simply relaxing in the well-appointed lounges and gardens.[20] The new hotel quickly attracted discerning visitors from elsewhere in Europe too, becoming popular especially with English travellers, like the dilettante writer Douglas Goldring, who, on the eve of the First World War, made what he described as an autumn tour of Italy and Dalmatia.

Hotels like the Imperial, few and far between on the Dalmatian coast, were honeypots for his privileged compatriots and one has to skip lightly over his notes on society 'tittle-tattle' exchanged over tea in the salons, to find something of what they thought of their surroundings. For cultured visitors, schooled in the splendours of classicism, the natural benchmark was whether this part of the world conformed to their imagined image of a glorious past. In his enthusiasm to find direct links with the Ancient Greeks, Goldring mistakenly believed that Epidaurum originated as an offshoot of that earlier civilization (as opposed to the later Romans), but he was on firmer ground when he observed the architectural treasures of Dubrovnik itself and the bustle in the streets. He saw it all as something of a charming timewarp from a lost past: 'the peculiar freshness, vigour, and delight of the Renaissance life is becoming increasingly difficult for us mentally to reconstruct; but here in Ragusa the aroma of a coloured past is as clinging and evocative as in a story of Boccaccio or an Umbrian picture of citizens talking together in some Italian market-place.'[21] It was the lifestyle of the city that captured his imagination just as much as the preserved buildings.

In spite of the dominance of tourism, everyday life finds its own spaces.

Unknowingly, Goldring touched on a theme that, nearly a century later, is at the heart of Dubrovnik's modern conservation. Is it enough to retain the exceptional townscape, much as it would have been in an earlier era? Or, in so doing, does it become little more than an empty shell, without other meaning? In one sense, this cannot be avoided: the original functions of the city when it was one of the Mediterranean's major trading centres and capital of a prosperous republic, have long disappeared. Its famous shipyards have closed, the merchants who skilfully managed its trade from harbour-side offices have departed, and its patronage of the arts is on an altogether diminished scale.

Tourists congregate daily in the Stradun and main squares.

There is still, however, an indigenous population of some 5000 within its walls, many of them working in the tourist industry but others leading quiet lives in the narrow streets and alleys beyond the main thoroughfare and squares, a world apart from the constant stream of international visitors. In their unassuming way, they bring at least a modicum of everyday life to what would otherwise be little more than an architectural museum. Incredibly, in its recent history there was a plan to convert a living neighbourhood into a wholly tourist venue, with new accommodation, craft workshops and boutiques; had it been implemented it would undoubtedly have stripped this historic quarter of its remaining authenticity.[22]

Without the people of Dubrovnik, there would be little to attract the critical visitor. Based though it is on its historical past, many of the present buildings are themselves replicas of their original structures. Given the circumstances, this was the best that could be achieved. Photographs of the city at the time of the recent war, in the early 1990s, show the extent of damage inflicted by direct hits and secondary fires. Rebuilding it as it was before bombardment represented an act of defiance, a statement of national resilience, as well as an investment in a new era of tourism. Regaining its UNESCO designation as a world architectural monument was no less essential to this programme of economic as well as physical recovery.

As such, the painstaking rebuilding that took place almost as soon as hostilities ended was in itself an outstanding achievement. Skilled craftsmen had to be assembled and authentic materials brought into the city to match as closely as possible what was there already. Twenty years on, a few repairs are still ongoing although most of the townscape is now restored; time alone will weather the new terracotta tiles that contrast with the old. The massive walls took a battering in the war but are once again intact throughout their circuit of two kilometres, affording remarkable views across the roofline of the old city and to the sea beyond. From these very walls, above the Pile Gate, one looks down along the length of the Stradun, the city's main thoroughfare and the route taken daily by streams of tourists. Beneath their feet the marble paving shines from years of wear and the imposing clock tower (dating from the fourteenth century but successively rebuilt) elegantly closes the vista at the end of the promenade, a textbook model of urban design. Café tables crowd onto the pavement, between a variety of shops and boutiques, some selling cheap souvenirs and others high-end designer clothes and accessories. Somehow it is like a cleverly designed stage set, complete in every detail yet also contrived. For all the attention to architectural restoration it is not the real thing, but that seems not to matter; it never does in a world of make-believe. This is a cameo of modern tourism, a scene repeated to differing degrees in every city visited on this journey around the Mediterranean.

Dubrovnik is a delight but is it real, and why do people come in droves to experience it? Japanese visitors and parties of central Europeans arriving in coaches; passengers from as many as nine cruise ships in a single day streaming along the Stradun; conference-goers freed from their programmes or small groups of Americans curious about their Croatian ancestry. For many it will be no more than an afternoon's experience in a crowded itinerary and quickly forgotten, for others something to value long after. Mass tourism is a strange phenomenon, easy in one sense to dismiss but also many-faceted. Dubrovnik asks all the right questions but, true to its Balkan connections, conceals most of the answers.

THESSALONIKI

Thessaloniki is a city that asks questions. Even its name is not straightforward. Originally, and since 1912, it has been known as Thessaloniki but for a long period it was, instead, Salonica (or Salonika).[1] It is physically a part of the Mediterranean but it belongs no less to the Balkans. It proudly claims historical ties with the ancient kingdom of Macedonia although that domain is now divided between the eponymous Slav republic to the north, Bulgaria to the east, Albania to the west and Greece itself. It is often cited for its long history of multi-culturalism and yet it has witnessed ethnic expulsions on a grand scale. It is the second city of Greece but for many centuries Greeks living there were in a minority. It is within Europe and yet at times it must have seemed more closely linked to Asia. Few cities illustrate more vividly the complex issues that arise from a location where so many different cultures cross paths.

On the Edge of Europe

Tourists do not come to Macedonia… but if they did they would find a show that no other part of Europe can produce.[2]

The very location of Thessaloniki should arouse suspicions that this is no ordinary place. In literal terms, the city is within Europe although it is on the very edge of that continent and only a short distance from the Black Sea and the opposite shoreline of Asia. Just as the winds blow westwards from the Asian landmass it is inevitable that the city has also felt the touch of this neighbouring continent. Visitors from the West were slow to discover Thessaloniki, deterred by the difficult journey overland across the Balkans or the long sea voyage to the head of the Aegean before the days of steam. When (in the second half of the nineteenth century) they did begin to arrive, their minds were already filled with exotic images of the Orient portrayed by European artists and writers.

The intrepid visitors were not be disappointed, for there on the skyline as their ship entered the harbour were the anticipated mosques and minarets, and the haunting sound of muezzins calling the faithful to prayer. As they disembarked they would immediately have been confronted with a hitherto unmet medley of cultures and colourful costumes, and the babble of a profusion of languages. In the narrow streets, porters pushed barrows, heavily laden with sacks of spices; brightly coloured fabrics imported from the East could be seen through open doorways; while groups of men sat in the lanes sipping coffee, smoking and playing backgammon. Those who might earlier have visited Constantinople would have found much in common with that better-known city. Somehow, the fact that they could step onto this oriental stage without leaving their home continent made it even more alluring: 'its anomalous character in a European setting ever more seductive'.[3]

If the city is shared in this way between two continents so, too, one can see within it elements of both the Mediterranean and Balkans. Thessaloniki, by reason of where it is, can lay claim to the sea as much as the land; in one direction, it faces the northern waters of the Aegean, itself an extension of the eastern Mediterranean. Its early settlement owed much to an expansive bay offering good anchorage for shipping, and trade routes were soon to link it to a host of other cities across the Mediterranean and beyond. Like many of its Mediterranean counterparts, Thessaloniki is fringed by mountains and, to add to the drama of its location, south-westwards across the bay one catches glimpses of the snowy heights of Mount Olympus, the 'home of the gods'. It also experiences the familiar rhythms of a Mediterranean climate, although with its own variations. Because of its adjacency to the Eurasian interior, temperatures are often colder in winter than in other parts of the Mediterranean, with freezing winds sweeping down from the north and east. In summer, the extreme heat of the region is moderated by sea breezes that waft across the bay.

View over the city walls to the northernmost waters of the Aegean.

It is, unmistakeably, a Mediterranean city but, at the same time, it bears hallmarks of the Balkans. All ports rely on a hinterland and Thessaloniki has traditionally looked to one that stretches deep into the heartland of eastern and central Europe. There are few good routes across the Balkans but the valley of the Axios (also known as the Vardar) is one—winding its way southwards from the neighbouring Macedonian republic, then across the coastal plain to the sea just west of Thessaloniki. To the east, a second river, the Strimon, rises in Bulgaria, and follows a parallel course to the sea. In both cases the valleys are narrow, and in places tortuous, but, compared with the surrounding mountains, successive generations of traders and soldiers have been grateful for their relative ease of access. The coastal plain itself, for long marshy and untended, was gradually reclaimed to provide a rich source of farmland from which the city has long benefited. It is the whole of this plain and mountains beyond that constitute the modern Greek province of Macedonia.

As a result of its geography, Thessaloniki has consistently been open to an extraordinary variety of influences. The city dates back to the fourth century BC, when it was founded as a coastal settlement within the kingdom of Macedonia. Its name is of Greek origin, after one of the daughters of Philip II (the father of Alexander the Great) to celebrate a famous victory over neighbouring Thessaly. Although fiercely independent, Macedonia was within the realm of Hellenic culture and Greek has been spoken in the city (though not always by the majority of the population) from the time of its formation.

These historic links with the rest of Greece have repeatedly been invoked to counter the claims of neighbouring Balkan states intent on appropriating portions of the original territory of Macedonia.

Excavated remains of the Roman period of occupation in the centre of the city.

Following the Greek phase, it was then the turn of the Romans to introduce their own culture. After fierce battles the Macedonians were finally overcome in 148 BC, and the Romans were then free to march eastwards, towards Byzantium and Asia beyond. The difficult itinerary taken by the Roman foot soldiers was subsequently consolidated as one of the great trans-continental routes of the day, the *Via Egnatia*, linking Rome to Anatolia. Thessaloniki lay directly on this path and, with its natural harbour and strategic location, the city was clearly too valuable a prize to pass by. For several centuries it thrived under Roman rule (the Latin version of its name being Thessalonica) and in the later years of the Empire successive emperors based themselves in the city. Although Thessaloniki was valued primarily as a base to support military campaigns, the conquerors made their presence known in other ways too. True to form, the Romans brought with them their renowned skills in town planning and architecture, passing on to later generations a grid system of street blocks and some typically grand public buildings and monuments (some of which have quite recently been excavated).[4] The importance of Thessaloniki could only have been enhanced as the balance of Roman power shifted eastwards, culminating in 330 AD in the designation of Constantinople as the new imperial capital. For a relatively short period, Thessaloniki was no longer in a marginal location, on the edge of the civilized world, but close to the centre of the most powerful empire of its day. Unfortunately, as the Roman Empire waned so did the importance of Thessaloniki, and for the best part of the subsequent millennium it faced barbarian attacks and an uncertain future largely on its own. Because of where it was—attractive to others yet, at the same time, vulnerable—there was a price to pay, but there was a positive side, too, in a unique mixing of different cultures.

The Meeting of Cultures

Five centuries of close proximity had brought about no unifying belief, no hyphen, no understanding.[5]

Even for the Mediterranean, where the whole region has always been a magnet for diverse cultures, Thessaloniki was an exceptional place. There are few other cities in this part of the world—Alexandria is an obvious exception, Smyrna another—where large groups of Christians, Muslims and Jews managed successfully to live side by side, over such a long period.

The arrival of so many groups was a long-term and generally gradual process. They came first from nearby mountain villages and hidden valleys, from along the lengthy coastline and from Aegean islands. As well as indigenous Greek Macedonians, the city was soon to host Slavs and Vlachs from as far away as Dalmatia, gypsies and Albanians, Serbs and Bulgars. Later, superimposed on this ethnic *mélange*, lines were drawn more sharply around adherents of the three dominant monotheisms of the Mediterranean: Christians, Muslims and Jews. For a crucial stretch of Thessaloniki's history, religion was at the heart of its daily life and the basis of its three major communities. It would be easy to paint a picture of uninterrupted harmony but the reality was more one of co-existence, of living alongside but in parallel worlds. Leon Sciaky was a Jew who grew up in the city shortly before the First World War and he recalls just that:

> *The Jew, the Greek, the Bulgarian, the Turk, each lived within himself. They were so many strangers, with as many distinct attitudes and ideas, with as many ways of life. They lived together within the same political boundaries, in the same city, in the same neighbourhood, yet separated from one another by divisions more unscalable than walls of stone and mortar; they were kept apart by barriers of language, customs and political dreams more insuperable than material obstacles.[6]*

Gold Crosses and Icons

It was lit by thousands of candles and lamps hung in front of icons, illuminating the coloured marbles and gold and blue mosaics.[7]

Thessaloniki was one of the early homes of Christianity. The message of Christ was brought to the city by the apostle, Paul, who journeyed far and wide across the eastern Mediterranean, speaking to all who would listen to him. The New Testament records that it was on his second missionary journey, from 49 to 52 AD, that he visited Thessalonica *[sic]* and entered the synagogue to make his case to the menfolk of the small Jewish community.[8] On three consecutive Sabbaths he argued with them from the scriptures, converting some to his cause but alienating others who refused to accept that the Messiah had already lived. As well as the small number of Jews who turned to Christianity he persuaded 'a great many of the devout Greeks and not a few of the leading women'.[9]

A foothold in the city was gained in this way, but for the next three centuries the Roman rulers were to keep a close watch on what was seen as a potentially disruptive creed. From time to time, this uneasiness erupted into systematic persecutions, as when the Eastern Roman Emperor, Galerius, made the city his base for military campaigns against barbarian aggressors. It was Galerius who put to death one of his own officers, Demetrios, for converting to Christianity. The Emperor's action provoked an outpouring of grief amongst the Christian community and led to something of a cult following for the martyr. By the sixth century, Demetrios had become the patron saint of the city, and was to be invoked at different points in its history in the hope of saving its population from epidemics, fires and enemy attacks.

At least, shortly after the rule of Galerius, the Christians were to be spared the enmity of the Romans, when his successor, Constantine (who was also based for some time in Thessaloniki), declared that the whole empire would convert to Christianity. Although his designation of Constantinople (formerly Byzantium) as the new capital of the Roman Empire was motivated by political and military factors, it was to have a profound effect on the future development of Christianity. Rome and Constantinople became rival centres of the faith and, over time, a sharp distinction opened up between the Catholicism of the West and the Orthodoxy of the East. In the latter, which attracted the Christians of Thessaloniki and held sway throughout much of the Balkans, there were differences of dogma as well as the manner of prayer. Rituals were generally more complex, paintings of Christ and the saints—the holy icons—took on a crucial role, and Byzantine architecture followed a new path. Characteristically, the great churches and cathedrals were distinguished by complex arrangements of domes, arches and columns; and by the use of a striking mixture of materials, with bricks in contrasting colours combined with plaster and stone. Domes were supported by massive pillars, the lofty space within representing heaven itself. Natural light was filtered by the use of thin sheets of alabaster across the windows, and in the poorly lit interiors intricate mosaics and glittering gold ornaments seemed to evoke an exotic notion of Asia rather than Europe.[10]

Churches, once no more numerous than synagogues and mosques, are now almost the only places of worship.

In a very different way, Christianity also came to the northern Aegean through the austere practices of monasticism. The very success of the Church in attracting a large following and accumulating its own wealth was for some a source of grief; they feared that the essential message of Christ had been lost and urged, instead, a return to the original principles of Christian community—where possessions were few and these were shared. Monasteries were established intentionally in remote and harsh conditions, like the deserts and mountains of Sinai and Syria. During the eleventh century, the advance of the Turks into Asia Minor and the Levant led to a dispersal of monastic activity from some of these early foundations. One new destination for exiled monks was the relatively isolated peninsula of Chalkadiki, to the south-east of Thessaloniki. Surrounded on three sides by the sea, various monasteries were established in the remotest part of the peninsula, on Mount Athos, which became 'a kind of self-governing monastic republic'.[11]

By one means or another, from early times Christianity became well established in the region and for some fourteen centuries its dominance went largely unchallenged. Through its religion, coupled with the Greek language and culture, Thessaloniki maintained its own identity throughout the rule of Rome, and was able later to look for inspiration to Constantinople. It sat well within the context of the Byzantine Empire. During the lengthy period of Christian hegemony, numerous churches and shrines were built within the city's walls, including the basilica in memory of St. Demetrios. It must have seemed that Christianity was, indeed, the natural order of things and that nothing would ever change. In fact, three events were to transform everything.

The first of these occurred at the start of the thirteenth century. Under the banner of the Fourth Crusade, an opportunity was seen by the Christians from the West to gain financial and political advantage through the capture of Constantinople, as a step towards securing the ultimate prize of Jerusalem. Diplomatic overtures soon gave way to outright conflict, when one Christian fighting force encountered another, and the prized city of Constantinople was ransacked in the process. It was an unforgiving campaign, 'an orgy of vandalism and brutality' only matched in history by barbarian invasions into Europe; never before 'had so much beauty, so much superb craftsmanship, been so wantonly destroyed in so short a space of time'.[12] It left a deep and irreparable rift between the Christians of West and East, Catholicism and Orthodoxy. Ironically, it also fatally wounded the Byzantine Empire and left it more vulnerable to subsequent attacks and its eventual capture by the Turkish Muslims, known as the Ottomans.

The second event to change the religious landscape (resulting from the first) was the relentless advance of the Ottomans, leading not only to the capture of Thessaloniki but also of Constantinople itself. The whole of Anatolia and the south-eastern Balkans fell under Ottoman control and Islam replaced Christianity as the dominant religion. At the same time, the Ottomans proved to be remarkably tolerant of other religions and, although non-Muslims were denied certain privileges, they were allowed to continue to worship in their own holy places. Thus, in Thessaloniki as in other cities in the Ottoman Empire, churches co-existed alongside mosques and many of its citizens continued to speak their native Greek. Gradually, Turkish peoples moved into the newly conquered city to take positions of authority and to share in its growing prosperity, bringing with them their own language and customs as well as their different faith.

Finally, to add to the impact of the Ottomans, the old order was to be further changed towards the end of the fifteenth century with the arrival of a large numbers of Jews, forced to leave their homes in Spain and Portugal (and, later, other countries in the West). The Jewish community soon became as numerous as those of the Greeks and Ottomans combined and the whole balance of population was radically changed. Greek Christians, not so long before the most numerous group, were shortly to be in a minority and would remain so until the twentieth century. Step by step, Thessaloniki had become a city not of one but of three cultures, with one foot still in Europe and one now in Asia; imams, rabbis and priests walked through the narrow streets, barely acknowledging each other but, equally, tacitly accepting their respective presence.

The Arrival of Islam

There was something quite specific in the meeting of Islam and Christendom that seemed to engender violence.[13]

Islam came to Thessaloniki by way of the steppes of central Asia. The religion that was born in a desert arrived with the Turkish tribes who made their way west, often fighting amongst themselves as well as confronting the Christian enemy in their path. They were soldiers of Islam, Sunni Muslims, although their adherence to the faith was not as uncompromising as with some other factions. With their fast-moving horsemen, effective fighting skills and a fervent belief in their cause, they proved more than a match for the defending Byzantine Christians. In terms of the territory that was won and the enormous changes that followed, the Turkish advance was remarkably rapid; whole lands were conquered and, one by one, turned to Muslim rule. Ottoman dominance was strengthened through the elimination of weaker tribal leaders and the emergence of a unified dynasty. By 1354 the Ottomans had crossed into Europe, their first conquest being the Anatolian peninsula of Gallipoli, and from there they advanced on the rest of the Balkans.

Thessaloniki came into sight of the Ottomans in 1383, and after a blockade lasting four years the city gave way to a peaceful occupation. A Turkish garrison was installed and, at first, life seemed to go on much as before. Christian practices were allowed to continue and only one church was converted to a mosque. It was only after an ill-considered rebellion by the Greeks, who brought in the Venetians as allies, that the Ottomans struck back, this time with a vengeance. A lengthy siege was followed by a brief episode of plunder before, in 1430, order was finally restored and the city began a period of Ottoman rule that lasted for nearly five centuries. At the start of its permanent occupation, Thessaloniki was in a poor condition, the morale of its people sapped by years under siege, most of its buildings and stretches of fortifications destroyed by the enemy, and then the pain of seeing many of its churches taken over for Muslim worship. Apart from those who were captured and sold as slaves, some of its people escaped and left the city for ever while others decided that the best course of action was to stay and convert to the religion of their occupiers. At the start of this new era, there were probably no more than 10,000 people living in Thessaloniki, barely a quarter the number before the siege. Recognizing the potential of its new conquest, the Ottomans quickly went to work to restore not only the buildings but also its economic and political life. For Sultan Murad II, the conqueror of Thessaloniki, 'no other city in his domain matched its imposing fortifications or its commercial possibilities. It was the key to the Balkans, and the Balkans were fast on their way to becoming the economic powerhouse of the empire.'[14] Part of the Sultan's plan was to bring in Muslims from other territories and within a couple of years their number matched that of the resident Christians. No less important was the accompanying process of establishing Islamic institutions of law and government, as well as religion. In the new Muslim communities, care was taken from the outset to ensure there was in each an imam and a proper place of worship; such communities were, in fact, better provided than the Christian ones, where for a time there was a serious shortage of priests willing to return to the city.

There were more mosques than churches, although Muslims themselves were never to be in a majority; indeed, with the arrival of exiled Jews in the years following 1492 the proportion was probably little more than a quarter of the total population. Being themselves in a minority, not only in Thessaloniki but elsewhere in the Balkans, the Muslims settled for a system of central control balanced by devolution of responsibility for the city's day-to-day business to local communities. To a large extent, not only the Muslims but also the 'non-believers', Christians and Jews, were each empowered to manage their own affairs, in relative isolation one from the other. They appointed their own councils, usually comprising representatives of notable families and religious officials. As time went on, they were able, too, to establish their own schools and hospitals, and to give support to the poor amongst them.

In most respects, the conquered communities accepted the rule of the Ottomans, although there were some instances of discontent and times of turbulence. The practice of forcibly taking selected sons from non-Muslim families, to convert to Islam and to fight for the Sultan, was bitterly resented. No less a cause of resentment in certain quarters was the appropriation of the main places of Christian worship for conversion to mosques; these included, in 1491, the basilica of the city's martyr, St. Demetrios, and in the following century two other buildings of note, Ayia Sofia and the Rotonda.[15]

From time to time, too, the sense of security afforded by stable government was shaken by mutinies of the Janissaries, the elite guard intended to protect the ruling Sultan and his family but which on occasions actually forced their deposal. Eleven such revolts were recorded in Thessaloniki in the eighteenth century alone, leading not only to changes in the higher echelons of government but also to episodes of violence in the city at large. Local disputes between communities also created ripples on an otherwise tranquil surface. Overall, though, Thessaloniki prospered under the Ottomans for most of the time that the city was part of their empire. For more than half a millennium it enjoyed its role as a valued imperial port and a commercial powerhouse of the eastern Mediterranean.

'Mother of Israel'

There is a city in the Turkish kingdom, which formerly belonged to the Greeks and in our day is a true mother-city in Judaism.[16]

The Jews who found their way to Thessaloniki were largely those expelled from the western Mediterranean, first from Spain and then Portugal.[17] They were known as the Sephardim, literally the Jews of Spain, and gave their name to the whole of the Mediterranean diaspora. Undeterred by their adherence to a different set of beliefs, the Ottomans saw commercial advantage in attracting these displaced communities.

Wherever the Jews had previously settled they had been industrious and made a success of their various businesses, so much so that the Ottoman rulers believed that the decision to expel them from Iberia was a grave misjudgement on the part of the two Iberian nations. The result was that boatloads carrying exiled Jews arrived to form a new community that was very shortly to become the largest of the three religious groups in Thessaloniki. 'With more than 30 synagogues, Talmudic schools and libraries Salonika became known as *the Mother of Israel*.'[18]

Evidence is slender but it is unlikely that, before this new influx, there was more than a handful of the original Jewish 'Romaniotes' still living in the city (those, largely Greek-speaking Jews, who had long ago left their biblical homeland to settle around the coasts of Anatolia and the Levant). Wars had taken their toll and the population level and prosperity of Thessaloniki as a whole had declined markedly; a major incentive in bringing in ready-made communities (especially as most were already used to living in cities) was to breathe new life into the once thriving settlement.

The immediate impact was significant: by 1520 the total population of Thessaloniki had doubled to 30,000, half of which was Jewish.[19] In both relative and absolute terms, the Greek Christian community became progressively less important, with the city largely administered by the Ottomans and run on a day-to-day basis by Jewish businesses and labour. An impression is often portrayed of Jews engaging solely in commerce but the reality in Thessaloniki (as elsewhere) was that they were present no less in a range of more mundane activities: the likes of 'porters and casual labourers, tailors, wandering street vendors, beggars, fishermen and tobacco-workers'.[20]

Against a background of persecution throughout most of Christian Europe, the Jews of Ottoman-ruled Thessaloniki enjoyed an unusual degree of security. The arrangement worked well because it was, effectively, contractual. Islamic Law was clear and precise on the issue: as a People of the Book (like Christians), Jews were guaranteed the same rights as other non-Muslim groups. Most important to them was that they could live and worship as they wished—so long as they refrained from challenging Ottoman authority. The situation was mutually beneficial for, in turn, the Ottomans benefited from their industriousness and ability to turn Thessaloniki into one of the great ports and workshops of the eastern Mediterranean. Only when Ottoman power waned in the early twentieth century—first in the face of an internal modernization movement (resulting from the Young Turks Revolution) and then as a result of a new wave of Greek nationalism—did things change for the worse. It was, in fact, the resurgence of Hellenism that proved the more decisive factor for the city, which was forcibly taken by the Greeks in 1912 and formally ceded by Turkey in the following year.

With the Greek flag flying high in the recovered territories of northern Greece, the Jewish community felt uneasy for the first time in centuries. Overnight, the certainties provided by Ottoman rule, and the religious tolerance that the Jews had enjoyed, disappeared. In fear of what might happen, some of the community decided then that it was time to leave.

One of the few remaining villas, typically owned in the past by Thessaloniki's wealthy families.

Leon Sciaky was a young boy in this time of change and was one of those who, just before the First World War, left the city of his childhood with his family for a new life in the United States. Later he wrote about his experience of growing up in the Jewish community of Thessaloniki, in another world.[21] His early recollections tell of a city that was still partly mediaeval, and which belonged as much to the Levant as the Balkans. He tells of watching the muezzins high above his garden; of street vendors with trays of pistachios and Persian sweets; of buttermilk sold from goatskins strapped to the sides of donkeys; and of copper being beaten into shape by craftsmen sitting cross-legged in the narrow lanes.

As a young boy he looked out of his window to see children in different costumes playing around the fountain in his square; and he recalls the sound of his father reciting Bulgarian verse as he struggled to learn the language that would help him in his trade as a grain merchant. His memories also give a good account of the ethnic geography of the city: of how the Jews from the end of the fifteenth century had occupied one quarter, the Greeks another, and the ruling Turks on chosen ground, on the hill of Chaoush Monastir, overlooking the sea.

It must have seemed to a young boy a world that was timeless, but year by year, under the strain of nationalist pressures, it gradually fell apart. In the following years, like the Sciaky family, many other Jews also turned their back on the city. There was a growing fear that Greek nationalism would have little time for such an influential minority, a fear that was given credence in the 1930s when a home-grown fascist movement was responsible for the burning of one of Thessaloniki's Jewish neighbourhoods.

As well as North and South America, France was a popular destination for the exodus and later some also made the relatively short journey to Palestine. Throughout the interwar period there was a steady outflow of population although, by the time of the Second World War, the Jewish community still numbered some 50,000. This was all to change in dramatic fashion when the Nazis occupied the city in 1941, and in just a few short years all but a couple of thousand had been sent to untimely deaths in concentration camps in Poland. By the time the war was over, most of the few remaining Jews, who had somehow escaped discovery, saw a life in Israel as their main hope of salvation. From its background as a cosmopolitan city—exceptional in its mix even by Mediterranean standards—Thessaloniki emerged in the middle of the twentieth century with an almost exclusively Greek population. Almost in defiance of this inexorable trend, a small Jewish community (currently of no more than a thousand in number) has re-made itself in the city, managing a well-resourced museum to tell the story of their predecessors and keeping alive otherwise lost traditions.[22]

The City that Never Was

Change is, of course, the essence of urban life and no successful city remains a museum to its own past.[23]

Successive events in the first half of the twentieth century transformed a city that had for much of its history been known for its tolerance, a shared home for peoples of diverse cultures. With the ending of Ottoman rule, the name reverted from Salonica to Thessaloniki, invoking its Hellenic origins even though by then the original state of Macedonia was no longer wholly in Greece. Then the Turks in the city were expelled (from as early as 1912 but mainly after the First World War) and, as they boarded ships to take them eastwards with their meagre belongings, they passed long lines of disembarking Greeks coming from Turkish territories in Asia Minor to replace them. With the later expulsion of the Jews, Thessaloniki became a predominantly Greek city for the first time in centuries: the second city of Greece and the effective capital of its northern provinces.

Traditional housing in the former Turkish quarter that survived the great fire.

As if that were not enough, during the twentieth century the physical fabric of the city was torn apart too. Most dramatically, an event occurred that initially had nothing to do with politics but which was to change the face of Thessaloniki. Localized fires were not unusual in old cities like this, with their wooden buildings dry with age, but no-one could have anticipated anything as widespread or damaging as the conflagration which swept through most of its inner districts in the summer of 1917. In just a few days the uncontrollable flames had done their work, destroying three-quarters of the old city and leaving 70,000 of its citizens homeless.

The Jewish neighbourhoods were almost totally devastated but the fire was indiscriminate and Turks and Greeks suffered too; synagogues, mosques and churches—including some of the city's finest buildings—were all lost to the flames. An international team of planners (chaired at first by the British landscape architect,

Thomas Mawson) was quickly commissioned, and political leaders saw in the tragedy an opportunity to rebuild Thessaloniki as a modern Greek city, an exemplar of the new nation, shaking off in the process vestiges of its mixed past.[24] As a challenge for the new profession of town planning there had been nothing like it before, and it was fairly proclaimed as 'the first great work of twentieth century European city planning'.[25]

Under Mawson's leadership a provisional plan was prepared within three months of the fire but at that point he returned to England.[26] It was a French colleague, Ernst Hébrard, assisted by Greek architects, who turned Mawson's work into a more detailed blueprint, the outcome being known thereafter as the Hébrard Plan. In the circumstances at the time, with the nationalist Prime Minister Venizelos at the helm, the brief for the planners could not be anything other than political. As they set about their work, there was little hiding the fact that Byzantine relics should be restored, that traces of the Ottoman legacy should be erased, and that the Jewish hold on the commercial life of the city should be replaced by Greek control. The result was a triumph for modernity, an opportunity eagerly taken to clear the city of its densely-packed, ethnic neighbourhoods and to create, instead, rectangular street blocks and wide thoroughfares, altogether more hygienic and manageable.

A new administrative and business district was designated, and an area of land behind the port was reserved for industry; on the gentle slopes beyond the eastern city walls, cemeteries were replaced with parkland and the site of a new university campus. Unlike the precedent of fire-torn cities elsewhere (like London in the seventeenth century), when plot boundaries and street alignments were kept largely as they were, the new plan treated the area as if it were a clean slate. Inevitably, the radical changes proposed were not universally welcomed, with the Jewish community particularly aggrieved by its relocation to the suburbs. In fact, the effects of the plan had as much to do with class as ethnicity, and those who could afford the higher rents in the central area continued to live there.[27] Whatever the reasons, the outcome was the same: Thessaloniki emerged from the drawing board as a newly aligned, modern city, with the Greeks well placed to assume the dominant role.

The trouble with blueprints is that events will always conspire to distort them and, sure enough, in 1917 no-one could have anticipated the scale and bitterness of an unprecedented episode of forced migrations. Within just a few years, by the end of 1924, the city would have to cope with the sudden departure of its entire population of 30,000 Turks while accommodating an influx of 100,000 Greeks ousted from Asia Minor. It was, inevitably, a chaotic process and the larger number of incomers to Thessaloniki, unable to wait for official directives, took direct action by occupying vacated properties and building ramshackle shelters in forsaken gardens. Symbolically, the departure of the Turks was followed by a systematic programme of demolition of the city's many minarets, seen as an unwanted reminder of centuries of Ottoman rule.

After the Second World War, the city experienced a second wave of rebuilding. As well as a programme of modernization, which would most likely have occurred in any case, there was the matter of how to fill the gaps left by the sudden departure of 50,000 Jews. No sooner had the Jews been taken from their homes than others moved in to help themselves to what was left; the occupying Germans made the first move but were quickly followed by the poor of the city, who stripped the former Jewish homes of useable materials, ransacked synagogues and dug up graves for buried treasures, and (with a constant influx of wartime refugees desperate for shelter) moved into the remaining structures.

Thessaloniki is now a thriving Greek city; the past is a foreign country.

Amongst the many clearance operations, the German occupiers destroyed the extensive Jewish cemetery, removing at a stroke the symbolic link with more than five centuries of continuous settlement. It was a dark period in the history of the city. Mark Mazower, in his admirable biography of Thessaloniki, believes that the motives of some Greek officials and interest groups at the time were less than honourable:

'They had not sought the deportation of the Jews, but they had not obstructed it either since it enabled them to complete the process which had started twenty years earlier—the Hellenization of the city.'[28] In the hands of postwar planners this process of 'Hellenization' proved to be just another excuse for a further phase of drab modernism.

Across Europe, cities were being rebuilt along similar lines, with the features that had once made them different lost in the process. In Thessaloniki, 'in an unregulated orgy of construction',[29] villas were replaced by apartment blocks, roads were widened, parks fell victim to new warehouses and factories, an old theatre was demolished, the site of the Jewish cemetery was used for the city's university, and the few remaining traces of years of occupation by the Turkish and Jewish populations all but disappeared. It was a time of rapid expansion—by 1971 the population exceeded half a million—and the surrounding slopes were quickly covered with rows of new apartment blocks.

In the wake of this frenzy of development, a visitor to Thessaloniki even as late as the 1980s would have found little of appeal. Its post-1945 architecture and wide streets were more akin to the grey cities of Sofia and Bucharest in its northern hinterland than those of the Mediterranean. The vitality that had once come from the rich mix of cultures had gone. Where were the Turks, one would ask, and where were the Jews? Answers were there none. Visitors would often make their way to a small section of the upper town known as Ano Polo, originally peopled by the Turks, which somehow escaped the destruction wreaked elsewhere by modernist planners. Here, in the narrow lanes and small cafes and bars one could find a lingering charm and reminder of a bygone age. Sitting under the shade of a tree in one of the little squares one might have reflected on how the city once thrived on its diversity. Those days were already long past, and largely forgotten in official histories and local folklore: hence Mazower's apt description of Thessaloniki as a 'city of ghosts'.

Since then there have been striking changes to the city. Contrary to the popular adage, time is not a healer of such deep wounds but for new generations the perspective is, inevitably, different. Visiting Thessaloniki now is a very different experience from that of even two decades ago. For much of this recent period It enjoyed boom years, helped by the collapse of communism in the neighbouring states to the north and the re-opening of borders; in a single throw of the geopolitical dice, the old hinterland that was always so important to the maritime city has been restored. Not everyone welcomes the new geography and some of the older residents blame the arrival of newcomers as a threat to Greek ways, just as former citizens would have resented the arrival of the alien Jews at the end of the fifteenth century. Only time will show whether stable communities will emerge amongst these latest groups, pursuing their own paths but learning to live side by side in peaceful tolerance, like past generations of immigrants.

Under the impetus of rapid growth, many of the formerly drab buildings of Thessaloniki were to enjoy a facelift, especially those along the fashionable corniche. The bars and coffee houses were soon full, and at weekends families walk along the restored promenade, meeting friends and enjoying the splendid views across the bay. Yachts set out from the vogueish sailing club, tacking against the unpredictable winds created by the meeting of sea and land at the head of the Aegean. Even towards the end of 2010, at the time when the Greek economy effectively collapsed under the weight of unsustainable debt, the scene along the waterfront was much the same. The full impact of economic decline had not yet struck and the citizens of Thessaloniki were not so easily to give up their newfound gains. Since then, the financial problems of the nation have taken hold, affecting the lives of ordinary people and sapping much of the energy that was evident in the first decade of the new century.

In any case, with its long history, there will always be deeper issues to contemplate. Across the bay, Mount Olympus looms dramatically above the skyline, with its classical associations a reminder of the immutability of Greek culture. Thessaloniki, even in crisis, seems to have retained an inner confidence as the undisputed capital of northern Greece. Here, surely, is one of the great cities of the Mediterranean. And so it is, until one catches murmurs from a now distant past—the sad voices of lost communities. Even these, however, will be muted as time moves on, until they will be heard no more amidst the din of modern life.

CHAPTER 4

GLIMPSE OF THE ORIENT

Along the stretch of coastline that was once known as the Levant—flanked by Europe to the north and Africa to the south—the nearest reaches of Asia meet the Mediterranean. As one would expect from this confluence of continents, the region is one of intense experience, where history, geography and culture all overlap. The presence of the three monotheisms—Judaism, Christianity and Islam—has served only to add to the combustibility of the mix.

It is a stretch of the Mediterranean that has always been of interest to foreign powers, attracted from the East as well as the West. Persians, Greeks and Romans were all to seek control, not least of all for trade, but its longest period of occupation was by the Turks, when it was brought within the orbit of the Ottoman Empire. Modern colonial powers, led by France and Britain, took over when the Turks gave way, while the formation of Israel in 1948 created a new imbalance. To this day, it remains one of the world's most volatile regions, the most recent illustration being the internal conflicts that in 2012 divided Syria.

The first of the three cities to be visited is Izmir. For most of its history known as Smyrna, Izmir is now a modern metropolis, the third city of Turkey; it has, in fact, embraced modernity with enthusiasm. Yet this is not the reason for its selection. Instead, the fascination is with its ability for so many years to accommodate different cultures in relative harmony, only for this to break down amidst a sudden outpouring of hatred and violence early in the twentieth century. Why did this happen and how has the city evolved since then, as a largely mono-cultural community?

Beirut is another city with a past measured in millennia but which has been selected more for what it can say about recent events. Here it is not simply the familiar rivalry between Muslims and Christians which led to modern conflicts, but also various factions within each. It is hard to think of another city which has so thoroughly torn itself apart, with the wilful encouragement of interfering neighbours. Equally, is there anywhere else that has so readily sought to rebuild itself, albeit on shaky foundations? Whether it will succeed in its mission to re-make itself again remains to be seen.

Finally, no coverage of the Mediterranean can be complete without a city to represent the modern state of Israel. Such is that nation's volatility that some of its neighbouring states still refuse to recognize it. Reflecting this enduring source of tension, Haifa was once predominantly an Arab settlement but when the Zionists chose it as their main port and industrial city there was a rapid reversal, with Jewish settlers soon in the majority. Today, the city has made a life of its own but the security of its future depends also on the wider fortunes of the Middle East. Geopolitics is part and parcel of its very existence.

IZMIR

Izmir, the third largest city of modern Turkey, is located in the eastern Mediterranean, midway along the west-facing stretch of the Anatolian coastline. Anatolia itself is a vast plateau that has also been known since classical times as Asia Minor, extending westwards to within bridging distance of the neighbouring European continent. Africa, too, has a part to play in shaping this edge of the region, for this is where the northward-moving African tectonic plate is forced against the Anatolian platelet, resulting in recurring earthquakes.

For most of its long history the modern city of Izmir has been known as Smyrna. Its origins date back to the third millennium BC and from about 1000 BC it came under Greek occupation. Like other cities of the Mediterranean, Smyrna has seen a succession of rulers and events of historic moment that have never been forgotten; repeated episodes of destruction and rebuilding have each left indelible marks on the collective memory.

The city has at different times been razed to the ground, destroyed by fire, shaken by earthquakes, and ransacked for political gain. It has also enjoyed an international reputation as a major port, at a pivotal point between East and West. Not unlike Thessaloniki, Smyrna has been home to a rare mix of peoples, although less than a century ago this cosmopolitanism was lost seemingly overnight and for all time in dramatic fashion. Its name was changed to Izmir, in keeping with its modern Turkish identity, but it is as Smyrna that it will forever be linked with its long history and its most painful episode.

'The Most Beautiful of All'

Their city is now the most beautiful of all; a part of it is on a mountain and walled, but the greater part of it is in the plain near the harbour…[1]

Strabo, the Greek geographer of the Roman Empire, was clearly impressed by what he encountered on his extensive travels, between 20 BC and 20 AD. He liked the physical order of Smyrna and its respect for culture:

> *The division into streets is exceptionally good, in straight lines as far as possible; and the streets are paved with stone; and there are large quadrangular porticoes, with both lower and upper stories. There is also a library; and the Homereium, a quadrangular portico containing a shrine and wooden statue of Homer; for the Smyrnaeans also lay especial claim to the poet; and indeed a bronze coin of theirs is called Homereium. The river Meles flows near the walls; and, in addition to the rest of the city's equipment, there is also a harbour that can be closed.*[2]

By the time that Strabo made his observations, the city could already tell of a long pre-history. Even if one takes up the story with the start of Greek colonization, a full millennium had elapsed. The contemporary historian Herodotus explained that the Greek chapter began with the Aeolians, an ancient tribe whose settlements on the Anatolian mainland grew at one stage to twelve, one being Smyrna.[3] Legend has it that during a festival when the Aeolians left the city for celebrations beyond the walls, the gates were closed behind them and power was transferred to another acquisitive tribe, the Ionians. Under the Ionians the city grew steadily, and something of the legacy of this phase of Hellenic occupation can still be seen in fragmentary remains of the city's *agora*. In about 600 BC the expansionist Lydians captured it, along with most of the remaining Greek possessions in Asia Minor, and duly demolished the buildings and walls of their predecessors. Smyrna then lay largely in ruins for three centuries, before the arrival of Alexander the Great, in the course of his eastwards military campaign. His deeds are surrounded by myth and it was said that he was urged by the goddess, Nemesis, to rebuild the city, although on the slopes of nearby Mount Pagus rather than the original site. That provided a fresh start although it was not until its conquest by the Romans in the second century BC that Smyrna really started to come into its own.

Roman rule was embraced rather than resisted, the citizens of Smyrna perhaps seeing the value of military protection and the prospect of a period of stability. It did, in fact, fare well in this era; the Romans established a province named Asia to mark their territory in the eastern Mediterranean, and they looked to Smyrna as its main port. Even the superior powers of Rome, however, could not prevent the destructive impact of natural forces and in 178 AD the city was destroyed by an earthquake. Under the direction of Emperor Marcus Aurelius, little time was lost in rebuilding it and there followed what was something of a golden era, with the city acquiring prestigious cultural and political institutions and becoming known as 'The First City of the East'. The Romans were in due course replaced by Byzantine rulers; good news for the surviving Christians (who had been the object of sustained persecution) and also for a new class of merchants who were to benefit from the opening of trade routes to the interior as well as seawards. During the eleventh and twelfth centuries, indigenous merchants were joined by seasoned traders from Venice, the Amalfi coast, Genoa and Pisa.[4] It must have seemed then that Smyrna was set fair for a future of political stability and commercial prosperity, but nothing is ever assured in the Mediterranean. In a repetitive cycle of destruction followed by rebuilding, the city suffered from successive incursions from the east, first, at the hands of the Seljuk Turks in 1084, then the Persians in 1130 and, yet again, when the Mongol warrior, Tamerlane, wreaked havoc in 1402. By this last date, the Byzantine era was all but over and Smyrna next found itself embedded in the Ottoman Empire, a situation that continued until the twentieth century.

Smyrna was visited at times by fire, plague and earthquakes but nothing could hold back its persistent growth as it became the busiest and most prosperous port in the region.

Like Thessaloniki, its good fortune attracted a mix of peoples. At first, with the arrival of the Muslim Turks, many of the resident Greeks, fearing for their Christian identity if not their lives, fled the mainland for the sanctuary of islands to the west. Gradually, however, they returned (especially in the seventeenth and eighteenth centuries), eventually to form the largest ethnic group in the city. By the early twentieth century there were more than twice as many Greeks living in Smyrna as in Athens.[5] In spite of their dominance they lived peaceably alongside sizeable communities of Turks, Jews and Armenians; it was a mixed religious as well as ethnic population, with Christians and Jews outnumbering Muslims in the order of two to one—an infidel city in the heart of a Muslim empire.

Nineteenth-century view of a Smyrna suburb (Caratach), with the busy port beyond.

The busy seaport would also have lured sailors, porters, street vendors and casual labourers from a myriad of places in nearby Africa and southern Europe, and from villages along the Levantine coast and interior of Asia Minor. From an early date, Smyrna attracted the attention of foreign powers with strong navies and an interest in international trade, notably France, Holland, England and the Italian city states. Recognizing the value of this commercial experience and also the prospect of political alliances, the Ottomans offered valuable incentives to encourage foreigners to establish permanent businesses. As a result, European communities were formed and some of the families, known as the Levantines, became enormously wealthy dynasties. A later addition to the mix of peoples in the city took the form of American evangelists and business interests, who lived together in a colony that they chose to name 'Paradise'. In spite of its name, the reality is that it was by no means always harmonious, with outbreaks of ethnic hostility in the area even before the twentieth century.[6]

Modern Konak Square retains landmarks from the Ottoman era.

Apart from periodic disturbances that were generally soon resolved, Smyrna flourished during the latter period of Ottoman occupation, especially around the turn of the nineteenth century. By 1900, more than half of all Ottoman exports were directed through this port, drawn not only from the city's own factories but also from the vast Anatolian hinterland. Agricultural products like figs and apricots, raisins and cotton, tobacco and opium were the mainstay of its traditional trade, along with carpets and valuable minerals.

British contractors built a railway to connect the port with the interior but even until the middle of the twentieth century, camels would wend their way across the mountains to bring their various loads onto the quayside. It was a hectic scene, with ships from different nations crowded into the harbour and lines of porters loading sacks and crates into their holds. It had all the appearance of a boom town and with the obvious prosperity came investment in all aspects of Smyrna's life. By the time of the First World War, it could boast an enviable reputation as an international city of commerce and culture, with a stylish mode of life that would last seemingly for ever.

An informed portrayal of its heyday, and subsequent transformation, has been compiled in a recent book by Giles Milton.[7] He shows that although it was in the early twentieth century still within the Ottoman Empire, the city was to a large extent autonomous; the nominal rulers in Constantinople knew better than to upset the goose that laid the golden egg. Alongside a benevolent and sympathetic Ottoman Governor, the real power in Smyrna lay with the leading Levantine families;

it was they who controlled the vital industries and trade, and their own lives were interwoven in a closed world of business partnerships and arranged marriages.

They lived in grand villas, mainly clustered in fashionable districts like Bournabat, furnishing their properties with the finest imports from Western capitals. In their spacious gardens they held extravagant parties and, when the heat became overbearing, they climbed aboard shiny motor cars or set sail in private yachts to take temporary residence in well-appointed retreats along the coast. In winter, the women wore expensive furs and the scent of Parisian perfumes filled the air. To the ordinary people of the city these exotic beings were akin to royalty. Little wonder that the Levantines pledged loyalty to the Ottomans for it was not only the neighbouring Americans who were living in Paradise. Smyrna, it was widely agreed, was a dream location: 'it had the climate of southern California, the architecture of the Côte d'Azur and the allure of nowhere else on earth.'[8]

The Levantines mixed in their own exclusive circles but the ethnic composition of the city and varied lifestyles was evident in other ways too. Providing almost a stage setting for its cosmopolitan population, the favourite venue to meet and mingle was the massive stone quay along the length of the harbour and projecting into the sea, known as the Cordon. Built between 1867 and 1876, it has been described as 'the greatest urban project in the history of the Ottoman Empire'.[9]

While its prime purpose was to enhance the importance of the port in a period of expansion, it also served the social life of the city. Every evening, it was the scene of fashionable groups promenading along the broad thoroughfare, lined by numerous hotels, cafes and restaurants. At the tables facing the sea, little was missed and news of who was doing this or that was eagerly exchanged. From sunset to midnight it was like 'a fairy-tale country, with a magic atmosphere which made the most sombre and depressed souls end by laughing'.[10]

This jewel of Asia Minor, the most prosperous city in the Ottoman Empire, was one of those places, by no means unique in the Mediterranean, which belonged to another era. With its elite of established families and seemingly impregnable institutions an illusion of permanence had been created, a world that would surely never change. It had managed *par excellence* to marry the best of East and West and to knit together so many different cultures, creating the nearest one could find to a cosmopolitan utopia. Sadly, if that is how it was seen at the time, the situation that emerged was altogether different; like a reflection in the placid waters of its harbour, this image of perfection would suddenly be shattered. The storm which changed everything came in the wake of the First World War, with old alliances ended and empires toppled, including that of the ruling Ottomans. Amidst the rubble and chaos that followed, the past was swept away and Smyrna was, in the space of a few years and at enormous human cost, reduced to ashes. Its recent grandeur was soon to become no more than a distant, and bitterly disputed, memory.

The Cordon remains a popular venue.

'Smyrna has Ceased to Exist'

I watched Smyrna burn from the ship that slowly sailed away.[11]

In a nutshell, the story of Smyrna's transformation to Izmir is the reverse of what happened in Thessaloniki. There, in the wake of insurgent Greek nationalism the Turks were forced to leave the city; in Smyrna it was the Greek population that was ousted, not to mention the separate fate of the Armenians and the forced departure of other ethnic groups too. If the storyline seems simple, the true text is quite different and there can be few episodes in world history more differently interpreted, depending on the standpoint of the narrator.[12] The kind of evidence that would normally be available to settle such differences is hard to come by, and the only certainty that emerges is that, effectively, Smyrna ceased to exist after 1922. From that year, its successor is the modern Turkish city of Izmir.

One central theme, however, is clear: Smyrna was used as a pawn on the international chessboard and errors by the playmakers proved decisive. It was not that the city tore itself apart from the inside; rather it was the object of a level of external interference, provocation and misjudgement that proved fatal. To be fair, the pot was already boiling before the First World War, some would say for centuries before. Historically, although they had co-existed well enough, there was little love lost between Greeks and Turks, the former with their proud record as a classical civilization bitterly resenting the many years of Ottoman rule.

A critical development came in the 1820s, when, in an explosion of nationalism, the Greeks succeeded in freeing the southern half of their peninsula; such was the birthplace of modern Greece, with Athens its capital. With the further waning of Ottoman power the Greeks looked for an opportunity to liberate the north too, finally achieved in 1912 with the recovery of Macedonia and its main city, Thessaloniki. Even that, though, was not the end of it. Why not, as well, the reclamation of the coast of Asia Minor, Smyrna included, historically a part of the Hellenistic realm and still peopled largely by Greek communities? For their charismatic leader, Eleutherios Venizelos, this was a legitimate cause, promoted under the banner of the Megali Idea, the formation of Greater Greece.[13]

Smyrna clearly featured in this ambition for what amounted to a new empire, with plans to extend it well into Anatolia—as far as Greeks could be found in the villages and tilling the land—and, as such, was to be fiercely contested. On the ground, the first signs of trouble were seen in the spring of 1914, when thousands of disaffected Muslims, displaced by wars in the Balkans in 1912 and 1913, made their way southwards along the Anatolian coastline. In a violent episode, Greek communities to the north of Smyrna were either massacred or forced to flee, leaving their properties open to Turkish occupancy. Surely, though, the good citizens of Smyrna believed, these were localized events that would not be allowed to encroach on their own city; indeed, for a while, well into 1914, life went on as normal, with its endless round of tea dances and evening promenades, operas and dinners in the fashionable clubs. Nothing, however, could disguise the growing schism after Turkey joined in an alliance with Germany, and in due course entered the war on that side. In a clumsy attempt to restore a balance of power in the region, the Western Allies looked, instead, to Greece for support, knowing only too well that little encouragement would be needed to hasten the downfall of the Ottomans.[14] Inducements were offered and, in a rash moment with little thought for the future, Greece was promised that part of Asia Minor where its own people were in a majority. Smyrna, of course, was the golden prize.

When the military left the field in 1918 the statesmen took over. By then, two mighty empires (Austria-Hungary and, more pertinently for Smyrna, the Ottoman Empire itself) had collapsed, Germany was defeated and Russia was in its own revolutionary disarray; the map of much of Europe and the Near East had to be redrawn. As if the situation was not complex enough it soon emerged that, in the heat of battle, sometimes the same promise had been made to more than one party. Not only Greece but also Italy believed it had the support of the Allies to appropriate the rich coastal strip of Asia Minor, and this was in addition to the longstanding interests in the region of France and Britain. That created problems enough but, even less excusable, in their eagerness to divide up the spoils of war, the international politicians badly under-estimated the real situation. There was no doubt that the Ottoman era was all but over—the Empire had, in fact, been disintegrating for some years before then—but it was a grave error to assume that Turkey itself was finished. On the contrary, within that country there was a dynamic modernizing movement that welcomed the fall of the traditionally minded Ottomans more than most, and was now poised to take over in a newly organized regime.

Asia Minor was most certainly not, as the Allies seemed to assume, a vacant territory just waiting to be occupied. In these circumstances, it is hard to understand how anyone could have imagined it was. The blame for this terrible misjudgement must, no doubt, be shared by a number of statesmen but amongst those who gathered at the post-1918 peace conferences the name of one person, David Lloyd George, the British Prime Minister, should be singled out. Seduced (as many West Europeans were) by the whole notion of Greek culture and history, it was Lloyd George who most directly encouraged the Greeks to believe that they could enter Asia Minor with impunity (not to mention with an implicit promise of British warships to support their venture). To the astonishment of the rest of the world, this is exactly what happened. In May 1919 a landing was made by Greek troops in Smyrna harbour, an ecstatic moment for the Greek population but also one that would only result in eventual tragedy.

Over the next three years most of the action took place in the Anatolian interior, a fearful struggle between the armies of Greece and Turkey that heightened age-old animosities and duly resulted in a humiliating defeat for the invaders. Communities were torn apart, atrocities were committed, and in the process any trust that had been nurtured over the years was instantly destroyed.[15] Yet, in Smyrna itself, while battles were raging in the countryside, there were times when one might have thought the conflict was on another planet, something to read about at leisure in the city's many newspapers but not enough to break familiar routines. Even when the Greek troops were finally routed, in August 1922, the cafes at first remained as busy as ever and in the evening audiences still filled the theatres and opera house. Not until a silent procession of maimed and war-weary soldiers entered the city did reality start to dawn.

Within days, the bedraggled troops were followed by huge numbers of refugees, forced from their villages and carrying their only belongings on their backs and in makeshift carts. A small number of wealthy Greeks and Armenians found ways to leave the city immediately, but for the rest of the vulnerable communities—as many as 200,000 Christians already living in Smyrna and tens of thousands more arriving each day from the interior—there was nowhere to go.

Kemal Ataturk urging his soldiers on towards the Mediterranean, in the face of the Greek invasion.

Within days, the situation deteriorated. First, the Greek authorities (who had held power in the city since 1919) closed their offices and boarded ships to return to their homeland, creating a temporary vacuum that aroused only fear and apprehension amongst those left behind. Then, in dramatic fashion, against a background of Allied warships in the harbour, the Turkish militia entered the city. It was, at first, a symbolic entry, an orderly line of cavalry along the Cordon, the mounted soldiers in smart uniforms with sabres drawn. In spite of a few shots fired from the crowds lining the streets, the situation seemed to be under control and an assurance was issued pledging that the citizenry had nothing to fear. This assurance proved shortlived and, with the later arrival of less disciplined Turkish infantry, the first incidents of looting and forced entries into private homes soon occurred.

Things very soon went from bad to worse, with the Armenian quarter cordoned off prior to the systematic persecution of its population and subsequent outbreaks of arson. Mustapha Kemal, the soldier and modernizer who had by then joined his forces in the city, saw the future of Turkey as one cleansed of non-Muslim minorities, which many of his soldiers interpreted as a licence to plunder. The Armenians in the north-east of the country had already been victims of a massive programme of genocide during the war years, and those who remained in Turkey were largely confined to Smyrna and Constantinople. Their days were clearly numbered as they were popularly portrayed as irreconcilable enemies of the Turks. Equally, there would be no place in modern Turkey for the Greeks, too, who were seen as aliens and were blamed for atrocities in the previous three years of occupation. There were also plans afoot to oust the Jews.[16]

As the Turks went about their business, the Allies, viewing events from the safety of their ships in the harbour, were no more than passive onlookers, determined to maintain a position of absolute neutrality. Above all, they were unwilling to upset the Turks, in the interests of longer-term access to that country's mineral and other resources, as well as its proximity to oil reserves to the east. They remained unmoved even when, before their very eyes, the city hitherto famed for its tolerance, its commercial vitality and its inherent sense of grandeur was, literally, taken apart. As well as summary executions, rape and widespread looting, fires rapidly spread from the Armenian quarter across the whole city. Soon, it seemed, there were no areas that were not in flames; in the words of George Horton, American consul and eye witness, 'the flames, raging now over a vast area, grew brighter and brighter, presenting a scene of awful and sinister beauty'.[17] Journalists, who had been hitherto instructed by their national politicians to play down the actions of the Turks, now broke ranks, like George Ward Price, who filed the following for his newspaper in London:

> ... *picture a constant projection into a red-hot sky of gigantic incandescent balloons, burning oil spots in the Aegean, the air filled with a nauseous smell, while parching clouds, cinders and sparks drift towards us—and you can have but a glimmer of the appalling and majestic destruction which we are watching.*[18]

There was nowhere for the people to run and many of those who were not burned alive in the narrow streets were drowned in the dark waters of the harbour. Most of the city's inhabitants who survived the fires crowded onto the quayside, at one time as many as half a million, looking in vain for help from the Allied ships at anchor.[19] Only belatedly was assistance to come from that source (a result of compassion by the ships' captains and crews rather than a change of political heart) and, later, more were rescued by the arrival of a flotilla of Greek boats. The killing, though, was far from over and men of fighting age were rounded up by the Turks and forced to march into the Anatolian interior, where many were either slaughtered or died of exhaustion.[20]

In the aftermath of the fires, a journalist on the scene wired back his chilling storyline: 'Except for the squalid Turkish quarter, Smyrna has ceased to exist.'[21] For George Horton, what had happened was unforgiveable and a cause to reflect on humanity itself: 'One of the keenest impressions that I brought away from Smyrna was a feeling of shame that I belonged to the human race.'[22]

The Making of a Metropolis

Slowly… a new Izmir arose from the ashes of Smyrna.[23]

So much of what happened in the destruction of Smyrna was lost forever in the ashes of its buildings and in the memories of its former minorities. For those who survived the conflagration, their suffering was still not over as hundreds of thousands of displaced Greeks turned their backs on Turkey for the last time, in favour of refuge in their true homeland. Their exodus, by land and sea, was matched by the expulsion at the same time of Turks living in Greek territories, in a population exchange of biblical proportions.[24] Meanwhile, in the year when all of this was taking place, 1923, the Turkish Republic was established with Mustapha Kemal (soon to be known as Ataturk) the first President.

A small Jewish community has remained in Izmir, served by a number of synagogues.

Modern Turkey was born and Smyrna itself would, in due course, rise from the ashes, under the new name and identity of Izmir. First, though, there was the question of addressing the past, if necessary of rewriting the records to make the city's recent history more palatable. In the interests of their newly formed nation, the wordsmiths were soon at work to devise a story line that went something like this: the years 1919 to 1922 represented a time of enemy occupation, followed by the liberation of the Anatolian interior and then the city of Smyrna by Turkish forces.

In the course of the latter, it was claimed that the great fire that swept through the old quarters had been lit by the escaping Greeks and Armenians.[25] Future generations of historians would revisit the facts, time and again, in search of the truth, only to find that possible insights were buried ever deeper in a tangled mass of conflicting claims. To neutral onlookers it remains a terrible episode, memorable even in a century when genocide became a recurring nightmare. It is unlikely that there will ever be agreement on what really happened.

One can, at best, reflect on the undoubted human cost of the episode and then turn the page to see what happened at the start of the city's next chapter. If there is a watchword for that it has to be modernity.

High-rise apartment buildings push the city's boundaries further up the mountain slopes.

With the birth of modern Turkey in 1923, Izmir itself, along with the rest of the country, was about to be remade. Due largely to the lead taken by Ataturk, in the new Turkey the past was quickly swept away. With most of the minorities no longer in the city it quickly lost its cosmopolitan charm and inherent diversity, along with a proud record for tolerance. Traditional costume was replaced in government and business circles by western fashions, for women as well as men.

Rather like Thessaloniki in the same decade—as a result of physical destruction of a large swathe of that city too by fire, dramatic demographic change, and nationalist aspirations—an early programme of rebuilding was urged. The Turkish mayor at the time, Sukru Kaya, called in French planners—René Danger and Henri

Prost—to show how the new Izmir could achieve a radical break with the past. Their proposals, which envisaged a city with wide streets, urban plazas and parks, were approved in 1925.[26] Kaya's successor, Behcet Salih Uz, from 1931 to 1940 enthusiastically followed his lead, equally determined to erase the past and build a modern city. Amongst his projects was the conversion of the former Armenian quarter into the Kültürpark (likened at the time to Moscow's Gorki Park), which was later to host Izmir's renowned international fairs—a prestigious venue 'built on rubble and bones'.[27] It was also on his watch that in 1932, amidst what were still the ruins along the Cordon, a statue was unveiled of Kemal Ataturk on horseback. The statue faces the sea and contains the inscription 'Soldiers! Your first goal is the Mediterranean.'[28]

Urban motorways along the southern waterfront were given priority in Izmir; in contrast, a scheme to the north was halted at the eleventh hour.

In the view of Mayor Uz, modernity had yet to be wholly embraced and with this in mind in 1938 he commissioned the arch-modernist, Le Corbusier, to prepare a new master plan. Because of the advent of war in the following year, it was not until 1949 that the Swiss architect was able to present his plan, designed for 'a green city with a population of 400,000'.[29] By that time, without the leadership and support of Mayor Uz to champion the scheme, Le Corbusier's proposals were dismissed as unrealistic. Instead, in 1951, alternative designs were invited through an international competition for yet another master plan.[30] The figure of 400,000 was retained as the target population to be reached over the coming fifty years.

This time the commission was given to a group of Turkish architects, who prepared a plan with what remained of the historic core to be conserved, and with a new civic centre alongside. Beyond this inner area, development would be characterized by a series of neighbourhoods separated by green corridors. The plan was lauded at the time but was soon overtaken by events. Instead of growing at a measured pace, a flood of migrants from the Anatolian countryside led (as in Istanbul) to far more rapid expansion.

From a figure of some quarter million in the middle of the twentieth century, Izmir's population now stands at close to four million. Many of the newcomers were commonly forced at first to find homes in squatter settlements (gecekondu) in peripheral areas or in overcrowded tenements in the older parts of the city. More recently, the authorities have built closely-packed clusters of high-rise apartments, rising ever higher up the slopes of the surrounding rim of mountains. Meanwhile, more people still arrive daily from the vast interior, in search of a better way of life.

Modern Izmir is a far cry from the kind of well-planned metropolis envisaged by Le Corbusier or, indeed, any other of the city's twentieth-century planners. In the face of exponential population growth on this scale, no plans could possibly keep pace. As a result, what has emerged is far from ideal, with heavy traffic, air pollution, high densities, and new suburbs that are constantly stretching the boundaries further into the countryside. This is not a place that at first appeals—just another Mediterranean city that is struggling against the odds to come to terms with the scale of modern growth. Yet, as with most places, not all is lost. For one thing, although Izmir's traffic engineers seem to have had their own way for too long there are at least signs of a popular backlash, demonstrated by the success of a former mayor in halting a potentially damaging urban motorway. It was an eleventh-hour victory for the mayor and his fellow campaigners as the first of the platforms were already in place in the district of Alsancak, designed to carry an elevated motorway along the northern section of the Cordon itself, following the line of the sea. The platforms remain as both a reminder and warning of how easily the quality of the coastal environment could have been diminished.

Another redeeming feature of the city is that, although planners appear to have only a marginal impact across the city at large, there are various localized projects that make a difference.[31] Konak Square, for instance, generally regarded as the heart of the city, is a public space that works well enough, a natural link between the sea and the adjoining bazaar. Office workers from the neighbouring governmental buildings and tourists visiting the city make good use of the square during the day, although the absence of homes in the area reduces its vitality in the evenings. Nearby, the historic Konak Pier—a unique steel structure designed originally by Gustav Eiffel as a customs house for the busy Levantine port—has been tastefully restored to create a lively venue for the city's better-off residents as well as tourists. Historic sites, notably, the well-preserved agora and the impressive Kadifekale Castle that overlooks the centre, are also obvious nuclei for urban design schemes. At a more strategic level, Izmir has presented itself effectively as an attractive venue for international exhibitions and festivals, mostly centred on the Kultur Park.

In spite of Izmir's modernity, traditional cultures are still evident.

To add to it all, there is a trump card that sets it apart from many other cities of this size, namely, its exceptional setting between mountains and sea, combined with the sunny climate and dazzling light of the eastern Mediterranean. The broad Bay of Izmir and the surrounding mountains are sufficient in scale to embrace even a metropolis of four million people.

One can see why this setting was so dearly loved by the Levantines who lived here in a previous era, believing that Smyrna was as well-endowed as anywhere on earth. In a very different, more democratic, context its coastal location remains so today, equally treasured by the present population. One can see this in the open-air cafes along the harbourside, where men play backgammon and smoke nargilehs; where on a warm evening families from the crowded neighbourhoods come to enjoy the gentle breeze; where fishing lines are often no more than a pretext to stand and look out to sea; and where, along the seawall, groups simply sit and watch the constant throng of passers-by.

Just as one feels in Thessaloniki, however, history despatches its own chill wind to remind one that all is not quite what it seems. Is this really the same harbourside where, not a century before, people fled to escape the fires that raged across the old city? Was this where crowds huddled on the very edge of the quayside, some falling to their death in the black waters? And is it where, instead of the cheerful ferries that now work their way round the bay, the dark outlines of Allied warships could be seen, silently obeying the command of distant statesmen rather than the urgent cries of common humanity? Or is history simply an unwanted intruder? Is it not time to move on, respecting the rights of new generations to enjoy what is here now and not what belongs to the past? Izmir, like Thessaloniki, has found a new identity, in its own way accepting of different cultures and certainly more open and democratic than many other modern cities in the Mediterranean.

BEIRUT

The eastern Mediterranean is known more exotically as the Levant.[1] It marks a geographical region but it is about more than location; the very thought of the Levant evokes powerful cultural associations. Here, along the eastern shores of the 'middle sea', many of the seeds of early civilization were sown: the Phoenicians first set sail in search of new lands; the Crusaders confronted the soldiers of Islam in a battle for religious hegemony; generations of traders exchanged goods between East and West.

This is the stretch of coastline about which the Egyptian poet, C.P. Cavafy, wrote: a romantic world of bright moonlight seen through open windows, of young men encountered in cafes and bars, of the constant presence of ghosts from a classical past. Language, dress, architecture, cuisine, music—all mingle in a veritable *pot pourri* derived from the meeting of Orient and Occident. It is a mix that is alluring but often far from harmonious, for the coastal cities of the Levant are no strangers to the pervasive effects of territorial and doctrinal conflict.

Nowhere better illustrates this long and contested history than Beirut itself, capital of Lebanon. It is an extraordinary city which has been witness to successive stages of human development, each one physically layered beneath the modern streets and now partly revealed through archaeological excavations. In spite of Beirut's longevity it remained relatively small until the second half of the nineteenth century, after which it emerged as one of the most dazzling cities of the Mediterranean. More recently, and in complete contrast, it became almost a byword for urban dissolution, when in a savage civil war lasting fifteen years rival factions reduced much of the city to ruins; even since then there have been further outbreaks of violence, from within and as a result of foreign interference. In spite of the nightmare of its recent past, Beirut has gained a reputation for recovery, with an ambitious and still evolving process of reconstruction. As the locus for so many interlocking themes, past and present, Beirut is, arguably, of more contemporary interest than any other Mediterranean city.

Levantine Palimpsest

… archeologists have uncovered layers of Canaanite, Phoenician, Hellenistic, Roman and Ottoman civilization.[2]

Wartime destruction not uncommonly reveals long hidden archaeological remains. That was certainly the case in the centre of Beirut in the 1990s, when damaged buildings were swept away and the excavation of ground for new foundations unearthed hitherto concealed remnants from earlier periods. These relatively recent finds confirmed what was already suspected, namely, that there is evidence of permanent settlement on the site stretching back over five millennia.

Recent excavations in the face of modern construction have revealed a rich legacy from earlier eras.

Had this been anywhere other than the eastern Mediterranean such a discovery would have aroused astonishment, but in this part of the world extraordinarily long timelines are almost expected. Just along the coast, to the north, the ancient town of Byblos claims continuous occupancy for seven millennia, while there are gnarled olive trees in Lebanon reputed to have first broken ground 6000 years ago.

Although early settlers came to the Mediterranean shores over a long period of pre-history, it now seems fairly certain that the first recognizable group belonged to the tribe recalled in the Bible as the Canaanites. The later Phoenicians are generally thought to be an offshoot of these pioneers, building their own civilization around maritime skills and enjoying most influence between roughly 1200 and 800 BC. Beirut was one of a string of Phoenician coastal settlements that included Byblos and Tripoli to the north, with Sidon and Tyre to the south. Then came the Greeks and, although the city did not loom large in the expansion of Hellenic culture, they, too, left their mark. Late in that era there is evidence in Beirut of the geometrical alignment of thoroughfares that was characteristic of Greek planners, and the city was then named Laodicea. Only with the arrival of the Romans in the first century BC does it start to come into its own, enjoying a new status as a colony (named Colonia Julia Augusta Felix Berytus, after the daughter of Emperor Augustus). The Romans did nothing in half measures and endowed the city with elegant public buildings, noble monuments and a respected school of law; attending as they always did to practical matters, they also built impressive aqueducts and canals to ensure a fresh water supply. Demonstrating its importance as a strategic base, the Roman fleet of the eastern Mediterranean could frequently be seen in the harbour. For half a millennium Berytus played its part in the region, first as a defensible stronghold in the eastern reaches of the Roman Empire and then, with the consolidation of Christianity, under the direct control of Byzantium. The latter, however, was shortlived and left few marks on the city, other than the legacy of a cathedral (later rebuilt by the Crusaders, before being converted to a mosque). In the year 551 the early history of Beirut effectively came to an end, when it fell victim to a devastating earthquake that killed as many as 30,000 of its citizens and left most of its buildings in ruins. It was in this depleted state that its next conquerors, Arab Muslims from the East, found it in the following century, marking the start of a new, and lengthy episode in its history.[3]

The Muslim conquest of the Mediterranean shoreline came just three years after the death of the Prophet Mohammed in 632, the Arab conquerors arriving with the urgency of their new message. In its diminished state, Beirut itself was of little immediate interest, compared with other settlements along the coast. From the outset, however, there would have been tensions between the resident Christian community and the messengers of Islam. Beirut's new rulers were at first content to leave their conquest as no more than a walled garrison town, under the jurisdiction of Damascus. Only from the tenth century, with the revival of sea trade (which had waned following the fall of the Romans and the security offered to merchant shipping by their powerful navies), were there fresh signs of growth. The arrival of the Crusaders in the region brought its own uncertainties but Beirut gained directly from the First Crusade; it was not simply that in 1100 its Muslim conquerors were expelled from the city but trade increased across the Mediterranean with the subsequent opening of routes to western ports such as Genoa. Apart from a period of some ten years, when it was retaken by the Muslims, Beirut remained a Crusader stronghold until late in the thirteenth century. It was then the turn of the Mamluks (armies of former slaves, mainly from Persia) who in 1291 captured Beirut and (like their Muslim predecessors) placed it once more under the administration of their province of Syria. Beirut prospered from the ensuing trade between the interior (from where caravans brought silks and spices, as well as other luxury products prized in the West), meeting ships from Europe in the safe waters of its harbour. In due course, early in the sixteenth century, control changed hands once again, this time when Beirut (along with the rest of Syria) became part of the Ottoman Empire, a situation that continued for some 400 years. For most of this era, in spite of its commercial value to the Ottomans, Beirut remained relatively small. Even by the middle of the nineteenth century, the population was little more than 6000. Then, largely in response to the growing demands of European economies for products from the region, the pace accelerated, and by 1915 the number of people living in the city had reached 130,000.[4]

This rapid growth changed the whole nature of Beirut, from a relatively sleepy backwater to a thriving port, and from a largely Muslim population to one with a Christian majority. Migrants arrived from the nearby mountains and from Syria beyond, bringing with them a mixed baggage of religious beliefs and tribal loyalties.

Most of the newcomers belonged to a variety of Christian sects, which soon outnumbered the previous majority of Sunni Muslims; the Shi'ites remained a small minority until the second half of the twentieth century. At the start of this era of growth, Beirut still had a mediaeval appearance. Away from the openness of the harbour, the streets closed in:

> ... *narrow and winding and badly paved, if paved at all. They were also filthy, with animal hides and offal heaped along the roadway. Traffic was a mixture of people and camels, horses and donkeys. Even in the daytime the streets were dark.*[5]

It was also prone to regular epidemics, like cholera and typhoid. Western visitors were quick to condemn the primitive conditions, although it is unlikely that their own cities would have been dramatically different at that time. In any case, relatively few of those who conducted trade with the Levant chose then to take up permanent residence.

Beirut's subsequent growth might well have eluded it but for two events. The first was the Ottoman response to intense lobbying on the part of the city's indigenous merchants and businessmen, resulting in its re-designation in 1888 as a major provincial capital in its own right.[6] Immediately, a direct line was opened to Constantinople and the city benefited from the arrival of senior administrators and a flow of investment to modernize its infrastructure. In the same period, as well as the stimulus of imperial preferment, Beirut also attracted the interest of the West, notably Britain and France. Apart from longer-term designs on the region, an immediate lure was the trade with its rich hinterland, extending into Syria and further into the interior. For the French, the supply of silk was a particular inducement. Stealing a march on their British competitors, they were quick to invest in the region. First, between 1859 and 1863, a French company built a new road across the mountains to Damascus, replacing what had been little more than a track suitable only for caravans of mules and camels.[7] Later in the century, from 1890 to 1895, the French were also responsible for major works undertaken to the harbour, greatly extending the landing space as well as increasing the depth; as a result, there was immediately a sharp increase in both commercial and passenger traffic.[8] Not to be completely outdone, British engineers made their own contribution by replacing the Roman aqueduct system with a modern system of water supply.[9] The rival nations trod a fine line, trying, on the one hand, to prop up the ailing Ottoman Empire as a bulwark (albeit increasingly fragile) against Russia, and at the same time staking their own claim to the region when the eventual collapse of rule from Constantinople occurred. As well as their contribution to Beirut's infrastructure they also played a part in the cultural activity of the city, and they encouraged missionaries to build schools and churches in the Christian communities. In the event, it was the French who came out ahead, and who were to assume the major role in the next chapter of the city's history.

French Connection

France long had coveted Greater Syria… for its empire in the Arab world.[10]

The First World War saw the final collapse of the Ottoman Empire, and for Beirut a new era opened. As a Mediterranean nation itself, France now seized the opportunity to further strengthen its hold on the wider region. The State of Greater Lebanon was formed in 1920 and, together with the adjoining coastal territories of Syria, a mandate was awarded to France for their joint protection. Just six years later, in 1926, Lebanon became a democratic republic with Beirut as its capital. France, however, was not so soon to relinquish its own powers and full independence for the embryo nation was not ceded until 1943.

Perhaps because of its coastal location, coupled with a large non-Muslim population, Beirut has always been more open to Western influence than landlocked Arab cities like Damascus. Although Europeans with business in the city were at first reluctant to settle there permanently, the situation changed and by the turn of the century it was home to small communities of foreigners. Numbers grew and, especially when it came under French stewardship, Beirut soon gained a reputation as a modern city, a beacon in what was still regarded in the West as a backward region. France enjoyed good relations with the Christian Maronites and, with this influential source of support, was keen to stamp its own cultural mark on the city. Indeed, what could be better than to make Beirut the kind of city that might be found in France itself? As well as the ubiquitous use of their language, French personnel arrived to teach in the schools and support the work of its churches. In terms of the urban fabric, the colonists found the city at something of a crossroads, with much of the mediaeval core recently demolished by the last generation of Ottoman rulers. Further destruction of the most historic parts was halted but in the remaining downtown areas the French were keen to do things their way. If not exactly *Haussmanesque*, there was a familiar ring about the introduction of a 'star-shaped, *beaux-arts* grid',[11] with new axial highways named after some of the military and political leaders of the recent war in Europe (including Foch, Clemenceau, Gourau and Monot). Characteristic of such grand designs, these routes converged on a renovated *Place de l'Etoile*, with the parliament building symbolically located at the physical heart of the young nation. Another iconic feature, announcing the future of Beirut as a venue for the wealthy traveller, was the flamboyant Hotel St. Georges (designed by Antoine Tabet and opened in 1930); many years later, following its destruction in the country's longest civil war, a poster defiantly illustrated a fashion show amidst the ruins, telling the world that Beirut was once again open for business. Elsewhere, in the style of the apartment blocks, with ornamental ironwork around the balustrades, and in the individual shop fronts and displays in the windows, there was more than a hint of provincial France; it was indeed, as one commentator has observed, 'an architectural environment more in keeping with the vernacular of southern France than a truly Arab oriental style'.[12]

Beirut enjoys a spectacular setting, between snow-capped mountains and the sea.

Under French patronage, Beirut emerged from its background as a busy but relatively humdrum port, dirty and dusty, into one of the most vibrant and cosmopolitan cities in the eastern Mediterranean, equipped for a luxurious lifestyle. It has always helped, of course, that it enjoys a spectacular setting, with the heart of the city on a promontory, overlooking the sea in one direction and a backcloth of mountains (in winter, snow-capped) in the other. Like most visitors to Beirut, the allure of it all was not to escape the sensitivities of the fictional Harriet Pringle, the neglected wife in Olivia Manning's trilogy set in the Levant during the Second World War. Finding herself at her friend's expense staying in a Beirut hotel reputed at the time to be the best in the Middle East, she wandered through the gardens, lush with semi-tropical plants and flowering orange trees, to be confronted with a view of the city below:

> *She saw Beirut itself stretched beneath her, a sharply-drawn maze of streets set with pink and cream buildings, delicately coloured in the early sunlight. The streets, flashing with traffic, converged towards the water-front where ships were gathered on the glittering Mediterranean. On the southern side of the town, beside the road, there was a wood of dark trees, each a stiff arrangement of branches with wings of closely packed foliage, standing like crows in affected attitudes. These, she realized, were the Cedars for which the hotel was named.*[13]

With the departure of the French and the introduction in 1943 of national autonomy for Lebanon, a new era opened for the capital. For every citizen who celebrated independence, there must have been just as many fearing for the future. After all, there had not been a long history of nationalistic fervour and there was no obvious rationale behind the creation of Lebanon as a nation state; nor, indeed, were there any obvious boundaries to contain it. Much of its history had been as a minor province of Syria, under external rule. Of more immediate concern, the country hosted a remarkable range of ethnic and religious groups; at the birth of the nation, no less than eighteen different faiths were formally recognized. Most were grouped into Christians and Muslims, roughly equal in numbers, but within each of these were sharp sectarian divisions. Amongst the Christians were the Maronite Catholics (named after their founding saint, Maroun), Copts, evangelical Protestants and Orthodox Christians; while the Muslims were divided between Sunni and Shia. There were also the secluded Druze communities in the mountains, the origins of which are still disputed.[14] Under Ottoman rule potential conflicts between the various groups had largely been contained, although as recently as 1860 there had been fierce fighting between the Maronites and Druze, resulting in some 10,000 fatalities amongst the Christians alone. If this basic inheritance was not complex enough, the neighbouring state of Israel was formed in 1948, one immediate effect being that 100,000 Palestinian refugees made their way north across the border into Lebanon, while most of the Jews who had lived in Lebanon for centuries chose to leave for their new homeland. The future for the new nation was clearly not going to be an easy ride.

In spite of the portents, however, the post-1943 era started well enough. Precarious though it might seem with hindsight, the young nation put its faith in the constitution that had been introduced in the 1920s, based on a simple formula of power-sharing between the largest minorities: the President would always be drawn from the Christian Maronite community, the Prime Minister a Sunni Muslim and the Speaker of the Chamber of Deputies a Shia Muslim. In celebrating the nation's independence, there was hope that a common commitment to Lebanon as a whole would be enough to overcome potential divisions. Initially, at least, a coalition of interests held together, bound as much by the sheer momentum of economic growth as by the abstract idea of nationhood.

Beirut in the middle of the century emerged as the leading financial centre for Arab countries in the region, successfully bridging political and ideological differences between East and West. A concentration of banks in the heart of the city became *the* place to do business;[15] Investors felt secure in depositing funds there, especially wealthy exiles from seemingly less stable states like Egypt, Syria and Iraq. No less, Beirut became the modern playground of the eastern Mediterranean, offering beaches, nightclubs and casinos, with the bonus of ski slopes in the mountains just an hour away. The international airport was expanded to meet an increasing number of tourists, five-star hotels were built along the corniche, and shops selling luxury goods brought a suggestion of Paris or New York. It emerged, too, as a place of culture, with museums and art galleries as well as respected universities; and also as an attractive location for international conferences.

The corniche has for long attracted luxury developments and, in spite of political uncertainties, continues to do so.

With so much to offer, Lebanon itself (essentially because of its international banking) was promoted as the 'Switzerland of the East'. Several decades ahead of the emergence of Dubai, Beirut was beginning to perform a key function in the Middle East as a global hub.

In one respect, Beirut even benefited from the formation of Israel and the refusal of Lebanon and other Arab states to recognize its existence. Traditionally, Haifa, to the south of the Lebanese border, had served as the entry port for the whole of the region, but with that no longer possible the shipping facilities in Beirut were upgraded to capture this valuable trade. With heavier traffic through its port and access to a regional market, factories and refineries in the city prospered. Lured by the prospect of jobs in construction and other industries, large numbers of migrants arrived from the Lebanese countryside, and these were joined later by workers and their families from Syria. As a result, the population of Beirut grew rapidly; during the 1950s from half a million to 600,000, and by the time of the 1975 civil war to an estimated one million.[16] Hemmed in by the mountains, physical expansion would never be easy and one obvious consequence was for more people to crowd onto available land at higher densities. Additionally, most of the migrants in search of work were forced to live in squatter communities around the periphery, alongside the Palestinian refugee camps.

The city's planners were never a match for the sheer volume and pace of development and growth in this period. Post-colonial French consultants engaged with local planners to produce plans to guide future development but these proved inadequate to the task. Especially after 1958 the government was more interventionist although, on the ground, attempts to impose a degree of order were largely thwarted by a natural resistance to regulations amongst the business community and by the irresistible influence of property speculators. Beirut surged ahead with only minimal guidance and the outcome was predictable: housing that failed to keep pace with demand, serious traffic congestion and few distinguished buildings or public places. High-rise blocks cut a swathe across the skyline, ignoring the cultural specifics of a Levantine city and its spectacular setting between mountains and sea. Then, in 1975, to the sound of gunfire, everything changed.

Plans Laid in War

Beirut has become its own metaphor, a self-parody even.[17]

From 1975 to 1990 the city was at the heart of an unforgiving civil war, its streets a battleground for numerous oppositional factions. When peace finally returned, Beirut then became the scene of an interrupted process of reconstruction. As well as damage resulting from internal fighting, it was periodically a target for bombing by the Israeli air force. In the summer of 2006, much of the progress achieved in the preceding years was undone in the face of repeated aerial attacks on the city. Beirut has paid a heavy price, internally, for its ethnic diversity, and, externally, for its involvement in the continuing conflict with Israel, but the remarkable thing is its ability to rise, time and again, from its own ashes; true to the words of a poster in the war-torn streets in 2006, 'that which was once built will be rebuilt'.[18]

The damaged Holiday Inn remains as a reminder of its place in the midst of hostilities.

To the outsider, immured in a belief in constant progress, it is hard to explain the sudden collapse of a city of Beirut's status. Although the history of the Mediterranean is all too full of accounts of urban destruction and decline, there is a mistaken notion that such episodes belong only to the past. Perhaps the early twentieth-century record of two other cities in the eastern Mediterranean, Izmir and Thessaloniki, should have been read as a warning of what could still happen. Perhaps, too, observers should have known that different ethnic and religious groups seem unable to live together without the kind of overall control that the Ottomans, and later the French, once provided in Lebanon. For the people themselves there were early enough signs of the political ground cracking beneath them.

A civil war had threatened to erupt in 1958; the Palestinian refugees had their own agenda and were seen as a destabilizing force for the country; the Shi'ites, once a minority in the city, were growing fast in number (partly due to the influx of fellow migrants from the country) and were becoming increasingly disaffected with the original constitutional arrangements; while the Maronites were suspected of being too much in league with France and other Christian nations in the West. There was also something unsustainable about the glaring juxtaposition of rich and poor, of the hedonistic lifestyle in the centre compared with the poverty around the periphery. Even more fundamental, there was a basic clash of cultures, between traditionalists from the mountains and modernists in the city; 'in the end the mountain, with its clan loyalties and vendettas, proved stronger than the city, particularly when things started to go wrong'.[19] There was, it is suggested, something almost tribal about the way things were emerging.

Although these were clear enough warnings, most of the outside world was caught by surprise by the sheer speed and extent of the collapse. The civil war (more precisely, civil wars, on account of disputes between a myriad of groups) broke out in April 1975 and it was to be fifteen years before the incessant sound of gunfire in the city ceased. To add poignancy to this episode, it was the very centre of Beirut—the financial district with its renowned banks that was at the heart of the apparent success of the first few decades of independence—which served as the main battleground. Geographically, positions were drawn up sharply along what became known as the Green Line, dividing the predominantly Christian east of the city from the Muslim west.[20]

In contrast to the sharpness of this division, battle lines were altogether more complex with separate militia and private armies formed by opposing factions, each one controlling different street blocks and even individual buildings. With the international airport and main docks out of action, with hostage-taking a matter of course, and with a breakdown in conventional government, Beirut rapidly degenerated into a dangerous state of anarchy for its citizens and largely a 'no-go' territory for foreigners.

Those intrepid journalists who reported the situation on the ground were universally horrified by what they saw:

> *The destruction of Beirut does not really strike home until you get right inside the city. Its sheer mindlessness takes the breath away. An apartment block here, half a street there, houses are reduced to stumps and shops to gutted caves, while youths barely in their teens tote guns and rocket launchers in sentry posts made of burnt-out cars and old bedding, or on balconies turned into sandbagged crows' nests... The urge to destroy has been staggering. Beirut was one of the finest commercial ports on the Levantine coast; it is now a ruin, an echoing charnel house inhabited by rats.*[21]

Successive attempts to broker a ceasefire failed but eventually, in 1990, with Syria's intervention, a deal was struck and the fighting ended. Large tracts of the city had by then become a wasteland, more than half the population had been displaced (many leaving the country altogether), and even more lasting was a loss of trust between religious and political groups. To add to uncertainties about the future, the presence of Syrian troops and that country's longer-term intentions was a matter of concern, while, looking to the south, the city remained within range of Israeli bombing in the event of a fresh outbreak of hostilities between the two countries. For all these reasons, the likelihood of early reconstruction seemed remote. But this was Beirut and even during brief interruptions in the fighting there had been ill-fated and, inevitably, piecemeal attempts to build afresh. With the final signing of a truce that seemed likely to hold, ambitious plans were very soon revealed to rebuild the city. By any measure, the scale of what was envisaged was spectacular, embracing not only the ravaged downtown area but also major infrastructure works including new highways, the international airport and port facilities.

Even more remarkable to anyone from outside the region is the fact that investors were ready to risk their funds in a city which could erupt again at any time. Land values, one might have expected in the circumstances, would have plummeted and yet the reverse has been true. Fuelled by Arab oil revenues and offshore Lebanese investors (many of whom live in the United States), land, particularly in the centre of the city and along the corniche, was from the outset keenly sought. In consequence, with constantly rising values, the whole thrust of new plans has been towards 'high end' development.[22] Nothing but the best would do as Beirut announced its intention to regain its regional role as the business hub of the eastern Mediterranean. Rather like Dubai, the city's own 'hype' led to further rises in land values which, in turn, precluded anything but the most prestigious schemes. Beirut, investors promised, would become the world's newest and most glamorous 'destination'.[23]

Out of the Ashes

It will be rebuilt: Lebanon will be back.[24]

For any venture on this scale, coupled with the bitter taste of the city's recent history, it is hardly surprising that successive plans would arouse controversy, some aspects especially so. For one thing, a key element in the new approach was to wipe the slate clean, if necessary erasing previous patterns of plot ownership and street alignments. Inevitably, there would be legal challenges, perhaps none more notorious than that of the former St. Georges Hotel (an icon of the city's earlier days of glory), which is still contesting rights to the harbour waters alongside.[25] A second area of controversy is that when the first master plan was presented it seemed possible that all traces of Beirut's history and remaining areas of character would be lost in the process of wholesale redevelopment.

This approach was soon moderated with a more tolerant treatment of old buildings but still there were limits; with so many remnants of the past below ground level, it seemed as if every new excavation would reveal another archaeological find. An additional source of public concern was the key role assigned to private developers and, especially, powers that allowed them to convert property values into company shares.[26] Any sense of impartiality was further jeopardized when it emerged that the largest shareholder in the principal company working on the central business district, Solidere, was none other than the country's Prime Minister, Rafik al-Hariri.[27] With so much of the city still in ruins, it was also questioned why most of the attention should be directed to the central area at the expense of the poorer residential districts.[28] A failure to respond effectively was one reason for the initiative later taken by Hezbollah, which exercises control over most of the hitherto neglected southern suburbs.[29]

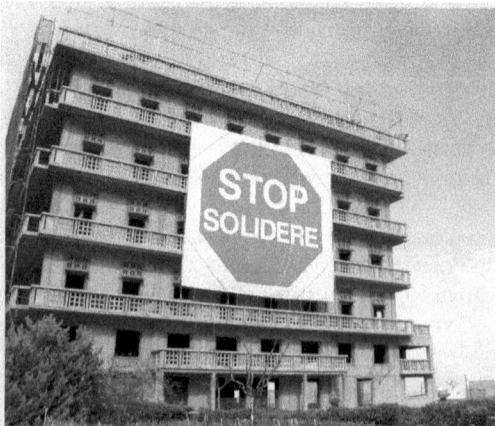

The former St. Georges Hotel is known now for its opposition to Solidere rather than its earlier reputation as the city's most stylish place to stay.

Beirut is being remade, again: the so-called Beirut Souks with their luxury shops; Saifi Village, a mixed development close to the former Green Line; and part of the new downtown area.

In the event, and in spite of understandable concerns, the people of Beirut are nothing if not pragmatic and after all that had gone before there were few who would finally stand in the way of recovery, in any form. As a result, the first substantial building works were evident in 1994. Some account was taken of public disaffection and, with growing confidence, the developers promoted their plans under the rubric of 'Beirut: Ancient City of the Future'. More attention than at first intended was paid to traditional features, like the city's souks; a controversial proposal to replace the popular public space, Martyrs' Square, with a wide boulevard was dropped; while, elsewhere too, the wings of modernist enthusiasts were clipped, although not enough to prevent flight. The guiding concepts, claimed the company's planners, 'reflect a city that combines Eastern and Western influences at the end of a period of cataclysm'.[30] Yet, in spite of the preparation of elaborate plans, the subsequent process of rebuilding was characterized more by a sequence of projects: 'sometimes huge, perhaps, but actual projects rather than plans, nevertheless.'[31]

Largely on this basis, street by street, block by block, the new heart of Beirut started to pump some of its old energy through the city. Then, after more than ten years of progress, disaster struck again. First, in 2005, a thousand tons of explosives tore through many of the new buildings, and amongst the lives that were lost was that of al-Hariri himself. In the following year, in response to actions by Hezbollah, Israeli war planes returned to Beirut, destroying parts of the reconstructed airport and the harbour, as well as numerous newly built structures in the city centre.

Predictably, the resilient people of Beirut barely waited for the bombing to end and for the dust to settle before returning to the recurring task of laying new foundations. Several years on, Beirut is once again a city of cranes, its economy boosted by the dynamo of construction. Tourists (mainly from neighbouring Arab countries and the Gulf region, as well as former Lebanese nationals who now live abroad) have returned in large numbers, lured by modern hotels, restaurants and a lively nightlife in a city that, even in the darkest days of the fifteen-year civil war refused to sleep.

It is certainly not to celebrate a triumph of cultural harmony that visitors have returned to Beirut, for the continuing reality is that it is still a divided city, effectively zoned along religious lines.[32] It is a fragile arrangement where, one feels, new fissures could open up at any time and it can be argued that urban planning has reinforced rather than cut across old lines of sectarianism. Equally, relations with Israel are far from settled. Nor do tourists come to admire its architectural splendours, although some of the rejuvenated areas are attractive in their own *pastiche* way and provide a pleasant enough setting for shopping. Many of the older buildings and historic neighbourhoods were either devastated in warfare or subsequently cleared as a prelude to urban renewal.

The first phase of the city's 'modern souks' was opened in 2009 amidst much publicity for their ingenuity in knitting the past to the present, but souks they are not; at most, one might conclude, the new complex is no more than an up-market shopping precinct. Towering hotels have arisen along the corniche, replacing all but a few surviving buildings from the past—where cocktails were once sipped on the ornate balconies, facing the sea—to remind one of days of real elegance. There is, indeed, little on the emergent skyline to lift the spirit, other than the important fact that the city is remaking itself. This last fact is not to be dismissed easily for the alternative of leaving the centre as a pile of rubble would really have sounded Beirut's death knell. Sceptics who doubt this should do no more than stand beneath the charred exterior of what was once the busy Holiday Inn, its walls ripped out by constant rocket fire, to see which is preferable.[33]

Beirut is still a city of contrasts.

It is a belief in the future—rather than the details of development—that is the most alluring feature of modern Beirut; it is the resilience of a city that has simply refused, against all odds, to die; it is, in spite of all that has been lost, the last Levantine city, where:

> ...with its conflicts and conjunctions, universities and refugee camps, on the fault lines between East and West, clericalism and secularism, city and state, coast and hinterland, at once vulnerable and resilient... [it is] at the heart of the world's debate, and an experimental laboratory for the future of the Middle East.[34]

It would be all too easy to dismiss what has emerged from the ashes but that misses the point. Instead, it is this simple fact of emergence itself that should be celebrated.

HAIFA

Haifa is a Levantine city with a difference. It shares with other settlements along that coast a long history of conquest and occupation by successive powers, but in the middle of the twentieth century its whole make-up and orientation took a completely different turn. With the formation in 1948 of the State of Israel, historic ties with the rest of the region were cut overnight. The previously extensive hinterland of its busy port was effectively truncated and while, until then, it had been a predominantly Arab city, Jews arriving from Europe and North Africa very soon formed the majority of the population. Haifa's subsequent development has been inextricably bound up with the modern history of Israel itself. Although trailing both Jerusalem and Tel Aviv in size and importance, Haifa offers revealing insights into that stretch of the eastern Mediterranean which has changed most since 1948. The city's continuing economic development is not enough to conceal the fact that it sits astride the region's most unstable geopolitical fault line. Visiting Haifa, one soon becomes aware of the vulnerability of its location.

Levantine Past

I know of no locality in the East which offers greater attractions of position, climate and association than this spot.[1]

The eastern Mediterranean has spawned more than its fair share of ancient cities, with Haifa just one example. Its pedigree extends back to the second millennium BC, when it first emerged as a tiny settlement, Tell Abu Hawam, around a natural harbour; it also had the advantage of the wooded slopes of Mount Carmel inland. The Greeks took an interest in the settlement but quickly abandoned the original harbour (which was by then silting up) in favour of an alternative haven nearby. A contemporary observation in the third century tells only of a resident Jewish population and Greek merchants, with records of a lively trade in dyes (produced from marine shells) that were especially prized by priests for their robes; so much so that the Greeks even named the settlement Porphyrion, town of the purple shell.[2] Unusually for a Mediterranean port with obvious potential, the Romans passed it by, preferring to establish outposts in other locations along that coastline. Few changes occurred in the subsequent Byzantine period and it was not until the end of the seventh century, when advance parties of Arabs arrived to spread the word of Islam, that the potential of Haifa was recognized as a port with a rich hinterland. Over the next few centuries it specialized in trade with Egypt and, as it prospered, small shipyards were built around the harbour. This first era of steady progress came to a sudden end in 1100, when European Crusaders entered the settlement and destroyed its fortifications and shipyards, reducing it once more to the status of a small fishing port. Then came the Mamluks (powerful armies of soldiers who were once slaves), who forced out the Christians and, in an endeavour to prevent them from returning, inflicted even more damage by destroying completely the recently restored harbour facilities. The situation only began to improve with the defeat of the Mamluks by the Turkish Ottomans in 1516, marking the start of an interrupted but relatively benign period of rule over the next four centuries.[3]

The German Colony, at the time of its inception, compared with a current view (showing the gardens of the Bahai'i Faith beyond).

For the first three hundred years of Ottoman rule, Haifa remained a small town overshadowed by its historic neighbour, Acre, which gave its name to the broad bay that both settlements share; at most, Haifa provided an additional facility for ships waiting to anchor in the more important port to the north. It was not until the eighteenth century that the order was reversed, with Haifa then chosen by the Ottomans as its principal harbour in that part of the Levant. Asserting its newly assigned role, the old core of Haifa was abandoned and a new settlement established nearby, within strongly fortified walls and with the added protection of a fortress on the lower slopes of Carmel. In spite of its stronger defences, Napoleon had little trouble in taking the city briefly from the Ottomans in 1799 and, some thirty years later, it succumbed to nine years of Egyptian control. Apart from these relatively short-lived incursions, for most of the Ottoman era it looked to Constantinople as the heart of the Turkish Empire and to Beirut for its regional administration. Its harbour was busy but in the first half of the nineteenth century Haifa itself remained relatively small, with a population even in 1860 of no more than 4000. Rapid growth, however, was to follow, spurred by the modernization of the harbour to accommodate the larger steam ships that were by then plying the Mediterranean and, later, the building of the Hejaz Railway, which linked Haifa to Damascus and from there continuing into the very heart of Arabia.

The house in the German Colony where Laurence and Alice Oliphant lived.

Typically, for an eastern Mediterranean port with a growing network of contacts, it attracted a varied mix of ethnic groups and religions. For most of its history Haifa had been peopled mainly by indigenous Arabs (many of them having converted to Christianity) and Jews, while successive periods of conquest left their own mark on the population when small groups of soldiers and administrators stayed on.

Early in the nineteenth century, Haifa started to attract a new wave of Jews from North Africa (whose ancestors had originally been exiled from Spain and Portugal), and later in the same century the first trickle of Ashkenazim Jews arrived from Russia and Romania. A contemporary description of Haifa as a home for disparate groups is provided by the eccentric Laurence Oliphant, who lived for a while in the city and travelled in the region in the 1880s[4].

Although not to be relied upon for some of his views,[5] his accounts of the different groups he encountered offer interesting insights. He met some of the newly arrived Jews from Eastern Europe and, noting their frail physique and inexperience in farming, doubted their ability to make a fresh start on the land. The fact is that tilling the soil and living in rural communities was an important strand of Zionism—the movement dedicated to securing a Jewish homeland in Palestine—even though much of Jewish history (at least around the Mediterranean) was associated with the commercial life of cities. In contrast to what he saw as the ill-suited Jews, Oliphant waxed lyrical about the progress and influence of several hundred German colonists, the Temple Society, who had been lured to Haifa by a messianic belief that the Second Coming would be in Palestine.

They established small settlements across the barren country, including in 1869 one on the lower slopes of Mount Carmel, now in the centre of modern Haifa. There, in what was known as the German Colony, they created 'a most agreeable and unexpected picture of civilization upon this semi-barbarous coast'.[6] An avenue of substantial, three-storey houses was built, and their gardens were farmed as smallholdings. As well as cultivating the land, they engaged in a variety of trades that increasingly served the surrounding population and they started a number of industries, like soap manufactured from olive oil. According to the Eurocentric Oliphant, the Germans transformed more than their own estate:

> *Thanks to the efforts of the colonists, it has become an oasis of civilization in the wilderness of Oriental barbarism... Prior to the arrival of the colonists of the Temple Society, Haifa was as dirty as most Arab villages. It is now well paved throughout. The houses, all constructed of white limestone, quarries of which abound in the immediate vicinity, give it a clean and substantial appearance, and contain a bustling and thriving population of about six thousand inhabitants.*[7]

So enamoured was Oliphant that he and his wife, Alice, themselves occupied one of the houses, which they turned into something of a spiritual centre for likeminded pilgrims in search of a higher order of life. The couple had not long before, while living in America, suffered at the hands of a manipulative visionary but appear to have found a more amenable existence in this balanced community. It was not just the messianic zeal of their neighbours but the traditionalism of the German way of life that appealed to them; by honest labour, Laurence concluded, the colonists set an example that others were already following. In contrast, the point was not lost on him that the community of monks (the Carmelites) in a nearby monastery on Mount Carmel, established seven centuries earlier, had for most of that time remained aloof and apart from the city, bringing no obvious material benefits.[8]

Apart from the messianic sect, Haifa was home to a variety of other religious groups. As well as the Jews and Muslims, Oliphant pointed to different denominations of Christianity—principally, Roman Catholics (known locally as the 'Latins'), Greek

Catholics (the 'Melchites') and Greek Orthodox. Of the three, the Melchites were the largest single group and their unconventional practices were an obvious source of interest for the curious observer. Originally part of the Greek Orthodox Church, they had been drawn towards Rome by the persuasive powers of Jesuit missionaries and Catholic priests.

The gardens of the Bahai'i Faith are prominent on the lower slopes of Mount Carmel.

The outcome was a mix of Oriental and Occidental interpretations of Christianity, with both Arabic and Latin used in services. While living in Haifa, Oliphant was also encouraged to visit the Bab, the leader of a Muslim sect who resided in partial seclusion in the countryside near Acre. The sect evolved into the Bahai'i Faith, and in 1909 an elaborate shrine and terraced gardens were built on the slopes of Mount Carmel, immediately above the German Colony.

For all the changes he noted, Oliphant's Haifa already belonged in many ways to the past, one that had evolved only slowly over centuries. Soon, however, the pace quickened and the Levant was to become part of a new world order. With the old Ottoman Empire in a weakened state, various powers were positioning themselves to take advantage when the predicted collapse occurred. There was fear in the West that Russia would seize every opportunity for a Mediterranean presence, but resistance to that was far from unified. Apart from a widening gulf between Germany and the rest, both Britain and France were in open competition for prospective gains. With hindsight, though, it was not directly these powers that had the greatest impact; instead, there was one other faction, at first barely visible in the world of international diplomacy, that more than any other was to change the whole balance of power in the region. This new actor on the Levantine stage was the Zionist.

Zionism has its roots, towards the end of the nineteenth century, in the large and often oppressed Jewish communities in Russia and the countries of central and eastern Europe. Typically, Zionism was fuelled by a romantic notion of nationalism mixed with revolutionary strains of socialism and communism. It was not so much a unified movement (as there were organized factions) so much as a shared belief that the destiny of the then dispersed Jews lay in a return to the biblical land of the Israelites. Only through nationhood would they end persecution and establish their own rights and freedom. Even before the emergence of Zionism as such, non-Jewish visionaries, including Napoleon at the time of his campaign in the eastern Mediterranean and, later, English reformers and politicians like Lord Shaftesbury, Benjamin Disraeli and the Victorian novelist George Eliot, invoked the idea of a return to the Holy Land.[9] In those heady days, few at the time took account of the indigenous Arabs nor of likely conflicts ahead; some of those who did have an understanding of the region's demographics naively believed that they would be welcomed by the Arabs as long-lost Semitic brothers and sisters.

For all Zionists, Jerusalem would be unquestionably the symbolic heart of the new nation but there was also a realization that other cities would be needed too. One of the movement's intellectual leaders, Theodor Herzl, turned the spotlight away from Jerusalem with a seductive portrayal of Haifa as a future urban powerhouse. In his utopian novel, *Altneuland*, published in Germany in 1902, Herzl painted an optimistic picture of a new, pluralistic society set in Palestine, making the most of the latest technologies, and rooted in co-operative principles of government and organization. Astonishingly, the far-reaching changes he envisaged take place over no more than a twenty-year period. Borrowing from fellow utopians of his time (notably, Edward Bellamy in *Looking Backward*, 1888, and William Morris two years later in *News from Nowhere*), Herzl uses the simple device of his central character falling asleep with thoughts of a better society churning in his mind, only to awaken in a transformed world: 'dreaming, he sailed through the Red Sea to meet the future'.[10] The yacht in which our narrator and his companion are travelling arrives in Haifa, where 'a magnificent city had been built beside the sapphire blue Mediterranean'.[11] Stepping ashore they make the first of a series of encounters with people from the discriminated Jewish community they had known in a previous life in Vienna; now, of course, everyone is free and singing the praises of their new land in an old country, *Altneuland*.

Haifa and everything within it was a revelation. The whole bay, all the way north to Acre, seemed like one great park, with white villas showing through the luxuriant vegetation. Acre itself had retained its historic skyline of golden cupolas and slender minarets. Within Haifa, they entered the bustling space known as 'The Place of the Nations', the cosmopolitan heart of international commerce, 'thronged with people from all parts of the world... There were many Chinese, Persians and Arabs in the streets, but the city itself seemed thoroughly European.'[12] The brilliant blue of the sea and sky reminded visitors of the French Riviera, 'but the buildings were much cleaner and more modern'.[13] Around the square were arcades to provide shade, and lines of palm trees in which were set electric lights. Although busy, the streets were quieter than they had previously experienced, largely because of the use of overhead railways and automobiles with rubber tyres; the visitors, as yet unaware of future problems of road traffic in cities were suitably impressed. Elsewhere, they were told of an intricate railway system that connected Palestine—'lying at the exact centre of traffic between Europe, Asia and Africa'[14]—with the rest of the world.

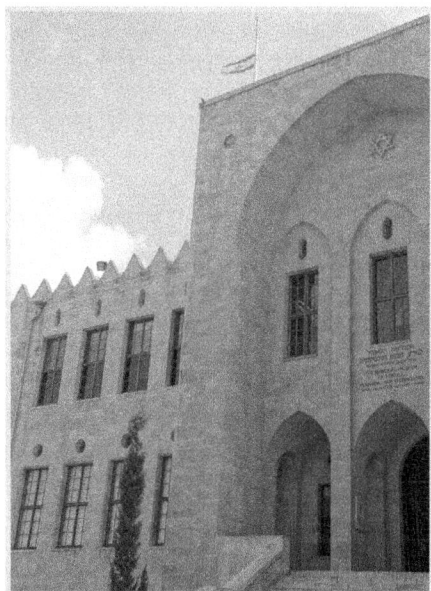

The Technion was inspired by Herzl's vision of Haifa as the industrial powerhouse of the Zionist future.

Herzl's recognition of the future importance of Haifa was encouraged by some of his Zionist contemporaries, when it was discussed as an appropriate location for a prospective technical university (which, in fact, materialized in due course as the Technion):

> *Haifa was destined to be the city of the future, a great port center of industry and shipping. With the building of the Hejaz railroad it would be linked to Damascus and Baghdad, and would become an important crossroads for land transport as well.*[15]

It is one of the quirks of history in this region that such faith in Haifa's future found common ground with a quite different set of interests, in the form of British imperialists who were soon to oust the Turks and make their own mark on Palestine's destiny in the coming years.

A Colony by Another Name

His Majesty's government view with favour the establishment in Palestine of a national home for the Jewish people.[16]

In December 1917, General Allenby led a contingent of British troops into Jerusalem, marking a seminal moment in the changing fortunes of the region. As the First World War neared a close events quickly unfolded, with the Ottoman Empire one of the old dynasties soon to disappear and with the map of the conflict areas redrawn. France and Britain both saw opportunities to pick over the remains, with the latter quickly securing its hold on Palestine, which it then ruled for the next thirty years under a Mandate arrangement brokered by the League of Nations.[17] As it transpired, however, the acquisition of this particular territory proved to be something of a poisoned chalice.

Emotionally, the idea of adding the Holy Land to the already expansive British Empire was of enormous popular appeal; this was not just another place on the world map but the land of the Bible, the birthplace of both Judaism and Christianity. The very names of Bethlehem, Nazareth and, of course, Jerusalem, the golden city, had a magical ring about them in the West. Since early times, though, it had been a troubled land, overrun repeatedly and at different times coveted by a ring of neighbouring powers: Turkey and Syria to the north, Persia to the east and Egypt to the south-west. Most of the original tribes of Israel had long departed from the region in an historic diaspora, leaving Palestine predominantly an Arab land. It was a rugged, arid landscape, tailing into desert in the south, and without the River Jordan it would have been largely uninhabitable. The real problem, though, that beset the area, then and since, was one of international politics. During the First World War conflicting promises were made to both Arabs and Jews. For the former, inspired by the efforts of Colonel T.E. Lawrence, the British, in exchange for Arab support during the war, lent their name to the idea of a pan-Arab nation that would extend over much of the Middle East. Shortly after that pledge, the then British Foreign Secretary, Lord Balfour, in 1917 issued an historic declaration that expressed his Government's support for the eventual formation of a Jewish homeland in Palestine, while at the same time acknowledging the continuing rights of existing Arab communities to the land in question. In a further attempt to appease all parties, the disputed territory was to be divided between Palestine (west of the Jordan) and the much larger area known as Trans-Jordan, to the east of the river. It was always intended that the latter would be excluded from any plans for a Jewish homeland. For the next three decades, the region was governed on this dual and highly precarious basis, on a collision course between newly aroused Arab nationalism and the Zionist movement with its single-minded mission to secure a Jewish homeland in Palestine ('Eretz Israel').

Although it was only a small colony in their much larger domain, the British were quick to recognize the future importance of Haifa to their plans for the region. In spite of the populist message of protecting the holy city of Jerusalem and other cherished sites, the real lure of Palestine had more to do with a perennial power struggle. Apart from keeping out the French, with their own designs on the Levant, Palestine was an important stepping stone into the Asian interior and a further means of securing vital routes to India. Haifa, especially, was seen as a useful industrial port that could be linked by a pipeline to the vast, and then largely untapped, oil resources of Iraq. One confident assertion during the Mandate period was that Haifa was 'likely to develop faster than any other town in Palestine';[18] another was that 'Haifa has a promising future. It is a natural gateway for the exchange of goods and ideas between East and West.'[19] As a show of confidence, the British took prompt action to strengthen rail links with the rest of the region; as early as 1918 the existing line from Damascus to Haifa was extended to complete a direct route to Egypt and the Suez Canal. It took nearly ten years, though, to agree a plan to further modernize the harbour, which in the last days of the Ottoman era had been allowed to fall behind its competitors.

In spite of this kind of commitment, British rule was later to end in tears, in the face of militant opposition by Zionists impatient to see the formation of their awaited nation state and of Arab resistance to the new settlers. Until then, Haifa itself had good reason to see the years of the Mandate as a time when it was well governed, with a sound basis laid for its economic future. Attention was paid from the outset to its physical planning, although the approach was somewhat disjointed and shared between different bodies.[20] At a strategic level, the policy-makers in London were keen to ensure that Haifa performed the role that was cast for it—as the major port for Palestine (in preference to Jaffa, to the south of the country) and as a vital link to the interior. To serve these ends, improvements to the city's infrastructure— especially the railway and harbour, and new oil refineries—were at the top of the list. At a different level, the Palestine Administration based in Jerusalem was concerned to set standards for the whole of their area of responsibility, and basic procedures were introduced to promote good planning in the various municipalities. The Administration also took the step of appointing the English Arts and Crafts architect, C.R. Ashbee, as Civic Adviser for planning in the mandated territory as a whole. Ashbee, something of a maverick who had formerly instigated a progressive community of craftsmen and their families in his own country, might seem now an odd choice, but there were few enough individual planners of note at that time and he had already served in similar posts in both Egypt and Jerusalem.[21]

Meanwhile, the various Zionist organizations in this same period focused attention on particular development schemes. Even before the Balfour Declaration, Jewish sponsors had been quietly buying land from Arab owners and now the pace quickened. Zionist leaders recognized the importance of planning and, when it came to an especially prestigious project—the proposed Hebrew University in Jerusalem—they were determined to get a 'first class man' on board.

The upper slopes of Mount Carmel were favoured by garden city planners, with views of the rest of the city below.

Their choice was a contemporary of Ashbee, and in his own way another maverick, Patrick Geddes.[22] He was at the time, in 1919, on his way to a university post in India but was unable to resist the chance to make his own mark on such hallowed ground. In the event, his brief was extended to include advice on Haifa as well. Jerusalem would always be a favoured location for the development of key institutions but, partly because of the attention drawn to it by Herzl, Haifa was also very much in the sights of the Zionists. At first, an early interest in urban development might seem at odds with the Zionist philosophy of settling in small colonies on the land. It was recognized, though, that there would always be a need for an industrial port, with Haifa best placed to perform that role. In any case, it was not impossible to envision urban growth while at the same time keeping a balance with the countryside, and one way to reconcile the different objectives, it was decided, was through the garden city.

It is significant that two important centres for Zionist activity were England and Germany, where, in both countries, the garden city was then very much in vogue. In England, in 1898, Ebenezer Howard published his blueprint for garden cities, *To-Morrow: A Peaceful Path to Real Reform*; while in Germany important steps had been made even before then to regulate urban land use and to promote a garden city type of development. Planners from each country travelled to see for themselves the achievements of their counterparts, the English parties visiting schemes like Hellerau and Margarethenhöhe and the German groups to the likes of Letchworth and, later, Welwyn. For the Zionists, who were aware of these achievements, it was a question of choosing the best people from both countries to prepare plans for chosen parts of Haifa, particularly the middle and upper slopes of Mount Carmel. Geddes was duly invited to present his own ideas for these areas. Taking account of a scatter of existing development on the middle slopes, he proposed a form of settlement that has been described as 'somewhere between garden suburb and garden city';[23] Geddes himself dubbed it 'the Garden Village of the Polytechnicum'.[24] On the top slopes where he was less constrained, Geddes was in his element, admiring the grand views across the bay and the native vegetation that had to be protected; for this exceptional location his vision was for a string of garden villages, ideally, connected to the city below by cable car. In a remarkable foretaste of New Urbanism (which emerged some sixty years later), Geddes decried layouts that were determined by roads and argued that 'the garden village planner settles for narrow streets, even pedestrian footpaths as shortcuts'.[25] It was not Geddes, though, but a young German-Jewish architect, Richard Kauffmann, who was responsible for most of the detailed designs that followed in the 1920s.[26]

Beyond Carmel, the Zionists were keen to shape a future for the whole length of the coastal plain that extended around the bay as far north as Acre. Kauffmann came down from the slopes of Mount Carmel to prepare what amounted to a regional plan for this stretch of land, attempting to balance the competing need for a complex of refineries and oil storage with a parkland setting for residential areas. The proper development of the bay was seen as critical to the future of the Jewish homeland but it proved to be difficult to win agreement.

Against a background of debate and uncertainties, once again the Zionists opted to bring in a big name, this time the renowned English planner, Patrick Abercrombie. If both Ashbee and Geddes had a sense of the unconventional about them, the same was not true of Abercrombie, an establishment figure through and through. He was at that time, 1929, Professor of Civic Design at Liverpool University, founder member of the Council for the Preservation of Rural England, and an early proponent of regional planning. Abercrombie warmed to the challenge of contributing to the transformation of 'the oldest country into the newest'[27] and knew how to captivate his paymasters: 'Haifa appears to have a future before it somewhat similar to that of Liverpool as the outlet for an industrial hinterland.'[28] In a later writing he spoke of Haifa as one of the world's emergent cities that would one day become a great Mediterranean port, rivalling even Marseille. 'At length, freed from the paralysing hand of the Old Turk, Palestine becomes the meeting point of East and West and Haifa the commercial centre of the country.'[29]

From the outset of Zionist occupation, the harbour and adjacent industries have been at the heart of the local economy.

Abercrombie's plan was not approved until 1938, by which time the city had already expanded well beyond its old boundaries: from a population of some 15,000 at the start of the Mandate to 100,000 in 1938. The change in ethnic composition in the same period was no less dramatic, with the balance shifting from 90% Arab and 10% Jews in 1918 to an equal balance twenty years later. To some extent this was a concerted change, a deliberate goal of the Zionists. Recognizing the importance of Haifa to the proposed Jewish state, its future leader, David Ben-Gurion, worked hard to achieve what was called the 'Judaization of Haifa'.[30]

The outcome was geographical as well as demographic, with each group occupying different parts of the city; the Arabs tended to cluster in the Old City and in tightly-packed housing close to the harbour, while the Jews favoured the slopes of Carmel and new neighbourhoods near the industrial areas. Ringed in this way by Jewish settlement, the Arab population found the situation oppressive.[31]

Increasingly, too, Jewish workers took industrial jobs, often at the expense of Arabs, forming unions to further their own interests and acquiring a reputation for militancy. As a result, the city became known as 'Red Haifa'.[32] Thus, in the course of little more than two decades, Haifa had changed out of all recognition: it was much larger, no longer with an Arab majority, and driven by a more aggressive brand of politics.

'An Episodic City'

Haifa remains as it was, an episodic city, a city of separate areas and neighbourhoods...[33]

In 1939, once again, everything changed. After little more than two decades of peacetime administration and planning for a bold future, Palestine was plunged into the melée of a second world war. There was fighting in the region but it was in Europe that its destiny was really shaped. Through their own actions the Nazi regime in Germany advanced the cause of a Jewish homeland in a way that was never intended. As a direct result of the massacre of six million Jews in concentration camps, the emotional arguments to support the survivors became irresistible and in 1947 the United Nations voted to fulfil the Zionist dream of a Jewish homeland in Palestine. Those who were less drawn by the emotional case could see inevitable problems ahead but their warnings were ignored; in May 1948 the British were forced to withdraw and the State of Israel became a reality.

As the main port of entry, Haifa would play a key role in the early days of the new nation. However, until the period of the Mandate ended, the British, with an eye to future relations with the rest of the Middle East, had resolutely refused to allow unrestricted Jewish immigration. In human terms, for most of the world the policy was deeply unpopular; in darkened cinemas in Europe and America, audiences saw newsreel pictures of overloaded, rusting ships crowded with destitute migrants on deck looking anxiously towards their Promised Land, from which in the last minutes of their journey they were turned back. One effect of British policy was for those Jewish settlers already in Palestine to organize themselves into terrorist groups, putting pressure on their colonial rulers to relent. In the event, it took the formal establishment of Israel before free immigration was allowed, although by then the Arabs within the country and in neighbouring states had pledged to destroy the new nation at birth. At the very time of its inception Israel was invaded, this war being just the first in a series of interventions, coupled with regular outbreaks of internal terrorism and political instability across the region.

Haifa's post-1948 history mirrors that of the nation as a whole, a time when its people were determined to make a success of the venture yet one of constant uncertainties. The early years of nationhood in the city were marked by considerable disruption, with a majority of resident Arabs, in the face of hostilities and the threat of more, leaving to cross the border into Lebanon. Fewer than 5000 remained, of an

Arab population that once totalled 70,000[34] — to be replaced by new arrivals from war-torn Europe. Most of the Arabs had lived in the Old City, which the authorities now used for emergency housing for incomers before progressively demolishing most traces of the former world. The observation that 'a visitor [today] would be hard pressed to unearth the remnants of Arab Haifa, its churches, mosques, cemeteries, market places and even its streets' is broadly true as well as poignant.[35]

Former Arab neighbourhoods have sometimes been overwhelmed by surrounding development.

Additionally, oil no longer flowed along the pipeline from Iraq, and the hinterland of the port was drastically diminished in other ways too as all around Israel borders were closed. This was to have a lasting impact, with Haifa, once the centre of a large region, now on the edge of a nation where the political focus was shifting more to Tel Aviv and Jerusalem. For the socialist municipal government in Haifa the problems were stark. The city's workers were dependent for their jobs on the port, and on the associated oil refineries and petro-chemical production; now there were doubts whether even pre-1948 levels could be sustained. Moreover, although many Arab workers had left the city their number was more than matched by a constant stream of Jewish incomers, most of whom were in any case unused to this kind of work. Jobs had to be found and so, too, did housing. Temporary camps were set up and these were followed by permanent apartment blocks and new factories. The finer points of the interwar plans were quickly forgotten and new development was often of a poor quality and no more than utilitarian. Only later, when the economy had stabilized, was serious thought given to questions of aesthetics and environment but by then the situation was in many parts of the city too late to recover.

In spite of the best hopes of garden city planners, much of Mount Carmel is now the scene of high-rise development.

Haifa today tells a mixed story, a city blessed by the presence of Mount Carmel and the expansive bay but also one where much of its development is, at best, mundane. It offers something of a patchwork rather than a unified entity, 'a city where the sense of the part is always much greater than the perception of the whole.'[36]

Amongst its favoured locations one can point to the conservation and revitalization of historic areas like the German Colony, where most of the houses (often in a poor state of repair from the time the colonists were expelled by the British during the Second World War because of suspected Nazi sympathies) have quite recently been refurbished. Additionally, the main street of the old colony (now known as Ben Gurion Avenue) has been the subject of a facelift in other ways too, with a renewal of street furniture and surface materials. The result has been the emergence of an avenue of popular restaurants and bars, attracting a hedonistic lifestyle that stands in stark contrast to the piety of the original settlers.

On the upper slopes of Mount Carmel, where British and German planners had visions of a Mediterranean garden city, it is private wealth that has secured the attractive environment. Spacious houses and gardens enjoy the breezes and scent of pine from the remaining forests, coupled with magnificent views, in what is ostensibly a garden suburb rather than a garden city setting. In the neighbourhood shopping centres of Carmel, fashionable boutiques are interspersed with cafés, where tables spill onto the pavements under brightly flowering trees.

The effects of planning are no more than regulatory, preventing excesses to spoil the idyll, but for those who can afford it the Carmel suburbs offer most of what the earlier planners would have envisaged.

Elsewhere, Haifa has the hallmarks of a working city, built (as it had to be) in a rush and where the imperative was for new housing and industrial units at any cost. Together with outlying settlements, Haifa now has a population of some 600,000. Particularly to the north of the downtown area, in the direction of Acre, the hillside is scarred with clusters of inelegant tower blocks and even Haifa's main university has been allowed to break the skyline. Similarly, the coastal plain is marked by a seemingly unplanned ribbon of factories and warehouses, with few places where one can gain access to the waterfront. Gradually, as less space is needed for the docks and associated industries, sites will be released for more varied uses; one example is an area that has been designated for Haifa's university port campus, as yet only in the early stages of renewal.

In spite of its spectacular location Haifa is not, in the main, a beautiful city. It might become more so in the future with a measured pace of redevelopment although much will depend on the wider political setting. Likewise, in spite of its Levantine location its population no longer reflects the diversity of the region. In some ways, Haifa looks and feels more like a city from the old Soviet bloc—a resemblance that is strengthened by the presence of so many with family roots in that part of the world[37]—than an expression of the eastern Mediterranean. It has a powerful presence but is somehow one-dimensional, a city with a purpose but in its endeavour to succeed perhaps too single-minded.

During the war with Lebanon in 2006, parts of Haifa itself were bombed, a reminder of the fragility of the political situation and its proximity to a neighbouring country that refuses to recognize Israel. There are many fundamental issues to settle before Haifa can even begin to realize the kind of potential that the Ottomans, Zionists and British have all in the past envisaged. The potential is still there to create a more significant and truly multi-cultural Mediterranean city but, without dramatic changes to its geopolitical context, such a vision remains as distant and illusory as ever.

CHAPTER 5

SHORES OF THE SAHARA

The North African shoreline is very different from its European counterpart, with relatively few indentations and nothing like as many natural harbours. Although it was once more mixed, culturally it has become more uniform, now essentially Arabic and Muslim. To differing degrees, the nations on this side of the Mediterranean are economically less prosperous that those to the north, fiercely nationalistic and politically new to democracy. In most cases, too, they are characterized by a rapidly growing population, resulting in high proportions of young people, many without adequate employment. To add to the challenge of modern development, there is an inherent shortage of water in a region with sparse rainfall, and in places the Sahara Desert itself reaches to the sea.

It is along this stretch of the Mediterranean that in early 2011 popular protests quickly led to the so-called Arab Spring. Three nations—Egypt, Libya and Tunisia—were quickly embroiled in the political *melée* and in each country their long-serving dictators were forced to relinquish power. The stories of the three cities that were visited shortly before these changes bring past and present into close juxtaposition.

Alexandria, the second city of Egypt, is now a world apart from its glorious past. Twice in its very long history it has been a truly international centre, once as a capital of the classical world and, more recently, a cosmopolitan city to rival its Levantine neighbours. Over the past six decades it has grown at an exponential rate into a modern metropolis yet as a vibrant cultural centre it has, at the same time, regressed. Alexandria is now but a pale shadow of its former self.

In the west of neighbouring Libya is Tripoli, a city with its own long history and an especially fascinating story to tell of more recent times. Muammar Gaddafi ruled the country with an iron hand for more than four decades, until falling victim to the popular uprisings of the Arab Spring. In spite of its very long history, it has never been one of the great cities of the Mediterranean, and it remains to be seen whether a new democratic system can inject fresh life into it.

Finally, for most of its early history in the shadows of nearby Carthage, Tunis has emerged in its own right as a modern North African city. While the latter has grown and prospered, the site of Carthage itself is now no more than a coastal suburb. In a carefully managed change of fortune, the city has thrown off its colonial mantle—it was until the middle of the last century the capital of the French colony of Tunisia—to become a major point of contact with the West. As the latest twist in its long history following provincial unrest, it was on the streets of Tunis that the protests of 2011 led to the first changes of the Arab Spring.

ALEXANDRIA

Fervent advocates of Alexandria rank the classical city above even Athens and Rome as the true birthplace of modern civilization. It certainly has a glittering history and was for a time, without question, the largest and most richly endowed city in the world. No expense was spared in its heyday to make it the uncrowned monarch of the Mediterranean. Those glorious days have, however, long gone in the wake of a seemingly inexorable process of decline. In spite of its present size—it has a population of more than four million and in modern Egypt is second only to Cairo— it is hard to reconcile the present with its legendary past. Few places can more vividly illustrate that nothing is permanent, that seemingly solid foundations may quickly crumble. Nor is this just a matter of material decay; Alexandria is yet another Mediterranean city where a colourful tradition of cosmopolitanism and tolerance of difference has given way to the louder voices of nationalism and religious purity. Modernity has cast a pall of sameness over an exceptional place that was once a byword for diversity in all its forms.

The Rise and Rise of Alexandria

Few cities have made so magnificent an entry into history as Alexandria.[1]

E.M. Forster was one of a number of Westerners who retained fond memories of Alexandria; while he was there, working for the Red Cross during and immediately after the First World War, he wrote of its seductive charms.[2] As the opening quote in this section suggests, he found the story of the city's classical past compelling but, no less, he enjoyed the cosmopolitanism (verging on bohemianism) of his everyday experience when he mixed in a stimulating literary circle. Like anyone who traces the short but exceptional life of Alexander the Great, Forster could not but be impressed by the story of the young ruler, who left his native Macedonia in his twenties on a course of military campaigns that would take him ultimately to Afghanistan and India. Egypt was acquired along the way and, intrigued by its pivotal position between the known Hellenic world and the largely unknown Orient, he determined to create a city that would have no equal. The outcome of his ambition and impulsiveness was Alexandria.

Like the outstanding soldier he was, Alexander knew the importance of choosing his ground well, whether for battle or for city-building. Apart from its strategic location in the eastern Mediterranean, the natural features of his preferred site seemed ideal. Positioned just to the north-west of the Nile Delta, he liked, especially, the presence of a limestone outcrop extending into the sea that would serve well to lay sound foundations, with a protective island just beyond. Fresh winds blew inland, making it healthier and more amenable than cities in the sultry Egyptian interior. Through the construction of a causeway to the island (Ras-el-Tin, later to be known as Pharos) two deepwater harbours could be created, one on either side, leaving a freshwater lake between the city and the Delta. When Alexander paced the barren shoreline in 332 BC the area was largely deserted. There had once been a small Bronze Age settlement, Rhakotis, but this had by then largely disappeared. The site was, effectively, a clean slate and offered a golden opportunity for Alexander's chosen architect, Dinocrates of Rhodes, to fulfil the extravagant vision of his master. Ironically, Alexander himself was soon to leave, to meet the Persians in battle, and was never to see even the first buildings before his untimely death at the age of 32. The city named after him, and where he was later to be buried, was, however, everything and more that Alexander could have envisaged.

Statue of Alexander, founder of the city.

Although Alexander hailed from Macedonia his mission was to spread to the rest of the world the finest qualities of Hellenic culture, and he knew that in Dinocrates a design would be prepared in the best traditions of Greek town planning. Dinocrates himself followed in the footsteps of Hippodamus, acknowledged by Aristotle in the previous century as the greatest authority of 'the art of laying out towns'.[3] Although examples of gridiron planning pre-date Hippodamus, he is rightly accredited for popularizing and refining its application.

The basic idea of gridiron planning is really very simple, seen by the Greeks as a device to incorporate the various components of the polis and then to replicate them easily from one location to another. As a means of advancing the cause of colonization it was invaluable, enabling the whole complex of Greek political and cultural life to be transferred from one place to another in an orderly and consistent fashion. So it was, in this tradition, that Dinocrates and his surveyors marked out on the ground appropriate sites for the agora and temples, theatre and gymnasium, government offices and fortifications—essential building blocks for a new metropolis by the sea.

View from the mainland towards the former island of Pharos.

Alexander's early death did nothing to halt progress and the ensuing dynasty of Ptolemaic rulers in Egypt, dating from 323 BC, initially carried forward the torch with no less enthusiasm. Within its first hundred years, Alexandria could boast not simply the usual landmarks of a Hellenic city but structures and cultural activities that were immediately a source of wonder. The causeway that Alexander had earlier anticipated was itself a triumph of engineering, a massive construction some 200 metres in width and seven times the length of a Greek stadium (hence known as the heptastadion); at either end it was cut and bridged to allow shipping to pass between the two harbours. Into these sheltered waters was brought cargo from the whole of the then known world: from the African continent and the Asian interior, from the nearby Levant and across the Mediterranean from the European mainland, along inland waterways from the Nile Valley itself and by way of the Red Sea from India. Dominating the skyline and safeguarding navigation was a formidable lighthouse, the Pharos (on the island of that name), 130 metres high, used for defence as well as to guide shipping along the low coastline and around the offshore sandbanks. It was built with granite and limestone blocks, faced with white marble, and crowned with a bronze statue of Poseidon. The light itself was reflected from a giant, parabolic reflector of polished brass, set against the sun in the day and lit by a bonfire within the tower at night. Pharos famously became one of the seven wonders of the Ancient World.

Classical remains are limited in extent and surrounded by modern buildings.

Elsewhere, within the city there was a royal precinct with palaces and centres of government; a giant mausoleum to meet the extravagant needs of the rulers' after-life; the temple of Serapis, which was to inspire a common cult of worship; a racecourse and a theatre; and, most significant of all, the intellectual powerhouse of Alexandria, the Mouseion. The latter was based on the Athenian Mouseion but on a much larger scale to house laboratories and lecture halls, observatories and shaded courtyards, a park and a zoo; at the heart of it all was the famous Library, reputed to include everything that had previously been published in the ancient world. Alexandria, it has been said, was built on knowledge rather than stone, luring scholars from around the Mediterranean and beyond to exchange and advance ideas:

> *Egyptians. Greeks, Jews, Babylonians, Persians, Gauls, Phoenicians and Romans flocked here, stimulating huge advances in mathematics, astronomy and astrology, alchemy, optics, medicine and anatomy, grammar, geography, philosophy and theology.*[4]

Alexandria in its heyday was a revelation, 'more Greek than Greece [itself]... brand new, gleaming white, a calculated marvel of marble.'[5] The city was large enough to be broken into districts, and as well as the royal quarter there were separate residential areas for Egyptians, Jews and Greeks, and later for newcomers from further afield. Local thoroughfares were linked to a processional avenue, Canopic Street, more than thirty metres wide and six kilometres long (the entire length of the promontory); along its course on either side were impressive colonnades offering shade as well as a sense of enclosure. In these various ways, most of the city took shape during Alexander's lifetime (albeit in his absence) and under the direction of the first three rulers of the subsequent Ptolemaic dynasty. As time went on, the energy of the endeavour began to wane and, left in the hands of a succession of less competent kings, the prized city became increasingly vulnerable to the ambitions of the ascendant Romans. In an endeavour to retain Egyptian autonomy an uneven alliance was struck with the potential aggressors; the terms offered a period of respite although, inexorably, the power of Alexandria declined while that of Rome increased. In a final attempt to stop a complete surrender, the last and only female ruler of the dynasty, Queen Cleopatra, famously used her personal charms to encourage rifts between the Roman leaders themselves. The plan only partly worked and in spite of a legendary web of romance, subterfuge, suicide and murder, the dynasty came to an end in 30 BC, with Alexandria reduced to the status of capital of a Roman province. Cleopatra's material legacy was confined to the Caesareum, a temple intended to honour Julius Caesar (but completed after her death by Augustus, and dedicated to him instead). It was later flanked by two lofty obelisks, subsequently known as Cleopatra's Needles.[6]

In spite of its reduced political status, Alexandria as a large city in the eastern Mediterranean continued to flourish for several more centuries; its major institutions of scholarship and culture still functioned and the twin harbours remained at the heart of its busy trade. Even during the period of Cleopatra's dealings with Rome the population stood at the extraordinary figure of around one million.[7] It fared less well, however, as a spiritual haven and the coming centuries were marked by sharpening divisions on religious grounds.

Until the Emperor Constantine's conversion to Christianity, the followers of Christ suffered repeated bouts of persecution at the hands of the Romans. When this finally abated, the Christians turned in on themselves, establishing rival sects based on an Egyptian brand of the faith (the Copts) and those who looked instead to Greek Orthodoxy; and when they were not struggling with each other the Christians combined to persecute the city's pagans. Into the mix, too, came the Jews, who saw from an early date the importance of Alexandria as a trading centre, not only within the Mediterranean but also through Egypt's inland waterways to the Red Sea and beyond.

Religious differences between the various groups distracted the city from a growing need to maintain its all-important defences and, with the decline of the Roman Empire and the protection it once afforded the city, Alexandria became dangerously exposed to Arab armies from the east, the vanguard of Islam. In 641 the inevitable happened and Alexandria fell to the conquering force; a message was duly sent by the victorious general to the Caliph in Arabia: 'I have taken a city of which I can only say that it contains 4000 palaces, 4000 baths, 400 theatres, 1200 greengrocers and 40,000 Jews'.[8] Undoubtedly exaggerated and strangely selective, the message was at least indicative of the reaction that here indeed was an exceptional place. It was, indeed, exceptional but that would soon change; the golden days of classical Alexandria were already by then largely over.

In contrast to more tolerant times, churches now have to be closely guarded.

'This City Will Follow You'

You will find no new land; you will find no other seas. This city will follow you.[9]

For all their admiration of Alexandria at the time of its conquest (even in its diminished state), the new Arab rulers chose instead the inland site of Cairo for their Egyptian capital. Alexandria was left largely as they found it although natural catastrophes before and after their arrival—a destructive tidal wave in the fourth century, periodic earthquakes, coastal subsidence and silting of the freshwater lake and inland waterways—together with the effects of time itself took their cumulative toll. Progressively, the city's unrivalled reputation became a distant memory, the vigour of its intellectual life gone and the prestigious buildings crumbling into unrecognizable mounds of sand and mud. Many centuries later, it took a spirited romantic, Emperor Napoleon, to visualize just what had been lost and to recall its glorious past; on his ill-fated Egyptian campaign at the end of the eighteenth century it seemed to him that to capture Alexandria would be to recover the very soul of Western civilization. By then the number of people living in the city had fallen to little more than 4000. Napoleon had high hopes of bringing it all back to life but his quest proved to be shortlived, with the British fleet soon ousting the French adventurers. The British proved to be of an altogether less romantic bent, causing irreparable damage to what was left of the old city in its re-conquest and, also, in a later episode in quelling the first rumblings of Egyptian nationalism.[10] The destruction resulting from these interventions sealed conclusively the fate of a long period of physical and cultural decline. Alexandria would never again recover the glories of its classical past.

The rebirth of Alexandria as a modern city dates from the middle of the nineteenth century.

Cities, however, have a life of their own and it was to be another military strategist from Macedonia (albeit this time an Albanian by birth), Mohammed Ali, who, like Alexander long before, saw the potential of the coastal site. Fighting for the Ottomans in the early nineteenth century, Mohammed Ali won favour with the rulers in Constantinople for defeating the troublesome Mamluks. With the title of pasha, he soon turned his attention to ways of rebuilding Alexandria; without an efficient Mediterranean port, he argued, the world would continue to pass Egypt by. With the help of French engineers, a new canal was excavated to restore access to the natural waterways of the Nile and to bring to the city once again a supply of fresh water, while modern docks were installed to revive trade across the sea. Foreigners were once more given privileged status to encourage them to live and invest in the city. The momentum was started and, later in the nineteenth century, under successive Ottoman governors (and the impetus of a reform programme emanating from the Tanzimat Edict of 1839)[11] a new city arose from the dust of the old. Wealthy patrons were free to instruct their own architects—some Egyptian, some European—to build in whatever style took their fancy: neo-classical and neo-pharaonic, neo-Byzantine and Art Deco, sometimes even combined in a single building looking both to the past and future. Little thought was given to the few remaining historical features, and a largely new street pattern was introduced piecemeal without the careful planning that had accompanied the original work of Dinocrates and his successors. E.M Forster viewed the outcome philosophically: 'It does not compare favourably with the city of Alexander the Great. On the other hand it is no worse than most nineteenth-century cities.'[12]

As well as emotional grounds for encouraging Alexandria's renaissance there were also sound economic reasons. A flourishing trade in good-quality cotton was itself enough to lure foreign merchants and manufacturers to this long-forgotten city. Throughout the nineteenth century its population grew rapidly, reaching 180,000 in 1860 and rising to more than half a million in the 1920s. Its renewed prosperity attracted labourers and aspiring professionals from across Egypt and from neighbouring countries in the Levant, as well as giving rise to lively communities of Armenians and Jews. Elsewhere, foreigners from Greece and Italy, and from France and Britain, made Alexandria their home, congregating generally in distinct European quarters. 'I know a city that everyday fills to the brim with sunlight, and in that instant everything is enchanted', wrote the Italian poet Giuseppe Ungaretti, offering one good reason why it became such a favoured venue.[13] Forster, who knew that it was certainly not the hallowed place it had once been also lauded Alexandria's 'perfect climate'.[14] The cooling winds across the sea certainly made it more amenable to foreigners than, say, Cairo, but that was not the real reason why they settled there.

For the businessmen and their families the irresistible lure was the money that could be made at one of the world's busiest crossroads. It became more, however, than a material mecca and for the likes of Forster what appealed most was the city's relaxed and cosmopolitan ambience. Until at least the end of the Second World War it was the kind of place where Europeans could find a quiet corner of a disappearing world. It offered an alluring mix of Oriental fantasy, of outlets for sexual mores not so easily practiced in Europe, and a luxuriant lifestyle enjoyed by colonists. The Mediterranean as a whole has proved, especially, a magnet for writers and artists, for *habitués* of cafe society, for bohemianism in a balmy climate, and for a time few places were more conducive to the flowering of artistic culture than Alexandria.

A succession of visiting writers passed judgement on what they saw. In the middle of the nineteenth century, Gustave Flaubert made a brief visit and even then his impression was that Alexandria was 'almost European, there are so many Europeans here… everywhere is full of English, Italians, etc.'[15]

Flaubert saved most of his observations on Egypt for Cairo and the classical sites, although a fellow Frenchman who visited Alexandria two years later deplored the disappearance of so many ancient monuments: it offered no more than 'a prospect of ruins and low mounds, a few scattered tombs on an ashen soil'.[16] Most of the tangible remains of its classical past had, indeed, disappeared but later writers contented themselves with its enduring spirit, moved by the fact that they trod the very ground ennobled, first by Alexander and then the intellectual giants of the classical age. Constantine Cavafy was born in the city in 1863 and his poems recall not just enduring historical themes but also a sense of pride in its former achievements: 'This city is the teacher, the crown of all Hellas, wisest in every subject and every art.'[17]

Alexandria was his home although he came from a Greek family and spoke only that language (at a time when French, not Greek, was the *lingua franca* in the higher echelons of society). When E.M. Forster arrived in 1915 he was immediately taken by the force of Cavafy's poetry and ensured it was soon known more widely in the English-speaking world. Although Forster's first impressions of the city were ambivalent, he slotted easily into its life—invisible at times when he found his way into a homosexual world denied him in middle-class England, but also making an impact in the glittering salons of polite society. The war got in the way of some of the normal routines but in 1916 Forster could write quite happily to Virginia Woolf, telling her that 'in Alexandria it still seems possible to read books and bathe'.[18] In its vivacity it was as if the Levant, where European influences were mixed with indigenous Arab, had been extended those few extra miles westwards across the mouth of the Nile, a stretch of coastline 'so small in area, yet first and last it has produced so much that is good'.[19]

Developed in the 1930s as a modern bathing resort, Stanley Bay is now a relic of a past era, largely cut off from the sea by a busy road.

Forster's sensitive appraisal and experience of Alexandria was not necessarily matched by a subsequent generation of foreign residents, seduced in the interwar years not least of it all by the social whirl of garden parties and exotic balls in some of the great houses, gala performances by international theatre companies and the excitement of polo tournaments and sailing regattas. An impressionable young American wrote to her mother in Memphis, Tennessee, describing:

> *Great tall palm trees and arabs [sic]—thousands of arabs in long great robes that look like shirts and red fezzes. There are the most wonderful street noises, birds chirping and cries—they sound like the negroes selling fruit at home and yet they are long drawn out and of course in Arabic. It's so hard to remember the servants are Arabic and not negro...*[20]

Later she tells how they were taken to the desert in open-top motor cars:

> *miles from civilization... There were eighteen people for lunch—ten nationalities! We had shrimp, chicken, wines, the most delicious dessert you've ever tasted... We got home about five o'clock and then Johnny and I had to dash off to a cocktail party on a British warship. Doesn't that sound exciting?*[21]

When the 'long weekend' of the inter-war years ended, the initial reaction was that the new conflict of nations might well pass Alexandria by, a naïve response soon discredited by the presence of Italian troops in neighbouring Libya and the more effective threat of General Rommel and his desert forces. At one point, the latter were camped just sixty miles from the city and its future was very much in the balance. If only as a staging post, however, Egypt still offered something of a sanctuary for foreign exiles from more vulnerable locations in southern Europe; with the Nazis advancing rapidly through Greece, ships were commissioned to carry stranded groups of Europeans to the welcoming port of Alexandria. Amongst one boatload in 1941 was the young writer, Lawrence Durrell, and his family who had previously been living in Corfu. Durrell's wife and daughter were immediately moved to Cairo but the author stayed in Alexandria, soon to assume a post to provide information to the Egyptian press. The significance of his residence was not what he did to help the war effort in that part of the world but the observations he made of the city and its characters, subsequently immortalized in the only partly fictional volumes comprising *The Alexandria Quartet*.

The Alexandria of Durrell's quartet was a city that bore the imprint of the tangled relationships that flourished in the steamy atmosphere like exotic plants in a hothouse: 'a city that is at once princess and whore... the royal city and the *anus mundi*. She would never change so long as the races continued to seethe here like must in a vat.'[22] In the four books, the reader is led, in turn, through the dense alleyways of the indigenous neighbourhoods and into the sumptuous villas of foreign dynasties, contrasting worlds largely unknown to each other.

It was for most of its people a city of 'a thousand dust-tormented streets':[23]

> *streets that run back from the docks with their tattered rotten supercargo of houses, breathing into each others' mouths, keeling over. Shuttered balconies teeming with rats... The smell of the sweat-lathered Berberinis, like that of some decomposing stair-carpet. And then the street noises: the shriek and bang of the water-bearing Saidi, dashing his metal cups together...*[24]

Just a short distance away from these teeming alleys was the Grande Corniche, 'the magnificent long sea-parade which frames the modern city, the Hellenistic capital of the bankers and cotton-visionaries—all those European bagmen whose enterprise had re-ignited and ratified Alexander's dream of conquest after the centuries of dust and silence...'[25] From the previous century, these 'bagmen' had been returning to the Egyptian shoreline: to make their fortune, to find freedoms denied them at home, and to engage in battles against one imperial force or another. Little seemed to have changed by the time of the Second World War, and yet within a few short years the whole political order was about to be overturned. For Alexandria, as for the country as a whole, a new era was about to begin.

'Scarcely a City of the Soul'

Modern Alexandria is scarcely a city of the soul.[26]

Forster's above dismissal of modern Alexandria was based on an earlier version of modernity. He went on at the time to attribute its economic foundation to little more than cotton, onions and eggs, and he described the modern city as 'ill built, ill planned, ill drained'.[27] If he thought of it then as 'scarcely a city of the soul', without doubt his language to describe it now would be more intemperate; to the modern observer it is, indeed, a soulless place. This is not just a result of its phenomenal rate of growth, from a population little more than 800,000 just half a century ago to a sprawling metropolis of more than four million. Undoubtedly, what would have most concerned the likes of Forster is the obvious loss of its once vibrant cosmopolitanism. Alexandria illustrates as starkly as any of the region's cities a marked trend in favour of a dominant ethnic and religious culture. There were times when a ship could dock at any Mediterranean port and find on the quayside a medley of peoples from the three adjoining continents, all speaking their own language, and on the skyline the intricate shapes of magnificent cathedrals alongside the shining domes of mosques. That is no longer the Mediterranean norm: as Paul Theroux concluded towards the end of his own littoral journey, 'the great multiracial stewpot of the Mediterranean had been replaced by cities that were physically larger, but smaller-minded'.[28]

Alexandria's break with its own past had been brewing for some time but when it finally came it was sudden and dramatic. Under the banner of nationalism, power was seized in 1952 by a group of army officers, from which Lieutenant-Colonel

Gamal Abdel Nasser emerged as leader. The unpopular monarch, King Farouk, was promptly exiled, leaving an uneasy arrangement with the British (whose remaining concern was to maintain safe passage through the Suez Canal). When, four years later, Nasser announced the nationalization of the canal, the British, French and Israelis intervened with military force, only to be restrained by the United States and the Soviet Union. Initially, Alexandria itself was to be the target for intensive bombing but the venue was switched, instead, along the coast to Port Said. In the event, the episode marked a diplomatic triumph for Egypt, one result being that the British, French and Jewish communities (all mainly in Alexandria) were finally forced to leave the country. Nasser's socialist and nationalist policies, strengthened by the Suez debacle, bit deep into remaining foreign interests, and by the early 1960s Greeks, Syrians and Lebanese had also departed. 'It was the end of the foreign communities, and the end of the cosmopolitan city in which Nasser, who spent part of his youth there, had never felt comfortable.'[29] Alexandria would never be the same again, its colourful traditions replaced by a single, Islamic culture and Egyptian aspirations. Durrell's world where 'communities still live and communicate—Turks and Jews, Arabs and Copts and Syrians with Armenians and Italians and Greeks'[30] now belong to a romanticized past.

The ensuing years in Alexandria, since the Nasser regime, reflect the path followed by Egypt as a whole.[31] Although the more extreme nationalist and socialist policies favoured by Nasser were reined back, the country was until recently led firmly from the centre, first by Anwar Sadat and then Hosni Mubarak. One of Nasser's first decisions was to centralize all of the government departments in Cairo, at the expense of Alexandria with its obvious Mediterranean outlook. It was a sign, according to one observer, that 'Egypt had turned inland, both literally and metaphorically'.[32] Nasser was popular but there is little evidence that he or his autocratic successors improved the lot of their people. Instead, over nearly six decades, the country experienced relative economic decline coupled with an unsustainable rate of population growth. Egypt is now the most populous Arab nation but this was not matched by increased material opportunities and progress.

As a result, many of the nation's most talented young professionals and entrepreneurs left the country for good. Moreover, there was less religious harmony than had been formerly commonplace, with the Christian community becoming a smaller segment of Egyptian society and under increasing pressure in the face of Islamic hegemony.[33] Religious extremism was vigorously opposed by the authorities but the influence of Islam became steadily more pervasive. In the 1960s it was uncommon to see a woman in the streets of Alexandria with her head covered, now it is almost universal; moreover, prayer mats are regularly laid on the pavements for men in the crowded markets when the mosques overflow. Bars which once were popular meeting places have now all but disappeared. Following the Arab Spring, the emergence in 2012 of the Muslim Brotherhood as the largest single party raises critical questions of religious tolerance and gender equality.

Along with the rest of the country, Alexandria has grown rapidly in the past half century and around the city are numerous factories and workshops; nearly 40% of jobs are in industry but there is also widespread unemployment, encouraging mainly young men to try to enter Europe in search of work. Tourism has not contributed to the local economy to the extent that is evident elsewhere around the Mediterranean. In spite of its attractive location fronting a broad bay, once so admired by foreigners, Alexandria is not an international tourist destination—remaining primarily a place for Cairenes, who enjoy the cooler temperatures by the sea in the summer months. Meanwhile, the boundaries of the city constantly expand, with new development forcing its way along the coast, extending over some thirty kilometres. Planning has done little to channel these pressures, nor to preserve what little remains of its classical past. It has also been unable to meet the challenge of squatter settlements around the edge, where new migrants gain their first foothold in the metropolis. Bearing in mind its exemplary origins as a planned metropolis, modern attempts to guide its growth have compared poorly. Hassan Abdel-Salam is a professor in Alexandria who has traced the morphological evolution of the city, including the relative influence of land-use planning.[34] He explained that in 1982 a 'comprehensive master plan' was drawn up to address the various problems; nearly thirty years on, there is little or no evidence on the ground to show that it has been effective.

The impressive Biblioteca Alexandria is seen as a focus for cultural revival in the city.

It is not surprising, given Alexandria's phenomenal rate of growth, that recent plans have made such little impact. The city brings to the Mediterranean issues that are evident elsewhere in recently developing countries across the world, where a rapid increase of population is not matched by adequate resources; where global forces come face to face with traditional cultures and impoverished economies. There are other cities in the Levant and North Africa that share these tendencies but not on the scale of Alexandria. Inevitably, in the eye of the storm, one finds currents flowing in different directions, a situation eloquently described by the Egyptian architect and author, Yasser Elsheshtawy, who explores some of the contradictions of the modern Arab city. The term 'Arab city' itself evokes:

> *a multitude of images, preconceptions and stereotypes. At its most elementary it is for many a place filled with mosques and minarets; settings characterized by chaotic, slum-like developments; a haven for terrorists; maze-like alleyways; crowded coffeehouses where people sit idling their time away smoking a nerghile; sensuality hidden behind veils and mashrabiy'yas. But it is also a place of unprecedented development, rising skyscrapers, modern shopping malls, unabashed consumerism. Most importantly, it is a setting where one can observe the tensions of modernity and tradition; religiosity and secularism; exhibitionism and veiling; in short a place of contradictions and paradoxes.*[35]

This anticipated mix of tradition and modernity is certainly evident in contemporary Alexandria, but there are variants too; the fact that it has such a long and exceptional history, coupled with the more immediate impact of nationalism, are no less significant. As a result, there is a complexity about the city that denies easy characterization. Antiquity, tradition, modernity and nationalism all contribute in different ways to its present *persona*. For all that has gone before, antiquity is now a lost treasure. Across the city, one comes across isolated excavations, invariably encircled by noisy traffic and overlooked by tall buildings. In a central location, for instance, are the extensive remains of a Roman amphitheatre, set in what was known in pre-Roman times as the Park of Pan but which is today little more than a dusty site below the surrounding streets. Tourist coaches line up to bring daily visitors but the real treasures from the past are to be found elsewhere, in one of Alexandria's dedicated museums; some of the most precious artefacts in these collections were recovered from the sea, where ancient structures like the Pharos long ago crumbled beneath the waters. For the most, though, this is a city divorced from its ancient past, with names like the Cleopatra tram station and Alexander the Great Street no more than tenuous reminders. Only in the acclaimed Biblioteca Alexandria has an imaginative attempt been made to reconnect the present with its past splendour, the great library of the early city. Located not precisely on the original site but close by, foreign investment (mainly from philanthropic Arab sources) has supported the building of an iconic structure to house a new international collection of books and documents. Claimed by the architects to resemble a second rising sun in the Mediterranean it can only be seen to full effect from the air, to the obvious disadvantage of its terrestrial visitors. In all other respects it represents a wonderful addition to a city that has few enough places of this calibre to celebrate, and it could yet serve to stimulate further sources of cultural revival.

There are still small pockets of the city that the likes of Forster and Cavafy would recognize.

In contrast with antiquity, tradition (mainly Arab and Ottoman) still has its own part to play, albeit now most evident in particular localities. The most vibrant of these is the old Turkish neighbourhood of Anfushi, an area between the two harbours. Here the narrow streets are permanently crowded with stalls and donkey carts, with boys weaving their way around obstacles, balancing trays filled with small glasses of tea for thirsty traders, all viewed by lines of men on chairs along the pavements outside the many coffee shops. In one street the women—their heads covered or, more commonly in these older parts of the city, wearing the full-length *burqah*—go to buy a live chicken or quail, in another they choose from piles of colourful fruit and vegetables brought in from the fertile Delta. Everywhere, stallholders shout to attract attention, car drivers hoot impatiently as they nudge their way through the crowds, and there is the constant sound of hammers on metal and the sawing of wood from rows of dark workshops. At different times of day, one hears the call of *muezzins* (now electronically recorded and amplified) from the minarets and, in response, men often choose to place their prayer mat on a pavement, ignoring in their devotion the continuing life of the street. This remains a world that the likes of Forster and Cavafy would still recognize although it is now typical of just a small part of the modern metropolis.

Yet again, there is another side to Alexandria, a city that has long succumbed to modernity in its various forms. First there were the infrastructural and other improvements introduced by Mohammed Ali early in the nineteenth century, followed over a century later by the investments of European and Levantine companies and wealthy families. During this latter period, modernization ran in parallel with the city's growing prosperity: well-appointed commercial buildings in the centre, sumptuous villas in the eastern suburbs and stylish apartments along the Corniche, grand squares with trees and fountains, and an electric tram system that was equal to any in Europe. Driving it all was the cotton trading that took place in the Bourse, in what was then Alexandria's main square—home to other important buildings too, as well as French-style *patisseries* and fashionable shops selling imported goods. This was a place to meet, a place to be seen, a place to tell the world that here, indeed, was a modern, successful city. Even as late as the 1930s, Alexandria could be described as 'a European style city with its Corniche, gardens, hotels, electrified transport, cinemas and theatres. It was a seaside resort with its sandy beaches, well-appointed cabins and *délicieuses excursions dans les environs*. Alexandria was Nice.'[36]

Varied modes of transport add to the city's traffic problems.

All of that, of course, was swept away by the wave of nationalism that broke on its shores in the late-1950s, with the subsequent departure of the city's foreign population. The achievement of independence undoubtedly engendered a new sense of pride amongst its population, just as the increasing influence of Islam (and a diminishing presence of Christianity) has marked another break with the European era. In economic terms, though, it is widely evident that there has been a heavy price to pay; cotton is no longer king and investment has slowed to a trickle. The dilapidated state of Alexandria's buildings and neglect of its infrastructure are telling indications of this change of fortune.[37] Once fashionable, the main section of the Corniche is now but a faded representation of its past, the former gaiety of a cosmopolitan lifestyle that it once displayed a distant memory. Even the narrow beaches that would formerly have attracted bathers cannot offer respite, degraded as they are by piles of litter washed ashore by the sea. The rest of the European legacy bears similar marks of deterioration, as if, in the half-century since the new occupants moved into the vacated properties everything has been left as it was. Elsewhere in the city, the closely-packed apartment blocks in the working-class suburbs offer a poor living environment for the large families that inhabit them; plaster has commonly fallen away from the exteriors, wires criss-cross the alleys from one building to another, entrance halls are neglected, lifts no longer work. Pavements everywhere are broken and the streets are heavily polluted, largely a result of the constant streams of traffic. Noisy black and yellow taxis (typically, Lada 2107s, their angular shape and utilitarian interiors quickly revealing their age) compete for trade with numerous private minibuses, while ploughing between them all are the original trams (permanently coated in thick dust and scarred by numerous scrapes experienced over the years) following routes along the linear axis of the coastal city.

Somehow it is as if the clock has stood still, its hands still at the hour when Nasser berated the foreigners and set his country on a new course. Alexandria has grown rapidly since then, making intensive use of its inherited capital, but—on a visit to the city on the eve of the Arab Spring—it was all too clear that time was running out. In the words of another recent observer: 'many Alexandrians feel they are living on a volcano. It could explode any time.'[38] And that, of course, is exactly what happened, with the immense forces of disaffection forcing out the old order. Regardless of the political regime, however, if Alexandria is to recover some of its former energy and reposition itself as a vibrant Mediterranean city, there is an urgent need for fresh investment as well as a strong sense of direction. Nearly six decades after the nation gained its independence, Alexandria still feels like a place in search of a new identity. It remains to be seen what this will be. Will a cultural revival lead the way forward or will this be constrained by dogma, religious as well as political? Will the future of this historic city be found in its Islamic hinterland or facing westwards across the Mediterranean? Will Alexandria take its place, as it has done in the past, at a busy crossroads between continents, or will it languish in the sluggish waters of the Delta? The course that it chooses will be of interest not only to Alexandrians but, no less, to other cities in the region.

TRIPOLI

Tripoli offers another extraordinarily long Mediterranean story, extending back over nearly three millennia. For most of its history, however, it has been in the hands of foreign powers and it was only in the middle of the twentieth century that it emerged as the capital of an independent nation.

Libya itself is an ancient term that used to signify the whole of the undiscovered African continent beyond Egypt. This is what Herodotus wrote about in the fifth century, when he drew on the limited descriptions of the Phoenicians, who took three years to sail around the African coastline.[1] Several centuries later, Strabo demonstrated that little more was known then about the southern continent that 'lacks so much of being a third part of the inhabited world'.[2]

In spite of its long and eventful history, there is little to be seen in modern Tripoli of past episodes. It is a classic palimpsest city, where most of the evidence of former times lies hidden beneath the new; literally under the pavements are multiple layers that tell of earlier eras. Even in the faces of its people there are traces of Arab and Berber, sub-Saharan Africans and Phoenicians, not to mention distant offspring of colonists (European as well as Ottoman). No less intriguing than the distant past is what has happened in Libya's post-colonial era, with the country's first experience of independence. Following the deposal after eighteen years of the country's one and only monarch, Libya was then guided by a single ruler—Muammar Gaddafi—with a unique brand of Islamic, socialist and autocratic tenets. In 2011, in the wake of the Arab Spring, he too was overthrown, marking the end of one chapter and the start of a new one.

Religion and politics, in a highly unusual mix, have made their own distinctive mark on modern Tripoli—and, no doubt, will continue to do so. It is a fascinating place that, in spite of recent events, is still relatively little known to outsiders. For more than four decades, the combined effects of an autocratic regime, fiercely independent policies and (for some of the time) externally-imposed sanctions did little to encourage visitors and a free flow of ideas. As such, there is now a great deal to unravel.

City of Desert and Sea

Tripoli, set on its tongue of sand surrounded by the waves, and crowned with palms, seems to have all the allure of an oriental city... But the enchantment is shortlived.[3]

To the north of Tripoli is the sea, to the south seemingly endless desert, and each, the Mediterranean and Sahara, has played its own important part in the way the city has evolved. The sea has traditionally brought trade as well as invading armies, and ideas in the wake of different cultures. In contrast, the desert has formed a natural barrier although even this has never been totally inhibiting. Over time, a string of caravans has navigated difficult routes across the inhospitable terrain, bringing goods and once, too, a lucrative traffic in slaves, from the African interior to the coastal markets.

The Arch of Marcus Aurelius is one of the few reminders of the Roman era in Tripoli.

Of the two, desert and sea, for most of its early history it is the latter that was the main influence on the emergence of Tripoli. The very foundation of the city was the outcome of a landing by seafaring Phoenicians from Lebanon, who established a trading post on the site in the seventh century BC. They named their new settlement Oea.[4] The Phoenicians were attracted by the natural harbour and defensive peninsula. Later visitors were also to be lured by these features, and it was the unfortunate lot of the city to find itself in the sights of a succession of conquerors. After the Phoenicians it captured the interest of the Greeks, already present on the North African coast to the east, in their colony of Cyrenaica. Oea was accordingly brought within the orbit of Greek culture, but this was not to last for it fell shortly after that to its powerful Carthaginian neighbours. Only with the rise of Rome were the Carthaginians ousted, in the second century BC, ushering in a long period of rule (some 700 years) from the opposite continent. The city was initially administered as part of the Roman province of Africa, a century later re-named Regio Tripolitania' ; Oea was thereafter known as Tripoli (one of three cities, *tri-polis*, the other two in the province being Sabratha and Leptis Magna). All three were advanced cities for their day and in each the Romans invested heavily in the type of infrastructure and facilities for which their architects and engineers were renowned.

A long period of relative stability came to an end in the sixth century, when the fall of the Roman Empire opened the way to raids by Vandals from northern Europe. Byzantine armies from Constantinople, the eastern branch of the waning empire, at first forced back the Vandals but they were never able to exercise the same level of control as their Roman predecessors. In the seventh century it was the turn of the Arab Muslims, with Tripoli on their path as they advanced westwards along the North African coastline. Indigenous Berber tribes, although with a strong sense of independence and tradition, were quickly converted to the new religion of Islam and, more gradually, to the Arab language. Under this new order, Tripoli itself looked first to the Umayyad caliphate in distant Damascus for its religious and political instruction and later to Cairo in neighbouring Egypt. From time to time, outsiders tried to turn back the march of Islam and win the provinces of Libya for Christianity, as in the twelfth century when Tripoli was held for a while by an invading army despatched from the then Norman kingdom of Sicily. The Christian monarch had plans for an African empire but the Muslims proved too powerful, forcing the infidels to return across the sea. More significant was an incursion in the sixteenth century by the Spaniards who, after just thirteen years, in 1523, handed the city for safekeeping to the Knights of St. John. The Knights promptly barricaded their new possession with sturdy defences, although not sturdy enough to keep out the Ottoman Turks who regained it for Islam in 1551.

The Old City in the sixteenth century. (Jamahiyra Museum).

For most of the period from 1551 until early in the twentieth century, Tripoli was answerable to the Supreme Porte in Constantinople. The name of Tripoli was used by the Turks to refer to the whole of northern Libya; in its early days of occupation the province was given the exalted status of a regency, governed by a *pasha* appointed directly by the sultan in the imperial capital. This arrangement was regularly challenged by tribal and other leaders in the region who pressed for greater autonomy. Tripoli was seen from Constantinople as being on the margins of their empire, part of a vast but impoverished land that was hard to defend. As a result, when local leaders claimed more powers these were usually conceded and the indigenous ruler would attract the title of *dey*; thus, at times Tripoli remained only loosely within the Ottoman realm. The few firsthand accounts of the city itself at the time of early Turkish occupation tell of a place that, other than its harbour, had little to commend it. In 1550 the exotically named Leo Africanus (a Spanish Muslim who converted to Christianity with the personal blessing of the Pope) produced a book describing his travels in the region.[5] Tripoli, he observed, was surrounded by desert where only date palms grew, and its people suffered from a constant shortage of grain; legend had it that a once-rich coastal plain had been lost to the advancing waters of the Mediterranean. In spite of the country's relative poverty, Africanus was impressed by the stature of the buildings and public spaces in the city itself. Tripoli's main asset was still its harbour, one of the few with such qualities along the eastern reaches of the North African coast. Accounts in the following century fill in some of the missing details of who, apart from the Turkish officials, lived in the city. We learn from the armchair traveller, John Ogilby, that it was 'full peopled with Turks, Moors and Jews' and that there was a large prison for Christian slaves.[6] It was not, in the sixteenth century, a great city—'sorely decay'd through the Cruelty of the Wars'—but it prospered as a result of a regular traffic of slaves from the heart of Africa and from its profitable dealings with Barbary pirates.[7] By the end of the seventeenth century it had a population of some 40,000, mostly Arab.[8]

Disruption to merchant shipping from the pirates (or, more accurately, corsairs) who navigated the waters along that coast was, in fact, one reason why the Spaniards had been eager in the sixteenth century to bring Tripoli and its valuable harbour under their own control. Nominal rule of the city by one power or another had previously proved insufficient to restrain the activities of the widely feared brigands, who gained as much from protection monies and ransoms as from the actual seizure of cargo. From time to time, foreign navies intervened on behalf of their merchant fleets, one colourful instance being in 1685 when the English commander, Sir John Narborough, sailed brazenly into Tripoli harbour with instructions to sink all ships at anchor.[9] He duly did this, largely by setting fire to the offending craft, and when the authorities refused to compensate the English for earlier losses he returned with a ground force to burn a vast stock of timber set aside to build a new fleet. Such events, decisive though they were at the time, created only a temporary lull and piracy along the coast continued largely unabated. Matters only reached a head in the nineteenth century when the pirates met their match in the face of an American government no longer willing to pay to keep open international shipping lanes.

In 1803 (when European powers were otherwise engaged in rebutting Napoleon's expansionist plans) America forced a blockade of Tripoli, heralding the start of two Barbary Wars. Together, these American interventions largely cleared the waters of pirates, a mixed blessing for the people of Tripoli who (in cahoots with the brigands) lost an important source of revenue. Anticipating a decline in fortunes from the ending of both piracy and the slave trade, the Ottoman rulers recognized an urgent need to fill the gap. Thus, they responded with various improvements to what was still a very basic infrastructure in the area under their control, they introduced some social reforms, and encouraged settled forms of agriculture to replace nomadic practices.[10]

The Grand Tour failed to include extensive Roman ruins in both Sabratha and Leptis Magna.

Most of these changes attracted little attention outside the region. In spite of its proximity to Europe, Tripoli in the nineteenth century remained off the beaten track. Those privileged young men and women who made the Grand Tour of classical sites in southern Europe would seldom have ventured further than Sicily, despite the exceptional Roman ruins that could be seen in Tripolitania, most notably at Sabratha and Leptis Magna.

From time to time, European consuls were appointed to safeguard national interests, and a limited number of explorers set out from Tripoli to cross the uncharted desert in search of Africa's hidden wealth. Their reports and letters home provided a patchwork account of what they found. For example, the letters of one Miss Tully (sister of the then British Consul), published as an illustrated volume in 1817, offer the most lucid account to date of Tripoli and its surroundings.[11] Like other visitors arriving for the first time in the harbour, she is at first seduced by the dazzling white of the buildings and rows of date palms surrounding the city. The cupolas above the bath-houses catch her eye, as do the small plantations around the mosques which present 'an aspect truly novel and pleasing'. On closer inspection of the streets, she remarks on the piles of stone and rubble which were all that remained from buildings dating from earlier periods of settlement. The coffee houses are denied to her as a woman but her informants tell her of the part they played in the life of an Arab city, and she describes their intimate atmosphere as if she had been an *habituée* herself. With her companions she explores the bazaars, one of which she discovers traded only in slaves—a discovery that was 'repugnant to a feeling heart'. At the time of her residence in Tripoli, the population seems to have declined to no more than 15,000.[12]

The small population was indicative of the poor state of the city. Well into the nineteenth century—and in spite of the Ottoman reforms—it saw little change, other than a slow decline in its fortunes. There was even then no running water and periodic famines and outbreaks of plague merely added to the hardships of everyday life. European communities were small—mainly Maltese and Italian traders, as well as the various consuls and their families—and, apart from engaging in its business, 'life in a city so far from and in such limited contact with the civilised world is inevitably rather monotonous'.[13] One visitor quickly saw behind the impressive skyline of dazzling white buildings, experiencing everywhere 'an insipid, sickening smell of rotting foodstuffs, stagnant water, and the filth lying in the streets'.[14] Given reactions such as these, it might be thought that there was little enough to attract fresh settlers to this barren shoreline, yet even while it remained under Ottoman rule European powers were looking ahead to the inevitable demise of the old empire and opportunities this would bring to stake their own claim. Italy, France and, later, Britain all had their own designs on this under-populated, and largely undefended, northern edge of their neighbouring continent. Most of Africa had already been claimed by one colonial power or another, leaving the extensive Libyan territory a rare and irresistible exception.

France made the first move, occupying adjacent Tunisia in 1881 and putting the Ottomans in Libya on alert. The main threat, though, came a little later, from the newly unified nation of Italy. Largely as a result of its proximity across a narrow neck of the Mediterranean, and a tenuous (though oft-repeated) claim based on the ancient presence of the Romans in North Africa, Italy assumed the role of Libya's natural custodian. With the Ottomans no longer the military power they once were, the Italians saw an opportunity and in 1911 claimed Tripoli for their own. Domenico Tumiati was an Italian journalist at the time who, a few months before the occupation, had fanned nationalist flames with a book which offered a totally unrealistic vision of Libya as the promised land.[15]

Italian architecture in Tripoli from the period of colonization.

Its ports, he claimed, would soon be busy with ships loading African riches in exchange for Italy's industrial products; railways would fan out from Tripoli, connecting the port with plantations and mines in the interior; and links would be made with Italian possessions further afield, in the Horn of Africa. Irrigation would bring a newfound fertility to the land, and factories would fill the air with the sounds of production. In his enthusiasm, Tumiati neglected to say that an earlier exploration of the country by a Zionist group had reported back that, in their view, it was not suitable for large-scale settlement.[16] Not surprisingly, the Italian occupation proved an ill-gotten venture. For a start, the colonists met stiff opposition, less from the weakened Turks and more from local tribes whom they had underestimated, and it was not until the late-1920s that most of Libya was finally brought under unified control. In the process of repressing their opponents, the Italians were responsible for a string of atrocities that cast a shadow over nearly three decades of occupation and soured relations between the two countries for many years more.[17]

On the domestic front, though, the acquisition of the colony was portrayed as a victory for the Italian nation. In the interwar years, Libya was treated as an integral part of Italy and was known as the 'fourth shore', a notion that appealed to the Fascist leader, Benito Mussolini, but which had little substance in practice. When Mussolini visited the colony in 1926 he invoked the spiritual, rather than practical, importance of the venture: 'It is destiny which pushes us towards this land. No one can check our destiny and, above all, no one can break our infallible will.'[18] In the following decade, to popular acclaim, ships left the Italian ports crowded with families seeking a new life in this new land across the sea. On the crossing their spirits were high and they sang enthusiastically:

The sea is ours; We cross it as if it were a piazza; And where we land we still find Italy.[19]

In spite of extensive archaeological work, particularly during the Italian colonial era, there is still much to be done.

Undoubtedly many of these settlers came from good peasant stock and worked hard to tame the desert; so, too, the Italian nation invested in an impressive network of roads and railways, and an urban infrastructure that it could ill afford. To reinforce the notion of an enduring Roman heritage in Libya, Mussolini personally initiated a series of important archaeological excavations, mainly at Sabratha and Leptis Magna, which have not been matched since. Such achievements, however, were overshadowed by costly military and political failures and, in the eyes of the rest of the world, barely disguised plans to eliminate all but a tiny minority of the indigenous population. Moreover, hopes within Italy that Libya would absorb many of the impoverished emigrants who were otherwise making their way to North and South America were to be sorely disappointed.

With the coming of the Second World War, Italy had little choice but to join the Germans in North Africa and defend their own colony. The immediate task of the combined force was to oust the British from Egypt, with the aim of ending control of the shipping route (through the Suez Canal) to India. In the event, hostilities were extended across the whole of North Africa, which became one of the main theatres of the war. Tanks from both sides rolled across the desert terrain, clashing in a series of decisive battles. Both the Germans and Italians suffered heavy defeats and their withdrawal led to Britain in 1943 taking direct control of two of Libya's three provinces (Tripolitania and Cyrenaica, both with a shoreline), with the French assuming responsibility for the third (Fezzan, in the interior). For the Italians, forced out by the Allies, their Libyan adventure was over.

Divide and Rule

In social terms, the family society is better than that of the tribe, the tribal society is better than that of the nation and the society of the nation is better than world society.[20]

Britain assumed control of the whole country until 1951, in which year Libya gained independence for the first time in its history.[21] With its traditional tribal and provincial divisions, the transition to a unified state was not easy but after lengthy negotiations a monarchy was chosen as the preferred system of rule. Idris I, the new king, came from the eastern province of Cyrenaica but in an attempt to reconcile opposing groups he designated two capitals: Tripoli, in the north-west, became the home of Parliament, and Benghazi (1000 kilometres to the east) the meeting place for the king and his cabinet. In his eighteen-year reign, however, the main challenge to the throne came not so much from the different tribal groupings within the country as from growing disaffection amongst his people, who were unhappy that the king still saw Libya as little more than a colony beholden to Western powers. Paradoxically, it was the discovery of rich reserves of oil that fostered this discontent for, in spite of the newfound wealth, the main beneficiaries seemed to be the foreign oil companies. Responding to the popular mood, a group of young army officers led a coup in 1969, forcing the king into exile. From within the ranks, Muammar Gaddafi emerged as the country's new leader, quickly establishing a revolutionary council and declaring a republic. The rest, as they say, is history, with Gaddafi's Libya emerging, even for its Arab neighbours, as one of the most maverick states of the modern world. It turned out to be something of a roller-coaster ride, and Tripoli's own development was subjected to an unusual mix of policies born of revolutionary theory and autocratic rule. As Libya's capital, it also had to face the full impact of international sanctions; far from being at the crossroads of the region, a catalyst for trade and development on the North African coastline, for much of the Gaddafi era it languished in a Mediterranean backwater.

On the face of it—with a constant flow of oil revenues and a charismatic leader— one might have expected that Tripoli would have been transformed from a relatively underdeveloped city to a symbol of socialist modernity. The reasons why this did not happen stem from one aspect or another of Gaddafi's changing ideologies and political machinations. Part of the problem, too, was the fact that, at root, he never favoured, perhaps even feared, urbanism. He presented himself as a man of the desert with little time for the trappings of the city; the motivation for the coup from which he emerged as the country's leader was characterized as 'a revolution of the oases and interior against the established society of dominant tribes and prominent coastal families'.[22] This is evident when one looks at Gaddafi's ideas as well as his actions. For a start, for someone who was keen to make known his ideas on a wide range of topics, Gaddafi said remarkably little on the place of the city in his grand scheme of things. It is only by reading between the lines that one gets a sense of what was in his mind on this subject. An important source is *The Green Book*, a collection of his ideas published some six years after he came to power.[23] In spite of its title it is, in fact, in three separate (albeit short) volumes, the first dealing with democracy, the second with economic issues, and the third with social topics. Together these add up to what he called the Third Universal Theory, a middle way between capitalism and communism.

In the first book, on democracy, Gaddafi starts by dismissing the western model of parliamentary majorities and elected representatives, favouring instead a system of 'direct democracy'. There is talk of people's committees and popular congresses that would not be out of place in an orthodox Marxist-Leninist tract, but there are also sharp differences. For instance, he distinguishes between laws that are 'man-made' and those that arise from custom and tradition; he asserts that religious laws, which embrace the latter, will always provide a fairer basis for administering justice. Gaddafi was wary, even paranoid, about any one centre of power becoming dominant (other than his own), something that was to have direct implications for Tripoli in its assumed role as capital city and symbolic centre of the nation. Rather than allowing Tripoli a strong municipal leader he advocated, instead, decentralization into neighbourhood committees. Likewise, instead of concentrating all of the nation's government offices in the capital he progressively dispersed these between a number of smaller settlements. In 1988, he took the step of removing all but the foreign and information ministries from the capital: to Benghazi, Kufra and Sirte. The last of these is close to his own birthplace and it is no coincidence that Sirte was where the National General People's Congress was held each year. Five years later, the foreign ministry too was relocated, to the small town of Ras Lanouf.

The second book sets out (in a very incomplete way)[24] a basis for economic development. At the heart of it is the axiom that 'the purpose of the new socialist society is to create a society which is happy because it is free'. And freedom, it is explained, results from no longer being exploited by unscrupulous employers and landlords. Those elements of the economy which enable the fulfilment of basic needs should not be used to advantage by one party over another; for instance, 'land is no one's property but everyone has the right to use it'. Gaddafi covers well-trodden socialist ground, alluring in principle but too often already discredited in practice; his tract would have been more universally received in the nineteenth century, before socialism was put so widely to the test. Finally, in the third book, an eclectic range of social issues is addressed, from nationalism at one level to horsemanship at another. The nation state is all-important, argues Gaddafi, and within it there should be just one religion. Unlike some of his socialist counterparts, he does not dismiss the family as a bourgeois relic but, together with the tribe (likened to a large family) sees it as the bedrock of society. Neither families nor tribes, however, would be enough to cement relations beyond their own boundaries and for this one has to look to a higher order, the nation. Libya, composed of various tribes and without natural boundaries other than the sea, is far from being an obvious nation so it is not surprising that Gaddafi was at pains to press the case.

With the departure of European residents, the cathedral built by the Italians was duly converted into a mosque.

One reads *The Green Book*, in this context, not for its political insights nor literary enjoyment—most of it is tired rhetoric, written in tedious prose—but because it reveals something essential about Gaddafi and, by implication, his approach to Libya's cities. He offers an impression (at least when he wrote the books) that he had retained his Bedouin roots, valuing those traditions that in previous generations enabled survival in the desert. The Bedouin were renowned for living in small groups where tribal loyalties counted for everything; their life was hard and dependent on rules that applied, without question, to everyone. Outsiders were welcome within their camp but they were viewed as potential enemies in other ways. Cities were exotic, faraway places, rarely visited except for their markets, essential for some functions but outside the orbit of everyday life. If much of this is merely implied in his official texts, all becomes explicit in less inhibited writings; thus, in one of Gaddafi's short stories he contends that:

> *City life means stress as you chase after certain desires and unnecessary, yet necessary, luxuries. When we see these social sicknesses spread throughout the city, and laws passed to combat them, we are not surprised. We do not believe that they will end, and that we will gain victory over them, for the nature of city life is thus, and these sicknesses are inevitable. The city is dizziness and nausea, madness and loss, fear of insanity, fear of confronting urban life and its urban problems.*
>
> *Leave this hell on earth, run quickly away. In complete happiness, go to this village and the countryside, where physical labour has meaning, necessity, usefulness, and is a pleasure besides. There, life is social, and human; families and tribes are close. There is stability and belief.*[25]

Until his overthrow in 2011, Gaddafi's presence was evident throughout the city.

In his actions, too, Gaddafi's ideologically driven approach did little to favour the development of Tripoli. On coming to power he wasted little time, for instance, in expelling some 20,000 Italians and appropriating their property, on the basis that they represented an unwanted link with earlier colonialism. At the same time, his violently anti-Zionist policy led to those Jews who had remained in the country after independence (mostly in Tripoli) leaving for Israel and other safe places, regardless of whether they were themselves Zionist. In a stroke, taking a lead from his similarly ultra-nationalistic Egyptian neighbour, President Nasser, he rid the country of those foreign influences that had in the past contributed in important ways to the economic and cultural life of Tripoli.

The city's isolation from the West was later increased in the face of international sanctions, initiated by the United States in response to terrorist attacks emanating from Libya; for more than a decade, flights from the West were largely stopped, cultural ties were cut and trade similarly curtailed. For Tripoli (which also at one stage experienced targeted bombing by the United States) these were hardly the best conditions to encourage measured growth and planned development. Because of Gaddafi's policies, the city—in contrast with much of its history—now turned its back on the sea, looking instead to the desert and greater reliance on the interior.

The Old City still retains something of the exotic that intrigued earlier visitors to Tripoli.

In spite of inimical policies during the first decades of Gaddafi's rule, the city grew defiantly. Its population increased, year on year, from little more than 200,000 in the

1960s to a total of some 1.5 million by the end of the century and an estimated two million for the city region ten years later (a number significantly more than for the whole of the nation at the end of the Second World War). While this transformation might, at first, be interpreted as a sign of the city's dynamism the reality was rather different, for it only matched the rapid rate of population growth for the nation as a whole. By 2010 Libya's population exceeded six million, seriously challenging the country's natural means to support it. The fact remains that Libya is still predominantly a desert environment, with a limited (and increasingly unreliable) rainfall restricted to the winter months, becoming almost negligible in the interior; only two per cent of the land has sufficient rain to provide an economic basis for settled agriculture without the support of irrigation. In the cities, even with the most careful measures to conserve water, it becomes increasingly difficult to meet modern demands on a sustainable basis.

In an attempt to overcome this longstanding natural obstacle to further development, Gaddafi put his name to a project that was, in fact, conceived before he came to power but only started under his auspices in the 1980s. Through a series of pipelines the project was designed to bring water from vast underground reservoirs in the south of the country, beneath the Sahara, to serve the most densely populated parts of the country in the north. Gaddafi described it as the eighth wonder of the world but environmentalists look askance at the enormous capital investment and energy costs to run it, coupled with the fact that such reserves can never be inexhaustible. Like other cities in the southern Mediterranean, Tripoli is surely ignoring constraints that will undoubtedly become critical over time.

Opening the Gates

Tripoli has waited, beautiful, picturesque, glowing, but as it were in a state of suspended animation, holding her breath for the next stage.[26]

Until at least the beginning of the twentieth century, Tripoli was regarded by visitors as an exotic city: 'a city of enchantment, white as dreams of Paradise, fringed by palms and olives, and steeped in memories of the centuries'.[27] Western observers were loathe to see this oriental idyll change, although, in reality, its whole history had been one of periodic transformation in the hands of successive conquerors.

Mabel Loomis Todd was an American astronomer who with her husband visited Libya on two occasions (in 1900 and 1905) to witness solar eclipses in the desert. She chose to write of her love of Tripoli just a year after the Italian invasion that marked the start of yet another chapter of colonial rule.[28] Even with the arrival of battleships in the harbour, it seems that none of her expatriate friends in the city at first took the threat too seriously. It was only when the ships opened fire with heavy artillery that their complacency was shaken, and they were hurriedly forced to flee. The tranquil days of sipping mint tea beneath a palm tree in the late afternoon and of playing tennis in the shade of the medina walls were over.

Whatever the future held, she concluded, Tripoli would never be the same again. Just as had been the case many times before, the new rulers would force on the city their own changes.

For the incoming Italians, modernization of their new colony was the order of the day and Tripoli was the obvious place to start. Symbolically, it was important to demonstrate the superiority of their imported culture—the expression of a young nation eager to cast off old ways in their own country too—in contrast to the sluggishness of the former Ottoman regime. With little delay, the colonists drew up plans to extend the city into a new district to the east of the medina.

It was some years before they felt sufficiently in control to implement their plans, but within a decade development was underway. A regular street pattern was laid out, soon to be flanked by lines of white buildings with balconies from which the residents could view the business of the neighbourhood, just as they might have done in Naples or Rome. At ground level, the commercial development invariably included colonnades along the pavements, providing welcome shade from the high sun. To complete the picture, an imposing cathedral was built on one side of a piazza, announcing in splendid terms the presence of Catholicism; this very cathedral, however, would later become a mosque, with the crescent replacing the cross on the towering dome.

High-rise development and urban motorways have largely severed the city from the sea.

Beyond the modern shops and government offices, a new residential area assumed the name of Garden City. Although it was no more than a distant cousin of Ebenezer Howard's original idea of what it should be, Garden City was aptly characterized by villas set in gardens, bordered by tree-lined streets. People who lived there would later recall it fondly for the tranquility of the gardens, where fruit trees bore oranges, figs and pomegranates, and brightly coloured bougainvillea covered the high surrounding walls. The new housing was intended at the time for senior members of the Italian colonial administration and wealthy businessmen and their families. After 1945 it was favoured by British officials and American military officers from the nearby air base; and it has since become the main location for foreign consulates.

The Italians made their mark on the colony although their tenure was to be relatively shortlived (little more than three decades), leaving behind a country that would go through further convolutions. First came the British, then a Libyan monarch, before Colonel Gaddafi took control with his own ideological aspirations. As if this succession did not bring enough change, at the start of the twenty-first century a bigger surprise was yet to come. After some three decades of homespun Arab socialism, combined with belligerence on the world stage, the capricious leader of Libya announced a *volte face*. On the domestic front, it was time to be more pragmatic, exchanging an overly doctrinaire approach for policies that would be more likely to attract much-needed foreign investment. He omitted to say that socialism had run its course but that was the underlying message. No less important, following years of confrontation with the West and political isolation, Gaddafi declared his country's return to the international arena. Symbolically, it was as if the gates of the citadel were suddenly, and unexpectedly, flung open.

For Tripoli itself, now assuming the role of *de facto* as well as *de jure* capital of the newly defined Libya, the release of its pent-up metropolitan energy led to a surge of growth and development as never before. Goods from around the world filled the previously empty shelves and it seemed as if every young man (gender divisions are still sharp in Libya, reflecting the hold of traditional ways) wanted to run his own business. It would never regain the charm and mystery that caught the imagination of early visitors but the city that started to take shape marked a new phase in the country's development. For years almost a forgotten city in Western eyes, there were signs that it could emerge in its own way as another Mediterranean hub—open to different cultures and seeking stronger links with Europe as well as its traditional partners along the North African coast. Propagandist posters in prominent places on the eve of Gaddafi's downfall boldly declared that Libya was a bridge between Africa and Europe, with Tripoli as the obvious bridging point.

Nothing better illustrates how much things had changed than the ending of Gaddafi's resistance to the concentration of economic and political power in Tripoli. Instead, he declared that the previously dispersed government ministries would return from the provinces to a dedicated district within the city. As if to signify the fresh approach, a firm of German architects was selected in 2007 to design the modern complex, which they named Tripoli Greens.[29] If the name itself is unimaginative the concept is quite the opposite: an attempt to combine tradition with modernity, to express the spirit of a more open era, and (seemingly impossible in Libya's harsh physical environment) to meet exacting standards of sustainability. The site itself is located between the international airport and the city centre. It extends over 230 hectares and was intended to contain the People's Congress Palace, the various Ministries and the official residence of the Prime Minister, together with a hotel and conference centre.

Elsewhere, ahead of Tripoli Greens, new office blocks and high-rise hotel developments were already—before the overthrow of Gaddafi—changing the face of the city. Tripoli had once been contained wholly within its high walls, adjacent to the harbour that was its main resource and link to the rest of the world. In spite of the destruction of most of the walls, the old city (the medina) remains to this day not only largely intact but also a vibrant district of trade and craft workshops, of mosques and coffee houses, as well as a traditional neighbourhood where many people still live. The sea, however, has been forced back through an earlier, ill-conceived reclamation scheme that separates the old city from its harbour, with an urban motorway cutting sharply across the new land. A former corniche to the east of the old city, fondly recalled for its elegance in the Italian era, has been left, literally, high and dry. No less intrusive, a group of socialist era residential blocks and more recent commercial development to the west of the medina, creates another unwelcome barrier.

There are few, if any, instances of a Mediterranean city where sea and land have become so needlessly divided; the symbiosis that one looks for and which would otherwise enhance Tripoli's maritime location is entirely missing. Once described as the 'daughter of sea and desert',[30] it is as if there is still an uneasy relationship with the former, an unwillingness to open itself to the sea which has in the past so often brought unwelcome change. Gaddafi's departure has ushered in the start of a new era and time alone will show whether Tripoli will choose, in a positive way, to look outwards to the Mediterranean and, beyond that, to the rest of the world.

TUNIS

Above the modern terminal building of the international airport there is a sign, in French as well as Arabic; it reads simply 'Aéroport de Tunis-Carthage'. For the visitor to Tunis, it is as if the whole of the city's history and modern development is introduced in this single announcement: the inseparable association of Tunis with ancient Carthage; a reminder that, in spite of its Berber heritage, it has for many centuries been part of the Arab world; and evidence of a more recent period of French colonization, now over but still with a strong imprint. It is the capital of Tunisia, a small nation in that stretch of North Africa known as the Maghreb, the region that extends westwards through Algeria and Morocco. Traditionally, the term has referred not to the full extent of these three nations but only to the land north of the Atlas Mountains and the Sahara. With such formidable natural barriers inland the coastal cities have for long been encouraged to look outwards, towards the sea and neighbouring continents.

There are local differences between the various countries of the Maghreb but they also have much in common: at best a semi-arid climate, a shared history of indigenous Berber and other tribal groupings, a predominant Arab and Muslim culture, and successive periods of foreign control. As such, Tunis can tell a story that other cities along the North African coastline would recognize. It has a long and often eventful history, in a country that for much of the time maintained a fair degree of political autonomy—although it was not until the second half of the twentieth century that Tunisia achieved full independence. Like other cities in the region that have so recently experienced revolutionary political change, its contemporary challenge is one of coming to terms with globalization, encompassing democracy and meeting the demands of a fast-growing, young population.

Delenda Est Carthago

This broken beauty is all we have of that ancient magnificence...[1]

Delenda Est Carthago—'We must destroy Carthage'—were the words allegedly repeated by Cato the Elder at the end of every speech he made to the Roman Senate. Little wonder that the Romans were apprehensive, having suffered a costly (although by no means decisive) defeat at the hands of the Carthaginians on their own soil, in the second Punic War, and being only too aware of the enduring strength of their enemy. Even after incurring heavy losses in two wars against the Romans, the home city of the Carthaginians was a power to be reckoned with; in the first century BC it was a metropolis, with a population of 750,000. Their fighting forces had more than proved their worth, and Rome—with only open sea between the two cities—felt constantly under threat of further invasion. The proximity of the two continents in this stretch of the Mediterranean, a narrow channel between its eastern and western basins, was an obvious source of concern. Little more than 120 kilometres separated Carthage from Sicily, with Sardinia not much further.

Carthage: some of the few remaining ruins of a once great city.

With Rome's aspirations as the supreme power of the Mediterranean at stake, pre-emptive action was called for and the battle was taken to the walls of Carthage itself. For two years, in the third Punic war, the city suffered a fearful siege until, in 146 BC, the Roman army broke through and proceeded to demolish every building and every sign of its former glory. Those inhabitants who survived the ordeal were not allowed to return to the site. An observer reported that the Roman general, Scipio Africanus the Younger, was greatly saddened by the city's demise, not for sentimental reasons but because the spectacle brought home to him the mortality of cities and their respective civilizations.[2] He was right, of course, for the

Mediterranean was even then an unforgiving place where cities and empires had come and gone in short order. More than 2000 years later, the name of Carthage persists, but now to denote no more than a suburb of Tunis, an area of fashionable villas by the sea and a few surviving ruins from its heyday as the home of one of the great powers of the Mediterranean.

Carthage's inland neighbour, Tunis, is another of those Mediterranean cities with nearly three millennia of history, an extraordinary fact in itself but one that is almost taken for granted in this part of the world. The original settlement pre-dates Carthage and was probably established by a Berber tribe; located on the inner shore of an extensive lagoon behind the shoreline, it offered safe waters for fishing. Carthage itself, some fifteen kilometres away, on a coastal site, was founded as a Phoenician colony in the eighth or ninth century BC, the name given to it meaning 'new town'. These natural sailors from the shores of Lebanon eschewed the tiny cluster of buildings that constituted Tunis in favour of a new site directly fronting the sea (in a broad bay that later became known as the Gulf of Tunis), although the sheltered waters behind were an added attraction to protect their ships in times of bad weather. So long as the Phoenicians ruled the waves, Tunis was destined to play second fiddle.

Although temporarily ousted by the Greeks, the Phoenicians were soon to return to strengthen their hold on the region. In the eyes of the Romans, Tunis was inseparable from Carthage and when they levelled the latter to the ground they destroyed Tunis too. Under the Romans, in a strange turn of fortune, Carthage was then to enjoy a new lease of life, being rebuilt and favoured as a stronghold to secure their prized African colony; additionally, the farmland in the region was valued for its rich grain harvests and for oil (used mainly for heating and lighting) from the abundant olive groves. Tunis was rebuilt, too, by the Romans but is mentioned as no more than a staging post for their new roads leading to the interior. When the Romans eventually left, the Vandals from northern Europe succeeded them, in turn to be evicted by the Byzantine army of Count Belisarius in the sixth century. It was only with the arrival of the evangelizing Arabs in the seventh century that the roles of the two cities were reversed, with Carthage permanently falling into decay while Tunis assumed a hitherto unknown status. With its more protected site the latter was preferred by the Arabs and new fortifications were built. In spite of successive changes resulting from factional rivalries between its rulers, Tunis over several centuries steered a steady path of political and economic growth, at one time designated as capital of a province that extended from Tripoli in the east to Fez in the west. Under the Hafsid dynasty, between the thirteenth and sixteenth centuries, it recorded a population of 100,000 and was recognized as one of the great cities of the Islamic world.

Its growing importance, though, along with its location so close to the European mainland, was certain to be seen as a threat to other powers and, sure enough, it attracted enemy forces carrying the banner of Christianity. Early in the reign of the Hafsids, King Louis IX of France briefly captured Tunis but (allegedly in the face of an outbreak of plague) was soon forced to retreat. Later, during the sixteenth century, it was Spain that tried to conquer the region but after several attempts the Christians were once again forced back. By then the new custodians of Tunis were the Ottoman Turks, who remained nominally in control until the nineteenth century; in reality, so far from Constantinople, the city enjoyed a considerable degree of autonomy during this long period. As elsewhere under the Ottomans there was toleration of different religious and ethnic groups, and a Jewish community that dated back to the original diaspora from the Holy Land—later augmented by exiles fleeing Spanish intolerance—was an important element in the city's population. To these were added large numbers of Moors, also expelled from Spain in the fifteenth century; and a long-established group of Muslims forced to leave Malta. Tunis under the Ottomans was well placed to prosper, with short shipping routes to Europe and a rich hinterland of agriculture. The fact that, like other ports along the Barbary Coast, it was also a home for pirates, did not deter foreign traders from taking advantage of the commercial opportunities.

By the nineteenth century, just as the Carthaginians had found in an earlier era, the proximity of this shoreline to Europe was again proving to be a mixed blessing. Anticipating the continuing decline of Ottoman power, Italy, Tunisia's nearest neighbour, considered itself the natural heir to the region. By the middle of the century, Italians represented the largest number of foreigners in Tunisia. As it later discovered to its cost in Libya, however, it was not yet in a strong enough position to convert its newfound national pride into effective colonial policies. France, on the other hand, was better placed. Morocco, Algeria and Tunisia all lay just across the sea and, with Ottoman power on the wane, the beginnings of her own North African adventure took shape. First, in 1830, France invaded Algeria, overcoming local resistance as a prelude to large-scale colonization. In spite of this early initiative, it was to be another half century, in 1881, before French troops entered Tunisia and subsequently imposed protectorate status. Morocco was later to follow suit to complete French control of the Maghreb.

When they occupied Tunis, and then the country's interior, it is likely that the colonists found a world that had changed little over centuries and was still largely unknown to most Europeans. An arrangement struck with Constantinople had previously ensured that, so long as levies were paid on time, the local ruler effectively had *carte blanche* to run his territory as he wished. By all accounts it was an autocratic regime with corruption endemic; however, as most accounts at that time were by Europeans—who tended to believe that anything to do with Africa could only be primitive—their reliability has to be questioned. Take, for instance, the findings of an English gentleman traveller, the Hon. Lewis Wingfield who, in 1868, in the comfortable surroundings of the Garrick Club in London, reflected on his own recent visit to Tunis and neighbouring Algeria. He spoke tellingly of arriving at 'a spot fully a thousand years behind all its neighbours in progress and civilization; a phenomenon, bordering, as it does, on the very skirts of refined Europe.'[3]

Even the respected regional geographer, Ellen Churchill Semple, later reflected that:

> *stimuli which have reached its shores [North Africa] have been blunted against its vast inertia. Phoenician, Greek, Roman, Vandal and Arab colonists have exploited its local resources here and there but in time succumbed to local conditions, without forcing from African soil any outstanding native achievement, except the elephant corps of Hannibal's army, the dauntless Numibian cavalry, and perhaps a winning horse for the races of the Greek games.*[4]

Clearly, the French, although they may have shared this disparaging view of Africa, had high hopes of their newfound acquisition and were looking for more than a few elephants and a winning horse.

The Making of Modernity

The old city found itself strangled from all sides by the symbols of French might, the menacing signs of power.[5]

Tunis, although it shares many features with its Mediterranean counterparts, is an unusual city. Unlike most others in the region of any importance, for reasons bound up with its long history, it does not face directly onto the sea; instead it fronts the shallow waters of a wide lagoon. The separation of its coastal port (La Goulette) was an immediate source of irritation for the Hon. Wingfield and his party, who were told on disembarking from their sea-going vessel that the onward journey overland would take an hour and a half.

There was no connecting railway then (Italian investors and engineers have later to be thanked for that) and, instead, it was an eventful carriage ride 'swaying over the uneven ground of arid sand, splashing now and then through the waters of the marshy lake, now through a wood of stunted, blasted olives cut out against the jagged blue hills, now past a herd of camels browsing peaceably by the water's edge'.[6] Eventually, 'Tunis the white'[7] came into view — 'a vista of white buildings and brilliant minarets, with here and there a palm, cool against the turquoise sky, while groups of promenaders were wandering about in all the brilliant dresses for which Tunis is celebrated.'[8] Pre-colonial Tunis was everything the Western visitor would have imagined of an Arab settlement on the margins of the declining Ottoman Empire. Fuelled with preconceptions of primitive lands and fortified by a 'hasty breakfast', Wingfield soon left his hotel to discover its mysteries. It was a city, he quickly concluded, 'ill-provided with ways of communication' but, with the help of a guide wearing a large red tarbouche, he proved more than equal to the challenge of finding his way around and describing what he saw.

> *Winding alleys and dark courts, narrow pavements, and narrower*

footpaths, long straggling bazaars, with vaulted roofs, which open out one into the other in a hopeless maze and intricacy, rendering a saunter alone a work of impossibility, unprovided with some silken string in the tangled labyrinth.[9]

Most of the houses were single-storey, with an inner courtyard, 'so that the streets look sombre and uninhabited to a European eye'.[10] Apart from the fact that they were oriented away from the street, he was also intrigued by the roof terraces, which he quickly appreciated were used to collect rainwater in large cisterns. In contrast to the tranquillity of the residential areas, the bazaars were a constant source of fascination with their profusion of colour, intensity of business, mingling crowds and perpetual noise. Like the good tourist he was, he let his guide lead him to a booth to buy a *tarbouche* for himself, to wear on his further travels in the country.[11]

Wingfield, like other visitors at the time, understandably draws attention to what was different from the European experience. The fact was, however, that on the eve of French colonization, Tunis had for long been influenced by its northern neighbours. Although most of its population was Arab, with a much smaller number of Turks from its long history of Ottoman rule, there were also significant minorities from the countries of southern Europe and Malta, together with a long-established Jewish community (many of whom had brought with them some of the traditions of Spain). Perhaps surprisingly, despite the imminence of French occupation, the number of that nation's own countrymen then living in the capital and in Tunisia as a whole probably amounted to no more than five per cent of the foreign population. Their cause was not particularly helped by the visit made in 1807 by the French man of letters and dilettante, François-René Chateaubriand, a romantic, Byronesque figure who weaved his way round the warring navies of the Napoleonic Wars in a year-long tour of the Mediterranean. In his subsequent account of his travels he finds little of interest to say about Tunis (apart from a few dismissive comments about its people), saving his enthusiasm for the ruins of nearby Carthage.[12] The latter, he notes, is *'ici le seul objet intéressant'*, duly spending most of his time amongst the ruins and claiming originality for his insights.[13]

Later in the nineteenth century, in 1846, the French authorities, keen to arouse greater interest in the idea of emigration to that part of North Africa to support their colonial aspirations, commissioned the popular author, Alexandre Dumas, to make his own visit and subsequently to tell the nation of his experience. Rising to the challenge, Dumas insisted that he be transported along the coast aboard a fully-manned corvette, *Le Véloce*. Ignoring protocol, his arrival on the approaches to Tunis was announced with a 21-gun salute, before he was taken ashore to meet the Turkish governor. Crossing the shallow lake, Dumas admired a flock of pink flamingos and had to be restrained from shooting one to take with him as a souvenir. Perhaps forgetting the more serious nature of his mission, he then took delight in describing the guard of honour lined up on the quayside, composed of soldiers of different heights in single-size uniforms. There were snatches of *gravitas* but, in the main, he seemed to see his excursion as no more than a government-sponsored adventure. Many years later, when his account was translated into English it appeared as a paperback with words taken from a review on the cover, proclaiming 'Colour, Sensation, Magnificence'.

The St. Vincent de Paul Cathedral and the Municipal Theatre were two of the early civic buildings built in the French colonial era.

It is very unlikely that the exploits of Dumas, amusing though they were, did much for recruitment to the French colonial cause. Italians continued to constitute the largest European community (comprising about half of all foreigners in the country), leading to the later allegation that it was really 'an Italian colony occupied by France'.[14] Having formally secured their new territory, if only to put paid to Italian claims, one obvious thrust of French policy was to try again to persuade more of their own people to settle there. This time they relied on more than the distracted efforts of a novelist; instead, vast tracts of land were bought by the government and then sold in smaller parcels to colonists, who were exhorted to concentrate on growing the vine and olive trees and exporting their products, mainly to France. Even with these inducements, the French were still slow in coming to this new land and it was to be the Italian settlers who took greater advantage of the opportunities.[15]

Tunisia remained a French protectorate from 1881 to its year of independence, 1956. During this time, Tunis itself was transformed from a still largely traditional city to one that, if not wholly modern, became largely so. To some extent, old and new were able to co-exist, for the original medina was left largely as it was. The French encircled it with a ring road, thus preserving 'a spatial and structural order attuned to the way of life of medieval and early modern Tunis'.[16] Muezzins continued to call their congregations to prayer in the many mosques, the colourful souks did business as they had always done, and the maze of narrow lanes and alleys (with houses facing inwards to preserve privacy) was left untouched. Most of the residual walls disappeared with the construction of the ring road but even that created its own sense of enclosure. It was on the land outside — in what became known as the *ville neuve* — where the real changes were to take place.[17]

Pictures of the new thoroughfares at the turn of the century evoke images of any large city in the south of France: tree-lined boulevards, fine shops selling artisan and imported goods, the domes of the new cathedral, and the formal architecture of government offices invariably with the *tricolore* fluttering proudly above. These grand avenues, an early expression of French modernity, were to be found between the outer limits of the medina and the inner shores of the lagoon, by then its narrow outlet sealed off from the sea and called the Lake of Tunis. The new neighbourhoods housed most of the Europeans although, in contrast, many of the Jews and Maltese still lived alongside Arab neighbours in the old city. Symbolism is an important weapon in the colonizer's armoury and imposing buildings play their own part in reinforcing the identity of the dominant culture. It was no coincidence that the St. Vincent de Paul Cathedral was built in the first year of occupation, dwarfing the mosques in the old city that had previously caught the attention of visitors. Over the next quarter century the cathedral was joined by a host of other buildings signifying French cultural and political life: the Central Market opened for business in 1891 and the Treasury in1900, the flamboyant *art nouveau* Municipal Theatre in 1903 and, as well, numerous banks and offices, the Town Hall, and *beaux-arts* (and, later, art deco) apartment blocks and hotels. Some institutions like the barracks and prison were sited close to the boundaries of the medina, as if to emphasize who was in control.

In terms of its impact, the building of what amounted to a new city alongside the old expressed not only the presence of the colonists but also represented an obvious contrast between tradition and modernity, between Africa and Europe. It was this contrast that intrigued a steady stream of European visitors, who would enjoy the comforts and familiarity of Tunis before taking a mandatory tour to the meagre ruins of nearby Carthage or, for the more intrepid, excursions into the desert. Unlike the rough conditions that awaited the likes of Wingfield and his party just a few years before, the path of the modern tourist was made all the smoother with the opening in 1902 of an office in Tunis of the respected travel organizer, Thomas Cook & Son.

Although the new neighbourhoods were attractive to middle-class Europeans, the wealthiest families often chose to live in villas in one of the salubrious suburbs near the sea, a choice that was helped by access to the railway that skirted the lake. Still further out, European settlers made their life in the countryside, mostly within fifty miles of the capital. Colonization of this immediate hinterland proved to be a mixed blessing for the city itself. In a commercial sense, it was an undoubted boost as Tunis could add to its existing functions the lucrative role of serving the large European population.

On the other hand, the displacement by these settlers of traditional farmers and of nomads who had roamed the area freely for centuries forced many indigenous families to come to the city in a largely vain search for work. It was the start of a process of migration from the countryside that, spurred later by a rapidly rising population, continues to the present day. Tunis is not alone in North Africa in spawning impoverished communities, the *bidonvilles*, characterized by self-made dwellings largely untouched by planning and government controls.[18]

Contrasting styles of architecture from the French era.

It was, of course, inevitable that the interests of colonizers and colonized would be opposed; such is the nature of the process, of one group seeking to dominate another. Colonization came late in this case, well into the nineteenth century, and from the very time of its arrival the mere presence of a foreign culture only served to hasten the rise of Tunisian nationalism. Undoubtedly, the colonizers brought material benefits, in the form of an improved physical infrastructure (such as roads and modern port facilities), and there were also some in the Protectorate Administration in favour of enlightened policies to give Tunisian children a basic education and better opportunities to qualify for professional jobs. Equally, there were others, encouraged by the fiercely resistant settlers, who showed only contempt for the native population. On balance, it was the latter faction that won the day and which, unintentionally but unmistakeably, strengthened the nationalist cause. In the years ahead, a political party was formed (the Dustur), trade unions lent their support, nationalistic literature was circulated and people not infrequently took to the streets. Hopes were raised briefly after the First World War, as a result of talk amongst international statesmen in Versailles of self-determination, but for the occupied countries of North Africa it proved to be the sound only of distant voices. The achievement of independence still lay well into the future.

In Tunis, scene of much of this nationalist activity, the interwar years saw the emergence of the country's future leader, Habib Bourguiba. He was one of a new generation of Tunisian professionals who, by dint of exceptional abilities and perseverance, had found a way through the restrictive education system, in his case to go to Paris and qualify as a lawyer. Forming a radical offshoot of the Dustur, the neo-Dusturians, these 'young Turks' kept the ultimate goal of independence firmly within their sights, while at the same time recognizing there would be no quick and easy resolution. Much of their work amounted to taking the message into the countryside but, particularly towards the end of the 1930s, many also took to the streets of Tunis to express their growing disaffection with French rule. The advent of the Second World War threw everything into a new perspective, with far-reaching consequences for the nationalist cause, and Tunis itself was to occupy a key position in the unfolding drama.

With France quickly over-run by Nazi forces, Bourguiba was one of a minority in his circle to urge restraint; to pledge loyalty to the Axis Powers, he believed, would not be in the country's longer-term interests. It was a prescient view if only because, by 1943, German and Italian forces had been forced out of North Africa, the last stand of many of them being in Tunis to await rescue ships to take them to Sicily. In the words of the victorious British commander, relaying the news from the war-torn city to his Prime Minister: 'Sir, it is my duty to report that the Tunisian campaign is over. All enemy resistance has ceased. We are masters of the North African shores.'[19] The wisdom of Bourguiba's caution in retaining links with France could now be seen; with the ending of the war, the French nation was seriously weakened but still in control of its colonies. It was to take another eleven years of negotiations, and arguments amongst the nationalists about the pace and extent of change, before full independence was finally achieved, in May 1956.

In spite of a generally pro-Western stance adopted by the new nation, its inherent Arab-Islamic roots were allowed to flourish. In the course of what amounted to a cultural as well as a political transition, the country (and Tunis in particular) lost much of its previous cosmopolitanism. Foreigners saw most of their privileges removed so that in just four years, from 1955 to 1959, 170,000 Europeans (mainly French and Italians) decided to leave the country.[20] Gradually, too, the large Jewish community dispersed.

Some left at the time of the formation of the State of Israel, others followed in the wake of Tunisian independence; the largest exodus, though, came with the Arab-Israeli war of 1966 and an associated wave of anti-Zionism that threatened their security. For many of those foreigners who left, looking to the fate of Tunisia's neighbours as a sign of what might happen, it was not so much their actual situation at the time as a fear of worse to come that really drove them out. In fact, had they been encouraged to stay, at least until the radical changes of early 2011, they would have experienced a long period of political stability and relative economic progress.

In the event, Bourguiba outstayed his welcome and, in 1987, under the banner of 'The Change', was usurped by his then Prime Minister, Zine-el-Abidine Ben Ali. The incoming President followed more or less the same course as his predecessor. Like Bourguiba, he was keen to espouse Tunisia's Arab heritage while keeping radical Islam at bay; his country remained essentially on good terms with the West but also retained an independent view when called for; and the economy yielded a higher *per capita* income than others in the region, while a dialogue was maintained with some of the poorer African nations.

A feature of Tunisia's modern economy is the close and reciprocal trade links that have been developed with Europe. Unlike its North African neighbours, there have been attempts to control the rate of population increase although this was largely a question of too little, too late. The number of young people has grown disproportionately and it was especially from disaffected youth, desperate for jobs, that the call came in January 2011 for Ben Ali to be removed from office. Anger about unemployment in the country at large proved to be the catalyst for ensuing events which questioned all aspects of the autocratic regime, and which rapidly led to the ousted President fleeing with his family to Saudi Arabia.

Until this recent turbulence, Tunisia had been widely regarded from the outside as something of an oasis in a difficult region. As the travel writer, Paul Theroux observed on his visit there in the 1990s: 'Tunisia is another Mediterranean island, surrounded on one side by water and on the other by pariah states—fanatic Libya on the south-east, blood-drenched Algeria on the west, and the blue Mediterranean on its long irregular coast, scalloped by gulfs and bays'.[21] In the event, it proved to be more like its neighbours than was popularly thought, its apparent stability underpinned by autocratic rule and subsequently challenged by young people who wanted something better. Notwithstanding its changing political context, Tunis remains a city with long roots and its essential character is no less evident now than it was before.

Journey Through Time

Arriving at the Tunis-Maritime station after a run of some fifty minutes and fifteen miles, the train has passed by sites associated with three millennia of history.[22]

The medina continues to play an important role in the life of the city.

Every twelve minutes a local train leaves Tunis-Maritime station, on a route that takes it across the causeway built by the French to the string of settlements along the coast.[23] Soon after the port of La Goulette, one of the stops is Carthage Hannibal. Thus, in under half an hour one is transported on a long journey back though time to the site of one of the greatest cities of the ancient world. Today there are only remnants of this glorious past, a result of comprehensive destruction by the Romans and later invading forces.

Those reminders that can still be found are carefully conserved and well presented by the authorities. One can also identify the two inlets where, literally, hundreds of ships might once have been at anchor: the outer one for trading vessels and, beyond that, an even more protected harbour accessible only through the merchant port, where the famous Carthaginian navy took shelter. These are now empty waters visited, if at all, by lone fishermen.

Modern buildings share the skyline with traditional structures.

For the most part, it is enough to sense the former presence of the Phoenicians and their slaves, and to reflect quietly on the thought of the sustained siege of the city mounted by the Romans, culminating in the starvation and slaughter of tens of thousands. Once, the walls of this metropolis extended over more than thirty kilometres, and an intricate street plan contained numerous buildings that have long ago crumbled into the ground. In contrast, modern Carthage is little more than a fashionable suburb by the sea, a place of luxurious white villas with guards in sharp suits sitting outside the gates. Trees heavy with oranges and pomegranates overhang the high walls. Meanwhile, the little railway continues on its way, stopping at brightly painted stations and calling at the even more picturesque coastal suburb of Sidi Bou Saïd, once favoured by artists and writers.

Returning back along the coast and across the causeway, there is time to reflect that it is unusual to find in a Mediterranean city different periods of history displayed alongside each other rather than layered beneath the ground. Tunis is a mosaic in which all of the pieces retain their own integrity. The site of ancient Carthage is on the coast, detached from the rest of the city. Meanwhile, on the original site of Tunis, the historic medina remains more or less intact. Instead of invading this space, the French colonists built on adjoining land beyond the old walls. Further development, especially in the second half of the twentieth century, led to an outer rim of new suburbs while, more recently, the shallow lake itself has been the site of reclamation and planned expansion.

Thus, the medina, although now surrounded by modern development, continues to play a vibrant role in the life of the city, still fulfilling many of its traditional functions. A spate of demolition and street widening in its northern area was soon stopped in favour of a protective policy for the whole of the medina that has led, in turn, to extensive but sensitive building renovation. Walking through the narrow lanes it is common to see small teams of builders renewing timeworn structures and revealing inner courtyards offering shade and respite from the ambient noise and heat. It would be easy to label this as yet another example of gentrification but the careful modernization of housing has not reduced the vitality of the souks and the abundance of craft workshops; through one door one can see a craftsman pressing material around a mould to form the distinctive red *tarbouche*, through another someone is beating metal. In the various souks, local shoppers mingle with tourists hunting for bargains, all finding their way through what at first seems a maze but is, in fact, organized into specialist quarters. Leatherware, kitchen pots and pans, clothing, shoes, meat and vegetables can all be found in different, covered alleys— in its way a kind of ethnic department store that has stood the test of time. The air carries the contrasting scents of tobacco from *sheshas* smoked at tiny tables along the walkways, of coffee beans roasting and sweet perfumes mixed in dark rooms. At appointed hours of the day, the call to prayer encourages one to look upwards to admire the exquisite shapes and colours of the medina's historic mosques and minarets.

Leaving the medina and crossing into *la nouvelle ville* it is striking how, more than half a century after the colonists returned to their homeland, the French character of the area remains. The original colonial buildings have largely been left in place and the bi-lingual nature of Tunisian society means that street names and institutions like the *lycées* are still as they were. Pavement cafés are crowded, most passers-by favour Western dress, and (at least before the Arab Spring) women seemed relaxed about covering their heads or not. Foreigners left in droves in the 1950s but the anticipated political turbulence and intolerance of Western nationals did not, at the time, materialize. Far from stagnating (as it might have done, had it deterred international investors), Tunis then enjoyed a period of rapid growth.

This, too (as were earlier phases), is reflected on the ground. Initially, the most obvious area for further development was on land immediately beyond the new quarters, extending into the countryside. More recently, however, reflecting the city's continuing appetite for expansion, attention has been focused on reclamation of the lake itself. Physically, this was once a mere inlet of the Mediterranean proper, until in the sixteenth century a spit across its entrance finally separated it from the sea. Over the years, a combination of natural silting and dumping of urban waste reduced its depth and created a foul, contaminated expanse of shallow water, no more than a metre in depth. Gradually, the geography of this natural feature has been changed.

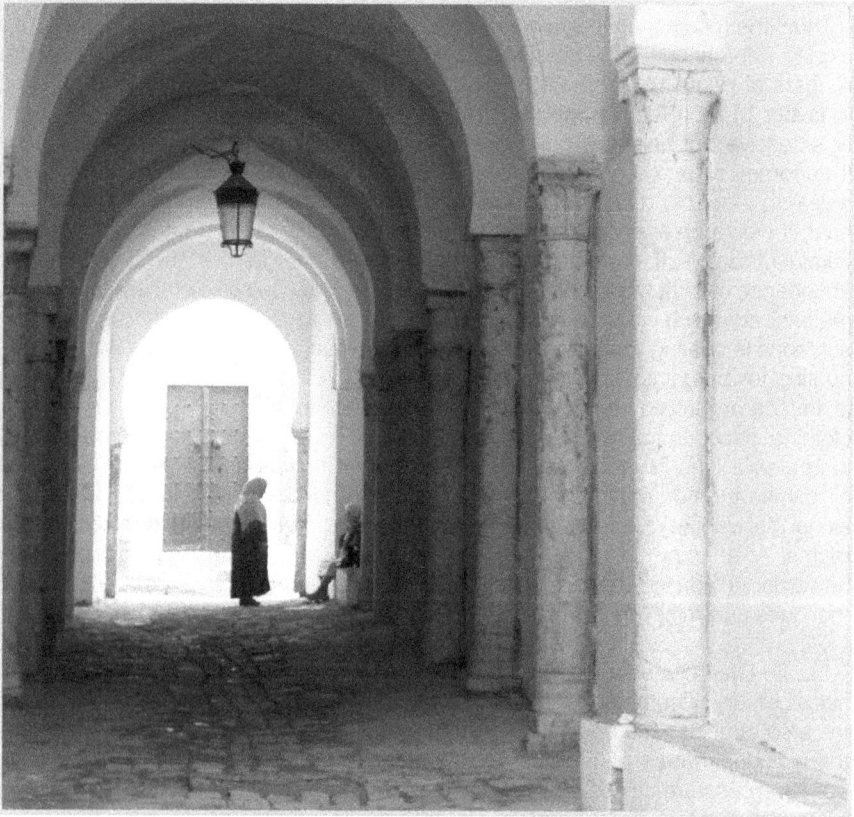

Questions remain to be answered about the country's future.

Firstly, in 1885, a navigation channel was built by French engineers to connect the city with the coastal settlement of La Goulette, dividing the lake into *Lac Nord and Lac Sud*. Excavated material from the canal was used to create a parallel causeway, later used for a road and direct rail link to the coastal settlements. It was, however, to be a century after the first ships sailed through the canal before a scheme was introduced to make better use of the shallow waters on either side. The *Projet du Lac* was launched in the 1980s with two objectives: one was to reduce pollution and create a more acceptable environment for the city, and the other to reclaim land for new development. It has been enthusiastically reported by one informed resident of Tunis that a 'new city is taking shape around the shores of a long-forgotten lake, confidently looking towards the Mediterranean Sea, somehow turning its back on the old medina and European city'.[24] Tunis, in its history, has had something of a love-hate relationship with the open sea, at once preferring its more protected location yet also seeing itself as a Mediterranean city. Increasingly, it seems to be displaying more of the latter side of its character.

Each of the two lakes, north and south, is the subject of separate plans. Plans for *Lac Nord* were started first, with the aim not simply to provide dormitory housing but also to create new manufacturing sites to rival the older industrial quarters. Work on *Lac Sud* followed a decade later, towards the end of the 1990s. Pollution was even more of a problem in this part of the old lake, much of it the result of adjacency to industrial sites, and the first phase of restoration was aimed at reducing contaminated outflows. With that under control, there are even more ambitious plans than for *Lac Nord*, to be known as the Mediterranean Gate.[25] Led by a Dubai investment company, the rhetoric is every bit as expansive as it would be in the company's homeland. Out of the shallow lagoon, claim the investors, will arise a third Tunis, 'the metropolis of the twenty-first century', a Dubai-type development of luxury hotels and high-rise housing (some more than 100 storeys) with a vibrant technological and financial centre. The whole site will be ringed by a fourteen-kilometre waterfront with marinas and an emergent café life.

Underlying the Mediterranean Gate, and other major projects including a new international airport which will be the largest in North Africa, was a basic belief in the stability of the regime. At the launch ceremony for 'Med Gate' in 2008, it was acknowledged that a key factor in the investment was the Tunisian Government's commitment in 'developing Tunisia as a hub for international business and a vital engine for economic growth'.[26] On the surface at least, there were grounds for this confidence. After all, since achieving national independence Tunis had emerged as one of the most stable points on the North African coastline. In effect, it became something of an urban hub for the region, taking advantage of the resistance in the neighbouring capitals of Algiers and Tripoli to allow free flows of people and capital. It grew rapidly (to a present population of some two million),[27] it accounts for the greater part of the country's new technology services and industries, and it has enjoyed a constant flow of visitors not only from Europe but also its Maghreb neighbours.

Yet, for a more observant and perhaps sceptical onlooker, not everything was as might first have appeared. Clouds had been forming on the horizon for some time. With only two leaders since 1956 would it be possible to effect a peaceful transition to a new regime? In the event of a change, could radical Islam still be contained while at the same time balancing moderate opinion?

What could be done to provide enough high-level education and jobs for an aspiring young population? How would a cumbersome autocracy respond to opponents with unlimited information through the internet and a keen knowledge of events in other parts of the world? Such questions were for too long ignored and it was left to violent events on the streets of the capital in early 2011 to demand answers. Tunisia was the first of the countries of the Arab Spring to hold democratic elections, revealing popular support for Islamic parties. It remains to be seen whether this preference will be tempered to create a more open society, or whether the country will, increasingly, follow a conservative path. The outcome will have a direct bearing on the future of Tunis as a Mediterranean city.

CHAPTER 6

ISLAND CROSS-CURRENTS

More than eleven million people live on the 12,000 or so islands of the Mediterranean.[1] The spread is very uneven, with only a relatively few large islands and by far the greatest number scattered in Greek waters, many of them little more than rocky outcrops. Sicily is not only the largest island but also the most populous. Proportionately, the islands represent only a small part of both the landmass and population of the Mediterranean whole and yet their role over the years cannot be ignored. Islands are an essential element of the story of this region, hardly surprising given its seafaring traditions. The three cities selected are intended to reveal different aspects of the past, as well as present developments, of this striking landform of the Mediterranean.

It is fitting that Sicily is the first to be visited, with Syracuse the city in question. Originally a Corinthinan colony, Syracuse emerged to become one of the most powerful cities of the classical world. Even with the demise of ancient Greece it held its own and later, albeit for only a few years, was favoured over Constantinople as the Byzantine capital. If the first half of its history is one of grandeur, however, the subsequent era is a tale of steady decline. Modern Syracuse contains well-preserved reminders of its past but also signs of decay; as the evidence testifies, its golden days are long over.

Dating from the sixteenth century, Valletta, on the small island of Malta, is, in Mediterranean terms, a relative newcomer. There are good reasons, though, for its inclusion. One is that its wealthy founders ensured that their creation was well planned and endowed with fine buildings. Another reason is that its very origins were linked to the defence of the Christianity against Muslim invaders, so that it was from the outset on the frontline of that familiar Mediterranean divide. More recently, as Malta's capital, it is adjusting well to a new economic role in the region.

Cyprus is the third-largest island in the Mediterranean but it is politically divided. To the north is Turkish-occupied territory and to the south the people are Greek. The line between the two runs right through the centre of Nicosia. Where better, then, to conclude this odyssey than in a city that bears the continuing scars of a divided past: Turks against Greeks, Muslims opposed to Christians? It is a depressing note to finish on but also a poignant reminder of the persisting problems of the region.

SYRACUSE

By modern standards, Syracuse, on the island of Sicily, is not a large city. It has a population of only 125,000 and is today no more than a provincial capital. Approaching it from the landward side, it has all the appearances of just another Sicilian settlement: ragged at the edges, noisy traffic in the centre, and buildings with plaster peeling from their walls. Do not be misled, however, by first appearances, for as an exemplar of urban change the story it tells is as eventful as any. Occupying a strategic location between the eastern and western basins of the Mediterranean, and between the nearby African coast and the mainland of southern Europe, few cities are more obviously at the crossroads of continents. Once the capital of the Mediterranean's largest island, there were times when Syracuse was at the very heart of the region's wars and commerce. Not only was it for a period even more populous and at the centre of events than mighty Athens, but so it is claimed by one enthusiast, in its heyday it was, indeed, 'the greatest city in the world'.[1] Although that is no longer the case—and perhaps never was—one finds within its boundaries exceptional physical relics to remind one of former glories

Not Quite Atlantis

Now in this island of Atlantis there was a great and wonderful empire which had rule over the whole island and several others...[2]

Islands, real and imagined, are at the very heart of the epic story of Greek colonization if not of the Mediterranean more generally. Quite apart from the material attractions of a large and fertile island like Sicily, there is something symbolic about the physical separation of islands and the prospect of discovering a hidden idyll. More practical minds, however, have pointed to their obvious shortcomings, open to the sea on all sides. When Cicero thoughtfully weighed up the pros and cons of a maritime location it was not especially Syracuse he had in mind but, more inclusively, the whole process of colonization. 'Maritime cities', he warned, 'are always exposed, not only to many attacks but to perils they cannot provide against.'[3] Why then, he asked, had the Greeks persisted in locating new outposts by the sea when such places had clear disadvantages, not least of all their vulnerability to attack? Compared with an inland site, where an enemy would find difficulty in taking a city wholly by surprise, the sea offers no such protection: 'a maritime and naval enemy can fall upon a town on the sea-coast before any one suspects that he is about to come; and when he does come, nothing exterior indicates who he is, or whence he comes, or what he wishes.'[4]

Syracuse was very much a case in point, selected by the Greek city state of Corinth as an ideal location for a colony because of its commanding position at a prominent point on the Sicilian coastline, which is itself in the centre of the Mediterranean. For the commercially-minded Corinthians here was a gateway to the island's rich hinterland, as well as a potential hub in an emergent network of seaborne traffic. At the same time, in their haste to establish a new foothold the colonizers rather neglected the question of its obvious vulnerability.

Looking across to the tip of Ortygia, which offers sheltered waters beyond.

It was in the eighth century BC that Corinthian ships first sailed into the western-facing bay, protected from seasonal storms in the Ionian Sea by the protruding island of Ortygia. When they explored the interior the invading force discovered evidence of scattered tribes that had for long occupied the remote mountains and valleys, but their own arrival marked the start of a totally new chapter in the island's history. The Corinthians settled first on Ortygia, a landform more like a promontory than an island, barely detached from the mainland and easily bridged. In time, as Syracuse grew in importance it would spawn its own colonies along the neighbouring Sicilian coastline but none were to rival the parent itself. Not only was Syracuse to become the most important city in Sicily but it also dominated *Magna Graecia*, the wider realm of Greek settlement that extended into southern Italy. During the first five centuries of its long history, Syracuse was regarded not simply as a colony but a fully-fledged Greek city in its own right. It was drawn into wars between city states in the Hellenic homeland, defeating the Athenian navy in battle as well as rebutting repeated attacks by the Carthaginians from North Africa; it was also successful in turning back the Etruscans and other armies from the Italian mainland. Nor was its reputation purely military; intellectually, it was home to various scholars of renown, not least of all the inventor and philosopher, Archimedes. As a physical artefact, the city acquired most of the elements of classical Greek town planning, including a spectacular theatre where its citizens could watch new tragedies by the occasional resident playwright, Aeschylus, as well as other notable dramatists of the day. In the first century BC, following its occupation by the Romans, Cicero could still describe it as 'the greatest of the Grecian towns. It was indeed a most beautiful city; and its admirable citadel, its canals distributed through all its districts, its broad streets, its porticoes, its temples, and its walls, gave Syracuse the appearance of a most flourishing state.'[5] The substance of what is quoted is correct but the many guide books that use this source to tell of the enduring attractions of Syracuse fail to point to the context and essential point that Cicero was making, namely, that such material magnificence is worth little if the ruler is despotic. Although at times it espoused democracy, that was certainly not always the case. Thus, 'while Dionysius its tyrant reigned there, nothing of all its wealth belonged to the people, and the people were nothing better than the slaves of one master'.[6]

Cicero's double-edged observation pointed straight to the heart of a dilemma that contemporary Greek critics had themselves already addressed: how could they be sure that their model of city life, exported through colonization, was indeed worthy of reproduction? The playwright, Aristophanes, for instance, voiced a view that Greek cities had become rather tiresome and over-planned, and hardly worth copying in their present form. In *The Birds* he cut closest to the chase, not simply because of what he wrote but also for the timing of the production.[7] First presented to an Athenian audience in 414 BC, these were anxious days for the city state of Athens, with its fleet at that very moment at anchor outside Syracuse, intent on overwhelming the colony. For his audience the play offered the welcome prospect of an escape from Athens, a city that had already known better days, and which had emerged the weaker following costly battles with Sparta. Rather like Thomas More was to do in England many centuries later, in his eponymous representation of utopia, Aristophanes was able to project his own sense of disaffection through the thinly veiled charade of a fantasy. Thus, we find on the stage two time-worn Athenians who journey far into the countryside, where they come across a population of birds and promise to create an ideal city in the clouds in which they could all live in peace. First they have to agree a name for this imagined paradise, and alight on Nephelococcygia, loosely translated to mean Cloud-Cuckoo Land. To a chorus of approval they then set to work on building their heavenly paradise or, rather, the birds are set to work to do this—only to be interrupted by a succession of unwanted visitors from the very society they are seeking to leave behind. Amongst these intruders is Meton, a town planner, who offers to survey the air and to parcel it into lots:

> *With the straight ruler I set to work to inscribe a square within this circle; in its centre will be the market-place, into which all the straight streets will lead, converging to this centre like a star, which... sends forth its rays in a straight line from all sides.*[8]

Meton's offer to plan their city in this way is firmly rejected and, like their other visitors, he is soon sent on his way. In ridiculing the town planner and his geometrical sense of order, Aristophanes was mischievously taking issue with the standard urban form used by the Greeks in the creation of colonies. Perhaps he was especially offended by the influence of the pioneer planner, Hippodamus, with his singular love of a grid layout; certainly, Aristophanes would have been familiar with the appearance of Piraeus, the port of Athens planned in this way by Hippodamus in the middle of the fifth century BC. More likely, though, Aristophanes—like a modern, anti-Establishment playwright—was simply giving voice to populist concerns and objecting to the heavy hand of regulation that was laid on his home city of Athens.

In contrast, there were respected voices at the time that spoke, instead, not of the desirability of less control but of more. Foremost amongst the Athenian philosophers who took this view was Plato (himself a former pupil of Socrates and, in turn, a mentor for Aristotle). By the time that Plato set down his ideas, the Peloponnesian War was behind him, with the former glory and invincibility of Athens irretrievably tarnished by Sparta. Unlike Aristophanes, though, his panacea was not to relax standards but rather to strengthen them. There was nothing wrong, he contended, with a political structure characterized by a privileged elite supported by a large under-class that included compliant slaves, and no reason why it should not continue to be reproduced elsewhere through colonization. For Plato, the strict regime of Sparta offered a better model than that of decadent Athens. While favouring order, however, he baulked at the idea of despotism.

It was fitting that Plato, who argued that philosophers had a crucial role to play in the practical operation of society, was duly invited in this capacity to visit Syracuse. On three occasions he attempted to persuade the despotic rulers, Dionysius I and then Dionysius II, to change their ways, exhorting them to allow the colony's citizens 'to be free and governed by the best laws'.[9] Nor was it just a question of abstract principles that motivated him, for Plato was disapproving, too, of the hedonistic lifestyle that he saw around him. Not surprisingly, on each occasion he visited the city his unwanted message and reproachful attitude led to the philosopher's early eviction and forced return to Athens. In spite of repeated rejection (and the personal hurt this undoubtedly caused him)[10] Plato was undeterred in continuing his search for a better society. Particularly in his later works, he was to explain in more detail his own improved version of the city state.

The essence of Plato's arguments (expressed through a series of dialogues) is to be found in the principles on which society rests and the institutions that need to be set in place. In an ideal world the rulers would be drawn from the privileged class of guardians and would, he contended, be philosophers. He accepts an uneven distribution of power as an inevitable legacy of either the deities or nature: 'the whole State will grow up in a noble order, and the several classes will receive the proportion of happiness which nature assigns to them.'[11] Of greater concern to him are the signs of material excess that too often emerge as a city becomes prosperous, only to threaten the very fabric of society. That is what he objected to in Syracuse and he returns to this theme time and again. Even locating a city close to the sea is seen as a moral threat, with the import of luxuries and avaricious merchants leading to 'degeneracy and discordance of manners'.[12]

Instead, Plato favours a less open society, with the most obvious material temptations removed. Property would be held in common, and wealth for its own sake eschewed. From his various writings one gleans that there would be 'no poets, no passionate music, no marital attachments, no parental solicitudes, no mixing of vocations, no luxury, no foreign intercourse. Restrictive, puritanic, authoritarian: such was his ideal.'[13] Undoubtedly, neither Athens nor Syracuse would have matched his exacting standards. One can only imagine that his ideal cities would be austere, tightly-regulated places. His preference was for a fixed population of some 5000 citizens (yielding a total population closer to 30,000 when one includes those who could not qualify for citizen status). The city itself would be sited centrally, so that it could draw on the surrounding farms and forests for its food and wood for fires. Unlike Aristophanes, he would have welcomed the likes of the town planner, Meton, to subdivide it dispassionately into lots according to a rational design. At the heart of the city would be the most revered temples, in the form of an acropolis, and elsewhere the lesser institutions. Everything would, no doubt, function with mechanical efficiency but it seems there would be little to lift the spirit.

Somewhere in his writings, however, there is at least a glimpse of humanity. In two of his later works, Plato uses an imaginary island to allow its people a modicum of waywardness.[14] His setting is the lost island of Atlantis, the origins of which he dates some 10,000 years before and locates beyond the Pillars of Hercules, in the open waters of the Atlantic. One might speculate that the myth was inspired by a real island such as Sicily—itself renowned for its natural abundance, evoking images that Plato would have retained—but the basis for that is no sounder than for other locations in the Mediterranean and beyond. Either way, in Atlantis Plato tells of various indulgences, like the royal palace, 'a marvel to behold for size and for beauty'; the different coloured stone used in the buildings, 'to please the eye, and to be a natural source of delight'; Poseidon's temple, faced in silver with golden pinnacles; and hot and cold fountains in beautiful gardens.[15] Elsewhere, truer to form, he describes 'guardhouses at intervals for the guards, the more trusted of whom were appointed to keep watch in the lesser zone, which was nearer the Acropolis, while the most trusted of all had houses given them within the citadel, near the persons of the kings'.[16] Even in Atlantis, Plato could not really free himself from thoughts of the imperfect world in which he lived.

Continental Crossfire

... more people have lived with one another and clashed with one another here than perhaps anywhere on the planet.[17]

Although Predrag Matvejevic, in the above quote, was reflecting on the whole of the Mediterranean this could well be directed to Sicily in particular. The experience of the island is in so many ways a distillation of the region at large, an intense history of one occupation after another—of accommodations found between different peoples as well as lasting enmities. After the Hellenic era, nothing could be more certain than that Syracuse, so close to neighbouring continents, would continue to be of interest to competing powers. Indeed, no sooner had the Greek sun passed its zenith than the Romans seized the opportunity, their first intervention being to place Syracuse under siege for two years from 214 BC. In spite of the defenders deploying a unique weapon, the 'claw'—a form of crane devised by the city's celebrated inventor, Archimedes, to lift enemy ships out of the water—the superior power of the Romans prevailed. Syracuse itself was largely destroyed after its capture, with buildings reduced to rubble and anything of value looted. Even the Roman consul and military leader, Claudius Marcellus, is said (according to Plutarch) to have been 'overwhelmed with compassion to see the riches accumulated in a long and happy epoch, vanish, in such a way, in the short space of an hour...'[18] Nor was it just Syracuse that suffered, for across the island fields were abandoned and corrupt government became the norm. Although Sicily was a rich prize for the conquerors, offering agricultural and mineral wealth as well as a strategic stronghold in the middle of the Mediterranean, the early experience of the new regime was not auspicious.

Once before, in the face of adversity, Syracuse had turned to a philosopher for advice; that, of course, was Plato but soon it was the turn of another wise man, Cicero, to offer his thoughts. There was a difference between the two as Cicero held an official position, as a senior administrator on the island, but he shared with Plato an outspoken dislike of obvious abuses of government. Following his appointment, he soon returned to Rome to present his case, the outcome being the forced resignation of Gaius Verres, the errant governor in question. It was to be another century, however, before Syracuse—which remained the capital of Sicily throughout these difficult times—experienced tangible signs of recovery. The Greek geographer, Strabo, was a contemporary observer who reported optimistically of a fresh wave of colonization and rebuilding:

> And in our own time, because [Sextus] Pompeius abused, not only the other cities, but Syracuse in particular, Augustus Caesar sent a colony and restored a considerable part of the old settlement; for in olden times it was a city of five towns, with a wall of one hundred and eighty stadia. Now it was not at all necessary to fill out the whole of this circuit, but it was necessary, he thought, to build up in a better way only the part that was settled — the part adjacent to the Island of Ortygia which had a sufficient circuit to make a notable city.[19]

Syracuse was never to regain its former glory as a cultural and commercial capital but the Romans at least brought to the city some of their own trademark structures. An extensive gymnasium was introduced, the old agora was converted to a Roman forum and, similarly, the Greek theatre was adapted to accommodate their own styles of production. In due course, a second amphitheatre was built nearby, amidst parkland, although, unlike the Greeks who dedicated their theatres to literary dramas, this was used primarily for gladiatorial contests and orchestrated representations of naval battles. Relics of this period remain to this day in the district known as Neapolis, originally developed by the Greeks for public performances and ceremonial purposes and now given over very largely to the gaze of tourists.

Alongside such material developments, Syracuse was an early home of Christianity. Following a brief visit by Paul the Apostle on his missionary travels around the Mediterranean, the seeds of the new religion were sown on the island. Its future was not secured, though, until the Romans some centuries later themselves embraced the teachings of Christ. As evidence of its formal acceptance, extensive catacombs were built beneath the city from the start of the fifth century. Christianity was by then firmly established although, with the departure of the Romans and the subsequent arrival of the Vandals and Ostrogoths—ostensibly Christian too but generally regarded as barbarians and dismissed as heretics—its hold on the spiritual life of the city was temporarily in question. Only when, in 535, the barbarians were expelled by the superior power of Byzantium could a longer period of stability be enjoyed; indeed, for five years, from 663 to 668, Syracuse was even designated as the capital of the Eastern Holy Empire (before the title reverted to Constantinople). During the Byzantine era in Sicily, extending over three centuries, Syracuse gained from the establishment of a number of important churches and its own cathedral. It was probably inevitable, however, if only because of Sicily's location and potential wealth, that Christian supremacy would in time be challenged by Islam. Indeed, throughout the rule of Byzantium there were raids emanating from the Arab-controlled lands of North Africa. Eventually, in the tenth century, the Muslims broke through, capturing Syracuse and, once again in the city's turbulent history, reducing most of it to rubble. To add to its woes, its recognition as Sicily's capital was ended in deference to Palermo, leaving the eastern part of the island in a political and economic backwater. With this decisive loss of power, Syracuse was never to regain its former importance.

In due course, Christian sovereignty was restored to the island, after a Norman force at the end of the eleventh century usurped the Muslims. Roman Catholicism gained the ascendancy over the Eastern Church and a feudal system of government and land management was introduced. Under the Normans, Sicily was recognized as one of the wealthiest kingdoms in Europe. Its very riches, however, were to deny the island stability as first one and then another European power claimed sovereignty. It was like a stage onto which stepped a parade of characters, invariably fighting amongst themselves as well as warding off others. At different times, France, Spain, Austria and (during the Napoleonic Wars) Britain, as well as various German and Italian states, were all to lay claim to the island. Marriages were arranged and alliances struck between respective European royal houses, shifting the balance of power with little or no regard to the wishes of the local population. For much of the time, Sicily was joined in a union with Naples that was known on the island as the Kingdom of the Two Sicilies (or on the mainland as the Kingdom of Naples). To add to the complexity of it all, various Popes treated Sicily as neutral ground, away from watching eyes in the Vatican, to broker secret agreements and to indulge in their own particular vices. With Sicily manipulated in these various ways, as little more than a pawn on the European chessboard, it is little wonder that the once grand city of Syracuse became increasingly marginalized; it was in the opulent palaces of Palermo that the island's future would now be forged.

Contrasting examples of Sicilian Baroque in Syracuse.

As if this turbulent political history were not enough, Syracuse suffered at different times from the devastating effects of plague and successive earthquakes, the most serious of the latter being in 1693, resulting in many lives lost and few buildings left standing. Other settlements along the east coast and in parts of the interior were also badly damaged. At least, some good was to follow, in the form of an extensive programme of rebuilding, characterized by a new style of architecture that came to be known as Sicilian baroque.[20] Even before the great earthquake, prestigious buildings in Palermo (but also to some extent in provincial Syracuse) were displaying baroque features, in a style emanating largely from Rome and Naples. By the time that Syracuse could commission its own architects, designs had become not only more intricate but also more refined than earlier examples. This later generation of home-bred architects 'used their intellect to produce buildings in which the energy and imagination of the south attained full and mature expression'.[21] According to the art historian, Anthony Blunt, Sicilian baroque was cleverly adapted to the island's traditions and to the varying qualities of local stone; thus in Syracuse the coarse, silvery-white limestone quarried nearby was not conducive to fine cutting and encouraged, instead, a bolder style than in neighbouring towns along the coast.[22]

Its manifestation could be seen at its best in the many ecclesiastical buildings and in *palazzos* owned by aristocratic families. Quite apart from its intrinsic qualities, the style spoke volumes for the island's Christian traditions and continuing attachment to the European mainland—so close, geographically, to the Islamic culture of nearby North Africa yet in other ways irrevocably separated.

By the end of the eighteenth century, this unprecedented spate of building development in Syracuse was largely over but any notion of restored grandeur for the city was misplaced. When its people protested to the authorities about their treatment in the face of an outbreak of cholera in 1837 (the island was still, nominally at least, under the control of the Spanish Bourbons) even its status as a provincial capital was removed. Not until 1865, when the many states of Italy were finally unified, could Syracuse at last breathe the fresh air of freedom, something it had not known since the Corinthians had first established it so many centuries before. Its future was now in the hands of its own nation.

Italian unification came in 1865, but for Sicily this still did not bring true independence. There was growing resentment on the island that the real power lay far away to the north, and that its own interests would be forgotten. In the event, the doubters were right: Sicily did not prosper from this political change and its endemic poverty led to a surge of emigration, with many of its inhabitants crossing the Atlantic to find new homes in the United States. Mussolini's centralist policies in the interwar period only added to a sense of being marginalized, encouraging the formation of a separatist movement. More misery was experienced during the Second World War, when the island found itself at the heart of Mediterranean operations: first, the retreating armies of Italy and Germany used it to regroup on their way from North Africa, followed closely by the Allies as they made their way in pursuit from Sicily up the very spine of Italy.

Only after 1945 was there at last a change in the island's fortunes. The previous years of fascist rule gave way to democratization, with a new constitution for Italy as a whole. Under these postwar arrangements, Sicily became an autonomous region, with its own Parliament and an elected President. In common with the whole of southern Italy, there were calls to redress the poverty and inequalities of the past, and hopes were placed in two new measures dating from 1950. One was a national policy of land reform, designed to transfer more holdings to peasant farmers, and the other was a massive development funding programme for the South (the *Cassa per il Mezzogiorno*). It would be cynical to suggest that these were wholly unsuccessful but critics have pointed to various failings, including the misdirection of funds, spurious projects of little value other than to favour the contractors, and political patronage on a large scale. Traditionally with a strong hold on Sicilian affairs, Mafia groups undoubtedly benefited from these various injections of government funds. [23]

Appropriating the Past

We must live in the future tense and not the past pluperfect.[24]

Syracuse, its days of glory and influence across the region long past, could only watch as a spectator the events which were to shape its modern destiny. Palermo, Messina and nearby Catania emerged as the new Sicilian powerhouses and, as each of these cities pressed ahead, it seemed that the former capital would be left with little more than its ruins. Albeit on a smaller scale its predicament was not unlike that of Venice; both had once played a leading role in Mediterranean affairs but in modern times it was as if they had little choice but to look to the past for economic salvation. In fact, the modern record of Syracuse is not without more intricate twists and turns; undoubtedly its history has crept up on the city and has only partially been resisted.

Ruins can sometimes be well integrated in the modern city.

Neapolis: the archaeological park that attracts most of the visitors to Syracuse.

It is inevitable that the past will always play an important part in shaping the modern history of Syracuse. The first stones were laid nearly three millennia ago and it has been continuously occupied since then. Such longevity cannot lightly be discarded. Yet in Syracuse there is a challenge that has to be faced by other Mediterranean cities too, with comparable layers of history, namely, to find ways to accommodate its past while allowing the present to breathe. If the evidence of former glories is allowed to take over, a city will suffocate; if it is erased, it will lose a potential and irreplaceable asset. Somewhere between the two extremes lies a balance that can, ideally, offer the best of both worlds—but it is a balance that is notoriously difficult to achieve and, in the case of Syracuse, the chance of its attainment is finely poised. Tradition and modernity face each other across a divide that has yet to be satisfactorily bridged.

Much of the housing in Ortygia is picturesque but also in need of improvement.

Of the former, the city's continuing love affair with the past is evidenced in the physical remains of the earliest settlement of Syracuse, the classical era. Relics continue to be unearthed in the course of modern construction, hitherto buried over the years beneath layers of rubble. Where possible, artefacts are removed to museums for safekeeping but there are also sites like the Temple of Apollo that are preserved *in situ*. Elsewhere, to the north-west of the two harbours—Porto Grande and Porto Piccolo—the land rises to an area of parkland that contains important relics of both the Greek and Roman eras. Still known by its original name of Neapolis, it was one of five districts that formed the ancient city.

Set amidst trees, this is where one finds well-preserved remains of both Greek and Roman theatres, the earlier one (although adapted by the Romans) so obviously designed primarily for dramatic productions and still used for this purpose, and the latter for spectacle. Within the park, there are also sites of ancient quarries and burial places, preserved for posterity. Throughout the day, coaches arrive with successive groups of tourists, each led quickly through the ruins before being taken to their next Sicilian venue. Modern tourism has created a strange relationship between visitor and object, between present and past, a relationship that relies on contrived itineraries—on places that one is required to see before being allowed to leave. It seems right that such places are protected and accessible but, somehow, the resultant interactions fall short of what should be a unique experience. The intellectual excitement of confronting the distant past and its enduring achievements is too often diminished by the routines of modern tourism.

In contrast, in the Baroque section of the city—on the island of Ortygia and (generally newer and less ornate) on the mainland in the nearest street blocks—the visitor becomes a participant as well as spectator. These are living neighbourhoods and the environment is altogether more vital. Inevitably, the finest examples of this flamboyant style are to be found in those structures built by the wealthiest sponsors. One sees this especially in the grand frontage to the city's cathedral and in neighbouring buildings around the Piazza Duomo, as well as the various palazzos on the island that were once home to aristocratic families and successful merchants. Perhaps more fascinating than these ostentatious exemplars of the period are the humbler structures in the narrow lanes, built for workers and their families.

Sometimes the buildings were designed specifically for artisans and included a workshop at street level, while above they were commonly divided into lodging rooms and apartments. Externally, they are still typified by decorative ironwork to frame the balconies, cleverly crafted doors and arches, and carved recesses with images of the Madonna. At first sight, such neighbourhoods retain the appearance of a long process of decay, modest (if not shabby) in appearance and seemingly untouched for decades if not centuries.

Much of the housing is still inhabited by low-income families, who originally found work in the same area. It is picturesque but cramped and the narrow streets were never designed for modern traffic or parking. In the absence of parks, boys kick footballs in the narrow alleys and courtyards, and washing is hung out to dry against the dusty walls. People have been slowly moving out when they can, not only in response to the deteriorating condition of the housing but also because of the loss of local employment. For instance, the once flourishing fishing industry of Syracuse largely collapsed in the 1950s and the close-knit community that used to live behind the waterfront emigrated *en masse* to Argentina. Likewise, most of the artisan workshops and specialist warehouses in the narrow streets and along the quays have long been closed.

Porto Piccolo with modern apartments on the waterfront.

In contrast with this process of inexorable decline, there are various signs that the area is remaking itself. Some of this change is more compatible with the traditional urban fabric than others. Syracuse, for instance, has a student population and the older, affordable housing is attractive to this group; likewise it is an area of choice for young professionals who want to live in historic buildings close to the centre of the city and quickly set about restoring them. In other respects, the change that is underway will be difficult to accommodate without jeopardizing the essential character of the area.

Increasingly, Ortygia is visited by tourists, and old buildings are being converted into boutique hotels, *trattorias* and, more recently, second homes. Around the harbours, there is a familiar pattern of smart waterfront restaurants and bars, and the presence of luxury apartments. The Porto Grande itself is being modernized to enable large cruise ships to dock, while the Porto Piccolo provides mooring facilities for small luxury craft. Progressively, Ortygia will be associated more with urban chic than the relaxed ambience that has weathered like the faded buildings themselves—in one sense an encouraging sign of revival but not without a cost. In their different ways, both the classical ruins and the remaining Baroque architecture are still central to the city's economic and cultural *raison d'être*. There will always be service functions for Syracuse, like local government, education and retail, but these will be more than matched by its 'unique selling point', the living remains of its long and fascinating history.

Popular recognition of this came in 2005 with UNESCO's designation of the historic areas of the city as a World Heritage Site. In making the award, the panel claimed that there is 'no other city that contains monuments of such exceptional value, ranging from the ancient Greek period to the Baroque and including the early Christian eras'.[25] Attention was also drawn to the cultural heritage of Syracuse, as a centre of ideas and literary works. Of particular interest is the importance attributed to the city's location in the centre of the Mediterranean, where it has absorbed influences 'down the centuries, of the different cultures of the western world'.[26]

The past, however, can never be enough for a city of this size and one must look as well to what has happened in the way of modern development. During the 1950s, in the wake of a slow postwar recovery, the discovery of oil nearby was welcomed as something of a bonanza. With the raw commodity came an associated development of petrochemicals and related industries along the coast to the north, offering a fresh source of employment for Syracusans. New housing was built in the 1960s and 1970s to the north of the old quarters, on the very slopes originally settled by Greek colonists in the days when Syracuse rivalled Athens. After years of decline the population started to increase. In the event, however, the supply of oil proved to be limited and the early promise of economic prosperity remained only partially fulfilled. Syracuse today is on the cusp. It possesses a built heritage of exceptional merit and is reliant on income generated by an increasing number of visitors. The past is, clearly, an essential element of the modern economy. At the same time, the potential gains of tourism are not easily won. Somehow a better balance has to be struck between attracting more visitors and, at the same time, successfully managing their impact on the fragile historic environment.

Somehow, too, the present gulf between old and new needs to be bridged, so that the urban fabric is once again unified rather than split. The task of getting this right is not insignificant and certainly not unique to Syracuse; it is a challenge that one sees, too, in other cities across the Mediterranean with a long history, but rarely if at all has it been satisfactorily resolved.

VALLETTA

Valletta, capital of Malta, with a population of only 7000 is the smallest of the cities in this study. It is also the youngest, dating only from the sixteenth century, a mere stripling compared with others in the region that measure their histories in millennia. Yet there are good reasons to include it as a vivid example of the mixed fortunes that can beset a city so close to different continents. Perched between the eastern and western basins of the Mediterranean, and just a short distance from Sicily and North Africa, the prime importance of Malta has always been strategic. Sometimes this has been to its advantage and sometimes not. As a result of its location, this tiny nation and its capital city have inherited a unique mix of cultural traces from their multi-ethnic neighbours—although, remarkably, instead of being overwhelmed Malta has managed to forge its own identity. Its show of independence—cultural as well as political—coupled with a proud history, has enabled Valletta to punch above its weight, making its own distinctive contribution to the evolving fortunes of the region.

Of Hostilities and Hospitals

History has cast Malta in the role of garrison and citadel, set in a sea of sieges.[1]

Long before the foundation of Valletta, events on the island set the tone for what followed. It was certainly not for any inherent riches that successive invaders were attracted. Malta itself is small, barely thirty kilometres across, although the modern nation of the same name includes two other inhabited islands, Gozo and Comino. Located close to the African coastline and the Sahara beyond, summer temperatures are invariably high; the *sirocco* blows across the island from the south, bringing the heat of the desert combined with the uncomfortable addition of moisture from the narrow stretch of intervening sea. Much of the landscape is barren with little or no surface water; supplies have traditionally been collected in cisterns and from dwindling underground reserves, now supplemented through costly seawater desalination. If once there were trees, these have long disappeared and timber has to be imported. Certain fruits and vegetables grow well if irrigated— the orange groves are invariably admired by visitors, and the vine flourishes if carefully tended—but, unlike in neighbouring Sicily, the soil is thin and not well-suited for grains in any quantity. Nor are the rocks renowned for gemstones or other prized minerals, although the prevalent limestone itself yields plentiful, honey-tinted stone for building. The real attraction of Malta, though, is not what is on the island so much as where it is; its location in the middle of the Mediterranean has always been the main lure.

From the earliest times, Malta experienced a familiar Mediterranean history of successive conquests.[2] The first occupants date back to prehistoric times, from as early as the sixth millennium BC, and probably originated in neighbouring Sicily. Much later, in around 700 BC, it is believed that a small group of Greeks arrived, settling in the area that is now Valletta but not attaching great importance to their newfound acquisition.[3] Of greater significance for the future of the island, they were followed a century later by Phoenicians who quickly recognized it as a useful staging post for more distant voyages that would take them beyond the Mediterranean. In spite of their seafaring activities the Phoenicians chose for their stronghold a site in the centre of the island, valuing its strategic vantage point and defensive position away from enemy fleets.

Then known as Maleth and now Mdina, this was, effectively, the first capital of Malta. With the departure of the Levantine Phoenicians in about 400 BC it was then the turn of the Carthaginians from nearby North Africa (themselves of Phoenician descent) to claim the island before, in turn, their defeat at the hands of the Romans. The latter, like the Levantine Phoenicians, also favoured Mdina, designating it a *municipium* and locating the Governor's palace there. With the eventual division of the Roman Empire in the fourth century into western and eastern realms, under Rome and Byzantium, Malta fell within the jurisdiction of the latter and remained so for the best part of 500 years. Even before that era, the island already enjoyed a reputation as a fount of Christianity, on account of its association in the first century with St. Paul. During his third missionary journey across the Mediterranean, Paul was allegedly shipwrecked off the coast and duly gave thanks for his salvation by performing miracles for the inhabitants.[4] There is little evidence of attempts by aggressors to capture the island in the post-Roman period, other than periodic attacks by Germanic tribes that were successfully rebuffed with the help of Byzantine forces.

Mdina was the first capital of Malta, chosen because of its inland location.

The next chapter in Malta's history saw the ending of Christian rule and the arrival of Islam, against the background of a broader conflict between Arabs and Byzantines in the eastern Mediterranean. Following the collapse of Christian resistance in nearby Sicily, Malta quickly succumbed to Arab domination, which lasted for nearly two centuries and brought to the island the cultural influence of different dynasties. Significantly, the Arabs introduced a number of innovations, including efficient methods of irrigation and new crops such as cotton. It was also the time when the language evolved to shape the modern hybrid, derived from a dialect spoken by Arabs in Sicily. As they did elsewhere, the Muslims allowed Christians to maintain their beliefs, albeit at a financial cost in terms of special levies. This period of relative stability, however, was not to last and the flags of Christian soldiers were soon to be seen again on approaching ships. In 1091, a Norman army led by Count Roger of Sicily recovered Malta from the Arabs and the island became part of the Kingdom of Sicily (which at the time included the southern mainland of Italy). Catholicism was installed as the dominant religion and, later in its history, all remaining Muslims were expelled from the island; even today, in spite of its proximity to North Africa, the presence of Islam is slight and there is only one mosque on the island.[5] With the subsequent demise of the Normans in Sicily, Malta was then to be treated as something of a pawn that was passed between various royal households—acquired first by Charles of Anjou and then the House of Aragon before Charles V of Spain handed it in 1530 to the Order of Knights of the Hospital of St. John of Jerusalem. It proved to be a decisive move, reinforcing the island's Christian pedigree and leading to the foundation of Valletta itself.

The arrival of the Order of Knights of the Hospital, the Knights Hospitaller, immediately brought to life memories of the earlier Crusades; indeed, the old battles between opposing religions were still far from over. Just as the Crusades had themselves attracted myth and legend, something of a mystical aura surrounded the Knights for whom chivalry was their very watchword. Their origins were, indeed, noble enough, with a reputation as a powerful fighting force combined with renowned compassion, expressed most famously in the foundation of a hospital in Jerusalem in the eleventh century to care not only for wounded soldiers but also for sick and wounded pilgrims. As a result, the Knights became a separate religious and military order, with its own charter, charged with the task of defending the Holy Land against the infidels. Defeated in due course and forced to leave Jerusalem, they sought a new stronghold, first in the Levantine port of Acre and then Cyprus, before a longer period of tenure on the eastern Mediterranean island of Rhodes. For two centuries they remained there, until ousted by the Ottomans; the relatively few survivors of the Ottoman raids were allowed by their conquerors to take refuge in Sicily, from where they made their eventual migration to Malta.

In fulfilment of their charter they were quick to establish a hospital in their new homeland, just as they had done previously in Rhodes and before that in Jerusalem. Far from ushering in a new era of peace and stability, however, it was as if the Crusades were still being fought. The decision of Charles V to grant the island to the Knights was itself hardly beneficent for he knew well that, in the event of an Ottoman attack on his own shores, the Christian soldiers in Malta would provide a first line of defence. Sure enough, seeing the Knights newly installed was sufficiently provocative to the Ottomans to warrant a fresh challenge. In 1546 and, again, in 1551 attacks were made and duly repulsed until, in 1565, the Ottomans arrived with forces in unprecedented numbers.

The resultant Siege of Malta ranks as one of the epic struggles in Mediterranean history, in which the greatly outnumbered Christians held out successfully against their Muslim foe. Throughout the searing summer of that year repeated attempts were made to breach the walls, with an enormous loss of life on both sides. Unusually for the Ottomans their military tactics were suspect. As well as divided leadership in the field they suffered increasing difficulties in maintaining supplies. Finding access to fresh water was a particularly pressing problem, aggravated by the fact that the defending forces contaminated enemy sources wherever possible. In due course, the spread of disease and low morale amongst the malnourished Turkish troops was a major factor in their eventual withdrawal.

For the Ottomans, turning their backs on the island was humiliating enough but the Knights, too, were left to count their own costs. They had lost many of their fellow soldiers and citizens, and suffered the wholesale destruction of fortifications and buildings within the walls. Most of the coastal settlements were left in ruins. Although the Turks had been rebutted there was a fear that they would soon return. In the circumstances, many of the surviving Knights thought it was time to leave the island. Largely to counter this, a decision was taken by the Grand Master, Jean Parisot de la Valette, in the immediate aftermath of the siege, to construct a new city. Valette had shown true leadership in the field of battle and was now doing so with the coming of peace; it was no surprise that the city (in spite of a subtle difference in spelling) would bear his own name, Valletta.[6]

Unlike the original choice of Mdina for the island's capital, this time the preferred location was on the north-east coast, with a commanding view of the sea. La Valette himself laid the foundation stone in 1566 but was to die just two years later. Posthumously recalled as 'once the scourge of Africa and Asia, and the shield of Europe'[7], his death occurred well before his visionary city could take shape. In fact, his parting wish for a great city to emerge on the barren headland was in good hands with his fellow Knights, who lost no time in continuing the work he had started.

The Making of Valletta

On getting on shore we found ourselves in a new world indeed.[8]

With the Ottomans forced to retreat to the eastern Mediterranean, and with Christian supremacy at sea endorsed by the subsequent naval victory in 1571 at the Battle of Lepanto, the Knights were now free to attend to the development of their island. Symbolically, the lifting of the siege was recalled as the start of a new era, with Valletta portrayed like Phoenix arising from the ashes. Befitting almost spiritual expectations, there was an understanding that this would, indeed, be an exceptional place.

Valletta, a fortified city, was the creation of the Knights of St. John.

Given the stark reminder of recent events, the immediate priority was to build a system of fortifications that would be as near impregnable as possible. It helped that the site itself was a defensible peninsula, not long before used by the Ottomans to mount their own attacks. The castle of St. Elmo, at the tip of the spur and with uninterrupted views of the sea approaches, had been destroyed during the siege but was rapidly rebuilt. Massive bastions and connecting walls were introduced, first on the landward approach (fronted by a deep cutting) and then along the other edges to deter future attacks from the sea.

Moreover, the site had the important advantage that on either side were two deep inlets, recognized already as exceptional harbours; one known as the Grand Harbour and the other Marsamxett. Both were natural formations, with the added attraction of numerous creeks and sheltered waters within them, and the siting of Valletta would ensure that they continued to play a key role in the island's commerce as well as defences. To the religious-minded, that these harbours should occur at the midpoint of the Mediterranean was surely a gift from heaven.

The peninsula had obvious advantages but, for all its defensive qualities, proved a difficult site for building a city. Initially, it was thought that the upper surface could be levelled but this idea was soon disbanded because of the sheer scale of stone removal and (even with the use of slave labour) mounting costs. As a result, there was no way to avoid steeply-sloping transverse streets that could only be reached from the harbours by steps. In two-dimensional form, the layout emerged as a geometrical grid, in stark contrast with the narrow, winding lanes and alleys that typified earlier settlements on the island and in the wider region. Credit for the plan is generally attributed to an Italian designer, Francesco Laparelli, who arrived with the impressive credentials of having worked as an assistant to Michelangelo and being deputed to Malta by Pope Pius IV. It is said that he took no more than three days to draw up the plans.[9] Laparelli broke with tradition in favouring a rectangular grid rather than the radial-concentric layout that was more commonly used at the time for defensive cities; no doubt the location of the site along a peninsula was the prime reason for the difference. The spine of the plan, extending through the centre from one of the three city gates to the castle of St. Elmo, was the main street, Strada San Giorgio. One by one, the new buildings took their place along the lines of the grid (twelve lengthwise streets and nine transverse) and around carefully planned squares at key intersections. The new buildings were invariably grand in appearance, as time went on increasingly in a pronounced baroque style to produce one of the most elegant skylines in the Mediterranean—described later as 'a gleaming unity of eighteenth-century grace'.[10]

In spite of early plans to level the site, there was to be no escaping the steep slopes along the main axis as well as across it.

Amongst the first buildings of note was the Cathedral of St. John's, the conventual church of the Knights, intended to rival the earlier cathedral in Mdina. Designed by a military engineer, it was handicapped with a frontage not unlike the entrance to a fort. Inside, however, the decor was later to become lavish and ornate to an extreme, a glittering collage of gold and mosaic, of exotic paintings and intricately carved stonework—quite 'the most striking interior I have ever seen'.[11] Other buildings soon followed, like the Grand Master's Palace, sited on one side of a square and planned not just as a place of residence but also with rooms for official receptions, a well-stocked armoury and its own chapel; works of art, including paintings by Carvaggio, adorned the walls. Elsewhere, in a comparable palatial style, offices were built for the various functions of government and administration, and an imposing structure for the Order's library. Churches were sited throughout the city so that no one community was far away from a place of worship. The Knights themselves were variously accommodated in one of seven Auberges (also known as palaces of the Grand Crosses), each one signifying a different provenance.

The Sacred Infirmary and the Cathedral of St. John: two buildings central to the mission of the Knights.

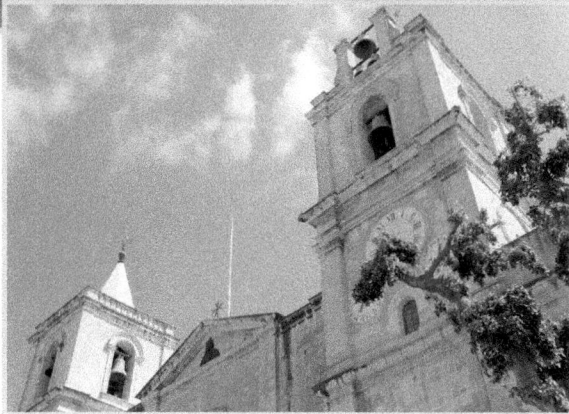

The hospital itself, the Sacred Infirmary, at the very heart of the Order, was widely acclaimed for the exemplary treatment of the sick; the beds (some 400) were in spacious surroundings within a ward that was at the time the longest room in Europe. Henry Teonge, an English navy chaplain who visited the hospital soon after it was completed, described what he saw:

> *The hospital is a vast structure, wherein the sick and wounded lie. This is so broad that twelve men may with ease walk abreast up the midst of it... [It is] extremely neat and kept clean and sweet; the sick are all served in silver plate.*[12]

A distinctive style of housing is evident throughout the city.

If the main buildings were palatial, at least the ordinary residences were not forgotten; they were, in their own way, of an equally high standard of design and construction and far in advance of what was found in most if not all of Europe. All new buildings, including private houses, were required to use a particular type of stone, quarried from the same source, to produce uniformity in appearance. Generally the houses were three storeys or more in height, with one or two enclosed balconies, characteristically in the form of projected timber-framed structures resting on ornamental stone supports. All of the homes were provided with roof terraces, to capture rainfall in cisterns and for the residents to enjoy the cooler winds on a summer evening. It is said that by the early 1570s some 2000 new houses had been built, a remarkable total in a short space of time.[13] Moreover, 'by the end of the century Valletta looked very much as it looks today—a stately, homogeneous Renaissance town of stone-built palaces and churches, regularly laid out with mathematical symmetry yet without monotony in draught-board pattern, deriving its artistic importance precisely from this homogeneity'.[14] Many years later, an admirer of Valletta acknowledged the importance of this European-derived regularity but suggested that the unique attraction was its mix with more spontaneous oriental characteristics (not least of all the colourful crowds milling through the streets).[15]

As well as the many fine buildings, the Knights invested, too, in a sturdy infrastructure, including a much-needed aqueduct to provide fresh water as well as newfound ways to drain the streets. The emergence of Valletta was a product of functionality as much as form. Time and again, European visitors (undoubtedly conditioned to expect the worst the further they travelled from their own homelands) expressed their delight and wonder at the cleanliness of the city. With the limestone gleaming bright in the morning light and breathtakingly golden in the early evening, was this, indeed, the mythical city on a hill? If that were so it had certainly not been without a high cost for its builders, for throughout the period of construction there was a constant concern that funds would be insufficient. In the event, enthusiasm for the project invariably outflanked caution. The Knights themselves were generally wealthy, often with an income from estates in their countries of origin (mainly France), and they were willing to invest generously. Modest donations were also received from the Catholic monarchs of France, Spain and Portugal, as well as from Papal reserves. It helped, too, that in time, as the fear of a fresh Ottoman invasion receded, military expenditure could be reduced—although there was still a need to protect the island from periodic raids by pirates from the Barbary Coast. Thus, for two centuries the Knights were in a strong position to exercise their own will, fulfilling La Valette's vision and building an outstanding model of early town planning.

If the rule of the Knights had started in this way as something of a golden era for Malta this, predictably, was not destined to last for ever. Other than the tiresome pirates, the island was no longer under serious threat of invasion; instead, the enemy lay within, not through possible subversion but rather a process of inner decay. Although the world around them was changing, the Knights continued to rule through a feudal system of government that was increasingly an anomaly. Far from adapting to the times, they tended, instead, to withdraw into their own sumptuous quarters, enjoying their amassed wealth and seemingly forgetting their spiritual mission. Life in their comfortable Auberges has been likened to a collegial existence, a protected world of unchallenging routines and the promise each day of fine dining. Lengthy dinners were taken together in convivial surroundings, in traditional halls complete with a high table presided over by the particular head (known as a Pillar), and with settings laid with silver plate and goblets. Visitors commented on the well-stocked larders, brimming with game of all description, together with fresh fish from the market and no shortage of vegetables and fruit. It is said that ice was delivered each day across the sea from the mountains of Sicily.[16]

With their original role as defenders of the faith against the infidels largely redundant, and now separated so far from the lives of ordinary people, the Knights became increasingly unpopular. Resentment simmered but the end came suddenly and from a different source when, in 1798, the Emperor Napoleon chose to commandeer the island to support his expedition to Egypt. In spite of the mighty fortifications surrounding Valletta, the Knights quickly succumbed to requests for French troops to enter the city. It proved to be a grave error of judgement. Far from showing gratitude, the atheist French revolutionaries had little time for this relic from a feudal age and ordered the Knights to leave Malta within three days. In their haste, and in the absence of strong leadership, they dispersed to various Catholic strongholds in Europe (the largest number finding their way to St. Petersburg, where the then Tsar offered them refuge).[17] Following their departure, the French made short shrift of the island's religious holy places as well as plundering its many treasures.

Their shortlived rule was harsh and, just two years later, when a combined British and Portuguese fleet appeared offshore, there was little support locally for the small garrison left by Napoleon to secure the island. The French forces at first held out, in the face of great hardships with the depletion of essential supplies, but were eventually overpowered. In spite of the assistance of the Portuguese, Britain claimed Malta for itself—a claim legitimized in 1814 in the international treaty that marked the end of the Napoleonic wars. There it remained, as part of the British Empire, until the middle of the twentieth century. Just as imperial powers had done before, the British acknowledged Malta's strategic location and the harbours of Valletta in particular. It was used as a holding point for troops during the Crimean War and, with the subsequent opening of the Suez Canal, the island became an important staging post for sea voyages to India and beyond.

One fascinating consequence of this change of regime was that suddenly the tiny, largely unknown, island appeared on the map for British travellers, a safe haven in the hitherto little explored southern reaches of the Mediterranean. Until the time of British occupancy, it had not been an easy place to reach. When Patrick Brydone, a Scottish traveller, led a small party of educated gentlemen from Sicily to Malta in 1770 he recorded a difficult sea journey in a small boat with six oars that was unable to navigate rough waters. In contrast, Brydone's successors more commonly enjoyed the relative security of naval craft or, later, passenger ships bound for distant destinations. Amongst the early visitors, in 1804, was the poet, Samuel Taylor Coleridge, who, most inappropriately, was appointed Public Secretary to the Administration. He was in poor health on his arrival, made worse by an addiction to opium, and appeared to have little interest in the tedium of government. Within a year he returned to England, where he could once again write verse. A short while later, in 1809, as part of his extensive tour of the Mediterranean, another Englishman of letters arrived, in the form of Lord Byron. His travelling companion, John Cam Hobhouse, as their ship entered the harbour, was overawed by his first sighting of Valletta: it was all 'very grand and surpassing every conception of that place'.[18] Byron, in contrast, found little in Malta to his liking, other than the daughter of an Austrian aristocrat, a married woman who taught him Arabic, with whom he purportedly fell in love and declared his undying devotion. In true Byronic fashion, this pledge of eternal love was forgotten as soon as he left the island and set his sights on new conquests. On his return journey, some eighteen months later, Byron's views of Malta were no more enthusiastic, and a verse written on his final parting was permanently to upset the islanders:

> *Adieu, ye joys of La Valette! Adieu, sirocco, sun and sweat! Adieu, thou Palace rarely entered! Adieu, ye cursed street of stairs!*[19]

When young Benjamin Disraeli made his own visit, in 1830, his foppish appearance—'long, hyacinthine curls, rings on his fingers, gold chains, and velvet dresses of the most gorgeous description'[20]—inevitably aroused more than a little interest wherever he went. Well before his statesmanlike manners had been honed, he was apt to give offence at well-attended receptions, but all was perhaps forgiven when he later wrote in glowing terms of the island's capital: 'Valletta equals in its noble architecture, if it even does not excel, any capital in Europe.'[21] Less controversial, but equally complimentary, was the much-loved romantic author, Sir Walter Scott, who arrived in the following year to popular acclaim. Although in poor health by then, he was captivated by the spirit of the island, imbued with reminders of chivalrous Knights and holy wars. Valletta held him in thrall, 'the splendid town quite like a dream'.[22] No less effusive was another Victorian, William Makepeace Thackeray, who in 1844, after enduring an uncomfortable sea voyage and a tiresome period of quarantine, still waxed lyrical about the splendours of Valletta. The Grand Harbour itself could always be relied on to take away the breath of most travellers, where:

> *round this busy blue water rise rocks, blazing in sunshine, and covered with every imaginable device of fortification; to the right, St. Elmo, with flag and lighthouse; and opposite, the Military Hospital, looking like a palace;*

and all round, the houses of the city, for its size the handsomest and most stately in the world.[23]

Nor was Thackeray content merely to view it from afar. Clearly, he took delight in exploring the various neighbourhoods and harbours, enjoying 'a scene of such pleasant confusion and liveliness as I have never witnessed before'.[24] Not everyone, though, was so adulatory. Rather like Byron before him, the moody D.H. Lawrence was less than impressed. Travelling in 1920 from the Sicilian resort of Taormina with his wife and a friend, he complained that what had been intended as a two-day visit was extended by a strike of steamer crews. His sourness might have had more to do with the state of his marriage at the time but, either way, the extra time on the island was not to his liking, as he found it a 'horrible' place, 'as stark as a corpse, no trees, no bushes even: a fearful landscape, cultivated, and weary with ages of weariness, and old weary houses here and there'.[25]

A statue of Queen Victoria, reflecting the island's importance in the British Empire; while Valletta's hostelries offered respite for Royal Navy sailors.

These early visitors were all, in their way, renowned figures, but for a carefully observed description of the island under British rule one can turn to the work of a lesser-known writer, George Percy Badger. Born in 1815, Badger displays all the eccentricity and spirit of enquiry of his age. He grew up in Malta, spoke Arabic and was later ordained as a priest, travelling extensively in the Middle East. Amongst his various achievements he wrote what is the first definitive guide to Malta, published in 1872.[26] His was very much a Eurocentric view, claiming that 'the sky, and air and country of Malta are African; but its life and civilization are European'.[27] For

Badger, the island was fortunate indeed when the Union Jack was unfurled on the heights above the Grand Harbour. Once the presence of the Knights had afforded protection but now the people could look to the British navy: they could once again 'enjoy the sea-breeze without dread of being dragged from their beds in slavery'.[28]

The advantages of British rule would not have been to everyone's liking, but at least in the popular mind at home Malta acquired a reputation not unlike that of Gibraltar as one of the fixed points in the Empire. Thousands of sailors spent time on the island while their ships were repaired and restocked, while passengers after the opening of the Suez Canal took the opportunity to go ashore to break the monotony of their long voyage to India. Trading vessels on their way to and from the Levant used Malta as a staging post, just as the Phoenicians had done more than two millennia before. Its importance to Britain was undeniable, yet it could never be more than a small colony and one that was too often misrepresented at that. Augusto Bartolo was a Maltese citizen, piqued like many of his countrymen by misleading reports in the British press which invariably dismissed the island as being nothing more than a useful harbour. Had they forgotten, he asked, that Malta was once all that stood between Christian Europe and the invading forces of Islam? Were they unaware of the island's long and distinguished history? And did they even know that it was not simply a part of Africa?[29] Bartolo's indignant questions, of course, remained unanswered.

Meanwhile, in the early twentieth century, new developments on the island served to strengthen Britain's hold. As well as modernizing the harbour facilities, colonial rule saw the growth of extensive shipyards and dry docks for repairs. With a growing population in the capital, thoughts also turned to how best to develop available land beyond the old fortifications. Possible layouts were invited through a competition in 1925, for which fourteen designs were submitted. Patrick Abercrombie arrived with a fellow architect, Edward Warren, to review the presentations and select one with the classically inspired name of 'Calypso' to guide future development.[30]

Domestic issues, though, were a sideshow to the real interest in Malta, which was always for its strategic value. This was clearly appreciated in peacetime but, as events were to show, never more than in times of war. Between 1939 and 1945, with the Mediterranean as one of the main theatres of conflict, Malta was used as an essential base for the British fleet. Located so close to the enemy in Sicily and, later, to the German and Italian presence in North Africa, it was not long before the island came under sustained attack. Once again it found itself on the front line of someone else's war, prized for its location but made to pay a heavy price. Malta, and Valletta especially, were subject to repeated air raids while at sea supply lines were effectively cut.

Many lost their lives and properties were destroyed but somehow—in one of the epic struggles of the war—the 'island fortress'[31] resisted enemy occupation, marking another colourful chapter in its long history as a coveted island in the middle of the Mediterranean.

Post-Colonial Capital

If you have an ear to listen, Valletta has lots of stories to tell.[32]

With the coming of peace, in 1945, talk of independence was soon in the air. Even before that there had been moves by the Maltese to secure greater control over their own affairs but now there would be no turning back. Different options were discussed, including the unusual one of integrating Malta wholly within the United Kingdom. In the event, the majority party on the island settled in 1964 for independent status within the Commonwealth. This was followed, ten years later, by the re-designation of Malta as a republic. The British were given due notice to quit its remaining dockyards and military base, and at the same time NATO was required to vacate its Southern Command headquarters in Valletta. Portraying the post-colonial Mediterranean as 'a sea of neutrality and peace', Mintoff encouraged other nations with an interest in the future development of the region to come to the island. To the dismay of the West, at the height of the Cold War, the Grand Harbour was soon host to Soviet shipping and China, too, took an active interest in the further development of the port. Meanwhile, alliances were struck with Libya, Syria and the Palestine Liberation Organisation. In fact, apart from a steady flow of Libyan investment, and the construction of dry docks by the Chinese, none of these links brought anything like the promised benefits. For a variety of geopolitical and other reasons, Malta's rejection of the West was largely reversed following the resignation of Mintoff in 1984. A treaty of friendship and security was signed with Italy—marking the end of a hostile stance dating from the Second World War—and a new reliance on tourism led to a more pragmatic approach to international relations. The entry of Malta, in 2004, into the European Union (an event long delayed because of divided views between the main political parties) effectively confirmed where the country's future would lie.

Throughout this period with its various changes, Valletta, as the nation's capital, was forced to respond to new demands. In the immediate postwar period there was work to be done in repairing damaged buildings and restoring the fine appearance of the city. Some notable landmarks, like the Royal Opera House, had been lost for ever as a result of the bombing. Later, it was recognized that independence would bring its costs as well as benefits. The city was heavily dependent on the jobs and income generated by the dockyards and no-one quite knew what would happen with the departure of the British. Politicians were quick to call for the complete evacuation of colonial forces but there was no guarantee that the economic loss could be countered. Moreover, as a sign of its previous dependence, it was estimated that up to a third of the country's income came from dockyard pensions, war allowances and other colonial subsidies.[33]

The island could also count for a while on the money spent by retired army officers and officials (known as the 'Ancient Brits') who had once served in the colonies and then found Malta an agreeable place in which to spend their remaining years. It seemed that overnight the economic lifeblood of the country would be lost and, with more than 350,000 people living on the three islands (now closer to 400,000, making it one of the most densely populated countries in the world), the way ahead would not be easy.

The former Royal Opera House site, now the subject of a major regeneration scheme.

In response to the challenge, Malta—and Valletta in particular—had to remake itself. The original city, within its defensive walls, had long spilled over, merging into a ring of neighbouring settlements. Planners were presented with familiar metropolitan issues of trying to contain further expansion while, at the same time, improving communications and the quality of life within. Because of its particular circumstances, Valletta's recent emergence as a new European capital in a post-colonial island state, the task for planners would have additional dimensions. One was a question of identity, for the capital to reflect Malta's new role rather than simply fossilizing its earlier form. Another challenge was to diversify the local economy, balancing a declining income from the shipyards and colonial administration with a new emphasis on tourism and services. Once again the location of the island would be a factor, with most of the heavily populated countries of Europe little more than two hours flying time away. For the tourist, Malta could offer all the advantages of the African shoreline without the political threats and uncertainties to be found in the likes of nearby Libya and Algeria. Valletta's self-promotion as an attraction in its own right was also helped by the city's designation in 1980 by UNESCO as a world heritage site. Especially valued was the close concentration of historic buildings, with more than 300 in a compact area identified as world class. Conservation is good for business and, coupled with expansive views across the sea and proximity to the waterfronts around the harbours (which would soon play their own part as an ideal anchorage for cruise ships that ply the Mediterranean), it ticks most of the boxes as a potential 'short-haul' destination. A balance, however, needed to be struck between the desire to bring in more visitors and protection of the delicate urban environment.[34] To achieve this, plans alone are never enough and the main thrust of Valletta's re-making has come less from city-wide solutions and more from a number of large capital projects.

A scheme known as Valletta Waterfront was the first of what will surely be more such developments in the future to take advantage of the harbour frontage. This particular scheme combines new landing facilities for cruise ships with the restoration of adjacent warehouses, combined with quayside bars and restaurants. More significant for the future of the city is the ambitious plan now underway to address the lingering issue of the bombsite that was once the Royal Opera House. Nearly seven decades after enemy bombers reduced it to ruins, the international architect, Renzo Piano, was handed the enviable brief to renew not just that site but its neglected surroundings too.

The area in question is at the inland end of the main axis of Valletta, known since independence as Triq Ir-Repubblika. Beyond the site of the former opera house is the main city gate, rebuilt in the 1960s without regard for its unique setting and now earmarked for demolition. Nor does the brief stop there, for outwith the gate one crosses a bridge of no particular distinction to find oneself amongst the bright yellow buses of the island's network, parked around an ornamental sculpture. Piano's plan will transform the whole area, with an open-air auditorium set in the opera house foundations coupled with a new building in Freedom Square for the nation's parliament. The city gate and the bridge beyond will both be replaced with more elegant structures and the makeshift bus terminus will be relocated. Piano aims to create a series of spaces that will, together, draw one into the rest of the city; his designs will be modern but it is tradition that will be enhanced.

When the regeneration project is complete it will provide far more than simply another tourist venue. A high-quality urban environment represents a shrewd investment, encouraging the co-location of new business activities (Malta has a growing reputation for international banking and other specialist services) as well as a venue for conferences. In this way, the declining population of Valletta will be reversed and, as younger people move in, the restoration of the city's traditional town houses will follow. One of the most intriguing examples of how this can come about is to be found on a large site across the harbour, where Dubai-based investors are developing the area for a complex of software businesses; in keeping with the Gulf city's love of thematic development it has been named Smart City. This will, in due course, generate some 5000 jobs as well as encouraging newcomers to settle around the bay.

There is, additionally, a further factor favouring Valletta. In spite of centuries of foreign influence the city exemplifies that powerful sense of identity retained by Malta as a whole. This makes it far more than an anonymous location for inward investment. Instead, as well as its outstanding urban setting, it is a place where the old language is used freely alongside English, where the many church domes and towers are not mere historical relics, and where Maltese culture is alive and well in its literature and festivals. In the centre of a sea where traditions are so often lost, Valletta is a remarkable exception, confident in itself and full of optimism.

NICOSIA

There is something poignant about concluding this odyssey with a visit to Nicosia, once capital of the whole of Cyprus.[1] It is now a divided city, separated by a controlled border crossing; to the north is the Turkish sector and to the south the Greek population. The border continues across the island, to the east and west of the city, marking the limits of different cultures and effectively creating separate nations. Nicosia is certainly not the only Mediterranean city to have experienced the pain of division in one form or another, but in the twenty-first century the situation endures as a persistent symbol of a troubled region. One instinctively feels that such conflicts have no place in the modern world but the reality tells otherwise. An Islamic crescent above the dome of a mosque (albeit once a Christian place of worship) can be seen on one side of the border, a cross over an ornate Orthodox church on the other: there is, to coin a phrase, nothing new under the Mediterranean sun.

Capital of the Plain

It was a place of high consideration...[2]

Cyprus is a large island (third in the Mediterranean to Sicily and Sardinia), for long a scene of conflict but only in modern times formally divided. For most of its history, its difficulties have stemmed, as in so much of this region, from external forces: the recurrence of invasions and subsequent occupations by one foreign power or another. Although this is a familiar enough Mediterranean story, few places can match the intensity of the process that one finds in Cyprus. In accounting for this, the island's geography has much to answer for. Not only has it lured invaders with its natural reserves of copper and other prized minerals, extensive forests and valuable agricultural land, but its location in the eastern Mediterranean—just south of the Anatolian coastline and west of modern Syria and Lebanon—has made it all too accessible to a host of acquisitive powers.

From the earliest times, events in Cyprus were closely linked to those of the ancient civilizations in the region and, later, to the colonial ambitions of more distant nations. It is, literally, at one of the busiest crossroads of the Mediterranean, hard on the shores of Asia, Europe and Africa. In cultural terms it has gained from this proximity but it has also paid a heavy price. The emergence of Nicosia as the island's capital reflects both sides of this turbulent past. Being 'a place of high consideration' has by no means been all to the city's advantage.

There is evidence that hunter-gatherers roamed the island some twelve millennia ago but enforced occupation by neighbouring powers started much later, towards the end of the Bronze Age.[3] First came the Hittites from nearby Anatolia, followed from about 1400 BC by Mycenaeans from Greece. The Mycenaeans were mainly interested in trade but, when their power waned, they were succeeded by a new wave of Greek migrants, looking instead to permanent settlement. These early colonists remained on the island throughout most of the first millennium BC, bringing their own ways and establishing Greek as the *lingua franca*. Other cultures followed, each leaving its own particular traces, like the Phoenicians who (just as the Mycenaeans before them) were more interested in trade than colonization *per se*. In contrast, the Assyrians had more enduring designs on the island; from their homeland of Mesopotamia they crossed the deserts of Syria to reach the Mediterranean, before making the short sea crossing to Cyprus. Their goal was nothing less than total conquest, which they duly achieved, imposing their rule on the island for at least the first half of the sixth century BC. After the Assyrians—and a half-century of relative freedom—it was the turn of the Egyptians, and then more decisively and over a longer period the Persians. Only with the rise of Alexander III of Macedonia in the fourth century BC and his successful campaigns across the region were the Persians evicted, bringing Cyprus firmly back within the Hellenic orbit. Following Alexander's death, however, the pendulum swung once more towards the Nile, where the Egyptians were able to resume control through the Ptolemaic kings. It was there that Cyprus remained until, predictably, the Romans appeared on the scene, adding the coveted island to their expanding list of conquests.

For all its might, Roman rule was not, however, wholly uninterrupted: both Julius Caesar and Mark Antony were to fall under the spell of Cleopatra and even agreed to cede Cyprus to her, a gesture that enjoyed little favour amongst their less emotional compatriots in Rome and was subsequently reversed. When the Roman Empire was divided into eastern and western realms, in the fourth century, the obvious home for the island was in the former, ruled from nearby Constantinople. Over many centuries Cyprus remained firmly Byzantine, a dedicated proponent of Eastern Orthodox Christianity with its own rituals and highly ornate brand of religious art and architecture. Even before its attachment to Constantinople, Cyprus had been home to numerous Christian communities on the island, the direct outcome, as so often in the Mediterranean, of Paul's missionary work in the first century. Yet, in spite of its religious certainty and the support of the Byzantine navy, stability throughout much of the first millennium of Christianity continued to be a stranger to Cyprus. Time and again it was invaded from the nearby coastline of western Asia, often by pirates in search of quick gains but sometimes, too, by enemies with more permanent intentions. A treaty signed by Christian and Arab leaders formally stayed in place for three centuries but, in practice, failed to prevent continuing raids on the island. It was only when Richard I, at the head of a force of Crusaders, arrived in the region that the situation was stabilized. He quickly saw the importance of Cyprus as a staging post for his onward advance to Jerusalem, and his superior forces were sufficient to repel further attacks.

Throughout this early period of successive raids and occupation, Nicosia itself was of little consequence. It remained a small settlement, distant not only from the coastal invasions but also from the political life and commercial development of the maritime cities. Originally known as Ledra (alternatively, Lefkousia—hence the modern version, Lefkosia, commonly used as well as Nicosia), it functioned as the capital of an insignificant kingdom of the same name that was effectively no more than a province. Its territory comprised the dusty plain of Mesaoria, with the mountain range of Kyrenia to the north.

Although dismissed as remote, in the face of Constantinople's failure to protect the island from repeated raids from the Levant, its inland location was increasingly recognized as a strength rather than weakness. Settlers in the ninth and tenth centuries gradually left the coast in favour of the more secure interior, a drift of population that contributed, in turn, to the emergence of Ledra as the natural centre of administration for the whole island. Significantly, towards the end of Byzantine rule, it was chosen as the home of the governor and a castle was built to defend the settlement. The last of the Byzantine governors, however, exceeded his powers, claiming Cyprus for himself, and was duly expelled by Richard 1.

Lurking not far behind the banner of high ideals, money was invariably a decisive factor in the Crusades, so when Richard discovered that the Knights of St. John, recently ousted from Jerusalem, were searching for a new home he offered them Cyprus. The Knights based themselves in the coastal town of Limassol but, unable to pay the high price demanded, they soon moved on to another large island, Rhodes. Richard, meanwhile, struck a deal with the dispossessed king of Jerusalem, Guy de Lusignan, a prominent crusader whose family hailed from south-western France. Lusignan quickly laid the foundations for a Christian dynasty (with the blessing of the Holy Roman Emperor, his successors assumed the title of sovereign); he introduced a rigid feudal system based on what he had known in his homeland, and Nicosia (as it was by then most commonly known) was formally designated the island's capital.

For three centuries, Cyprus prospered under the House of Lusignan: 'the most brilliant epoch of its varied history... its remarkable achievements in every domain of human activity invested it with an importance among the nations of Europe wholly out of proportion to its small size and population'.[4] In Nicosia itself, splendid churches and other exemplars of Gothic architecture were built, giving the city an appearance more akin to that of a European capital.[5] Nor were the new rulers slow to fulfil their duties as Christian warriors, lending support in various ways to the ongoing Crusades. In the event, though, the main threat to Cyprus was to come not from the east but the west. The island's importance as a trading centre and its cumulative riches attracted growing interest from the two rival city states of Genoa and Venice, both of them forces to be reckoned with throughout the Mediterranean. Genoa made the first move, claiming the eastern port of Famagusta, but it was eventually Venice which took control in 1489 of the whole island, evicting the Genoans in the process. For all the architectural splendours of their own city, however, the Venetians showed little respect for the Frankish legacy, wilfully destroying palaces and churches built by the Lusignans and replacing the existing walls with an elaborate system of modern fortifications.

Part of the Lusignan legacy, now used as a mosque.

Nicosia was totally replanned within a star-shaped perimeter, 4.5 kilometres in length with only three points of entry. It was an exceptional system of fortifications, a textbook model of defence, widely admired as being 'of the finest and most scientific construction.'[6] Although undoubtedly impressive in itself, there was a crucial flaw as the monumental scale of the walls required more troops to defend them than the city could easily muster. Thus, when Christian control was later challenged by the Ottomans, it was not a frontal assault but a siege that led to the city's downfall. In 1571, enemy forces broke through the gates, marking a victory for Islam and the start of three centuries of rule as part of the Turkish Empire.

As with any empire that over-reaches itself, the Ottoman record is a mixed story, in places one of considerable achievement but in others unrivalled neglect. Cyprus proved to be a dismal expression of the latter: 'from being a kingdom known throughout Christendom the island was to become an obscure Ottoman dependency... a story of provincialism and decay, of contracting commerce and un-enterprising administration, a story not regal but parochial'.[7] In cultural as well as economic terms it was a time of regression, relieved only by a degree of religious tolerance which allowed Christian worship to continue. Muslims remained in a minority across most of the island, except in Nicosia where they were 'inclined to assert their superiority'.[8] The Ottomans could not be blamed for natural disasters but incidents of plague and earthquakes during this period only added to the miseries of the islanders, and repeated outbreaks of cholera were a direct result of unsanitary conditions. Although Nicosia remained the capital, it, too, fell into relative decline, 'becalmed by the Turks, to drowse away its life on the dusty Mesaoria'.[9]

Nicosia 1610: Map by Giuseppe Rosaccio and Jacomo Franco. (A.G. Leventis Foundation b/200510, 244).

It was a miserable period in the island's history, eventually brought to an end in the stately rooms of a former palace in Berlin. Hosted by Chancellor Bismarck, the heads of European states took stock of the outcome of a war between the Russian and Turkish empires, ostensibly gathering in Berlin to establish a new balance of power in the region. Behind the scenes, however, each pressed their own national interests. The British Prime Minister, Benjamin Disraeli, was in his element in this world of intrigue, brokering a secret agreement with the Ottomans even before the conference opened. His plan was for the Turks to allow British administration of the island, in exchange for protection of their territories elsewhere in the event of renewed Russian incursions. Because of its location, Disraeli held the view that Cyprus was vital to the interests of the British Empire and, with Gibraltar in the west and Malta in the centre already secured, his navy could now enjoy free passage across the whole of the Mediterranean.[10]

A new addition to the Empire was always a source of interest at home, and it was not long before journalists and others were despatched to Cyprus to report on what was there. First impressions of Nicosia itself were not always favourable, as for instance in an early article in the *Illustrated London News*, where the streets were described as 'narrow, squalid, and wretched in appearance'.[11] Looking desperately for a saving grace, the journalist at least found favour in the city's surroundings: 'the situation, in a fertile plain sheltered by noble mountain ranges, has some natural attraction when viewed from outside the walls.'[12] It was not for the appearance of its capital, however, that the likes of Disraeli had negotiated so hard for this Mediterranean stronghold.

Britain's hold over the island was strengthened during the First World War when, following Turkey's alignment with Germany, the original agreement was replaced by a declaration of *de facto* control. In 1925 this was formalized through the re-designation of Cyprus as a crown colony. Away from the heady world of geopolitics, however, deep-rooted issues remained to be solved; with the population split nearly three to one in favour of Greek Christians, as opposed to Turkish Muslims, its future was far from certain. From as early as the 1920s there was talk of unification with mainland Greece, an aspiration of the majority that would never be tolerated by the smaller Turkish community. Antipathy between the two would only have been sharpened by events in Thessaloniki and Smyrna in that same period, with mass evacuations in each city of the respective minorities. Far from attempting to resolve the issue, the colonial power (in spite of growing unrest and, at times, itself the target for violent incidents) simply allowed poor relations to simmer. In something of a vacuum, in the ensuing years the situation deteriorated, with sections of the Greek community continuing to press the claim for unification with their homeland.

After the Second World War, the divergent interests of the two communities widened in the context of increasingly urgent calls for national independence, a cause promoted fiercely by the Greeks but approached more warily by the Turks. *Enosis*, the movement for the unification of Cyprus with Greece, became the banner raised by the majority, as opposed to *taksim*, the pursuit of partition that was favoured by the minority Turks. In these difficult circumstances, Britain tried to retain good relations with both communities. Widely criticized for its ambivalence, there was a sense in which British loyalties were genuinely torn.

On the one hand, well-educated staff in the colonial administration quite commonly nursed a patrician respect for Greek culture and classical civilization and, ignoring the realities of modern politics, believed that shared values would eventually prevail. At the same time, in the footsteps of Disraeli, they retained a more covert interest in keeping Turkey on side, especially in the deepening struggle against communism in the Cold War era. The delicate balance, however, could not be held for ever and in the 1950s things took a serious turn for the worse, in the form of an unrelenting terrorist campaign mounted by the Greeks. As well as hostilities between the two communities, Britain now found itself directly in the firing line. An agreement had eventually to be negotiated, resulting in independence for the island in 1960. Such was the birth of the Republic of Cyprus, the outcome of struggle and now poised on the cusp of opposing interests.

One City, Two Capitals

Cities are often located on the fault-line between cultures...[13]

Celebrations for the nation's newly won independence were, understandably, shortlived. The fact was that the constitution, in an effort to please everyone, soon proved to be unworkable. It required a greater degree of trust and willingness to cooperate between the two ethnic groups than, given their background, it was realistic to expect. To add to its unpopularity it contained a provision to allow for the continuing presence and territorial autonomy of the British in two military bases. It was not long before there were fresh outbreaks of violence between the two communities.

The Green Line itself cuts across former streets.

External powers looked askance at the deteriorating situation and in 1964 the United Nations despatched a peacekeeping force to separate the opposing factions and prevent a full-blown war. As if the challenge they faced in dealing with the situation was not difficult enough, the 'peacekeepers' were given very little room to manoeuvre. A demarcation line had been drawn by the British a decade earlier, recognizing but also hardening the division between the two sides. The line itself in Nicosia took the form of a barbed wire fence across the breadth of the city. To the north the majority community was Turkish, and to the south mainly Greek; access between the two was controlled by means of five checkpoints. This was known as the Mason-Dixon line and, although it was hastily enacted, it was more or less followed to the letter in later measures to divide the city.

With the arrival of the UN, the Mason-Dixon line was widened to include a buffer zone and, because it is reputed that the military commander drew a line on a map with a green crayon, this became the 'Green Line'. It snaked its way across the whole island, including a section from east to west through Nicosia itself. For ten years, based on this pragmatic arrangement, there was, more or less, a stand-off between the two sides, until the Greeks once again determined to seek unification with the mainland nation (encouraged by the then military government in Athens). In the face of what was seen as a threat to its own people, Turkey responded in 1974 by invading the island and occupying the northern sector (extending across some 37% of the overall landmass). Cyprus effectively became two nations: the Republic of Cyprus to the south and, subsequently, the Turkish Republic of Northern Cyprus to the north (still unrecognized by the international community). Nicosia, until then capital of the whole island, now found itself in the crucible of this conflict, literally split between the two.

The Green Line itself was immediately fortified and access between one sector and the other was even more heavily restricted than it had been before. UN troops controlled the buffer zone, with Greek and Turkish militia subsequently allowed to defend their respective frontline boundaries. For almost three decades the situation remained unchanged, until in 2003 the control of movement between one side and another was significantly eased. By then, however, the whole of Cyprus, and Nicosia in particular, had changed for ever. In part, these enduring changes were of the nation's own making.

There are local exceptions but, in general, Greeks and Turks have a poor record in the eastern Mediterranean of living peaceably together. In the case of Cyprus, the Greek community has always seen itself as the island's true heirs, with the Turkish minority an unwanted legacy of Ottoman occupation. Fired by extremists on both sides (but especially Greek nationalists), and not helped by Britain's earlier colonial policy of 'divide and rule', in which relations between the two communities were polarized rather than reconciled, the situation after political independence had gone from bad to worse. The repeated call by the Greek majority for full integration with mainland Greece only served to arouse fear and opposition in the Turkish minority. Meanwhile, the meddling of external powers, pursuing their own geopolitical interests, hardly helped matters. Cyprus had long been prized by the West because of its strategic location and, at the height of the Cold War, this became even more critical. Britain was resolute in safeguarding its military bases on the island (designated as sovereign territory, as if they were in the UK itself). Increasingly, the United States was determined that, through their sophisticated listening devices, NATO monitors would continue to keep a close watch on the troublesome countries of the Middle East. Just as Disraeli had done a century before, the West wanted advanced intelligence on Soviet intentions in the region.

So much of the present predicament, culturally as well as geopolitically, can be traced back to this crucial factor of location. Is Cyprus a part of Europe or the Levant? Should it look, if at all, to Greece or to Turkey for protection and political alignment? Are there historical grounds for hope that Greeks and Turks might one day be able to live side by side, or does the actual record suggest that this aspiration is ill-founded? Do the Orthodox Church and Islam have to be mutually exclusive? In seeking to resolve these perennial issues, it cannot be ignored that for most of its long history the island has been colonized. Only since 1960 has it been free to forge its own identity, and even then foreign powers have continued to interfere. It is, perhaps, little wonder, in these circumstances, that reconciliation has so far proved too much for all parties.

In its modern history, as in the past, the capital city itself could hardly escape the effects of these competing claims on the island. Indeed, the immediate effects were little short of catastrophic, with mass migrations of the ethnic populations from north to south and *vice versa*. Even at the time of the UN's first attempt, in the 1960s, to keep opposing factions apart, many Cypriots on both sides chose to move to communities where they would feel more secure. That, however, was nothing compared with the scale of change that took place following the Turkish invasion. Homes and land were left behind as families and often the inhabitants of whole villages fled *en masse* from one side to the other.

Figures vary according to their source but a fair estimate is that 180,000 migrated from north to south and nearly 50,000 in the reverse direction.[14] This was a human disaster on a global scale, and successive UN Secretary-Generals put their name to proposals designed to retrieve the situation—none of which were accepted by either of the rival Cypriot groups or their ethnic counterparts in Greece and Turkey.

The whole island was affected by this far-reaching process of displacement and Nicosia, already divided, felt the brunt of it as much as anywhere. Apart from reciprocal movements of its own population, it attracted newcomers who thought their future would be more secure in the city. To add to it all, in an effort to balance numbers, the Turkish government organized the resettlement of 100,000 migrants from the mainland to make their home in Cyprus. Although they were largely country people, many were directed to Nicosia, a source of concern for the original Turkish Cypriots as well as the Greeks.[15] As a result of these various exchanges, the population of the city grew rapidly.

Some of this growth would have occurred anyway because of a natural movement of people from impoverished villages in central Cyprus, but the rate of change and the chaotic nature of the process were largely beyond control. In the 1950s, when the British army was struggling to hold the balance of power, the population of Nicosia was probably little more than 60,000.[16] By the time of the Turkish occupation, the total had increased to 100,000, but in the immediate aftermath—a result of the forced movement of both Greeks and Turks—this figure increased to 180,000. Since then, it has continued to grow rapidly, to a present population of at least 400,000 (more than 75% of whom are in the southern half of the city). The effects on the form and functioning of Nicosia have been dramatic.

'No man's land': the former Ledra Palace Hotel, one of various buildings trapped between the two sides, now used as the United Nations HQ.

Until well into the twentieth century, most of the city was still confined within its historic Venetian walls, just as it had been for many centuries. This was where the main commercial district flourished and where most of the population lived. Here were the numerous workshops, many of them dependent on each other, and the places of worship.

So, too, were the offices of government and the law courts, the central post office and the transport hubs. At the heart of a productive agricultural plain, the markets flourished and, symbolically, one could even see remains of the former caravanserai, a busy focus for traders in past times. Most dramatically, since the Turkish occupation, Nicosia has burst its boundaries, in both sectors rapidly spreading beyond its walls onto the surrounding plain. The rate of change has been more rapid on the Greek side, where modernization is also more apparent. It is beyond the walls where new commercial centres have been built (mainly in the southern part of the city) and where most people now live, in modern apartment blocks and suburban villas. Many facilities, formerly shared by the whole of the population, have had to be duplicated and most of these, too, have been located outside the walls.

Add to this the drift of population from impoverished villages and outlying farms and the result is a sprawling metropolis, seemingly unchecked by planners. Long gone is the compact city nestled within its own fortifications and long gone, too, is any sense of unity, with the two sides following contrasting paths of development. Nicosia experiences the same pressures to accommodate growth as many other cities around the Mediterranean but, in addition to everything else, it remains physically divided.

It is cold comfort to the people of Nicosia to know that their fate as a divided city is not unique; around the world it has counterparts which remain an anachronism in an era of globalization, yet are still very much in evidence.[17] Jerusalem, even now, functions as two cities, just as Beirut and Sarajevo in recent years experienced their own war-torn divisions. Elsewhere, beyond the Mediterranean, the likes of Johannesburg, Belfast and Berlin all offer their own tragic stories of physical separation in modern times.

Some commentators stretch a point in seeing social segregation (although often based on the clustering of different ethnic communities) as a variation on this same theme.[18] The fact is, for whatever reason, dividing a city is a travesty, the severance of something that is intended to be whole and which, invariably, has evolved on that basis. Everything that has gone before has been designed for its citizens to share, almost certainly not equally but at least with a sense of common belonging. Division is alien to the very nature of a city, the splitting of a live organism.

Yet this is what has happened to Nicosia.[19] The reality of this artificial division is everywhere evident, yet nowhere more than along the Green Line itself. No visit to Nicosia can be complete without a closer look at the very source of this modern aberration.

Walking the Line

Don't touch the history, forget the history…[20]

Nicosia, it has to be kept in mind, has had its glorious moments in the past, winning praise for the fine Gothic architecture endowed by the Lusignans and, later, the outstanding fortifications built by the Venetians. For most of its history, however, it has made few waves. Even before its present division into two sectors, Lawrence Durrell, who during the 1950s lived in what is now the Turkish Republic of North Cyprus and loved the island dearly, was far from impressed. He bemoaned Nicosia's 'terrible shabbiness and inadequacy', comparing it for 'twentieth-century amenities with some fly-blown Anatolian township, bemused and forgotten on the central steppes'.[21] Less contentiously, he observed that it could not begin to compare with other cities in the region, like Athens, Beirut and Alexandria. If Durrell was right in his assessment then, what would he make of Nicosia now, so obviously damaged by political events? It is impossible to look at Nicosia without one's eye fixing on its terrible wound. Sadly, this is its defining feature. Nicosia, as posters in the city lament, remains the only divided capital of Europe.

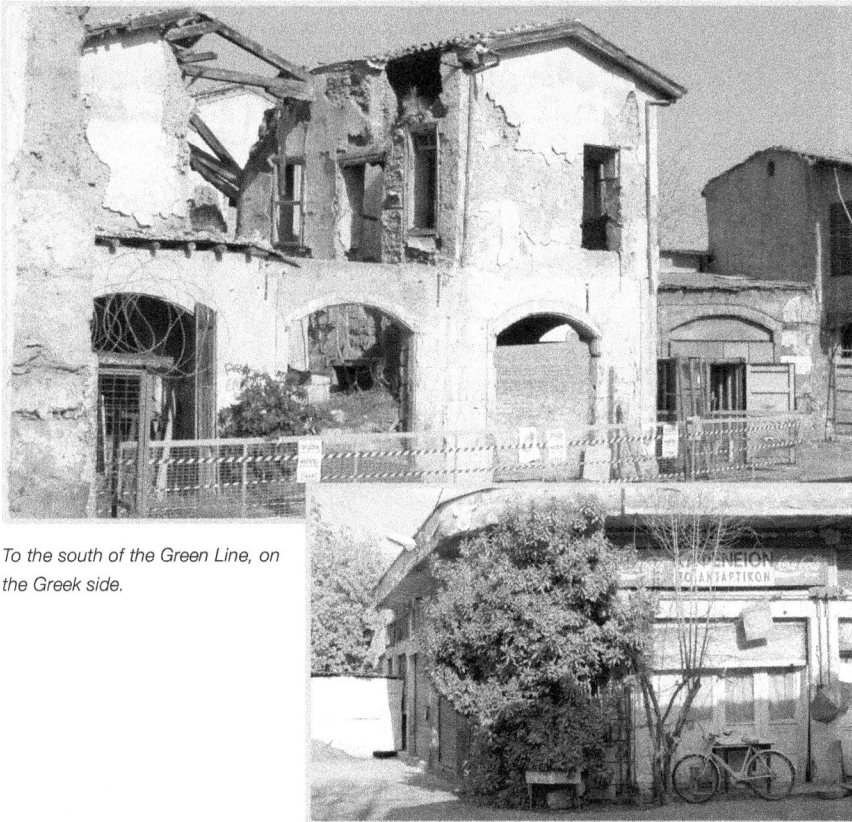

To the south of the Green Line, on the Greek side.

For nearly three decades the borders between the two parts of the city were effectively sealed, and only in 2003 were the regulations relaxed to allow easier access.[22] In spite of this step towards normality, the fact of division over so many years has created separate landscapes—not only different patterns of development between north and south but also the chilling reality of a 'no man's land' between the two. Still widely referred to as the Green Line, the latter has also been dubbed the Dead Zone, *Nekri Zoni*, to signify a lifeless void.[23] Snaking through the city it is fringed by watch-towers and barbed wire, oil drums weighed down with concrete and camouflaged sandbags, with controlled crossing points managed by Greek militia on one side and Turks on the other. Out-of-bounds to outsiders, the neutral ground itself is patrolled by UN forces, treading a fine line between conflicting ethnic groups on either side. Buildings along the borders have fallen into decay, leaving trees and untended shrubs to make the ground their own, producing a natural wilderness in the centre of the city. Symbolically, the once grand Ledra Palace Hotel was left isolated in the middle of this neutral ground, soon unrecognizable as one of the leading hotels of its day.[24] Understandably, it is a landscape that has drawn to it anthropologists and planners, intrigued by its complexity. A key question with an eye to the future is whether:

> *... in an urban situation where there are antagonistic, ethnic or racial groups, do city-builders encourage these groups to live together and interact, or do they facilitate the development of ethnically segregated neighbourhoods and districts?* [25]

It is a question that probably only politicians and the people themselves in a divided city can satisfactorily answer, but at least analysts and policy-makers can point to the daily costs that this kind of artificial division imposes. Thus, until the regulations were relaxed, someone living on one side of the line would, theoretically, have needed to make three separate flights, first to mainland Greece or Turkey, to reach the other side. This was not just a physical trial but no less an affront to human dignity; it illustrates how 'the static and semi-permanent feel of the ethnic buffer line in Nicosia belies the pain in people's hearts'.[26] At the same time, there are some who argue that the Green Line was not only inevitable but also, in a strange way, fortuitous. For one thing, since its inception at least the two communities have been able to live in relative peace, unlike the situation that existed before. Moreover, 'some feel that this may be a solution to ethnic conflict because it allows self-sufficiency and self-confidence to build on both sides... *[a prelude to]* collaboration between equals to meet basic urban needs'.[27] That indeed may be so but the experience of Nicosia is that, in human terms, such measures should surely be by choice rather than default.

The city remains divided but at least the control points are more porous than they used to be. Each day, Greek Cypriots cross into the Turkish zone and vice versa. Most of those who walk across do so where Ledra Street (the main shopping street on the Greek side of the walled city) meets the Green Line. Formerly this area was at the very heart of Nicosia, a thriving commercial hub. To see how much it has changed, instead of continuing north or south one must follow the line of the border to east and west, first in the Greek zone and then the Turkish. Starting on the Greek side, the bustle of Ledra Street gives way quickly to a hidden landscape that is all the more macabre the closer one gets to the border. Many buildings are in a state of ruin, open to the elements and damaged beyond repair. Even more evocative are traditional houses and workshops that are now heavily padlocked and mostly inhabited only by feral cats and pigeons. Everywhere is the pungent smell of decay. Once this would have been a mixed neighbourhood of Greeks and Turks, living side by side, but when the Turkish community saw their future to the north of the Green Line they packed their few possessions, locked their properties and hurried to safety. Now it is the silence of these streets that speaks most volubly of what has happened. As if to remind one what it was like before, there are also rows of workshops where Greek Cypriots still carry on their trades (often joiners and metal workers), just as they would have done before the barriers were erected.

To the north of the Green Line, on the Turkish side.

It is now an area, away from the public eye, where here and there red lights glow above the doors of decaying properties and battered limousines are parked outside. In between, too, are small coffee shops and bars, just a few metres from the fortified border. The irony of their location is not lost on some of the occupants, with one of the bars, for instance, named the Berlin Wall.[28] For others, though, there is no place for humour, as one finds in a popular restaurant where a Greek national flag flies outside and *enosis* leaflets are available to customers. Posters on the walls show little love for American politicians (like Henry Kissinger and Bill Clinton), who are accused of having shown favour to their NATO ally, Turkey.

In recent years, encouraged by a more stable political situation, confidence is creeping back into the area. Building restoration is much in evidence and in one particular area, Chrysaliniotissa, with the help of municipal and international funding, the streets and other public spaces are enjoying an attractive facelift. The nearby

On the Turkish side of the Green Line, the city is relatively low-rise; on the Greek side, high-rise development marks the emergence of a new downtown area.

Famagusta Gate (one of only three gates in the original Venetian walls) has been restored and to the rear is a new cultural centre. As a familiar sign of change in an area that is 'coming up', some of the houses and workshops are now occupied by creative professionals like architects and interior designers. Elsewhere, a cluster of craft workshops is grouped around a courtyard, along with a vegetarian restaurant. If all of this suggests the arrival of urban chic, it is only a matter of taking a few paces back to be reminded of the sombre presence of the border. Sentry boxes remain in strategic positions along the adjoining streets and bored militia seem almost grateful to see new faces on their watch. The barricades of oil drums and barbed wire have been in place now for the past three decades and are often overgrown with grass and trees climbing out of vacant buildings alongside. It all looks increasingly *passé*, somehow a remnant of an earlier era that is even more anomalous when each day thousands of people can now cross the line just a short distance away.

Much the same can be found on the Turkish side, where not all of the watchtowers are now manned. Signs of decay amongst the buildings are even more in evidence and it is said that some of them have been occupied illegally by newcomers to the city. Large families sit in the dusty yards eating their mid-day meal; cars are repaired in the streets while customers look on. Lanes peter out in the face of formidable barriers but, in spite of menacing signs to keep away, even these look as if they are no longer so rigidly enforced. There are also growing signs of confidence, just as one finds to the south. Notably, the main market, which abuts the border, is currently being restored.

To add to the irony of the situation, the market is popular with Greeks from south of the border as well as the local Turkish population. In what was once part of the downtown area for both communities, the Turkish sector contains the main post office (built by the British) and the original law courts. Turning west, away from the historic centre, one soon picks up the Green Line again. High on the old walls, the view from a parkland bastion is of the United Nations HQ, formerly the prestigious Ledra Palace Hotel. The hotel itself, like a number of domestic as well as commercial properties, was trapped in the buffer zone when the border was fortified on either side. At least a use was found for this one, unlike most of the buildings in 'no man's land' which are reputedly mined and left to fall apart. Beneath the walls, children are chasing a ball on a football pitch, against a backcloth of watchtowers and military signage.

The Green Line has been bad news for the city and it will take decades for the gaping wound to heal. Cities, however, are remarkably resilient and, sure enough, change will come in time. The first steps towards normality were taken in 2003, when crossing became easier, followed by the Republic of Cyprus joining the EU in 2004. If Turkey continues along the same path, eventually achieving its own EU membership, the present division will surely end. To draw a line under this whole sorry business, any reconciliation will have to include an agreement to compensate property-owners who lost their homes and businesses when they were forced to leave. One day, perhaps, the buffer zone will be cleared of its military and other debris, and the natural greenery which has flourished in the vacant strip of land will become a park to remind us all of an episode that will always defy belief.

AFTERWORD

ARAB SPRING, EUROPEAN WINTER

Not one of the fifteen cities visited on this journey has escaped a turbulent history. That is the lot of being in the Mediterranean, caught in the cross-winds between three continents. Geologically as well as geopolitically, the region lies along one of the world's most unstable fault lines. Earthquakes and volcanoes, ethnic and religious conflicts, civil wars and global conflagrations are in its very DNA. Its cities have suffered in bad times and prospered in good, but little has been constant. Change is endemic, uncertainty a by-word.

Even as I write these closing words, the Mediterranean continues to make headlines and outcomes are far from clear. All three coastlines have been the scene of tumultuous events. Thus, along the North African coast, in early 2011 popular protests erupted in three countries—Tunisia, Egypt and then Libya. Lives were lost but hitherto all-powerful dictators were usurped and plans were laid for a democratic future. Such was the episode that has been dubbed the Arab Spring. From the Saharan shores, it spread quickly to Middle Eastern states like Yemen and as far east as Bahrain.

Meanwhile, a later outbreak of protests in Syria led to a violent response from the authorities, determined to maintain power at all costs. Fired by the opposing stands of foreign powers, the situation soon worsened, resulting in a full-blown civil war. Alongside Syria, factions in the tinderbox that is Lebanon watched every move with keen interest and, as refugees poured northwards, Turkey, too, was drawn into the conflict. Israel monitored these unfolding events with growing concern, aware that the region as a whole was becoming not only more hostile to its interests but also less predictable. With Islamic majorities setting the pace in the countries of the Arab Spring, hopes that the popular revolutions so recently experienced would lead to more open societies and balanced policies were soon brought into question. One cannot but recall the words of Dickens: '...it was the season of Light, it was the season of Darkness, it was the spring of hope, it was the winter of despair.'[1]

As if these momentous events were not enough, in this same period a different kind of situation emerged on the northern shores. After years of overspending and poor management, the Greek economy was in a parlous state. As part of the Eurozone, and in exchange for a massive 'bail-out', Greece was required by the European Central Bank to introduce radical spending cuts. These cut deep into the lives of the whole population, and people took to the streets to protest, blaming corrupt politicians and overpaid bureaucrats for the crisis.

With the collapse of the Government and fresh elections, the country at one stage came close to withdrawing from the Eurozone. To add to the instability of southern Europe, Portugal was also forced to apply for a 'bail out', while the economies in Spain and Italy too were to falter, with Cyprus following suit.

In the scheme of things, serious though they are, these troubled times will soon be recorded as no more than blips in the long history of the region. Turbulence is a bedfellow of the Mediterranean, in the past just as now. *Rien ça change*. The cities at the heart of these latest events, economic as well as political, will all somehow weather the storms. They have known worse situations before. This, however, is not to say that the region will emerge unscathed into a sunlit future, for many questions still need to be answered.

Once the immediate constitutional issues of countries in the south and east are resolved, how will the elected leaders respond to the realities of democracy? What will they do to meet the economic challenge of finding work for their still rapidly growing populations and of pegging food prices to affordable levels? Is the region now entering a new phase of religious-driven conflict, with Islamic doctrine in sharp opposition to Western values? How would such a cultural shift affect international relations and power blocs across the Mediterranean? Especially with Iran stoking the fires, how will the interests of Israel be accommodated in this new geopolitical order?

Issues of comparable weight are emerging in the changing economic landscape along the European shores. Everything is connected in the modern Mediterranean, and those countries that were only recently perceived as havens of employment for migrant labour from the south have since firmly closed their doors. For the growing pool of unemployed young men and women in North Africa, there is no respite now in crossing the sea. How will the countries that so recently offered jobs to migrant labour cope with what are now large resident minorities?

Will the situation lead to a rise in extreme right-wing policies with an intolerance of incomers? Even with an eventual return to prosperity, new questions will arise. The issue of Turkey's entry to the Eurozone will be raised again and, if the bid is successful, will it simply sharpen the line between north and south, rich and poor? Moreover, the task of accommodating even larger numbers of tourists and incoming residents seeking a life in the sun will exacerbate existing environmental problems in the region—including the perennial issue of a potential water shortage, with natural supplies far outstripped by increasing demands.

So many questions remain. It would be satisfying, instead, to end this excursion on a more conclusive note. But this is the Mediterranean and, if one learns anything from the experience, it is that uncertainties are part and parcel of the region. Had this excursion been undertaken when the Romans and Carthaginians were locked in war, what could one reasonably have predicted then about the future?

When the Moors invaded Spain in the eighth century, who would have argued against the prospect of the whole of Europe escaping Islamic control? Or, say, in the seventeenth century, with economic power shifting inexorably to northern Europe, what role would one have cast for this obviously declining region? The new geopolitics of the south and east, with the coincident crisis of the Eurozone, together pose a new challenge but this, too, will be met, just as others of greater moment have been in the past.

The Mediterranean has been riven before and still is. It retains its popular image as an idyll but no less telling is its dark side. This is the birthplace of so many achievements but also of human failings. Perhaps it is this juxtaposition and these very uncertainties that make it unique, that give it an alluring edge. The Mediterranean is forever a place of contrasts, where one is constantly asking questions. It defies easy characterizations, easy solutions. Instead, it is complex, volatile, contested, more divided than whole. This has been its past; this will be its future.

---

[1] Charles Dickens, from the opening paragraph of his novel, A Tale of Two Cities, 1859.

NOTES

CHAPTER 1

[1] The word 'Mediterranean', translated from its Latin origins, means literally 'middle land' or 'middle earth' and in this sense it was used to describe an inland location. However, a late-Latin use of the term (seventh century), when combined with the word for sea, extends the first meaning. Thus, the notion expressed by *mare Mediterraneum* 'may originally have been *the sea in the middle of the earth* rather than *the sea enclosed by land*.' The Oxford English Dictionary, Second Edition (1989), Vol.IX, Oxford: Clarendon Press.

[2] Matvejevic (1999), p.10.

[3] Braudel (1966), p.276.

[4] J.M. Houston, in King *et al*, eds. (1997), p.7.

[5] Durrell (1962), p.213 *(Balthazar)*.

[6] Braudel (1966), p.17.

[7] Shakespeare, *The Tempest*, Act I, Scene I.

[8] Fox (1991), p.5.

[9] Durrell (1969), p.187.

[10] www.uwsp.edu/geo/faculty/ritter/geog101/textbook/climate_systems/mediterranean.html-.

[11] Theroux (1996), p.8.

[12] Allen Perry, 'Mediterranean Climate', in King *et al*, eds. (1997), p.31.

[13] *Ibid*.

[14] Braudel (1976), p.237.

[15] *Ibid*., p.241.

[16] Durrell (1969), pp.356-7.

[17] King *et al*, eds. (1997), p.5.

[18] Drinkwater (2007).

[19] Lawrence Durrell (1969), p.369, has suggested that the word 'Mediterranean' should be applied to all wine-drinking countries around the basin. Perhaps when he wrote this, in 1969, it would have had more credence than now, when alcohol is frowned upon or even forbidden in some of the Mediterranean countries.

[20] Rick Stein, chef and restaurateur, is a popular exemplar of this *genre*, having guided his readers and television viewers around the Mediterranean while advocating the merits of 'slow cooking'. His theme has a modern ring, decrying supermarket products in favour of food that is produced locally and lovingly handled by traditional methods. He looks for the real gems of the region to the rugged hinterland and finds in the mountains families who produce cheeses using recipes passed down from generation to generation, shepherds who are enjoying a revival of interest with the modern appreciation of regional meats, and locally-grown vegetables sold in busy markets. Stein shows that it is not just for the tourist that regional specialities are produced; they are, instead, an enduring feature of Mediterranean life and make their own impact on the towns that distribute them through their little shops and restaurants as well as through annual festivals.

[21] Norwich (2006), p.1.

[22] Semple (1931), p.3.

[23] Braudel (1998), p.60.

[24] Shakespeare, *Antony and Clepatra*, Act II, Scene VII.

[25] Mumford (1961), p.148.

[26] Norwich (2006), p.6.

[27] *Ibid.*, p.8.

[28] *Ibid.*

[29] Abulafia (2011), p.22.

[30] Dicaearchus, between the first and second century BC, in Mumford (1961), p.191.

[31] Macaulay (1953), p.26.

[32] Strabo (22 AD), *Geographica*, Book XVII, iii, pp.1-11.

[33] Virgil (19 BC), *Aeneid*, Book I.

[34] Braudel (1998), p.335.

[35] *Ibid.*, p.317.

[36] Dr Johnson, in Theroux (1996), p.2.

[37] Macaulay (1953), p.26.

[38] *Ibid.*, p.62.

[39] *Ibid.*, p.26.

[40] George Bernard Shaw, Preface, *Plays Pleasant*, 1898.

[41] It is commonly the case in Jewish and other histories to use the letters BCE (Before the Current Era) but, to be consistent with other references, the use of BC is preferred.

[42] de Lange (1984), pp.20-31.

[43] Smart (1989), p.246.

[44] *Ibid*, p.277.

[45] Braudel (1992), p.24.

[46] Book of Joshua, *Old Testament*, 4 and 28.

[47] Thucydides (1972 trans.), p.48.

[48] Norwich (2006), p.31.

[49] Wheatcroft (2004), p.198.

[50] The events in southern Europe will be dealt with in later sections, particularly in relation to the cities of Alicante and Syracuse.

[51] Fletcher (2004), p.77.

[52] An excellent source of this episode and of the place of Jerusalem generally in Mediterranean history is Montefiore (2011).

[53] Book of Revelation, *New Testament*, 14:20.

[54] Norwich (2006), p.205.

[55] *Ibid.*, p.204.

[56] *Ibid.*, p.138.

[57] Braudel (1976), p.234.

[58] Thucydides (1972 trans.), p.37.

[59] Norwich (2006), p.94.

[60] *Ibid.* p.282.

[61] Braudel (1966), p.865.

[62] *Ibid.*, p.866.

[63] Captain John Ward was one such renegade, who in 1605 made a deal in Tunis to raid all Christian shipping

except for that which flew the English flag and, in return for safe anchorage, to share the profits with the local ruler. His success at his trade earned him a grand palace, and he was soon to enlist a flamboyant second-in-command, the Englishman, Sir Francis Verney, who preferred a rough life at sea to the sedate routine of a landed aristocrat.

[64] *Lepanto*, a poem by G.K. Chesterton, 1915, celebrating a Papal-inspired victory.

[65] Virgil, Aeneid, c.29 BC, Book 6, lines 122-5.

http://classiclit.about.com/od/aeneidvergil/a/aa-aeneid.htm.

[66] See, for instance, Crowley (2008). Lepanto was the last major battle to be fought with ships powered by oars and with men fighting the enemy in hand-to-hand encounters with swords and archery. In the future, artillery would provide the mainstay of weaponry although, until the advent of steam power, sails continued in use to carry the extra load.

[67] Chesterton, *op.cit.*, n.38.

[68] For helpful accounts of Lepanto, see Norwich (2006), pp.321-330; Wheatcroft (2004), pp.3-38; and Crowley (2008).

[69] Contemporary chronicler, in Crowley (2008), p.285.

[70] Norwich (2006), pp.425-9.

[71] Moorehead (2007).

[72] Keegan (1997).

[73] Abulafia (2011), p.648.

[74] Norwich (2006), p.6.

[75] Abulafia (2011), p.211.

[76] *Ibid*, p.xviii.

[77] Professor Leontidou has written extensively on the geography of Mediterranean cities. Particular use has been made in this section of Leontidou (1990) and her chapters, 'Five Narratives for the Mediterranean City' and 'Cultural Representations of Urbanism and Experiences of Urbanisation in Mediterranean Europe', in King *et al*, eds. 1997 and 2001.

[78] 'Sarkozy's proposal for Mediterranean block makes waves', *International Herald Tribune*, 10 May 2007. http://www.iht.com.articles/2007/05/10/africa/france.ph.

[79] Alfred, Lord Tennyson, 'The Lotus-Eaters', 1832.

[80] *Ibid*.

[81] There are various estimates, such as the Mediterranean as host to 30% of the world's international tourists, in the Blue Plan report 2009, op.cit., n.8.

[82] These estimates pre-date the global recession that was formally recognized in 2008, the difficulties faced by Mediterranean countries in the Eurozone, and the political uprisings in 2011, all of which will inevitably lead to a downscaling of numbers (if only delayed).

[83] http://www.monachus-guardian/org/library/wwftou01.pdf.

[84] Arnold (2008), pp. 72-3.

[85] V.R. Rodríguez, P.S. Tomàs and A.M. Williams, 'Northern Europeans and the Mediterranean: a New California or a New Florida?' in King *et al*, eds. (2001), pp.176-95.

[86] King *et al* (2000).

[87] Jan Mansvelt Beck and Paolo De Mas, 'The Strait of Gibraltar: Europe's Rio Grande?', in King et al, eds. (2001), p.134.

[88] Russell King, 'Population Growth: An Avoidable Crisis?' in King *et al*, eds. (1997), p.168.

[89] See, for instance, figures prepared by the UN Population Division, in 'The End of the Population Explosion in the Mediterranean?' www.jstor.org/stable/2949165.

[90] *Ibid.*, p.172. Precise figures depend on different interpretations of what constitutes the Mediterranean basin; some authors estimate the population around the sea itself while others clearly refer to whole nations with a Mediterranean coastline. Thus, in another work, it is claimed that the population rose from about 212 million in 1950 to 298 million by 1970 and then to 497 million in 1997: Wainright and Thornes (2004), p.302. Actual numbers vary but, in all cases, the upward trend is unmistakeable.

[91] Osman (2010), pp. 5-7.

[92] 'Immigrant Odyssey', *Time Magazine*, 1 December 2008, pp.38-40.

[93] King, op. cit., p.164.

[94] Webster (2005).

[95] Chambers (2008).

[96] *Ibid.* p.39.

[97] *Ibid.*, p.3.

[98] *Ibid.*

CHAPTER 2

Gibraltar

[1] Disraeli, in a letter to his father dated 1 July, 1830, in Sanchez (2006), p.233.

[2] Michael Portillo, http://www.michaelportillo.co.uk/articles.

[3] With the subsequent occupation of Gibraltar by the British, the shrine was decommissioned and was not used again for religious services until 1962. In 1979, Pope John Paul II officially approved the title of Our Lady of Europe as Patroness of Gibraltar.

[4] The first landings on the Spanish mainland were in the previous year, 710.

[5] George Edward Woodberry, 'At Gibraltar', 1890, in Sanchez (2006), p.189.

[6] Garratt (1939), p.25.

[7] *Ibid.*, p.41.

[8] Lopez de Ayala, in Garratt, op. cit., p.43.

[9] Sanchez (2007), pp.125-50.

[10] In Norwich (2006), p.408.

[11] Garratt (1939), p.143.

[12] Extract from an early brochure for The Rock Hotel, currently displayed in one of the lounges.

[13] William Makepeace Thackeray, on a visit to Gibraltar in 1846, in Sanchez (2006), p.113.

[14] *Ibid.*

[15] In Sanchez, op. cit., p.233.

[16] A renowned specialist on Gibraltar, Peter Gold, explains that a small minority of Gibraltarians claim that their first language is a hybrid known as *Llanito*, 'combining English and Spanish but also incorporating lexical items from Genoese and Hebrew'. See Peter Gold, 'Identity formation in Gibraltar: geopolitical, historical and cultural factors', *Geopolitics*, Vol.15, No.2, 2010, pp.367 to 384.

[17] Theroux, op. cit., p.21.

[18] *Ibid.*, p.16.

[19] Garratt (1939), p.227.

[20] Waugh (1985), p.158.

[21] Theroux, op. cit., p.12.

[22] Some say that Gibraltar is gaining an unwanted reputation as a conduit for money laundering, a claim that is strongly denied by officials.

[23] Peter Gold, 'The tripartite forum of dialogue: is this the solution to the problem of Gibraltar?' *Mediterranean Politics*, Vol.14, No.1, 2009, pp.79-97.

[24] David Lambert, '*As solid as the Rock?* Place, belonging and the local appropriation of imperial discourse in Gibraltar', *Trans. Inst. Br. Geogr.*, Vol.30, No.2, 2005, pp.206-220.

Alicante

[1] W.H. Auden, in Fletcher (2001), p.13.

[2] Fletcher, op. cit., p.8.

[3] *Ibid*, p.65.

[4] *Ibid*.

[5] Webster (2005), p.122.

[6] Macaulay (1950).

[7] Pageants depicting battles between Moors and Christians take place in various towns and villages in the south of Spain; Alicante is just one such location.

[8] Irazabal (2007), p.24. The evidence is drawn from Latin America although common cultural ties with Spain remain strong.

[9] Jason Webster (2005) provides evidence of this.

[10] There is a twice-daily ferry from Algeria, which is believed to be a major source of illegal immigration. Additionally, Alicante has gained an unwanted reputation as an entry point for Eastern European prostitution and drug rings. The source for both these allegations is Leland L'Hote and Chad Gasta, 'Immigration and street entrepreneurship in Alicante, Spain', *International Journal of Iberian Studies*, Vol.20, No.1, 2007, pp.3-22.

[11] Matvejevic (1999), p.93.

[12] Macaulay, op. cit.

[13] Surveys have shown that young men who went from the land to the resorts for work became prone to mental illness. Hooper (2006), p.19.

[14] Theroux (1996), p.35.

[15] Macaulay, op. cit., p.137.

[16] As an icon of popular culture, Benidorm is the name and location for a UK TV series, originating in 2007.

[17] It is difficult to get precise totals as some permanent incomers still record themselves as domiciled in the country they have come from. These figures are taken from an article (p.129) by Ingo Zasada, Susan Alves, Felix Claus Müller, Annette Piorr, Regine Berges and Simon Bell, 'International retirement migration in the Alicante region, Spain: process, spatial pattern and environmental impacts', *International Journal of Environmental Planning and Management*, Vol.53, No.1, January 2010, pp.125-141.

[18] Rodriguez, V. R., Tomas, P.S. and Williams, A., 'Northern Europeans and the Mediteranean: A New California or a New Florida?', pp. 176-84, in King et al (2001).

[19] In 2006 there were fifteen golf courses with an additional thirty-three projected in the Alicante region. See Zasada et al, op.cit., p.132.

[20] Zasada et al, op.cit., p.132, contend that the older residents who predominate in these communities appreciate well-managed, secure open spaces—like golf courses—although they do not necessarily use them as such.

[21] A Spanish Arabist professor, in Webster, op. cit., p.122.

Marseille

[1] Alexander Dumas, in Agostini, J. and Forno, Y. (1997), p.210.

[2] Thucydides (1972 trans.), 13:1, p.44.

[3] Few cities in the Mediterranean escaped at least one serious bout of bubonic plague and in the fourteenth century it has been estimated that as much as half of the total population of the region was decimated by the disease. See Abulafia (2011).

[4] *Institut Français d'Architecture (1989) Marseille*. Paris: Bulletins d'Informations Architecturales.

[5] Laurent Morando, *'Les Expositions Coloniales Nationales de Marseille de 1906 et 1922: Manifestations locales ou nationales?'*, Provence Historique 2004, pp.229-52.

[6] Animals from the African wild had long before captivated the interest of the inhabitants of Marseille. Michael Allin's *Zarafa* (London: Headline, 1998) provides a charming account of the arrival of a giraffe in the city in 1826, winning the hearts of the local population before it was taken on the long trek by road to Paris.

[7] *'Marseille: Vue par une touriste allemande au milieu du XVIIIe siècle'*, in Bonillo (1991), p.134-35.

[8] Some figures of the present mix of population are provided by 'Andrew Purvis in 'Marseille's ethnic *bouillabaisse'*, *Smithsonian*, Vol.38, Issue 9, pp.86-93, December 2007. Within the municipal area of Marseille, with a total population of 800,000 he estimates that 200,000 are Muslim, 80,000 Jews and 80,000 Armenian Christians.

[9] Elizabeth Bryant, 'It's here that Le Pen draws his strength', *St Petersburg Times Online*, USA, 30 April 2002, http://www.sptimes.com'2002/04/30/Worldandnation/It_s_here_that_Le_Pen.shtml.

[10] *Ibid*.

[11] Arthur Schopenhauer, German philosopher, in Agostini, J. and Forno, Y. (1997), p.200.

[12] Bonillo (1991).

[13] Agostini, and Forno, op. cit., p.248.

[14] Kargon and Molella (2008), p.92.

[15] Albert Londres, French journalist, in Agostini and Forno, op.cit., p.279.

[16] http://www.nga.gov/exhibitions/2006/cezanne/motif3.shtm.

[17] http://www.marubeni.com/gallery/painting_f/paint_oz.html.

[18] Agostini and Forno, *op.cit.*, p.117

[19] For evidence of the location of key French and multi-national firms in Marseille, see, for instance, http://www.marseille-tourisme.com/fileadmin/user_upload/EUROMED_GB.pdf and http://www.euroméditerranée.fr. See also Bruce Grumley, 'Mediterranean Mecca', Time Europe, Issue 25, Vol. 157, p.32, 25 June 2001.

[20] Sources have been derived from a variety of material provided in the *Euroméditerranée* exhibition area in the centre of the project area.

CHAPTER 3

Trieste

[1] Powell (1920), p.47.

[2] Newby (1998), p.109.

[3] Morris (2002), p.65.

[4] McCourt (2000), p.26.

[5] Morris(2002), pp.50-1.

[6] An estimated 5000 Jews were taken to gas chambers within the environs of the city itself.

[7] Morris, *op. cit.*, p.13.

[8] *Ibid.*, p.29.

[9] *Ibid.*

[10] *Ibid.*, p.13

[11] *Ibid.*, p.32

[12] Joyce's time in Trieste is best accounted for in McCourt (2000).

[13] Paul Waley, in 'Introducing Trieste: a cosmopolitan city?', *Social & Cultural Geography*, Vol.10, Issue 3, May 2009, pp.243-256, distinguishes between this type of cosmopolitanism (which he describes as 'Oriental', on account of its likeness to that of the traditional ports of the eastern Mediterranean) and the modern mix of cultures (which he describes as 'European', being perhaps a model of a new form of multi-culturalism).

[14] Letter to Joyce's brother, Stanislaus, 2 or 3 May 1905, in Ellmann, ed. (1966), p.88.

[15] Morris (2002), p.65.

[16] Although, in the case of Trieste, the reasons were geopolitical, cities have declined for other reasons too, not least of all economic (the decline of traditional industries, etc.). Shrinking Cities is the name given to a project initiated in 2002 by a German research body, the Federal Cultural Foundation. Four interdisciplinary teams were commissioned to study and document urban shrinking processes in Detroit (USA), Manchester/ Liverpool (UK), Ivanovo (Russia), and Halle/Leipzig (Germany).

[17] Morris (2002), pp.153, 154, 161-2.

[18] *Ibid.*, p.45.

[19] Theroux (1996), p.231.

[20] Morris (2002), p.3.

[21] Theroux (1996), p.228.

[22] Morris (2002), p.97.

[23] *Ibid.*, p.3. See also, Claudio Minca, '*Trieste Nazione* and its geographies of absence', *Social & Cultural Geography*, Vol.10, Issue 3, May 2009, pp.257-277, where Trieste is described as 'the most *European* of Italian cities' (p.257).

[24] The new region was declared in November 2007 and named after the city. It extends over a large area, comprising the existing Italian administrative areas of Veneto and Friuli Venezia-Giulia; Carinthia, in southern Austria; Slovenia; and Croatian Istria. See Waley, *op.cit.*, pp.244-245.

[25] It is no coincidence that a modern version of the coffee machine was pioneered in Trieste, in 1933, by Francesco Illy.

Dubrovnik

[1] Mazower (2001) argues that the West's negative perception of the Balkans is based as much on myth as the facts of the region's long history.

[2] West (2006), p.21.

[3] Fox (1991), p.178.

[4] The origins of Dubrovnik have, most recently, been carefully traced by Harris (2003).

[5] Harris (2003), p.31.

[6] Braudel (1976), p.318.

[7] In *The Merchant of Venice* (Act 1), Shakespeare uses the term for any grand seagoing vessel: '... argosies with portly sail... Do overpeer the petty traffickers... As they fly by them with their woven wings.'

[8] Harris (2003), p.18.

[9] *Ibid*. Harris uses the term 'sunset years' as a chapter heading to cover the period from 1669 to 1792.

[10] Anica Kisić, 'Shipbuilding in ancient Dubrovnik', pp.10-13, in Salamon (2001).

[11] Mazower (2001), p.128.

[12] Fox (1991), p.160.

[13] Glenny (1996), p.43.

[14] The phrase is commonly attributed to Lord Byron (although there is no mention of a visit to Dubrovnik in Fiona MacCarthy's biography and account of his travels).

[15] Glenny (1996), p136.

[16] Foretić (2002), p.87.

[17] West (2006), pp.230, 231.

[18] *Ibid*., p.231.

[19] Harris (2003), p.402.

[20] *Ibid*., p.411.

[21] Goldring (1913), p.232.

[22] Colin Kaiser, 'When the war is over', pp.87-91, in Foretić (2002).

Thessaloniki

[1] Thessaloniki is derived from the ancient Greek word for victory, 'thessaly', and the city was named after the Macedonian princess, Thessalonike. For much of its history (especially the long period of Ottoman rule) it was also known as Salonica or, alternatively, Salonika. For the sake of clarity (although, admittedly, at the expense of cultural precision) the single term, Thessaloniki, will be used throughout.

[2] Mazower (2004), p.187, citing the observation of an American journalist in 1906.

[3] *Ibid*., p.191.

[4] Sakellariou (1988), p.208.

[5] Sciaky (2007), p.123.

[6] *Ibid*.

[7] Herrin (2008), p.51. Although this description is based on a mediaeval view of the Church of Hagia Sophia in Constantinople, it is indicative of the elaborate interiors (and the awe and wonder they provoked) elsewhere in the churches and cathedrals of Byzantium.

[8] Acts 17.

[9] *Ibid*.

[10] Smart (1989), p.255.

[11] *Ibid*, p.268.

[12] Norwich (2006), p.138.

[13] Wheatcroft (2004), Preface p.xxx.

[14] Mazower (2004), p.31.

[15] *Ibid*., p.33.

[16] Samuel Usque, a sixteenth-century poet living in Salonica, in Mazower (2004), p.50.

[17] Others in that period came, in 1493, from Sicily and Southern Italy, and from Provence in 1506. Sakellariou (1988), p.354.

[18] Lewkowicz (2006), p.43.

[19] Mazower (2004), p.49.

[20] *Ibid.*, p.7.

[21] Sciaky (2007).

[22] There is a young contingent that is determined to rebuild their community, not in the same numbers as before but as a meaningful representation of Judaism. The Jewish Museum of Thessaloniki, where some of these people work as volunteers, enables them to engage in conversation with visitors—explaining the past and looking to the future.

[23] Mazower (2004), p.5.

[24] A helpful source on the planning and rebuilding of Thessaloniki in this period is Alexandra Yerolympos, 'Thessaloniki (Salonika) before and after 1917: twentieth-century planning versus twenty centuries of urban evolution', *Planning Perspectives*, Vol.3, No.2, May 1988, pp.141-66.

[25] Pierre Lavedan, in Alexandra Yerolympos, *op.cit.*

[26] According to Yerolympos, *op.cit.*, Mawson had been brought in personally by Venizelos, in an attempt to balance the prevailing influence of French planners in the Commission.

[27] Yerolympos, *op.cit.*, .p.147, claims that the newly planned city was characterized by 'low, middle and high income group districts' rather than the traditional ethnic neighbourhoods.

[28] Mazower, *op.cit.* pp.457-8.

[29] *Ibid.*, p.459.

CHAPTER 4

Izmir

[1] Strabo, *Geographica*, XIV,1.37.

[2] *Ibid.*

[3] Rather like Strabo is acknowledged as the first geographer, Herodotus has been dubbed 'the father of history'. His account of the early development of Smyrna is to be found in *The Histories* (1998 translation), mainly in scattered references in Book 1.

[4] Dobkin (1998), p.22.

[5] These statistics and other information on Smyrna in the early twentieth century are derived from authoritative accounts in Dobkin (1998) and Milton (2008).

[6] Mansel (2010) reports on massacres in the city from as early as 1770, pp.5-55.

[7] Milton, *op.cit.*, builds on accounts in earlier works through the addition of interviews with survivors of the 1922 destruction and access to family records.

[8] This was the view, if not the exact words, of American consul George Horton, in Milton, *op.cit.*, p.9.

[9] Mansel, *op.cit.*, p.156.

[10] The Turkish writer, Naci Gundem, in Mansel, *op.cit.*, p.160.

[11] Recollection of a twelve-year-old boy, one of the fortunate ones to escape the city on its destruction, in Milton, *op.cit.*, p.331.

[12] Dobkin, *op.cit.*, in her introduction, provides the most revealing account of how the records of 1922 have been obscured and distorted and how difficult it is for the researcher to discover what really happened.

[13] The idea pre-dates Venizelos although he seized the opportunity to link it to his own military campaign.

[14] It is arguable whether the Allies manipulated the Greeks or *vice versa*; certainly, Venizelos seized the

opportunity to overthrow his king, Constantine, who was advocating neutrality. For Venizelos, joining with the Allies offered the best prospect to realize the dream of a Greater Greece.

[15] A fictional account of this episode, although based on actual events seen from a Greek perspective, is that of Themelis (2008).

[16] The Jews were never treated as badly as the Armenians and, although many chose to leave the city then and later, there remains in Izmir a small but thriving community of some 2500.

[17] Milton, *op.cit.*, p.325

[18] *Ibid.* The journalist in question filed his story with the Daily Mail.

[19] *Ibid.*, p.319.

[20] *Ibid,* pp.339-40.

[21] *Ibid.*, p.325. The description was written by John Clayton, a Chicago news reporter.

[22] *Ibid.*, p.326.

[23] Mansel, *op.cit.*, p.232.

[24] It has been variously estimated that as many as 1.2 million Greeks were forced to leave Asia Minor, while 0.4 million Turkish refugees arrived from northern Greece.

[25] Ways in which the past has been rendered innocuous are considered in the introductory and final chapters of Dobkin, op.cit.

[26] Ayona Datta and Sebnem Yucel Young, 'Suburban development and networks of mobility: sites in Izmir, Turkey', *Global Built Environment Review*, Vol. 6, No. 1, pp 44-55.

[27] Mansel, *op.cit.*, p.233.

[28] *Ibid.*

[29] Cana Bilsel, 'A pioneering city in the 20th century urbanism in Turkey: urban projects in Izmir', presentation to 14th IPHS Conference, 12-15 July 2010.

[30] Isin Can, 'Urban design and the planning system in Izmir', *Journal of Landscape Studies*, Vol. 3, 2010, pp.181-9.

[31] *Ibid.* Isin Can dates the new emphasis on project planning to the 1980s, in part a result of the failure of comprehensive plans.

Beirut

[1] The name is based on the French for rising sun, *soleil levant*, and then, because the sun rose in the east, the Orient.

[2] Douglas Jehl, 'Under Beirut's rubble, remnants of 5000 years of civilization', *New York Times*, 23 February 1997

[3] A helpful source on Beirut's early history is to be found in Fawaz (1983), Ch. 2.

[4] Tabet *et al* (2001), p.8.

[5] Fawaz, *op.cit.*, p.10.

[6] This episode is carefully explained in Hanssen (2005).

[7] *Ibid.*, pp.67-9.

[8] *Ibid.*, pp.71-2.

[9] *Ibid.*, pp.78-9.

[10] Rogan (2009), p.211.

[11] Angus Gavin, 'Heart of Beirut: making the master plan for the renewal of the central district', in Rowe and Sarkis, eds. (1998), p.218.

[12] Assem Salam, 'The role of government in shaping the built environment', in Rowe and Sarkis, op. cit., p.122.

[13] Manning (1982), p.482.

[14] The origins of the group remains a mystery to outsiders. Some observers believe that Druze beliefs are really an offshoot of mainstream Islam, others look instead to earlier links with Hinduism or Zoroastrianism. It remains an enclosed community into which no newcomers may enter.

[15] The banks of Beirut gained a reputation for their discretion, rather like the banks of Switzerland.

[16] Writers on Beirut repeatedly complain of a lack of reliable population figures, so that totals can only be estimates.

[17] Fox (1991), p.442.

[18] Sofia T. Shwayri, 'From Regional Node to Backwater and Back to Uncertainty: Beirut, 1943-2006', Chapter 4, in Elsheshtawy (2008).

[19] Fox, op.cit., p.447.

[20] The Green Line—which followed the line of the formerly busy Damascus Road—was so-called because (as a 'no go' zone) it was gradually reclaimed by natural vegetation.

[21] *Ibid.*, pp.441-2.

[22] The emphasis on 'high end' development is explored in Marieke Krijnen and Mona Fawaz, 'Exception as the rule: High-end developments in neoliberal Beirut', *Built Environment*, Vol. 36, No.2, pp.245-59.

[23] The city's promotional material, and Solidere's in particular, is replete with image enhancing slogans. Solidere's 2009 Annual Report contains many such phrases as 'modernity with historicity', 'revival of a world-class destination', 'a promenade architecturale *[sic]* that charms the spirit and enriches the mind', 'a cultural voyage in time and space', 'traditional fabric in a modern city', 'the climax of a citywide seaside corniche'.

[24] Slogan on the streets in the aftermath of Israeli bombing of Beirut in 2006. Shwayri, op.cit., p.70.

[25] A background to the saga is provided on the hotel company's website: http://www.stgeorges-hotel. com.

[26] See, for instance, Shwayri, *op.cit.*, p.89.

[27] The role of Rafiq Hariri and the confused lines between private and public investment are explored in Richard Becherer, 'A matter of life and death: the untold costs of Rafiq Hariri's New Beirut', *The Journal of Architecture*, Vol.10, No.1, February 2005, pp.1-42.

[28] In fact, a company, Elisar, was designated to improve conditions in the impoverished residential districts in the south of the city. Progress was slow, not least of all because of 'factional and intercommunal struggles': see Assem Salam, *op.cit.*, p.132.

[29] The role of Hezbollah in replanning Beirut's southern suburbs is explored in Mona Fawaz, 'Hezbollah as urban planner? Questions to and from planning theory', *Planning Theory*, Vol.8, No.4, 2009, pp.323-34; also Mona Harb and Mona Fawaz, 'Influencing the Politics of Reconstruction in Haret Hreik', in Al-Harithy (2010), pp.21-45. In addition to her written work, I am very grateful to Mona Fawaz for taking time out to meet me on my visit to the city and for advising me on important landmarks.

[30] Gavin and Maluf (1996), p.71.

[31] Rowe and Sarkis, *op.cit.*, 'Introduction'.

[32] Bollens (2012), chapter 13.

[33] The Holiday Inn opened only a few months before the outbreak of the civil war in 1975. It became a focus of intense fighting but was able to withstand heavy artillery without collapsing because of its anti-earthquake structure.

[34] Mansel (2010), p.356.

Haifa

[1] Oliphant (2005), p.22.

[2] Goitein (1967), p.127.

[3] For an account of Haifa during the Ottoman period, see especially Tal *et al*, (2009).

[4] During his time in the region, Oliphant wrote a series of letters for publication in the press, later brought together as a book, originally published in 1887: see Oliphant (2005).

[5] Oliphant's wife, Alice, died of a fever contracted by the Sea of Tiberias. As a believer in spiritualism he maintained that he had better communication with her after her death than when she was a mere mortal.

[6] Oliphant (2005), p.20.

[7] *Ibid.*, p.23.

[8] The criticism was not entirely true as the Carmelites had built a school and offered a refuge for pilgrims to the area.

[9] de Lange (1984), p.132.

[10] Herzl (1902), p.61.

[11] *Ibid.*, p.69.

[12] *Ibid.*, p.73.

[13] *Ibid.*

[14] *Ibid.*, p.96.

[15] Carl Alpert, explaining in 1982 the case made by the Zionists in the early twentieth century to locate the Technion (Israel's Institute of Technology) in Haifa, in Herbert and Sosnovsky (1993), pp.27-8.

[16] Extract from the Balfour Declaration, 1917.

[17] British rule effectively begins with the military occupation of Jerusalem in 1917. it was to be another seven years before the Mandate was formally approved by the League of Nations.

[18] Contemporary view (unattributed), in Ziva Kolodney and Rachel Kallus, 'From colonial to national landscape: Producing Haifa's cityscape', *Planning Perspectives*, 23:3, 2008, pp.323-48.

[19] Lionel Watson, British City Engineer for Haifa, in Kolodney and Kallus, *op. cit.*, p.329.

[20] A prime source for details of planning during the Mandate is Herbert and Sosnovsky (1993).

[21] Ashbee's colourful background in England is described in MacCarthy (1981).

[22] There are several accounts of Geddes but the one that focuses most on his planning experience is Meller (1990).

[23] Herbert and Sosnovksy (1993), p.50.

[24] *Ibid.*, p.49.

[25] *Ibid*, p.82.

[26] *Ibid*, pp.85-98.

[27] *Ibid*, p.189.

[28] *Ibid*, p.191.

[29] *Ibid*, p.198.

[30] Tamir Goren, 'The Judaization of Haifa at the time of the Arab Revolt', *Middle Eastern Studies*, Vol.14, Issue 4, July 2004, pp.135-152.

[31] Seikaly (1995) sees this encirclement as part of a deliberate strategy by the Zionists, repeated in other settlements in Israel over the coming years, p.257.

[32] Details of Haifa's changing population during the Mandate period are interpreted in Seikaly (1995). See also Ziva Kolodney and Rachel Kallus, *op.cit*.

[33] Herbert and Sosnovsky (1993), p.277.

[34] Rogan (2009), p.260.

[35] Seikaly (1995), p.xi.

[36] Herbert and Sosnovsky (1993), p.277.

[37] Nearly 30% of the population of Haifa has family roots in the former Soviet Union.

CHAPTER 5

Alexandria

[1] Forster (2004), p.19.

[2] He wrote two books on the city: *Alexandria: A History and a Guide* (1922) and *Pharos and Pharillon* (1923), the latter being a series of previously published articles for newspapers.

[3] Pollard and Reid (2007), p.24.

[4] *Ibid.*, p.xiv.

[5] Forster, *op.cit.* (2004), p.29.

[6] The two matching obelisks, along with a third on the site, were duly plundered: one to be taken in modern times to New York, one to Paris and the third to London.

[7] By then, within this total, it contained the largest concentration of Jews in the ancient world, perhaps as many as 200,000: Pollard and Reid, *op.cit.*, p.191.

[8] The Arab general, Amr, *ibid.*, p.54.

[9] Cavafy (2008), 'The City', p.25.

[10] In 1882 the British fleet bombarded the city, in the course of which remaining historical monuments were damaged or demolished.

[11] The Tanziman Edict was introduced in an attempt to buttress the Ottoman Empire, in the face of emergent nationalist and other demands from its various colonies.

[12] Forster, *op.cit.*, (2004), pp.78-9.

[13] From 'Silence', 1916, by Giuseppe Ungaretti, in Empereur (2002), p.142.

[14] *Ibid.*

[15] In a letter to his mother, 1849, in Empereur, *op.cit.*, p.137.

[16] Gérard de Nerval, in Empereur, *op.cit.*, p.136.

[17] Cavafy, *op.cit.*, 'The Glory of the Ptolemies', p.38.

[18] Haag, *op.cit.*, p.27.

[19] Forster, in Haag, op.cit., p.56.

[20] Haag, *op.cit.*, p.162.

[21] *Ibid.*, p.163.

[22] Durrell (2005), Clea, p.700.

[23] *Ibid.*, Justine, p.17.

[24] *Ibid.*, p.26.

[25] *Ibid.*, Clea, p.676.

[26] Forster, *op.cit.*, (2004), p.245.

[27] *Ibid.*

[28] Theroux, *op.cit.*, p.362.

[29] Empereur, *op.cit.*, p.120.

[30] Durrell, op.cit., *Balthazar*, p.314.

[31] The big picture of modern Egyptian history is most ably traced by Osman (2010).

[32] Mansel (2010), p.275.

[33] As a sign of growing tensions, on New Year's Day, 2011, a bomb exploded in the Coptic Church in Alexandria, killing Christians at prayer.

[34] Hassan Abdel-Salam, 'The historical evolution and present morphology of Alexandria', *Planning Perspectives*, Vol. 10 (2), 1995, pp.173-98.

[35] Elsheshtawy (2008), p.3.

[36] Ilbert and Yannakakis (1997), p.33.

[37] The deterioration of its buildings was evident even in 1966, when James Morris observed that 'all over the Levantine city an air of seedy neglect lies like a blight'. Mansel, *op.cit.*, p.289.

[38] Mansel, *op.cit.*, p.295. Since those words were written the feared explosion has taken place, starting in January 2011, in the form of a popular protest movement against the leader for more than three decades, Hosni Mubarak.

Tripoli

[1] This understanding of the extent of Libya is revealed in the following description by Herodotus: 'As for Libya, we know it to be washed on all sides by the sea, except where it is attached to Asia.' *The Histories: Book IV*.42-43.

[2] Strabo, *Geographica*, Book XVII Chapter 3.

[3] Paul Melon, a French traveller in 1884, in Wright (2005), p.188.

[4] There is, in fact, some dispute over the original name, the consensus being that Oea might have evolved from an earlier version, Uiat.

[5] *La descrizione dell'Africa*, in Wright, *op.cit.*, pp.19-25.

[6] Wright, *op.cit.*, pp.31-2.

[7] *Ibid.*

[8] St John (2008), p.32.

[9] Online edition of an account by Captain William Goldsmith, 1825, extracted from his book *The Naval History of Great Britain*, p.211, http://www.google.co.uk/search?q=john+narbrough+tripoli&hl=en&rlz=1T4ADBR_enGB293GB 294&start=10&sa=N.

[10] This was in line with the modernization of other Ottoman cities, encouraged by the Tanziman Edict of 1839.

[11] Miss Tully's first name is not known. Her letters were published in 1817 in a single volume, *Narrative of a Ten Years' Residence at Tripoli in Africa*. See Wright, op.cit., pp.42-50.

[12] A contemporary of Miss Tully, Ali Bey Abbassi, estimated the population as between 12,000 and 15,000. Wright, *op.cit.*, p.66.

[13] The German painter, William Heine, sent to Tripoli in 1859 by the US government to record aspects of the Barbary Wars. Wright, op.cit., p.160

[14] Wright, *op.cit.*, p.188

[15] Domenico Tubiati, *Nell'Africa Romana: Tripolitania*. Wright, *op.cit.*, p.236

[16] Report of a visit by the Jewish Territorial Organisation in 1908. Wright, *op.cit.*, p.233

[17] It was not until a visit to Libya in 2008 by the Italian President, Silvio Berlusconi, that more amicable relations between the two countries were formally declared.

[18] Segrè (1974), p.57.

[19] *Ibid.*, p.109.

[20] Gaddafi (1975), Part 3, p.15.

[21] Helpful sources on the modern period include Wright (1982), Vandewalle (2006) and St. John (2008).

[22] St. John, *op.cit.*, p.139.

[23] Gaddafi, *op.cit.*

[24] There are just four chapters, dealing in turn with the economic basis of the Third Universal Theory: need, land and domestic servants.

[25] *The Village*, in St. John, *op.cit.*, p.135.

[26] Todd (1994)

[27] *Ibid*, p.203.

[28] *Ibid.*

[29] www.leonwohlhagewernik.de/fileadmin/downloads/english/Press_Release_Tripolis_e.pdf.

[30] Todd, *op.cit.*, p.1.

Tunis

[1] Macaulay (1964), p.6.

[2] The firsthand observation was by Scipio's Greek tutor, Polybius. Streeter (2006), p.85.

[3] Wingfield (2005), Vol. 1, p.233.

[4] Semple (1931), p.6.

[5] Bechir Kenzari, 'Lake Tunis, or the Concept of the Third Centre', p.115, in Elsheshtawy (2004), pp 114-33.

[6] Wingfield, *op.cit.*, Vol. 1, p. 238.

[7] The term, 'Tunis the white' was coined by the Greek historian, Diodorus of Sicily, in the first century BC.

[8] Wingfield, *op.cit.*, Vol.1, p.239.

[9] *Ibid.*, p.273.

[10] *Ibid.*, p.275.

[11] The city is, in fact, renowned for the manufacture of this form of headwear, which at one time was an important source of exports.

[12] Chateaubriand (2007).

[13] *Ibid.*, p.18.

[14] Italian premier, Francesco Crispi, in Perkins (2004), p.44.

[15] Later the balance changed, although no more than half of the incomers were to be French, with large numbers of those from Corsica (especially in Tunis itself).

[16] Kenzari, in Elshestawy, *op. cit.*, p.115.

[17] Two useful accounts of how the city spread beyond the original core are to be found in Vigier (1987) and Woodford (1990).

[18] Kenzari, in Elsheshtawy, *op. cit.*, p.115.

[19] 'Alexander, Harold Rupert Leofric George, first Earl Alexander of Tunis', Oxford Dictionary of National Biography, http://www.oxforddnb.com/view/article/30371.

[20] Perkins (2004), p.144.

[21] Theroux (1996), p.478.

[22] Perkins, *op. cit.*, p.3.

[23] Completed in 1872, the original line was the work of Italian investors and engineers (who were originally offered a licence to build a long-distance line from Tunis into the interior but chose, instead, this cheaper

and more lucrative option).

24 Kenzari, in Elshestawy, *op.cit.*, p.125.

25 Michael Keating, 'Traditional Tunis and the City of the Century', *Washington Report on Middle Eastern Affairs*, Vol.26, Issue 9, December 2007, pp.39-40.

26 Dubai Holding press release, September 2008, 'Tunisian Government Approves Master Plan for Sama Dubai's US$25-Billion Mediterranean Gate Project'.

27 Kenzari, in Elshestawy, *op.cit.*, p.133. The estimated population is for Greater Tunis and compares with a total for the country as a whole of some ten million.

CHAPTER 6

Island Cross-Currents

1 Arnold (2008), pp. 361-64.

Syracuse

1 Douglas Sladen, 1901, in Dummett (2010), p.159.

2 Plato, *Timaeus*, http://classics.mit.edu/Plato/timaeus/html.

3 Cicero explores this argument as part of a Socratic dialogue, spoken in this case through the character of Scipio Africanus the Younger: *On the Commonwealth*, Book II, iv. http://www.gutenberg.org/files/14988/14988-h/14988-h.htm.

4 *Ibid.*

5 Cicero, *op. cit.*, Book III, xxxi.

6 *Ibid.*

7 Aristophanes, *The Birds*. http://classics.mit.edu/Aristophanes/birds/html.

8 *Ibid.*

9 Plato, *The Seventh Letter*, 360 BC, http://www.sacred-texts.com/cla/plato/seventh.htm.

10 *Ibid.*

11 Plato, *The Republic*, Book IV. http://classics.mit.edu/Plato/republic/html.

12 *Ibid.*

13 Mumford (1961), p.211.

14 Plato explores the theme of Atlantis in his two books, *Critias* and *Timaeus*.

15 Plato, *Critias*. http://classics.mit.edu/Plato/republic/html.

16 *Ibid.*

17 Matvejevic (1999), p.10.

18 Plutarch, Marcellus, 75 AD. http://classics.mit.edu/Plutarch/marcellu.html.

19 Strabo, *Geographica*, Book VI, Chapter II. http://penelope.uchicago.edu/Thayer/E/Roman/Texts/Strabo/home.html.

20 Blunt (1968) claims that 'almost all the Sicilian buildings which can be classified as Baroque date from a period covering the last half of the seventeenth century and the first three-quarters of the eighteenth century', p.12.

21 *Ibid.*, p.9.

22 *Ibid.*, p.24.

[23] Evidence of Mafia involvement can never be conclusive but it is well evidenced that such groups have for long operated on the island and that they had more than a say in the allocation of contracts. For example, see Finkelstein (1998).

[24] Hewison (1987), p.146.

[25] Dummett (2010), p.xxv.

[26] *Ibid.*, p.xxvi.

Valletta

[1] Fox (1991), p.367.

[2] My understanding of Valletta, historically and now, was greatly enhanced by the insights provided by my friend and former colleague, Steve Pelan, an historian who took time out to guide me through the city that he knows so well.

[3] In the nineteenth century, before subsequent archaeological finds, it was thought that the Phoenicians preceded the Greeks. Even now, some argue that was the case although there is evidence that the Greeks were in the region before the Phoenicians. Significantly, nearby Syracuse was a Greek colony from the eighth century BC.

[4] New Testament, Acts 28.

[5] There is probably no more nor less tolerance of Islam than in the rest of Europe, although past conflicts are not forgotten. There is also a keen awareness of the proximity of Africa and the potential for illegal immigration.

[6] The most credible explanation for the difference in spelling is that in the Maltese language 'Valette' would be pronounced 'Val-lette'.

[7] Part of La Valette's epitaph, coined in Latin by his English secretary, Sir Oliver Starkey, in Norwich (2006), p.309.

[8] Patrick Brydone, 1770, in Luke (1960), p.144.

[9] Hughes (1956), provides a unique account of the planning process (especially pp. 20-30) and the architectural history of Valletta.

[10] Fox (1991), p.369.

[11] Sir Walter Scott, in Luke, *op.cit.*, p.177. The quote is also recalled on a plaque on the site of the former Palazzo Britto, where Scott resided during his stay in Valletta.

[12] Hughes, *op.cit.*, p.156. Teonge did not disclose, though others did, that any of the Knights themselves who were patients were served on the silver plates twice as much food as anyone else.

[13] Luke, *op.cit*, p.58.

[14] *Ibid.*, pp.58-59.

[15] Zammit (1918).

[16] *Ibid.*, pp.61-2.

[17] The Russian Emperor, Paul 1, was himself a follower of the Orthdox Church rather than the Catholicism of Rome. In spite of that, the grateful Knights elected him as their *de facto* Grand Master.

[18] MacCarthy (2002), p.98.

[19] Luke, *op.cit.*, p.154.

[20] James Clay, one of Disraeli's travelling companions, in Luke, *op.cit.*, pp.161-2.

[21] Luke (1960), p.163

[22] *Ibid.*, p.165.

[23] *Ibid*, p.168.

[24] *Ibid*, p.169.

[25] *Ibid*, p.176.

[26] Badger (1872).

[27] *Ibid.*, p.5.

[28] *Ibid.*, p.44.

[29] Bartolo first submitted an article to the *National Review*, supporting the view of a previous contributor, 'An Englishman', who wrote that Britain was not always treating its colonies with due respect. Bartolo's article was later published in his own country as a pamphlet, 'Malta: A Neglected Outpost of Empire', Valletta: *Daily Malta Chronicle* Printing Office, 1911.

[30] Reports and other papers relating to the Valletta lay-out competition', Malta: Government Printing Office, 1925.

[31] Malta was described thus by King George VI, in awarding the islanders the George Cross for their bravery in resisting the enemy.

[32] Renzo Piano, the Italian architect commissioned to re-plan the Royal Opera House site and its surroundings, *Times of Malta*, 26 January 2009.

[33] Fox, op.cit., p.375.

[34] David Chapman and Godwin Cassar, 'Valletta', *Cities*, Vol. 21, No. 5, 2004, pp.451-63. See also David Chapman, 'Malta: Conservation in a transitional system', *Built Environment*, Vol. 25, No.3, pp.259-71.

Nicosia

[1] The city is still known internationally as Nicosia although the local preference is Lefkosia on the Greek side and Lefkoş in the Turkish sector.

[2] *Illustrated London News*, 27 July 1878: Ledra Museum and Observatory, Nicosia. The quote is directed specifically to its place in the Byzantine Empire although it applies equally to the interest in the island of successive powers.

[3] For a chronological account of the successive periods of foreign occupation, I am grateful for the availability of copious sources in the Leventis Municipal Museum of Nicosia.

[4] Luke (1921), p.1.

[5] The Lusignan legacy is commonly invoked by Greek Cypriots as sign of the island's early 'Westernization', making the political point that Turkey, in contrast, belongs to the East.

[6] Crowley (2008), p.222.

[7] Luke, *op.cit.*, pp.2-3.

[8] *Ibid.*, p.210.

[9] Durrell (2000), p.163.

[10] Mallinson (2009), p.10.

[11] *Illustrated London News*, 27 July 1878: Ledra Museum and Observatory, Nicosia.

[12] *Ibid.*

[13] Scott A. Bollens, 'City and soul: Sarajevo, Johannesburg, Jerusalem, Nicosia', *City*, Vol.5, No.2, 2001, pp.169-187.

[14] No two sets of figures are the same. Inevitably, in the circumstances, each side tends to exaggerate its own numbers (and, by implication, the extent of suffering). The figures used in the text represent a median derived from various sources.

[15] Yael Navaro-Yashin explains such differences in Papadakis, Peristianis and Welz (2006), pp.84-99.

[16] In 1946 the population was 46,000; in 1960 it had grown to 96,000. Source: Leventis Municipal Museum

of Nicosia.

[17] Bollens (2012).

[18] This is, for example, the view of the scholar of divided cities, Scott A. Bollens, *op. cit.*

[19] Bollens (2012), chapter 7.

[20] Turkish resident and engineer in the northern half of the city, commenting on a possible way forward: Calame and Charlesworth (2009), p.125.

[21] Durrell (2000), p.163.

[22] Access is relatively easy for most groups but recent Turkish immigrants (as opposed to indigenous Turkish Cypriots) are not allowed to enter the Greek sector. Additionally, passports (or equivalent identification) are required on the Turkish side.

[23] Yiannis Papadakis, Nicos Peristianis and Gisela Welz, 'Modernity, history and conflict in divided Cyprus', in Papadakis, Peristianis and Welz, eds. (2006), p.2.

[24] The former hotel has recently been restored to serve (more effectively than it had done for years in its dilapidated state) as the United Nations military HQ.

[25] Scott A. Bollens, op. cit., p.187.

[26] *Ibid.*, p.186.

[27] *Ibid.*

[28] There is also a shop on the edge of this area called 'No Border Underwear'.

BIBLIOGRAPHY

Articles, websites and other references are detailed separately in the chapter notes.

Abu-Lughod, J.L. (1989) *Before European Hegemony: The World System AD 1250-1350*. Oxford: Oxford UP.

Abulafia, D. (2011) The Great Sea: *A Human History of the Mediterranean*. London: Allen Lane.

Agostini, J. et Forno, Y. (1997) *Les Ecrivains et Marseille*. Marseille: Editions Jeanne Laffitte.

Ahmetović, S. (2008) *Curiosities of Dubrovnik from the Past Two Millennia*. Dubrovnik: Ahmetović.

Al-Harithy, H. (2010) *Lessons in Post-War Reconstruction: Case Studies in the Aftermath of the 2006 War*. Abingdon: Routledge.

Arnold, C. (2008) *Mediterranean Islands*. London: Survival Books.

Archer, E.G. (2006) *Gibraltar, Identity and Empire*. Abingdon: Routledge.

Baccar, A. B. (2008) *La Méditerranée: Odyssée des Cultures*. Tunis: Les Editions Sahar & Publications de l'ENS.

Badger, G.P. (1872) *Historical Guide to Malta and Gozo*. Malta: Bonavia. Reprinted in facsimile edition, Elibron Classics, 2005.

Benoit, G. and Comeau, A., eds. (2005) *Sustainable Future for the Mediterranean: The Blue Plan's Environment and Development Outlook*. London: Earthscan.

Blunt, A. (1968) *The Sicilian Baroque*. London: Weidenfeld and Nicolson.

Bollens, S.A. (2012) *City and Soul in Divided Societies*. Abingdon: Routledge.

Bonillo, J-L. (1991) *Marseille Ville et Port*. Marseille: Parenthèses.

Bradford, E. (1971) *Gibraltar: The History of a Fortress*. London: Rupert Hart-Davis.

Braudel, F. (1966) *The Mediterranean and the Mediterranean World in the Age of Philip II*, Vol. 1. First published in France, Librairie Armand Colin. Current edition New York: Harper Torchbook, 1976.

Braudel, F. (1966) *The Mediterranean and the Mediterranean World in the Age of Philip II*, Vol. 2. . First published in France, Librairie Armand Colin. Current edition Berkeley: University of California Press, 1995.

Braudel, F. (1998) *The Mediterranean in the Ancient World*. First published in France, Editions de Fallois. Current edition London: Penguin, 2002.

Brenner, N. and Keil, R., eds. (2006) *The Global Cities Reader*. London: Routledge.

Chambers, I. (2008) *Mediterranean Crossings: The Politics of an Interrupted Modernity*. Durham, USA: Duke University Press.

Connolly, C. (1936) *The Rock Pool*. First published in France, Parisian Obelisk Press. Current edition New York: Persea Books, 1981.

Crowley, R. (2008) *Empires of the Sea: The Final Battle for the Mediterranean, 1521-1580*. London: Faber and Faber.

de Bernières, L. (2004) *Birds Without Wings*. London: Secker & Warburg.

de Chateaubriand, F-R. (2007) *Voyage de Tunis*. Tunis: Cérès Editions.

de Lange, N. (1984) *Atlas of the Jewish World*. Oxford: Equinox.

Dobkin, M.H. (1998) *Smyrna 1922: The Destruction of a City*. New York: Newmark Press. First published as The Smyrna Affair, Harcourt Brace Jovanovich, 1971.

Drinkwater, C. (2007) *The Olive Route: A Personal Journey to the Heart of the Mediterranean*. London: Phoenix. First published by Weidenfeld and Nicolson, 2006.

Dennis, P. (1990) *Gibraltar and its People*. Newton Abbot: David & Charles.

Dumas, A. (1959) *Tangier to Tunis*. London: Brown, Watson. Originally translated in French as *En Véloce*.

Dummett, J. (2010) *Syracuse City of Legends: A Glory of Sicily*. London: Tauris.

Durrell, L. (1969) *Spirit of Place: Mediterranean Writings*. London: Faber and Faber.

Durrell, L. (1957) *Bitter Lemons of Cyprus*. London: Faber and Faber. Reprinted 2000.

Durrell, L. (1962) *The Alexandria Quartet*. London: Faber and Faber. Reprinted 2005.

Ellmann, R., ed. (1966) *Letters of James Joyce, Vol. 2*. London: Faber and Faber.

Elsheshtawy, Y., ed. (2008) *The Evolving Arab City: Tradition, Modernity & Urban Development*. Abingdon: Routledge.

Elsheshtawy, Y. (2010) *Dubai: Behind an Urban Spectacle*. Abingdon: Routledge.

Empereur, J-Y (2002) *Alexandria: Past, Present and Future*. London: Thames and Hudson. First published in France by Gallimard, 2001.

Fawaz, L.T. (1983) *Merchants and Migrants in Nineteenth-Century Beirut*. Cambridge, Mass.: Harvard University Press.

Finkelstein, M.S. (1998) *Separatism, the Allies and the Mafia: The Struggle for Sicilian Independence, 1943-1948*. Bethlehem, PA: Lehigh University Press.

Finlayson, C. and Finlayson, G. (1999) *Gibraltar at the End of the Millennium: A Portrait of a Changing Land*. Gibraltar: Aquila Services.

Fitzgerald, F.S. (1934) *Tender is the Night*. First published by *Scribner's Magazine*, January to April 1934. Current edition London: Penguin, 1997.

Fletcher, R. (2001) *Moorish Spain*. London: Phoenix Press. First published by Weidenfeld and Nicolson, 1992.

Fletcher, R. (2004) *The Cross and the Crescent*. London: Penguin. First published by Allen Lane, 2003.

Foretić M. (2002) *Dubrovnik in War*. Dubrovnik: Matica Hravatska Dubrovnik.

Forster, E.M. (1922) *Alexandria: A History and a Guide and Pharos and Pharillon*. The *Guide* was first published in 1922, and Pharos in 1923. London: André Deutch, reprinted 2004.

Fox, R. (1991) *The Inner Sea: The Mediterranean and its People*. London: Sinclair-Stevenson.

Garratt, G.T. (1939) *Gibraltar and the Mediterranean*. New York: Coward McCann.

Gavin, A. and Maluf, R. (1996) *Beirut Reborn: The Restoration and Development of the Central District*. London: Academy Editions.

Geisthövel, W. (2008) *Homer's Mediterranean*. London: Haus Publishing. First published in Germany, Patmos Verlag GmbH, 2007.

Gaddafi, M. (1975) *The Green Book*. www.geocities.com/Athens/8744/readgb.htm.

Glenny, M. (1996) *The Fall of Yugoslavia*. London: Penguin. Third edition.

Goitein, S.D. (1967) *A Mediterranean Society: The Jewish Communities of the Arab World as Portrayed in the Documents of the Cairo Geniza (Volume 1: Economic Foundations)*. Berkeley: University of California Press.

Gold, P. (2005) *Gibraltar: British or Spanish?* London: Routledge.

Goldring (1913) *Dream Cities: Notes on an Autumn Tour in Italy and Dalmatia*. London: Fisher Unwin.

Grenon, M. and Batisse, M., eds. (1989) *Futures for the Mediterranean Basin. The Blue Plan*. Oxford: Oxford University Press.

Haag, M. (2004) *Alexandria: City of Memory*. New Haven: Yale University Press.

Hanssen, J. (2005) *Fin de Siècle Beirut: The Making of an Ottoman Provincial Capital*. Oxford: Oxford University Press.

Harris, R. (2003) Dubrovnik: *A History*. London: Saqi.

Harris, W.V., ed. (2005) *Rethinking the Mediterranean*. Oxford: Oxford University Press.

Harvey, M. (1996) *Gibraltar*. Staplehurst, UK: Spellmount.

Herbert, G. and Sosnovsky, S. (1993) *Bauhaus on the Carmel and the Crossroads of Empire: Architecture and Planning in Haifa during the British Mandate*. Jerusalem: Yad Izhak Ben-Zvi.

Herodotus (1998) *The Histories* (trans. Robin Waterfield). Oxford: Oxford University Press.

Herrin, J. (2008) *Byzantium: The Surprising Life of a Medieval Empire*. London: Penguin. First published by Allen Lane, 2007.

Herzl, T. (1902) *Old New Land (Altneuland)*. Leipzig: Hermann Seemann Nachfolger. Reprinted by Filiquarian Classics, USA, 2007.

Hewison, R. (1987) *The Heritage Industry: Britain in a Climate of Decline*. London: Methuen.

Hooper, J. (2006) *The New Spaniards*. London: Penguin. First published by Viking, 1986.

Horden, P. and Purcell, N. (2000) *The Corrupting Sea: A Study of Mediterranean History*. Oxford: Blackwell.

Hourani, A. (2005) *A History of the Arab Peoples*. London: Faber and Faber. First published by Faber and Faber, 1991.

Hughes, Q. (1956) *The Building of Malta During the Period of the Knights of St. John of Jerusalem*, 1530-1795. London: Tiranti.

Ilbert, R. and Yannakakis, eds. (1997) *Alexandria 1860-1960: The Brief Life of a Cosmopolitan Community*. Alexandria: Harpocrates Publishing. First published in French by Les Editions Autrement, Paris, 1992.

Irazabal, C., ed. (2007) *Ordinary Places, Extraordinary Events: Citizenship, Democracy and Public Space in Latin America*. Abingdon: Routledge.

Isaac, B.H. (2006) *The Invention of Racism in Classical Antiquity*. Princeton: Princeton University Press.

Jackson, W.G.F. (1987) *The Rock of the Gibraltarians: A History of Gibraltar*. Cranbury, NJ: Associated University Presses.

Joutard, P., ed. 1988 *Histoire de Marseille en Treize Evénements*. Marseille: Editions Jeanne Laffitte.

Kadish, S. (2007) *Jewish Heritage in Gibraltar: An Architectural Guide*. Reading: Spire Books.

Kapuściński, R. (2008) *Travels with Herodotus*. London: Penguin. First published in Poland, Znak, 2004.

Kargon, R.H. and Molella, A.P. (2008) *Invented Edens: Techno-Cities of the Twentieth Century*. Cambridge, Mass.: MIT Press.

Keegan, J. (1997) *The Second World War*. London: Pimlico.

Kenny, M. and Kertzer, D.I., eds. (1983) *Urban Life in Mediterranean Europe: Anthropological Perspectives*. Urbana: University of Illinois Press.

Khalaf, S. and Khoury, P.S. (1993) *Recovering Beirut: Urban Design and Post-War Reconstruction*. Leiden: Brill.

King, R., Proudfoot, L. and Smith, B., eds. (1997) *The Mediterranean: Environment and Society*. London: Arnold.

King, R., Warnes, T. and Williams, A. (2000) *Sunset Lives: British Retirement Migration to the Mediterranean*. Oxford: Berg.

King, R., De Mas, P. and Beck, J.M., eds. (2001) *Geography, Environment and Development in the Mediterranean*. Brighton: Sussex Academic Press.

Klaushofer, A. (2007) *Paradise Divided: A Portrait of Lebanon*. Oxford: Signal Books.

Lane-Poole, S. (1890) *The Barbary Corsairs*. London: Fisher Unwin.

Leontidou, L. (1990) *The Mediterranean City in Transition: Social Change and Urban Development*. Cambridge: Cambridge University Press.

Levi, C. (1947) *Christ Stopped at Eboli*. First translation published by Farrar, Strauss and Company. Current edition London: Penguin, 2000.

Lewkowicz, B. (2006) *The Jewish Community of Salonika: History, Memory, Identity*. London: Vallentine Mitchell.

Luke, H. (1960) *Malta: An Account and an Appreciation*. London: Harrap.

MacCarthy, F. (1981) *The Simple Life: C.R. Ashbee in the Cotswolds*. London: Lund Humphries.

MacCarthy, F. (2002) *Byron: Life and Legend*. London: Murray.

Macaulay, R. (1950) *Fabled Shore*. London: Readers Union. First published by Hamish Hamilton, 1947.

Macaulay, R. (1977) *Pleasure of Ruins*. London: Thames and Hudson. This version contains photographs by Roloff Beny; the original edition was published in 1953.

Malkin, I. and Hohlfelder, R.L., eds. (1988) *Mediterranean Cities: Historical Perspectives*. London: Cass.

Mallinson, W. (2009) *Cyprus: A Modern History*. First published in 2005. London: Tauris.

Manning, O. (1982) *The Levant Trilogy*. Harmondsworth: Penguin.

Mansel, P. (2010) *Levant: Splendour and Catastrophe on the Mediterranean*. London: John Murray.

Marcuse, P. and van Kempen, R., eds. (2000) *Globalizing Cities: A New Spatial Order?* Oxford: Blackwell.

Marozzi, J. (2008) *The Man Who Invented History: Travels with Herodotus*. London: John Murray.

Matvejević, P. (1999) *Mediterranean: A Cultural Landscape*. Berkeley: University of California Press. First published by Grafički Zavod Hrvatske, Zagreb, 1987.

Mazower, M. (2001) *The Balkans*. London: Phoenix. First published by Weidenfeld and Nicolson, 2000.

Mazower, M. (2004) *Salonica*. City of Ghosts: Christians, Muslims and Jews 1430-1950. London: Harper.

McCourt, J. (2000) *The Years of Bloom: James Joyce in Trieste 1904-1920*. Dublin: Lilliput Press.

Megas, Y. (1993) *Images of the Jewish Community: Salonika 1897-1917*. Athens: Kapon Editions.

Meller, H. (1990) *Patrick Geddes: Social Evolutionist and Planner*. London: Routledge.

Milton: G. (2008) *Paradise Lost. Smyrna 1922: The Destruction of Islam's City of Tolerance*. London: Sceptre.

Montefiore, S.S. (2011) *Jerusalem: The Biography*. London: Weidenfeld and Nicolson.

Moorehead, A. (2007) *Gallipoli*. London: Aurum Press. First published by Hamish Hamilton, 1956.

Morris, J. (2002) *Trieste and the Meaning of Nowhere*. London: Faber and Faber. First published by Faber and Faber, 2001.

Mumford, L. (1961) *The City in History.* Harmondsworth: Penguin.

Newby, E. (1998) *On the Shores of the Mediterranean*. Oakland, USA: Lonely Planet. First published by Harvill Press, 1984.

Norwich, J.J. (2006) *The Middle Sea: A History of the Mediterranean*. London: Chatto and Windus.

Oldenbourg, Z. (1966) *The Crusades*. First published by Weidenfeld and Nicolson, 1966. Current edition London: Phoenix, 2001.

Oliphant, L. (1887) *Haifa or Life in Modern Palestine*. First published by William Blackwood, Edinburgh. Current edition New York: Elibron Classics, 2005.

Osman, T. (2010) *Egypt on the Brink: From Nasser to Mubarak*. New Haven: Yale University Press.

Pagnol, P. (1962) *The Water of the Hills and Manon of the Springs*. First published in France, Editions Julliard. Current edition London: Picador, 1989.

Pamuk, O. (2008) *Other Colours*. London: Faber and Faber.

Papadakis, Y., Peristianis, N. and Welz, G., eds. (2006) *Divided Cyprus: Modernity, History and an Island in Conflict*. Bloomington: Indian University Press.

Perkins, K.J. (2004) *A History of Modern Tunisia*. Cambridge: Cambridge University Press.

Pirenne, H. (1939) *Mohammed and Charlemagne*. London: Allen and Unwin.

Plato (2007) *The Republic*. London: Penguin.

Plato (1977) *Timaeus and Critias*. London: Penguin.

Pollard, J. and Reid, H. (2007) *The Rise and Fall of Alexandria: Birthplace of the Modern World*. New York: Penguin. First published by Viking Penguin, 2006.

Powell, E.A. (1920) *The New Frontiers of Freedom: From the Alps to the Aegean*. New York: Charles Scribner's Sons. Re-issued as E-book 17292 by Project Gutenberg, 2005.

Ribas-Mateos, N. (2005) *The Mediterranean in the Age of Globalization: Migration, Welfare and Borders*. New Brunswick, NJ: Transaction Publishers.

Rogan, E. (2009) *The Arabs: A History*. London: Allen Lane.

Rowe, P. and Sarkis, H., eds. (1998) *Projecting Beirut: Episodes in the Construction and Reconstruction of a Modern City*. Munich: Prestel-Verlag.

Said, E.W. (1978) *Orientalism*. First published by Routledge and Kegan Paul.Current edition London: Penguin, 2003.

Sakellariou, M.B., ed. (1988) *Macedonia: 4000 Years of Greek History and Civilization*. Athens: Ekdotike Athenon.

Salomon, V. (2001) *Experience of the Boat: Wooden Shipbuilding Heritage in Croatia*. Dubrovnik: Maritime Museum.

Sanchez, M.G., ed. (2006) *Writing the Rock of Gibraltar: An Anthology of Literary Texts*, 1720-1890. Dewsbury: Rock Scorpion Books.

Sanchez, M.G. (2007) *The Prostitutes of Serraya's Lane and other Hidden Gibraltarian Histories*. Dewsbury: Rock Scorpion Books.

Sassen, S. (2001) *The Global City: New York, London, Tokyo*. Princeton: Princeton University Press.

Sciaky, L. (1946) *Farewell to Salonica: City at the Crossroads*. First published by Paul Dry Books, Philadelphia. Current edition with introduction by Neil Barnett, London: Haus Books, 2007.

Segrè, C.G. (1974) *Fourth Shore: The Italian Colonization of Libya*. Chicago: University of Chicago Press.

Seikaly, M. (1995) *Haifa: Transformation of an Arab Society, 1918-1939*. London: Tauris.

Semple, E.C. (1931) *The Geography of the Mediterranean Region: Its Relation to Ancient History*. London: Constable.

Sepos, A. (2008) *The Europeanization of Cyprus: Polity, Policies and Politics*. Basingstoke: Palgrave Macmillan.

Simons, G.L. (1996) *Libya: The Struggle for Survival*. Basingstoke: Macmillan.

Smart, N. (1989) *The World's Religions: Old Traditions and Modern Transformations*. Cambridge: Cambridge University Press.

St. John, R.B. (2008) *Libya: From Colony to Independence*. Oxford: Oneworld.

Stein, R. (2007) *Rick Stein's Mediterranean Escapes*. London: BBC.

Sultana, D. (1969) *Samuel Taylor Coleridge in Malta and Italy*. Oxford: Blackwell.

Tabet, J. (2001) *Beyrouth: Portrait de Ville*. Paris: *Institut Français d'Architecture*.

Tal, N. (2009) *Ottoman Haifa: Aspects of the City, 1516-1918*. Haifa: Haifa City Museum.

Taylor, C. (2007) *Once Upon a Time in Beirut*. Sydney: Bantam.

Themelis, N. (2008) *The Quest*. Athens: Kedros.

Theroux, P. (1996) *The Pillars of Hercules: A Grand Tour of the Mediterranean*. London: Penguin. First published by Hamish Hamilton, 1995.

Thucydides (1972) *History of the Peloponnesian War*. London: Penguin. The original writings were contemporaneous to the events.

Todd, M.L. (1912) *Tripoli the Mysterious*. First published in 1912 (publishing house unknown).Tripoli: Dar Al Fergiani, 1994.

Towner, J. (1996) *An Historical Geography of Recreation and Tourism in the Western World, 1540-1940*. Chichester: Wiley.

Varanava, A. and Faustmann, H. (2009) *Reunifying Cyprus: The Annan Plan and Beyond*. London: Tauris.

Vigier, F. (1987) *Housing in Tunis*. Cambridge, Mass.: Harvard University Graduate School of Design.

Wainwright, J. and Thornes, J.B. (2004) *Environmental Issues in the Mediterranean: Processes and Perspectives for the Past and Present*. London: Routledge.

Ward, P. (1969) *Tripoli: Portrait of a City*. Stoughton, Wisconsin: Oleander Press.

Waugh, E. (1930) *Labels*. First published by Duckworth, 1930. Harmondsworth: Penguin, 1985.

Weber, M. (1958) *The City*. London: Heinemann.

Webster, J. (2005) *Andalus*. London: Black Swan. First published by Doubleday, 2004.

West, R. (1942) *Black Lamb and Grey Falcon: A Journey through Yugoslavia*. First published by Macmillan. Edinburgh: Canongate Books, 2006.

Wheatcroft, A. (2004) *Infidels: A History of the Conflict between Christendom and Islam*. First published by Viking, 2003. Current edition London: Penguin.

Wingfield, L. (1868) *Under the Palms in Algeria and Tunis, Vols. 1 and 2*. First published in London by Hurst and Blackett, 1868. Reprinted Elibron Classics, 2005.

Woodford, J.S. (1990) *The City of Tunis: Evolution of an Urban System*. Outwell, Cambs.: Middle East & North African Studies Press.

Wright, J. (1981) Libya: *A Modern History*. London: Croom Helm.

Wright, J., ed. (2005) *Travellers in Libya*. London: Silphium Press.

Zammit, T. (1918) *Valletta: An Historical Sketch*. Valletta: Critiens.

INDEX

www.ingramcontent.com/pod-product-compliance
Lightning Source LLC
Chambersburg PA
CBHW080548270326
41929CB00019B/3233